REGNUM STUDIES IN MISSION

Planting an Indigenous Church

The Case of the Borneo Evangelical Mission

REGNUM STUDIES IN MISSION

Series Preface

Regnum Studies in Mission are born from the lived experience of Christians and Christian communities in mission, especially, but not solely, in the fast growing churches among the poor of the world. These churches have more to tell than stories of growth. They are making significant impacts on their cultures in the cause of Christ. They are producing 'cultural products' which express the reality of Christian faith, hope and love in their societies.

Titles in the Regnum Studies in Mission series are the fruit of rigorous research to the highest international standards and always of authentic Christian engagement in the transformation of people and societies. These books have been created for the world. The formation of Christian theology, missiology and practice, in the twenty-first century, will depend to a great extent on the active participation of growing churches contributing biblical and culturally appropriate expressions of Christian practice to inform World Christianity.

Series Editors

The publication of this title is made possible through the generous financial assistance of The Commission on Theological Education of Evangelisches Missionswerk in Deutschland (EMW, Dr. Verena Grüter), Hamburg, Germany

REGNUM STUDIES IN MISSION

Planting an Indigenous Church

The Case of the Borneo Evangelical Mission

Jin Huat Tan

Foreword by Brian Stanley

First published 2011 by Regnum Books International

Regnum is an imprint of the Oxford Centre for Mission Studies
St. Philip and St. James Church
Woodstock Road
Oxford, OX2 6HR, UK
www.ocms.ac.uk/regnum

09 08 07 06 05 04 03 8 7 6 5 4 3 2 1

British Library Cataloguing in Publication Data
A catalogue record for this book is available from the British Library

ISBN 978-1-506477-52-7

Typeset by Words by Design Ltd

Distributed by 1517 Media in the US and Canada

Contents

List of Maps

Preface

This book began as a PhD thesis submitted to the University of Wales through the Oxford Centre for Mission Studies (OCMS). My interest in the BEM began when I first read an unpublished copy of Charles Hudson Southwell's memoir. It started me on my journey to explore about the BEM and the SIB.

My gratitude goes to Canon Dr Christopher Sugden, formerly Executive Director of OCMS, who gave me much encouragement to get this research project off the ground in 2001. I am privileged to have Prof. Dr Brian Stanley, currently Professor of World Christianity at the University of Edinburgh, as my supervisor who provided me with wise advice and invaluable guidance. The faculty at OCMS had given much invaluable help towards this dissertation.

A word of thanks goes to the staff at the Rhodes House Library, the Bible College of Victoria, and the archives of the Sarawak Museum who provided helpful assistance to make my research pleasurable.

My oral research took me to the retired missionaries of the BEM in Australia and the United Kingdom who willingly allowed me to interview them despite their very senior years. Not any less important were the interviews with the leaders of the SIB whose insights were extremely useful.

There are many friends who have made this study possible and space does not permit to mention them all. A special word of thanks goes to the Church Mission Society and the Singapore West Malaysia Diocesan Association for providing some support for my five months stay in Oxford in 2004.

Dr Beatrice Clayre, a former BEM missionary, had been helpful and was instrumental in introducing Colin Davis to me. Colin did a wonderful job with the maps in this book. The help of Hwa Mei Shen and Chang Tsyh Yong in editing and proof-reading this script for publication is greatly appreciated. The responsibility remains mine in the event of any error.

My gratitude is also extended to my wife King Shen who gave unselfish support and encouragement for this study to be completed. My children, Phoebe and Derek, proved understanding and encouraging of their father's research. To Derek, I wish to extend my appreciation for making his expertise with computers and his electronic gadgets available to me for my oral research in Sarawak and Australia.

Jin Huat Tan

Foreword

The publication of Tan Jin Huat's PhD thesis on the Borneo Evangelical Mission (BEM) and the Sidang Injil Borneo (SIB) is an event to be warmly welcomed. In important respects this work breaks new ground. Southeast Asia is still under-represented in the scholarly literature on the history of indigenous appropriation of Christian missionary traditions – at least so far as Anglophone scholarship is concerned. Equally neglected is the often strategic role played by Australian Protestant initiatives in foreign missions, particularly in southeast Asia. Sarawak, a unique example within the British empire of a private fiefdom administered for a whole century by the Brooke dynasty, is still given limited attention in the historiography of imperialism. More specifically, the BEM has almost entirely escaped the notice of historians of the 'faith missions', while the church which it helped to bring to birth, the SIB, has until now awaited its historian despite being the second largest Protestant community in Malaysia. Tan Jin Huat's research into the origins of the SIB illuminates the ways in which village peoples who adhered to a spirit-based cosmology reframed a conservative evangelical presentation of the gospel as a message about the superior power of Christ over the spirits.

This book also makes illuminating connections that have not been drawn hitherto. Behind the story of the BEM lie the distinctive missiological principles and stirring example of James Hudson Taylor's China Inland Mission, a mission that now only grew to become the largest Protestant mission in China but also functioned as a model for evangelical missionary initiatives in other fields. But Tan Jin Huat also reveals other lineages that shaped the character of this primarily Australian mission. The dominant spiritual influence on most of the early BEM missionaries was C. H. Nash of the Melbourne Bible Institute, who in turn was deeply influenced by his student years in Cambridge, particularly at Ridley Hall under the principalship of Handley C. G Moule. Through the Institute and the Upwey Convention, the Australian counterpart of Keswick, holiness revivalism shaped Melbourne evangelicalism and moved thence to the villages of Borneo. 'Revival' eventually came to the churches of the Orang Ulu in the 1950s and 1970s, though not necessarily in the form that the missionaries expected. Keswick enthusiast though he was, C.H. Nash also appears to have been the channel as early as the 1920s in mediating the principles of the High Anglican mission theorist, Roland Allen, to his students. Tan Jin Huat shows that for the BEM missionaries the goal of establishing a three-self church was no mere theoretical commitment, yet also that, as so often elsewhere, political events played a decisive part in bringing a genuinely autonomous church into being: the Japanese occupation of Sarawak and consequent internment of the missionaries were determinative in bringing forward indigenous leadership. Finally, he traces the impact on an originally rural church of migration to the coastal towns from the 1960s: even for a church planted by a 'jungle outfit', urban mission was now firmly on the agenda.

Brian Stanley,
Professor of World Christianity,
University of Edinburgh.
October 2011

Abbreviations

ADEB	*The Australian Dictionary of Evangelical Biography*
AJPS	*Asian Journal of Pentecostal Studies*
ANCC	All Nations Christian College
BCV	Bible College of Victoria (formerly known as MBI)
BEM	Borneo Evangelical Mission
BEM NL	*Borneo Evangelical Mission Newsletter*
BMJ	*Brunei Museum Journal*
BRB	*Borneo Research Bulletin*
CBFMS	Conservative Baptist Foreign Mission Society
CIM	China Inland Mission
C&MA	Christian and Missionary Alliance
EMQ	*Evangelical Missions Quarterly*
FEBC	Far Eastern Broadcasting Corporation
FES	Fellowship of Evangelical Students
IBMR	International Bulletin for Missionary Research
IMC	International Missionary Council
IRM	*International Review of Mission*
ISCF	Inter School Christian Fellowship
IVP	*Inter Varsity Press*
JAH	*Journal of African History*
JAS	*Journal of Asian Studies*
JCE	*Journal of Christian Education*
JICH	*Journal of Imperial and Commonwealth History*
JMBRAS	*Journal of the Malayan Branch of the Royal Asiatic Society*
JMBRAS	*Journal of the Malaysian Branch of the Royal Asiatic Society*
JMHS	*Journal of the Malaysian Historical Society* (Sarawak Branch)
JRA	*Journal of Religion in Africa*
KEC	Kuching Evangelical Church
KINGMI	Kemah Injil Gereja Masehi Indonesia
LBS	Lawas Bible School
MBC	Miri Bible College
MBI	Melbourne Bible Institute
MEC	Malaysia Evangelical College (formerly known as MBC)
MEC	Miri Evangelical Church
MS	*Mission Studies*
MTS	Methodist Theological School
NCF	Nurses' Christian Fellowship

NECF	National Evangelical Christian Fellowship
NZBTI	New Zealand Bible Training Institute
OMF	Overseas Missionary Fellowship
SAM	Sekolah Alkitab Makassar (Makassar Bible School)
SBC	Singapore Bible College
SDA	Seventh Day Adventists
SG	*Sarawak Gazette*
SIAC	Sarawak Iban Annual Conference
SIB	Sidang Injil Borneo
SMJ	*Sarawak Museum Journal*
SPABC	South Pacific Association of Bible Colleges
SPG	Society for the Propagation of the Gospel
SRD	Special Reconnaissance Detachment
SSEM	South Seas Evangelical Mission
SU	Scripture Union
TCF	Teachers Christian Fellowship
UMNO	United Malay National Organisation
WEC	Worldwide Evangelization Crusade
VBS	Vacation Bible School

Glossary

adat	custom or traditional culture
Alkitab	Indonesian Bible
Bahasa Melayu	Malay language
Batu	stone or rock
borak	locally brewed rice wine
bumiputra	the Malays and other indigenous people
dayong	shaman
guru	teacher
irau	feast
jimat	a charm
ketua daerah	district superintendent
kundung	rice ritual man
Negeri	State
pantang	taboo
penghulu	chief over a few villages
rumah	house
sekolah	school
sungai	river
tamu	government-organized market days
temenggong	high chief of a particular river system
tohad	blood compensation
tua kampong	village headman
tuai burong	Iban augur of the longhouse
ulu	interior

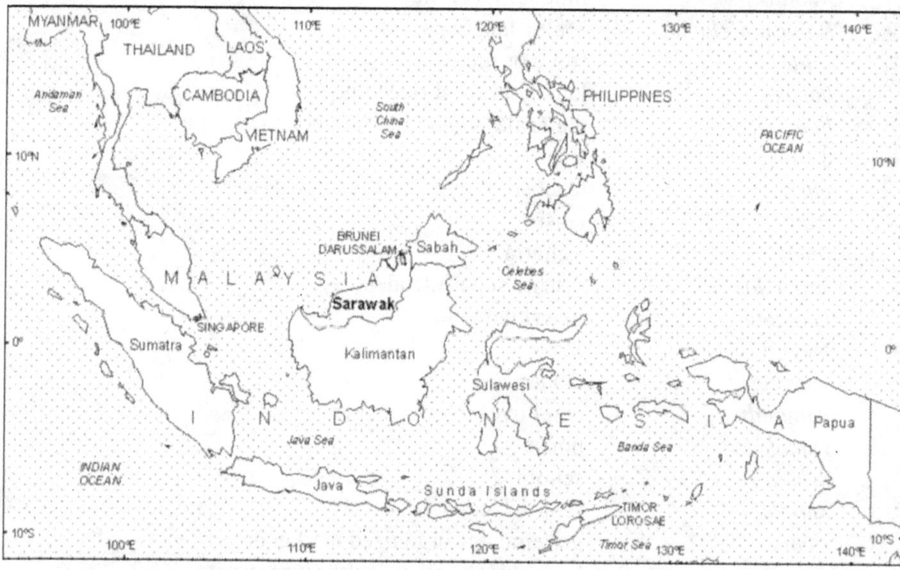

Map 1: Sarawak in Southeast Asia

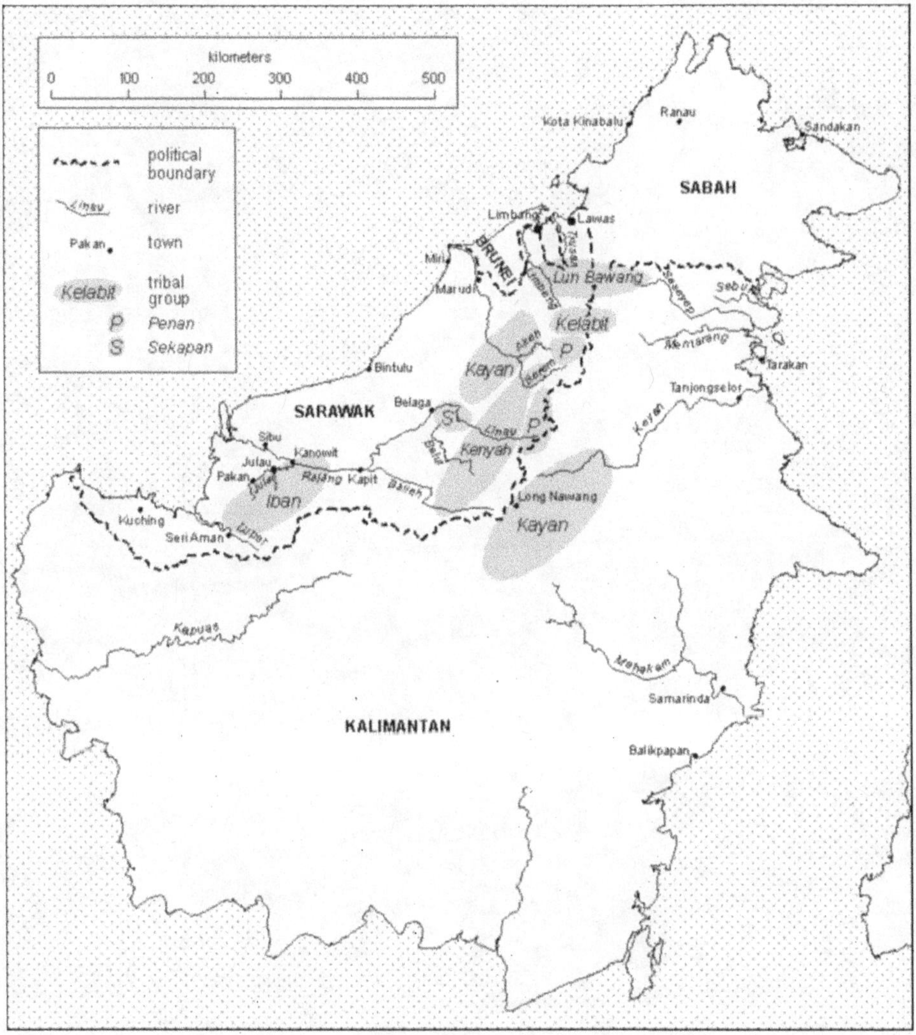

Map 2: Sarawak, Sabah and Kalimantan
(Distribution of the *Orang Ulu* consisting of the Lun Bawang, Kelabit, Kayan, Kenyah, Sekapan and Penan)

Chapter 1

Introduction

The Borneo Evangelical Mission (BEM), which began in 1928 as an Australian evangelical missionary society, facilitated the planting of the Sidang Injil Borneo (SIB) (or the Evangelical Church of Borneo) in Sarawak as an indigenous 'Three-Self' church. In 1959, the SIB was formally constituted as an independent indigenous church with an ecclesial structure autonomous of the BEM, the parent mission body. From 1959 to 1979, the SIB worked in close partnership with the BEM. By 1979, with the departure of the last BEM Field Director,[1] the SIB was on its way to becoming one of the largest Protestant denominations in Sarawak and later in Malaysia.[2] From the 1990s onwards, the work of the SIB expanded into Peninsular Malaysia.[3]

This study seeks to assess the strength and consistency of the commitment of the BEM to the planting and development of an indigenous church on 'Three-Self' principles, and will evaluate how far this goal was achieved.

The Planting of Indigenous Churches

Mission theorists such as Henry Venn (1796-1873) and Rufus Anderson (1796-1880) were well-known proponents of the theory that the goal of missions was to plant indigenous churches that were 'Three-Self', namely, self-propagating,

[1] The BEM had three Field Directors: the first was Charles Hudson Southwell (1939-1948), the second was Alan Belcher (1948-1968) and the third and last was Dr Bill Hawes (1968-1979).

[2] Though the data in David Barrett's *World Christian Encyclopaedia*, should be viewed cautiously, they nevertheless give us an important guide to church growth in Malaysia. In his 1982 book, Barrett estimates the SIB as having 278 congregations, 6,700 adult and 40,000 affiliated members; the Methodist Church in Malaysia with 240 congregations, 30,000 adult and 65,000 affiliated members; and the Anglican Church in Sarawak with 47 congregations, 25,635 adult members and 29,600 affiliated members. David Barrett (ed.), *World Christian Encyclopaedia* (New York: Oxford University Press, 1982), 475.

[3] The figures in Barrett's *World Christian Encyclopaedia* (2001) estimate the SIB at 500 congregations, 110,000 adult and 190,000 affiliated members, making it the second largest Protestant denomination in Malaysia. The Methodist Church in Malaysia is the largest with 300 congregations, 77,962 adult and 230,000 affiliated members. D.B. Barrett, G.T. Kurian and T.M. Johnson (eds.), *World Christian Encyclopaedia*, 2 vols. (New York: Oxford University Press, 2001), I, 475-78.

self-governing and self-supporting.[4] Their ideas were later adopted, modified and extended by others, such as John Livingston Nevius (1829-1893), Roland Allen (1868-1947) and Melvin Hodges (1909-1988).[5]

The planting of a 'Three-Self' indigenous church has been the goal of many Protestant missionary societies from the mid-nineteenth century, but this policy was generally not successfully implemented in Africa and Asia before decolonisation. The process of the devolution of authority from the parent mission society to the indigenous church has often being undermined or subverted, reversed or hastily implemented in situations of political crisis.[6]

For a newly planted church to be independent and viable, it should be a 'Three-Self' church. For it to be indigenous, it has to be in the control of the local people. The BEM's goal was to plant such an indigenous 'Three-Self' church. In this study, some comparative reference with other missions in Sarawak (notably the Anglican SPG and the American Methodists) will be made when it is appropriate.

The idea of 'the euthanasia of a mission', (that is, when the missionaries leave a mission field completely), was spelt out in Venn's concept of the 'Three-Self' church. The essential concept (though not the specific term) of the euthanasia of a mission appears to have been implicit in the minds of the BEM leadership from at least as early as 1939, as from that date the mission's literature makes explicit use of three-self language, committing the mission to the goal of planting a 'Three-Self' church. The closure of the BEM, as a mission, eventually became a reality with the departure of the last BEM Field Director in 1979.

Scope of the Study

This study examines the policies and practices of the BEM and also the processes and influences that have aided in the planting and development of the SIB as a 'Three-Self' indigenous church, particularly among the Orang Ulu. (Orang Ulu is a collective term in current usage which refers to the indigenous people of the interior of Sarawak, comprising the Lun Bawang or Murut, Kelabit, Kayan, Kenyah, Penan and Sekapan).[7] It also seeks to discuss the

---

[4] See Max Warren (ed.), *To Apply the Gospel: Selections from the Writings of Henry Venn* (Grand Rapids: Eerdmans, 1971); R. Pierce Beaver (ed.), *To Advance the Gospel: Selections from the Writings of Rufus Anderson* (Grand Rapids: Eerdmans, 1967).

[5] Warren B. Newberry, 'Contextualising Indigenous Church Principles', *AJPS* 8.1 (2005), 96-102. Everett N. Hunt Jr., 'The Legacy of John Livingston Nevius', *IBMR* 15.3 (July 1991), 120-24. C.H. Long and A. Rowthorn, 'The Legacy of Roland Allen', *IBMR* 13.2 (April 1989), 65-68. Gary McGee, 'The Legacy of Melvin Hodges', *IBMR* 22.1 (Jan 1998), 20-24.

[6] See examples of these cases in Chapter 6.

[7] See Chapter 2 for further details. The Lun Bawang or Murut in Sarawak are also known as Lun Dayeh or Murut in Sabah (formerly known as British North Borneo).

interaction of the policies and practices of the BEM and SIB with the following contextual influences: a) the administrative policies and style of the Brooke Raj and the subsequent colonial government; b) the character and self-governing leadership styles of the Orang Ulu; and c) the changing social, economic and political climate of Sarawak under independent Malaysia until 1979.

The study will also evaluate the nature of the distinctive strand of Australian Christianity from which the BEM originated, and of the growth and development of the BEM's work from its inception in 1928 till the establishment of the indigenous church, the SIB, in 1959. In the appropriation of Christianity among the Orang Ulu, attention will be given to understanding and analysing the nature of the conversion process among the tribal communities against their social, religious and cultural background. As anthropological insights are essential to understand the process of religious change, these will be discussed.

Another major concern will be to assess the role of the BEM and the implementation of its policies with regard to its approach to encouraging the 'Three-Self' movement within the SIB, the stages of its evolution towards autonomy, and the ways in which the BEM supported or hindered the emergence of local indigenous leadership within the SIB. There will also be an analysis of the response of the SIB leadership to the policies of the BEM and its implementation, and the development of the SIB as a 'Three-Self' church since 1959. Finally, an evaluation will be made of the responses of the BEM and SIB to social, economic and political challenges from 1959 to 1979. Particular attention will be given to the shifts in the policies of the BEM in response to social-economic and political factors.

This study is intended to place the work of the BEM within the wider canvas of other 'faith' missions so as to enable further comparative study, and also to situate the growth of the SIB within the wider picture of the growth of Christianity in South East Asia. The contribution of this study will be to elucidate the relationship between the BEM as the parent mission body, and the SIB, the indigenous church, which it helped to establish, and the processes and the influences that gave rise to the planting, emergence and development of a 'Three-Self' indigenous church.

Literature Review

The history of the BEM is relatively unknown in academic literature. Currently, there is a gap among scholarly works on the history of the Church in Malaysia. The published works omit the history of the Church in East Malaysia (Sarawak and Sabah, formerly known as Borneo), as is illustrated by the book Christianity in Malaysia (1992) by Robert Hunt, K.H. Lee and J. Roxborogh.[8]

---

[8] R. Hunt, K.H. Lee and J. Roxborogh (eds.), *Christianity in Malaysia: A Denominational History* (Kuala Lumpur: Pelanduk Publications, 1992).

There are a few theses on the BEM, which include Richard Samporoh's 'The Establishment, Growth, Strengths and Weaknesses of the SIB Church' (BTh thesis, 1992),[9] Brian Newton's 'A New Dawn over Sarawak' (MA thesis, 1988)[10] and Colin Reasbeck's 'The Growth of the Gospel among the Iban People of Sarawak' (MA thesis, 2003).[11] Of greater significance is Brian Michell's doctoral thesis on 'The Role of Missionary Partnership in Indigenous Church Development: A Malaysian Case Study' (DMiss thesis, 2004),[12] which examines 'the importance of developing mission-church partnerships (that is, OMF and SIB) and effective ways of preparing the church for smooth transition to national leadership and for continuing growth after missionary withdrawal'. The focus of Michell's study was on missionary closure and on developing on-going mission-church partnerships after missionary withdrawal from the SIB. It thus complements this study, discussing the themes from where this study ends. Michell's study shows that, on the effectiveness of the BEM/OMF for preparing the church for missionary closure, the SIB leadership rated a) the missionaries and b) their range of missionary activities, especially evangelism and church development, at 5.6 and 6 respectively on a scale of 1-7 (where 7 means very good). Theological education and missionary training were rated at 5.7. Based on the good scores obtained from his survey, Michell argues that the closure of the mission brought to completion a successful process of BEM/OMF partnership development with the SIB and a smooth transfer of operation to the SIB.[13]

Another relevant study is Gary Dean Roosma's thesis entitled 'Guiding Toward Independence: The Borneo Evangelical Mission and the Planting of the Borneo Evangelical Church' (ThM, 2006).[14] Roosma argues that the BEM was successful in guiding the SIB towards independence. In his view, 'a combination of external circumstances, intentional mission programmes and the divine work of God through renewal movement have all contributed to this

---

[9] Richard Samporoh, 'The Establishment, Growth, Strengths and Weaknesses of the SIB Church' (BTh thesis, Malaysia Bible Seminary, 1992).

[10] Brian Newton, 'A New Dawn over Sarawak' (MA thesis, Fuller Theological Seminary, 1988).

[11] Colin Reasbeck, 'The Growth of the Gospel among the Iban People of Sarawak' (MA thesis, University of Sheffield, 2003).

[12] Brian Michell, 'The Role of Missionary Partnership in Indigenous Church Development: A Malaysian Case Study' (DMiss thesis, Asian Graduate School of Theology Phillipines, 2004).

[13] Michell, 'The Role of Missionary Partnership', 261-62. See Appendix B and C in Michell's thesis for details of the survey.

[14] Gary D. Roosma, 'Guiding Toward Independence: The Borneo Evangelical Mission and the Planting of the Borneo Evangelical Church' (ThM thesis, Regent College Vancouver, 2006). A copy of this work came into my possession too late for consideration in my original thesis.

remarkable work'.[15] These factors will be dealt with in greater depth in this work.

There are also books of a popular nature such as Shirley Lees' Jungle Fire (1960) and Drunk before Dawn (1978),[16] Hudson Southwell's Uncharted Waters (1999),[17] which is substantially his unpublished memoirs, and more recently Ray Cunningham's Longhouses Open Doors (2002).[18] These are either official histories written for the Borneo Evangelical Mission/Overseas Missionary Fellowship constituencies or autobiographical histories of the BEM missionaries. There are also a couple of popular works by indigenous writers: Solomon Bulan and Lilian Bulan-Dorai, The Bario Revival (2004), chronicling the 1973 revival,[19] and John Edison Urud, Datuk Raja Umong (2004), focusing on the life of the first President of the SIB.[20]

There are however, references to the work of the BEM and the SIB in some anthropological studies; for example, James L. Deegan's 'Change Among the Lun Bawang, A Borneo People' (1973) on the Lun Bawang in Lawas;[21] and Sue Russell, Conversion, Identity and Power: The Impact of Christianity on Power Relationships and Social Exchanges (1999), on the Lun Dayeh in Sabah.[22] There are three other works on the Kelabit: one by Robert Lian Saging, 'An Ethno-History of the Kelabit Tribe of Sarawak' (1976/77);[23] another by Matthew H. Amster, 'Community, Ethnicity, and Modes of Association among the Kelabits of Sarawak' (1998)[24] and by Poline Bala, Changing Borders and Identities in the Kelabit Highlands: Anthropological Reflections on Growing Up in a Kelabit Village near the International Border

---

[15] Roosma, 'Guiding Toward Independence', 189.

[16] Shirley Lees, *Jungle Fire* (London: BEM, 1960) and *Drunk before Dawn* (Sevenoaks: OMF, 1978).

[17] C.H. Southwell, *Uncharted Waters* (Calgary: Astana Publishing, 1999).

[18] Ray Cunningham, *Longhouses Open Doors: God's Glory in Borneo* (Ormond: Hudson Press, 2002).

[19] Solomon Bulan and L. Bulan-Dorai, *The Bario Revival* (Kuala Lumpur: Home Matters Network, 2004).

[20] John E. Urud, *Datuk Raja Umong: Memories of the Great Rhinocerous Hunter Lives on* (Kota Kinabalu, Sabah: H and A Media Publishing, 2004).

[21] J.L. Deegan, 'Change Among the Lun Bawang, a Borneo People' (PhD thesis, University of Washington, 1973).

[22] Sue A. Russell, *Conversion, Identity and Power: The Impact of Christianity on Power Relationships and Social Exchanges* (Lanham/New York/Oxford: American Society of Missiology/University Press of America, 1999).

[23] Robert L. Saging, 'An Ethno-History of the Kelabit Tribe of Sarawak: A Brief Look at the Kelabit Tribe before World War II and After' (BA thesis, University of Malaya, 1976/77).

[24] Matthew H. Amster, 'Community, Ethnicity, and Modes of Association among the Kelabits of Sarawak' (PhD thesis, Brandeis University, 1998).

(2002).[25] Other than these studies, there has been no other serious comprehensive study of the BEM and the indigenous SIB church.

By way of contrast, there are scholarly published works on the history of the other missions or denominations in Sarawak. There is an excellent history of the Anglican SPG mission by Graham Saunders, Bishops and Brookes: The Anglican Mission and the Brooke Raj in Sarawak, 1848-1941 (1989).[26] The Roman Catholic Mill Hill Fathers Mission has been studied by John Rooney, Khabar Gembira: A History of the Catholic Church in East Malaysia and Brunei 1880-1976 (1981),[27] and there is a more general history of the Roman Catholic Church in Malaysia by Maureen K.C. Chew, The Journey of the Catholic Church in Malaysia 1511-1996 (2000).[28] Another doctoral thesis has been written on the Methodist Church in Sarawak by Yuk Chong Liong, 'A Historical Inquiry into the Quest for a Post-Independence Identity of the Chinese Methodist Church in Sarawak (CMCS), Malaysia, 1963-1988' (2001).[29]

Within the wider academic literature on 'faith' missions, there is no mention of the BEM, as is evident in Klaus Fiedler's book, The Story of Faith Missions (1994).[30] Nor is there any mention in Ruth Tucker's book, From Jerusalem to Irian Jaya: A Biographical History of Christian Missions (1983),[31] which emphasises the American contribution to world mission. However, there is a brief article on the BEM and SIB by Diana Shearer and Mina Tingan, 'Australians and the Indigenous Church of Borneo: An Overview of Australian Contributions to Sarawak and Sabah through the Borneo Evangelical Mission and Overseas Missionary Fellowship' (1997).[32]

---

[25] Poline Bala, *Changing Borders and Identities in the Kelabit Highlands: Anthropological Reflections on Growing up in a Kelabit Village near the International Border* (Kota Samarahan: University Malaysia Sarawak, 2002).

[26] Graham Saunders, *Bishops and Brookes: The Anglican Mission and the Brooke Raj in Sarawak, 1848-1941* (Singapore: Oxford University Press, 1992).

[27] John Rooney, *Khabar Gembira: A History of the Catholic Church in East Malaysia and Brunei 1880-1976* (London: Burns and Oates, 1981).

[28] Maureen K.C. Chew, *The Journey of the Catholic Church in Malaysia, 1511-1996* (Kuala Lumpur: Catholic Research Centre, 2000).

[29] Yuk Chong Liong, 'A Historical Inquiry into the Quest for a Post-Independence Identity of the Chinese Methodist Church in Sarawak (CMCS), Malaysia, 1963-1988' (PhD thesis, University of Birmingham, 2001).

[30] Klaus Fiedler, *The Story of Faith Missions* (Oxford: Regnum, 1994).

[31] Ruth Tucker, *From Jerusalem to Irian Jaya: A Biographical History of Christian Missions* (Grand Rapids: Zondervan, 1983).

[32] Diana Shearer and Mina Tingan, '"Australians and the Indigenous Church of Borneo": An Overview of Australian Contributions to Sarawak and Sabah through the Borneo Evangelical Mission and Overseas Missionary Fellowship', in Mark Hutchinson and G. Treloar (eds.), *This Gospel Shall be Preached: Essays on Australian Contribution to World Mission* (Sydney: Centre for the Study of Australian Christianity, 1997), 147-63.

Methodology

The approach of this study is historical. It traces, analyses and examines the relevant themes using a broadly chronological framework. However, in analysing the course of religious change, it is emphasised that anthropological perspectives are essential to understanding and interpreting the process of religious conversion and the distinctive nature of the indigenous Christianity that resulted.

Most previous studies on mission history have been written either from the perspective of the mission body or from the indigenous church.[33] Few studies give weight to both perspectives. This study attempts to study the processes, whenever possible, from the perspectives of both the BEM and the SIB in the light of the internal situations of the indigenous communities and the SIB church and the external context of socio-economic and political changes.

In this research, it is acknowledged that most of the surviving materials that were made available to me have been written from mission sources. This study analyses primary written sources from the BEM which are located at the Bible College of Victoria in Melbourne and at the OMF Centre in Kuala Lumpur. I was allowed limited access to the documents at the OMF Centre, and hence was not able to access all the private correspondence, though some of the more important letters were made available. Further, these materials were contained in uncatalogued boxes. These materials include official documents and publications, correspondence between the missionaries and between the Field Director and BEM Home President, Home Council minutes, Field Executive minutes, Field Conference minutes, reports and papers and other published BEM material.

A qualification needs to be made regarding the relative value of the BEM materials. It is self-evident that the BEM newsletters were written with the purpose of providing information to the BEM constituency about the work of the missionaries, as well as with the view to raise financial support. This means that matters that were more likely to interest the BEM constituency and to raise support for the Mission were highlighted and, at times, exaggerated. Conversely, setbacks, divisions and controversies were sometimes glossed over, omitted or described only in spiritualised or sanitized form. Hence, it is necessary to 'read between the lines' of these accounts. Some deconstruction of the accounts has been necessary, although such deconstruction always runs the risk of reading 'foreign' meanings into the accounts of the missionaries and not giving sufficient credence to what they have to say. Nevertheless, it remains the

---

[33] Early works on mission history focused mainly on the work of the missionaries. Later works such as A.D. Tom Tuma, *Building a Ugandan Church: African Participation in Church Growth and Expansion in Busoga, 1891-1940* (Nairobi: Kenya Literature Bureau, 1980) and Louise M. Pirouet, *Black Evangelists: The Spread of Christianity in Uganda, 1891-1914* (London: Rex Collings, 1978) focused on indigenous initiatives in the spread of Christianity.

case that the BEM newsletters provide a broad coverage of the happenings within the Mission and in the field, even though they were written from their narrow perspective of religious concerns.

Consequently, documents, such as the minutes and reports of the Home Council and Field Conference and private correspondence between the missionaries and between the Field Director and BEM Home President, reflect more accurately what was happening behind the scenes. However, the brevity of the minutes at times affects their usefulness. Of significantly greater value is the correspondence which gives the private views of the writers.

Unfortunately, primary written sources from the SIB are virtually non-existent. This is understandable, as literacy was only introduced into the Orang Ulu community in the post-war era. It is important to note that an oral tradition continued to dominate the Orang Ulu until there were sufficient numbers among their communities who became literate enough to appreciate the need for published written documents. As a result, this study exhibits heavier reliance than is desirable on the BEM newsletters. The newsletters clearly provide a perspective on the BEM and SIB that is partial and inadequately reflective of indigenous perspectives. This study makes a conscious attempt to counter-balance this problem by various means. First, and most important, interviews have been conducted among national and local SIB leaders and members, whose lives and ministries spanned the period from 1938 to 1980, and whose perspectives will serve as an additional source of information to the written sources.[34] Those interviewed were in leadership positions of the SIB, and they had a direct contact and working relationship with the BEM leadership and missionaries.

Second, oral history research was conducted among the surviving missionaries of the BEM, especially those who had played important roles in its work previously, whether by personal interviews or by correspondence. The oral research surveyed a cross-section of the surviving missionaries of the BEM in both the United Kingdom and Australia. The participants in this oral history research were asked to tell their stories through interviews and open-ended questions using a carefully designed questionnaire.[35] This oral research has uncovered additional information as well as providing different perspectives from those reported in the BEM newsletters. The purpose of these two sources is to find corroborating, supplementary and alternative perspectives to those in the archival materials and records.

Third, use has been made of other external sources such as the Sarawak Museum Journal (SMJ) and the Sarawak Gazette (SG), especially on the relevant and key themes or issues under discussion. As shown later in this book, the BEM missionaries started their work in Sarawak under a cloud of suspicion by the Brooke government. They therefore had to earn the respect of

---

[34] See Appendix 2.

[35] See Appendix 1.

the Brooke administrators. Recognition of their work began after a dramatic change occurred among the Lun Bawang. This change was reported in the Sarawak Gazette by Edward Banks, the Curator of the Sarawak Museum, and led to a visit to Trusan in 1940 by the Rajah, who was reported to have been surprised at the success of the work of the BEM. Hence, later writings in the Sarawak Museum Journal and Sarawak Gazette were generally less critical and more neutral in their tone in their assessment of the BEM's work. But it must be noted that the Brooke administrators and colonial officials were men who held opinions of their own, and they were not easily influenced, particularly by missionaries.

A search was also made at Rhodes House in Oxford into the SPG archives for any reference made to the work of the BEM. However, no reference was found in the SPG archival records.

An assumption in this study has been to take seriously the theology and beliefs of the missionaries and the implications for their mission policy and strategy, and not to treat them as being irrelevant, insignificant or of no consequence to their missionary work. As Andrew Porter has argued in his book, Religion versus Empire? British Protestant Missionaries and Overseas Expansion, 1700-1914, historiography should take due consideration of this aspect. Porter contends that 'missionaries viewed their world first of all with the eye of faith and then through their theological lenses' and therefore, we should allow 'the relevant historiography to be generously defined and that sources of missionary inspiration be given a full consideration, rather than be arbitrarily confined to their supposedly rational and secular components, generally found more comprehensible if not congenial by most of today's scholars'.[36]

Outline of Chapters

The next chapter of this study sets the political, cultural and religious context in which the BEM found itself when it first began work in Sarawak. There will be an examination of the attitudes of the Brooke and colonial regimes to Christian missions tracing the work of the different Christian missions such as the Anglican SPG, Roman Catholic Mill Hill Fathers and American Methodist Episcopal Mission. In addition, a study will be made on the ethnic, cultural and religious geography of Sarawak which includes consideration of the Orang Ulu and their constituent people, their worldview, the place of Islam in Sarawak, and the influences of modernity as well as literacy and education in Sarawak.

Chapter Three analyses the particular strand of Australian Christianity that gave rise to the formation of the BEM. The questions pertinent to this chapter

[36] Andrew Porter, *Religion versus Empire? British Protestant Missionaries and Overseas Expansion, 1700-1914* (Manchester: Manchester University Press, 2004), 11, 13.

are: What was the kind of the Australian evangelical tradition that lay behind the BEM as a mission? In what ways did this Australian evangelical tradition shape the nature of the BEM?

Chapter Four sketches the early history of the BEM, dealing with its work before the Second World War (WWII) but with a focus on the interaction between Brooke policy and BEM mission philosophy and practice. There are a few questions that this chapter wishes to explore. How and why did the policies of the Brooke government help, hinder or shape the work of the BEM? How did the BEM respond to these challenges?

Chapter Five continues to trace the BEM mission policies and practice as its work spread rapidly into the Baram, Fourth Division and into the Rajang, Third Division of Sarawak in the post-war era in tandem with mass movements into Christianity, especially among the Kayan, Kenyah and Penan tribes. Another focus will be to examine the nature of these conversions and the place of indigenous agency in the spread of the Gospel. The pertinent questions are: How and why were there mass movements into Christianity? Which people were particularly receptive to the Christianity offered by the BEM and why? Which were less receptive and why? In what ways did the indigenous people respond to appropriate and re-interpret the Gospel message presented by the BEM? What were the mission policies of the BEM and how were these worked out among the indigenous people?

Chapter Six discusses the relationship between mission policies and the establishment of the indigenous church, SIB and traces the changes in mission policies in response to the changing socio-political situation. The promotion of indigenous initiatives and the response of indigenous Christians are analysed. The key questions are: What was the BEM's approach to planting and nurturing an indigenous 'Three-Self' church, the SIB? In what ways did the BEM support or hinder the emergence of local indigenous leadership within the SIB? How successful was the BEM's approach, and why?

Chapter Seven discusses the role of revival movements in consolidating the SIB in the face of a changing social context and on the eve of the official closure of the BEM's work in Sarawak. After the formal establishment of the SIB in 1959, the BEM and SIB faced different political and socio-economic challenges from 1959 to 1979. It is necessary to ask: Why were revival movements a feature of the life of such a young church as the SIB? What were the consequences or impact of the revival movements on the SIB?

Chapter Eight discusses the response of the BEM and SIB to the challenges of socio-economic and political change under the Malaysian government. The relevant questions here are: How and why did the policies of the Malaysian government after 1963 help, hinder or shape the work of the SIB, and how did SIB respond to these challenges? What ongoing relationship did BEM have with the SIB after 1959? What form of external assistance (if any) did SIB receive after BEM ceased to function as a mission body in 1979, and what was its impact?

The concluding chapter seeks to assess the degree of success achieved by the BEM in the implementation of its philosophy and mission policy to establish and nurture an indigenous 'Three-Self' church.

Chapter 2

The BEM in Sarawak in Its Context

The BEM, working within a particular political, cultural and religious context in Sarawak, initially started its mission work in the Limbang Valley, Fifth Division, in 1928.

This chapter seeks to explore firstly, the political context in Sarawak by examining governmental attitudes and policies under Brooke rule, then Japanese rule, colonial administration and finally the Malaysian government; secondly, the indigenous socio-cultural and religious structures of the Orang Ulu in Sarawak; and thirdly, the work of other Christian missions in Sarawak, as they provide a useful comparison to the work of the BEM.

The Distinctiveness of Sarawak

In the early nineteenth century, direct contact with Western colonial powers was found only at the periphery of Southeast Asia. By the end of the century, nearly the whole region with the exception of Thailand had come under Western colonial rule. Of these powers, the British were the most dominant through the nineteenth century and into the early twentieth century.[1] The driving force of British global expansion during this era was primarily the pursuit of economic, strategic and political objectives.[2]

Within this context of Southeast Asia, Sarawak's history was distinctive from that of the other Southeast Asian countries. Though colonised as early as 1841, it did not come under direct British colonial rule until 1946, when it was officially ceded to the British. For a century from 1841 to 1941, Sarawak was ruled by the Brookes, a dynasty of three Englishmen;[3] namely, James Brooke (1841-1868), Charles Brooke (1868-1917) and Vyner Brooke (1917-1941). But it was only given official British recognition as an independent state in 1863

---

[1] Of the colonial powers, the British, Dutch and French played the largest role in the affairs of Southeast Asia. By the nineteenth century, Dutch influence had waned, giving way to British dominance with the French having an interest in Indo-China since the mid-nineteenth century.

[2] The promotion of Christianity was not among their primary objectives. Clive J. Christie, *Southeast Asia in the Twentieth Century: A Reader* (London, I.B. Tauris, 1998), 12.

[3] Otto C. Doering, 'Government in Sarawak under Charles Brooke', *JMBRAS* 39.2 (1966), 95.

and later, formal protection in 1888. In reality, it was 'a specific type of British colonialism' with a 'colonial administration',[4] which has generally been considered as anomalous in that it was governed as 'a private fiefdom'.[5]

Brooke rule sought to enforce strictly a geographical segregation of the races as well as to engage them in different roles; the Malays were mainly involved in the political and administrative affairs of government, the Iban (or Sea Dyak)[6] in the police force and the Chinese in commercial activities.[7] Their geographical separation enabled a better control and prevented a coalition of forces among them against Brooke rule. The establishment of forts at river mouths had the effect of isolating the Malays from the war-like Iban, whom the Malays recruited for their expeditions or piracy, confining the Malays to the coastal regions, and the Iban to the upriver territories. Only in the urban centres like Kuching, Sibu and Miri was there some form of mixing of the races. During Charles Brooke's rule, he reversed James Brooke's ban on the Chinese by encouraging a mass importation of Chinese into Sibu in 1901 for the purpose of stimulating the economic activity of the state.[8] As for the people of the interior or Orang Ulu, particularly the Lun Bawang, Kelabit, Kayan and Kenyah, they were too isolated from the others to have much meaningful contact until the BEM missionaries began to work among them.

This 'private fiefdom' of Sarawak ruled by English individuals for a century was unique in the history of colonial influence in Southeast Asia, in that it survived and thrived into the middle of the twentieth century, while the other Southeast Asian nations fell under the rule of the European colonial powers. Further, as an anti-colonial colonialist, James despised the manner of British colonial rule in India[9] and advocated his bold experiment of ruling over a large local population with just a handful of European officers.[10] It was initially

---

[4] Ulla Wagner, *Colonialism and Iban Warfare* (Stockholm: OBE-Tryck Sthim, 1972), 1-2.

[5] Craig A. Lockhard, *From Kampong to City: A Social History of Kuching, Malaysia, 1820-1970* (Athens: Ohio, 1987), xi. J.H. Walker, *Power and Prowess: The Origins of Brooke Kingship in Sarawak* (Honolulu: Allen & Unwin/University of Hawai'i Press, 2002), xvi.

[6] The term 'Dyak' was used during Brooke and British colonial rule to refer to two groups of people; 'Sea Dyak' refers to the Iban and 'Land Dyak' to the Bidayuh.

[7] Robert M. Pringle, 'The Brookes of Sarawak: Reformers in spite of Themselves', *SMJ* 19.38-39 (July/December 1971), 62.

[8] James Brooke banned the mass influx of Chinese after the Chinese Uprising in Sarawak of 1857.

[9] R. Mundy, *Narrative of Events in Borneo and Celebes, Down to the Occupation of Labuan: From the Journals of James Brooke Esq., Rajah of Sarawak and Governor of Labuan, Together with a Narrative of the Operations of HMS Iris* (London: John Murray, 1848), I, 12, 69-70.

[10] Letter of Brooke to Gardner, 10 December 1841 in J.C. Templer, *The Private Letters of Sir James Brooke, K.C.B., Rajah of Sarawak, Narrating the Events of His Life from 1838 to the Present Time*, 3 vols, (London: Richard Bentley, 1853), 176-77. 'The

thought to be a novel and seemingly preposterous idea, but it proved successful and left an indelible mark on the history of British colonialism.[11] This system of government was transplanted into the British Residential System in Peninsular Malaya through the influence of Hugh Low who became the British Resident of Perak from 1877 to 1889. 'A modified version of the Brooke model became the basis of Low's administration and through his example influenced the nature of colonial rule in the four Protected States of Peninsular Malaya.'[12]

The Political Context

During the rule of the Brooke Rajahs, Sarawak attained its present size in 1905 and was administratively divided into five Divisions.[13] The Japanese occupied Sarawak from 1941 to 1945. After WWII, Sarawak was ceded to the British colonial government until 16 September 1963, when Sarawak became part of the new nation of Malaysia, comprising Peninsular Malaya, Singapore, Sarawak and Sabah.

We will examine the attitudes of government to Christian missions during each stage of the political context in Sarawak.

Missions and 'Civilization': Brooke Rule (1841-1941)

JAMES BROOKE (1841-1868)

During the era of British global expansion in the late eighteenth and nineteenth centuries, it became a widespread conviction that Britain was marked out by divine providence as an instrument of universal progress, having a humanitarian and salvific role in the world and that the empire was a powerful means of bringing civilization to 'savage' natives through trade and the imposition of a superior moral code of conduct; the abolition of slavery being a prelude to the process.[14] Within this milieu, James Brooke himself was

---

experiment of developing a country through the residence of a few Europeans by assistance of its native rulers has never been fairly tried; and it appears to me, in some respects, more desirable than the actual possession by a foreign nation'.

[11] Barbara and Leonard Andaya, *A History of Malaysia* (London: Macmillan, 1982), 172.

[12] Andaya, *A History of Malaysia*, 172. Sarawak had the experience of successfully implementing James Brooke's experiment for some thirty-three years (1841-1874). Hugh Brooke Low was Resident of Third Division under Charles Brooke.

[13] The first to fifth divisions have their centres of administration at Kuching, Simmangang (now known as Sri Aman), Sibu, Miri and Limbang respectively. Under Charles Brooke, the borders of Sarawak extended to its present limits by acquiring the Baram River in 1882, the Trusan River in 1884, the Limbang River in 1890 and the Lawas River in 1905.

[14] Lawrence James, *The Rise and Fall of the British Empire* (London: Abacus, 1998), 170, 184-85. The campaign against slavery coincided with the growth of Christian missions.

convinced that he was fulfilling a divine liberating mission in the Malay Archipelago.[15] In his letter to his mother on 18 April 1841, he spoke of introducing civilization, commerce and Christianity into Borneo.[16] There was, within contemporary mission circles, a debate over the relative priority of civilization and Christianity.[17] But James' preference for civilizing before Christianizing showed in his liking for those American missionaries who tended to focus on civilizing the locals through education and social work.[18] Graham Saunders argues that, though his preference was indebted to Sir Stamford Raffles, James developed it further and saw that 'there was a role for Christian missions as part of an overall civilizing process'.[19]

James' appeal for a Christian mission to work among the Dyak was prompted by political and humanitarian concerns.[20] He viewed the Dyak as 'an

---

[15] As Brooke wrote, 'I see the benefits I am conferring. The oppressed, the wretched, the enslaved have found in me their only protector. They now hope and trust: and they shall not be disappointed whilst I have life to uphold them. God has so far used me as a humble instrument of his hidden Providence'. Mundy, *Narrative of Events in Borneo and Celebes*, I, 272.

[16] 'I have excellent hopes that this effort of mine will succeed and whilst it ameliorates the conditions of the unhappy natives and tends to the highest promotion of philanthropy, it will secure me some better means of carrying through these grand objects: I call them grand objects for they are so, when we reflect that civilization, commerce, and religion may through them be spread over so vast an island as Borneo'. See Letter of Brooke to Mother, 18 April 1841 in Templer, *Private Letters*, I, 97. Letter of Brooke to Templer, 31 December 1844 in Templer, *Private Letters*, II, 40-46. By 1840, Thomas Foxwell Buxton had already disseminated his idea of civilization, commerce and Christianity in his book, *The African Slave Trade and its Remedy* which was first published in 1839. Although it is likely that James Brooke borrowed Buxton's ideas, there is no firm evidence of his dependence on Buxton.

[17] According to Brian Stanley, 'the substantial majority of mission thought in English Evangelical tradition from the late eighteenth to mid-twentieth century subscribed to the priority of Christianity over civilization'. Brian Stanley, 'Christianity and Civilization in English Evangelical Mission Thought', in Brian Stanley (ed.), *Christian Missions and the Enlightenment* (Grand Rapids: Eerdmans, 2001), 176-77. However, Samuel Marsden appeared to hold to the priority of civilization before Evangelization; arguing that missionaries should initially refrain from preaching and devote themselves wholly to manual work or leave the civilizing task to secular agencies (185). On the other hand, Scottish evangelicals such as Thomas Chalmers viewed education as having a Christianizing role (180-81).

[18] Brooke noted that American missionaries 'live quietly, relieve the distressed, do not dispute or argue, and aim to educate the children'. Letter of Brooke to Mother, 16 October 1842 in Templer, *Private Letters*, I, 229-30. See Saunders, *Bishops and Brookes*, 7.

[19] As Saunders puts it, Brooke's views 'went further than Raffles in developing the theory that Britain had a duty to spread her civilizing and pacifying mission whether or not any profit accrued to British trade'. Saunders, *Bishops and Brookes*, 4-5.

[20] 'If the poor Dyaks who dwell on the coast were only to sufficiently numerous to protect themselves or lived under a government strong enough to afford them protection.... Now they are in constant peril of their lives, not only from the roving

unhappy race' under oppression of the Malays, and believed that the introduction of Christianity would 'ameliorate their unhappy condition'.[21] For Christianity to be successfully introduced into Sarawak, he wrote of the need of the mission to work on a moderate scale so as to remove any chance of arousing a feeling of distrust among the Malays. He disapproved of missionaries whose preaching of Christianity implied abusing the religious beliefs of others.[22] In Saunders' view, there was already a hint of future conflict of interest between Brooke and Francis McDougall, the pioneer Anglican missionary. Brooke believed in gradualism in mission work, whereas McDougall saw that his mission was to plant the apostolic Church in Borneo, and this aim did not necessarily preclude methods to which the Rajah might object.[23]

As Saunders notes, there was a contradiction in James' view. Though he expressed the desire to have missionaries to work among the Dyak, James was suspicious of the zeal that one would expect of a missionary. On the one hand, he desired to introduce Christianity as an agent of civilization; on the other, he did not want to disturb the peace.[24]

In his experiment of civilizing the indigenous people, James would not allow any individual,[25] any commercial enterprise[26] or power to jeopardise his grand vision or to pose a threat to him as Rajah. Neither did he want any interference from the British government, though he wished very much for British

---

tribes of their own nation, and from the treacherous Malays, but also from those terrible pirates, the Illanuns and Balalanini.... My anxiety and my desires to ameliorate their condition are boundless.... I must never dream of returning to my native land, until, at least, some measure of good has been accomplished.... Injustice and tyranny now stalk throughout the land. The Dyaks are slaughtered without mercy'. Mundy, *Narrative of Events in Borneo and Celebes*, I, 195-96. Max Saint, *Twenty Years in Sarawak 1848-68: A Flourish for the Bishop and Brooke's Friend Grant* (Kuala Lumpur: S.A. Majeed, 1992 [1985]), 15-16.

[21] Letter of Brooke to Templer, 10 November 1841 in Templer, *Private Letters*, I, 136.

[22] See Letter of Brooke to Mundy, 18 February 1850 in Templer, *Private Letters*, II, 269-70. 'Zealots and intolerants and enthusiasts with brains heated beyond the rational point, and who begin the task of tuition by a torrent of abuse against what the pupils hold sacred shall not come to Sarawak or if they come, I shall prevent the mischief they attempt at any cost'. For further discussion, see Saunders, *Bishops and Brookes*, 8-9, 11.

[23] At a meeting held on 22 November 1847, different views between Brooke and the Mission were already present. Revd H. Montagu Villiers expressed that the purpose of the Mission was not to civilize but to preach the Gospel: 'Mr Brooke would die to civilize, but Christ died to redeem'. Quoted in Saunders, *Bishops and Brookes*, 11-12.

[24] Saunders, *Bishops and Brookes*, 36-37.

[25] Graham Irwin, *Nineteenth Century Borneo: A Study in Diplomatic Rivalry* (Kuala Lumpur: University of Malaya, 1955), 132-35. Tom Harrisson, 'Robert Burns - the first Ethnologist and Explorer of Interior Sarawak', *SMJ* 5.3 (November 1951), 463-77.

[26] Ooi Keat Gin, *Of Free Trade and Native Interests: The Brookes and the Economic Development of Sarawak,* 1841-1941 (Kuala Lumpur: Oxford University Press, 1997), 28-29.

recognition and protection. Further, he viewed Christian mission as playing an integral but subservient role in fulfilling his plan of civilizing the local people, treating it as an arm of his governmental authority.[27] His purpose was to use Christian mission as a means of stabilising the politically unruly parts of the country; hence, his suggestion in January 1851 to Francis McDougall, the Anglican bishop, to increase the number of missionaries and to place them at strategic areas along the more distant rivers, including an area not under his jurisdiction like Kanowit.[28] Even his proposal in 1851 to have McDougall made bishop was more a means of controlling the Anglican mission through its head, the bishop, than a genuine concern for its development.[29] He further affirmed his right to direct new missionaries to places where they should work, and his preference for young rather than old men.[30] Further, his control extended to isolating the Dyak from the Malays, thereby lessening his fears about them converting to Islam. There seems to have been in Brooke a characteristic colonial preference for Christianity over Islam if animism was deemed fated for extinction.[31] His underlying motivation was his ambition to make his novel experiment a success;[32] thereby bringing him name and fame.[33]

A characteristic feature of British rule in general, and Brooke rule in particular, was to segregate Christian missions geographically. During James' rule, the area was considered too small to have more Christian missions;[34] hence he refused entry to Roman Catholic Chinese catechists from Singapore in 1850.[35] Also, as Saunders pointed out, James was opposed to 'Romanism' and the Oxford Movement.[36] Later, he discouraged the establishment of a Moravian mission at Quop in 1865.[37] In not allowing two Christian missions to work

---

[27] Charles J. Bunyon, *Memoirs of Francis Thomas McDougall and of Harriette, His Wife* (London: Longmans, 1889), 43.

[28] Letter of Brooke to McDougall, 28 January 1851 in Templer, *Private Letters*, III, 29-31.

[29] Saint, *Twenty Years*, 86. The Bishop, Francis McDougall admitted his disappointment with the Rajah Brooke by 1858: 'I cannot tell you how the Rajah has disappointed us, he cares for nothing about Christianity and *would only use us politically and kick us overboard if we did not suit his views*'. (Italics mine).

[30] Bunyon, *Memoirs of Francis Thomas McDougall*, 61.

[31] Saint, *Twenty Years*, 15-16.

[32] Brooke to Gardner, 10 December 1841 in Templer, *Private Letters*, I, 176-77.

[33] Brooke to Mother, 9 June 1840 in Templer, *Private Letters*, I, 85-86. He expressed his wish to be knighted. Brooke to Mother, 18 April 1841, in Templer, *Private Letters*, I, 103.

[34] Sarawak then consisted of First and Second Division, for which the Anglican mission (SPG) had sole charge.

[35] Saunders, *Bishops and Brookes*, 28.

[36] Saunders, *Bishops and Brookes*, 6.

[37] Owen Rutter, *Rajah Brooke and Baroness Burdett-Coutts* (London: Hutchinson, 1935), 245-46.

within the same area, Brooke aimed to ensure firm control and maintain peace over Sarawak.

CHARLES BROOKE (1868-1917)

As Charles Brooke subscribed to a policy of impartiality to all religions, Christian missions did not find themselves more favoured than the other religions in Sarawak.[38] He continued James' policy of no proselytization of the Malays by any Christian mission,[39] and adhered strictly to the policy of geographical segregation, allocating the First and Second Divisions to the Anglican mission and the Third Division to the Roman Catholic mission in 1881. But he allowed the Roman Catholic mission to have a headquarters in Kuching. Later, he allowed the Methodist Episcopal Mission to work among the Foochow Christians in Sibu in 1903, but made an exception to allow both the Roman Catholics and the Methodist mission to work among the Chinese immigrants in Sibu.

In regard to the work of 'civilizing' the indigenous population, Charles expressed an ambivalent attitude toward education. Initially, he took a more positive view that Christian mission work would slowly convert the Dyak through education[40] and also approved of their transition from a migratory lifestyle to a settled agricultural lifestyle.[41] But he later feared that the negative effects of western education and civilization, in the long-term, would destroy the indigenous culture and way of life,[42] so that he was careful to ensure that any measure taken 'shall not be contrary to native customs' and without their prior consent, espousing a philosophy of *ad hoc* action.[43]

Like James, Charles saw the political value of Christian missions and regarded the place and duty of missionaries as part of his governmental machinery: 'the conversion of the Dyaks would be the means of strengthening the government beyond measure.'[44] Hence, he exercised a very firm control

---

[38] 'It was the duty of the Government...to be a supporter of no religion in preference to another, and to protect all alike. If the Government had attempted to push Christianity, such a course would have inevitably led to the ruin of both itself and the Mission also'. Charles Brooke, *Ten Years in Sarawak* (2 vols, II; Singapore: Oxford University Press, 1990 [1866]), 325.

[39] Henry de Windt, *My Restless Life* (London: Grant Richards, 1909), 59.

[40] *Sarawak Gazette*, 16 January 1872. Brooke, *Ten Years*, II, 327.

[41] Sylvia Brooke, *Queen of the Headhunters* (Kuala Lumpur: Oxford University Press, 1990 [1970]), 61-62.

[42] S. Baring-Gould and C.A. Bampfylde, *A History of Sarawak under Its Two White Rajahs* (London: Henry Sotheran, 1909), 440. In his book, *Queries: Past, Present and Future* (London: Planet, 1907), Charles Brooke expressed his doubts about the relevance of western education for the Dyak.

[43] Robert M. Pringle, *Rajahs and Rebels* (London: Macmillan, 1970), 137. Charles Brooke was of the opinion that the common man of the early Industrial Revolution was not any better than the Iban or Malay in Sarawak. See Brooke, *Ten Years*, II, 214.

[44] Brooke, *Ten Years*, II, 325.

over Christian missions, more so than James, dictating where they were to work and using them as a means to bring stability to pacified but still unruly regions in the interior.[45] He further dictated how missionaries were to do their work among the people, which was very much patterned after his own experience in the outstation in his early ten years in Sarawak.[46]

One of his main concerns was the economic viability of Sarawak, especially when Charles inherited a state that was in debt.[47] In 1901 the Rajah encouraged a large immigration into Sibu of a thousand Foochow Chinese Christians under the leadership of a Methodist pastor, Wong Nai Siong, to develop agriculture along the Rajang, which met Brooke's economic objective of bringing prosperity to Sarawak. With the later immigration of other Chinese groups, the lower Rajang from Sibu to Kanowit was transformed into a lucrative farming area by 1916. There were both political and economic dimensions in using Christian missions, particularly the Roman Catholics and Methodists, in developing the country. Both these missions produced results that suited his objectives; the Roman Catholics in developing education and social work, introducing new methods of farming, and helping the Dyak to make the transition to a settled farming life.[48] Not only did the Methodist mission contribute to the economic prosperity of Sarawak through the Foochow Christians, but it also acted as an agent of modernization for Sarawak through James Hoover, the missionary from the American Episcopal Methodist Mission.[49] Hoover established numerous schools on a self-supporting principle with little help from the government, introduced modern facilities, amenities and technology, and handled land arbitration and disputes between the Foochow and the Dyak with the help of the Resident or Rajah.[50] By 1912, the Rajah was so impressed with the Methodist mission that he encouraged them to start a similar work in the Baram.[51] Hence, Charles was generally more favourable to the Roman Catholic mission and the Methodist mission.

---

[45] The Roman Catholic Mission was directed by Charles Brooke to Kapit in 1882 to act as a politically stabilizing force between the Iban of the Balleh and the Kayan. Pringle, *Rajahs and Rebels*, 257.

[46] Brooke, *Ten Years*, II, 323-24.

[47] Elizabeth Pollard, *Kuching Past and Present* (Kuching: Borneo Literature Bureau, 1972), 72. The state's expenditure of $126,161 exceeded its revenue of $122,840 in addition to a large public debt of fifteen thousand sterling pounds.

[48] See section on 'The Mill Hill Fathers' in this chapter.

[49] James Hoover was sent from British Malaya in 1903 to oversee the Methodist mission in Sarawak and was appointed the government's agent in charge of the Chinese settlements by the Rajah after Wong Nai Siong's return to China in 1904.

[50] F.T. Cartwright, *Tuan Hoover of Borneo* (New York: Abingdon, 1938), 106-108, 165, 121, 111-12. Daniel Chew, *Chinese Pioneers on the Sarawak Frontier, 1841-1941* (Singapore: Oxford University Press, 1990), 148-52.

[51] Cartwright, *Tuan Hoover*, 125-26 and 134-35. *SG* August 1912, 168. The project did not materialize due to a lack of interest by the Chinese.

VYNER BROOKE (1917-1941)

Under Vyner, the continuance of the Brooke tradition[52] and its ad hoc policy led Sarawak to lag behind in social and economic development when compared to British Malaya and Singapore. Feeling the dilemma between isolating his people and exposing them to the rapid changes in the world, Vyner expressed a cautious willingness in 1936 to adapt Sarawak to the conditions of a rapidly changing world.[53]

Though Sarawak was relatively peaceful and prosperous, the significant Kapit Peace-making in 1924 effectively ushered in an era of peace, ending the constant inter-tribal feuding.[54] From the 1930s onwards, travel into the interior became relatively safer; a factor which was to aid the travel of the BEM missionaries into the interior of the Fifth Division. In maintaining the Brooke zoning policy, Christian missions were used as stabilising forces in politically unstable areas. When the BEM started work in Sarawak in November 1928, it was directed to the Limbang River of the Fifth Division, making its base among a mixed Murut-Iban population at Sungai Pranga, the furthest government outpost into the interior. The BEM was refused permission to expand its work among the Lun Bawang and the Kayan and Kenyah in the Baram in the early 1930s, as the Brooke government felt that it was still unsafe for the BEM missionaries to settle in the Trusan.[55] Also, the Baram had already been allotted to the Roman Catholic mission, which had a mission base at Marudi since 1901 and at Miri since 1914.

However, the zoning policy underwent a subtle change under Vyner's rule. Vyner's proclamation speech as Rajah, saying that he 'will on no account interfere with the Mohammedan faith or with another religion or belief of the people', was an assurance to the local people that the Government would not interfere with the internal affairs of any religion, and each religious group could have its own work and place of worship among its adherents. This assurance provided a loophole for formal work by any mission body to be started in any area where the mission body had its adherents.[56] The Singapore mission of the

---

[52] *SG*, 1 December 1928.

[53] The Rajah's Speech to Council Negeri, 25th Meeting, 29 April 1937. *SG*, May 1937.

[54] The Kapit Peacemaking on 16 November 1924 was the last of the peacemaking ceremonies which ended the feuding between the Kayan, Kenyah and Kajang of the Appoh Kayan and Balui Rivers and the Sea Dyak (Iban) of the Batang Rajang and Batang Ayer headwaters. See *SG*, 1 December 1924, 1-2. Steven Runciman, *The White Rajahs: A History of Sarawak* (Cambridge: Cambridge University Press, 1960), 238.

[55] *BEM Fifth Annual Report*, 30 June 1933, 2. Southwell, *Uncharted Waters*, 83. Lily Chan, 'Christian Missions and the Ibans of Sarawak during the Brooke Rule 1840's to 1940's' (BA thesis, Australian National University, 1975), 25.

[56] Under Charles Brooke's rule, when R.P. Montgomery, director-designate of Borneo Mission of SDA tried to begin a work in Sarawak in 1915, he was summarily expelled four days after his arrival at Kuching. See Herbert Clarence Sormin, 'A History of the Seventh-Day Adventist Church in Sarawak from 1915 to 1956' (MA thesis, Philippine Union College, 1971), 25.

Seventh Day Adventists (SDA) applied and gained approval for formal work among a small group of its adherents, mostly Chinese in Kuching, which later resulted in the establishment of a church and school. Further, the SDA was allowed to work among the indigenous people where no existing mission work was present, but was discouraged from working in the same area already worked by another mission body. This resulted in the SDA establishing the Bukit Nyala station along the Tatau River in the Bintulu District, Fourth Division in 1930 and later the Ayer Manis Station on the 37th mile on the Kuching-Simmangang road in 1933.[57] So, the areas which had been assigned to mission bodies had become smaller, opening the door to any new mission body to work in any area where there was no existing mission work. The practical outworking of this policy later led to two mission bodies working next to each other, as in the First and Third Divisions. Moreover, in towns such as Kuching, Sibu and Miri, the implementation of this zoning policy became impractical due to population migration.[58] This small change paved the way for different mission bodies during the colonial era to work in the same area and often in competition with one another, particularly in towns. However, in the rural areas, the government administrators sought to continue the zoning policy unless approval came from the highest authority.[59] Despite the Brookes' restrictions, the BEM missionaries worked the area to the very limits of governmental permission. They directed their attention to the upper Limbang to work among the Kelabit in the Medihit after permission was refused them to set up a base at the next river, the Trusan, where there was a mass conversion of Lun Bawang to Christianity.[60] They continued to make visits to the Trusan from 1934 to 1937 to encourage and teach the Christians there. In November 1937, permission was granted by the Rajah to the BEM to establish a mission base at the Trusan,[61] and when the Rajah visited the Trusan himself in November 1940, he was reported to be duly impressed with the work there and remarked to the BEM leader, Hudson Southwell:

> I am amazed at the change in the Murut tribe.... It's remarkable! Very remarkable! And they seemed cleaner than I have ever seen them before... I believe you have done more good in a few years than the Government has done in

---

[57] Sormin, 'A History of the Seventh Day Adventist Church in Sarawak', 30, 32-35, 51-53.

[58] By 1941, the Roman Catholic, Methodist and Anglican Missions were working among the Chinese in Sibu. In Kuching, in addition to these three, there was the SDA Mission. In Miri, the Anglican Mission worked alongside the Roman Catholic Mission.

[59] Permission to start a base in the Baram in the post-war era had the approval of the Governor. See Chapter 5.

[60] This issue of mass conversion among the Lun Bawang or Murut will be discussed later. See Chapter 4.

[61] Saunders, *Bishops and Brookes*, 249. Permission was given to the BEM to work in the Trusan and Lawas districts.

forty (italics mine)… But the thing that surprises me is that your Mission does all this by methods of faith and spiritual means.[62]

Its success was later to earn the BEM permission to expand its work beyond the Limbang valley area.

Missions under Japanese Occupation (1941-45)

The Japanese Occupation of Sarawak from 1941 to 1945 saw the closure of Christian mission work with the internment of all foreign missionaries at the Batu Lintang Camp in Kuching.[63] All mission buildings, including schools, were commandeered to be used as military barracks, government offices and stores, and churches were targets of bombing.[64] By the end of WWII, all BEM buildings had been completely destroyed so that the immediate post-war era saw the need for the reconstruction of new mission buildings.

Indigenous leadership of the various missions in the coastal and sub-coastal areas rose to the challenge to maintain church activities under difficult circumstances. The BEM-established churches in the interior had little interference from the Japanese, who had generally confined themselves to the coastal areas of Sarawak except for occasional expeditions into the interior. The BEM missionaries, who hid in the interior for nearly a year before surrendering to the Japanese, started a school which was very popular, did much Bible teaching among the Lun Bawang and Kelabit. They conducted weekly services, visited, preached and encouraged them, appointed leaders (who were often community leaders) and trained them to manage the fledgling indigenous churches, besides translating the Scriptures into the vernacular.[65] After WWII, these churches were found to have continued reasonably well, partly due to local leadership initiatives and partly to the Mission's policy of lay leadership.

In the closing years of WWII, the Lun Bawang, Kelabit, Kayan, and Kenyah of the interior of the Third to Fifth Divisions were for the first time exposed to prolonged European contact due to the presence of the Special Reconnaissance Detachment (SRD), the British Allied forces who liberated them from the

---

[62] *BEM Twelfth Annual Report*, 31 March 1941, 3. See also Southwell, *Uncharted Waters*, 101-102. Lees, *Drunk before Dawn*, 67. See also Harold McCracken, *Summing Up: John Harold McCracken, 1906-1999* (Aranda, ACT: Heather and Paul Shelley, 2003), 170, 178. Harold McCracken, President of BEM Home Council from 1935 to 1971, mentioned a similar remark made by Vyner Brooke to him when the Rajah was in Australia during WWII. McCracken acted as the Rajah's solicitor in Melbourne when purchasing a property named *Castle Towers* for his residence in South Yarra, Australia.

[63] The BEM missionaries, interned at Batu Lintang, were Hudson and Winsome Southwell, Roland and Mary Bewsher, Frank Davidson, Alan Belcher and Brian Morcombe. Davidson died in internment on April 1945. After WWII, the Bewshers resigned from the Mission.

[64] Rooney, *Khabar Gembira*, 56, 84, 194.

[65] *BEM Thirteenth Annual Report*, 31 December 1946, 2. Southwell, *Uncharted Waters*, 118-26.

Japanese. The detachments that parachuted into the Kelabit highlands under Major Tom Harrisson (who after WWII became the Curator of Sarawak Museum) and into the Baram under Major Toby Carter, began enlisting the people to wage a war against the Japanese; for which task, they also enlisted the assistance of all the chiefs of the Lun Bawang, Kelabit, Kayan, and Kenyah in the Third to Fifth Divisions.[66]

This exposure to the Europeans had a profound impact on the indigenous people. They were astounded by the SRD in the following ways. Firstly, the SRD operated in a manner that disregarded traditional beliefs and practices. It seemed strange from the perspective of the indigenous people that the Europeans did not experience any harmful effects for breaking their taboos. Secondly, the indigenous people were for the first time exposed to aeroplanes, paratroopers dropping from the sky, and impressive modern weaponry and technology. Furthermore, as Harrisson noted, European military tactical skills and management in the jungle deeply impressed the Orang Ulu.[67] Moreover, as they were able to secure victory in the War, these European outsiders, who were regarded as Christians, were highly respected by the indigenous people. This outside western influence prepared them to be positively predisposed toward Christianity, western culture and education. In the immediate post-war period, there were mass conversions especially among the Kayan and Kenyah to Christianity, (whether Roman Catholic, Methodist or BEM), but the BEM was particularly successful in gaining converts. This issue of mass conversion in the post-war period will be explored later, examining the nature of indigenous response.[68]

Missions under the Flag: British Colonial Rule (1946-1963)

When Sarawak was ceded to the British Crown on 1 July 1946, the post-war reconstruction of Sarawak weighed heavily on the mind of the colonial government. The priorities then were the development of a viable political system that would enable Sarawak to reach its goal of self-government, the development of a viable economy, and the improvement of its social and educational services so that the standard of living would be steadily raised.[69] To this political development, there were two main obstacles; namely, the anti-cession movement from 1946 to 1951[70] and the communist threat, which was

---

[66] Tom Harrisson, *World Within: A Borneo Story* (Singapore: Oxford University Press, 1990), 176, 221. See also Southwell, *Uncharted Waters*, 239.

[67] Harrisson, *World Within*, 194, 251-52.

[68] See Chapter 5.

[69] Runciman, *The White Rajahs*, 248.

[70] The anti-cession movement was led by Anthony Brooke, the Rajah Muda and the Datu Patinggi, the paramount leader of the Sarawak Malays. Its activities created sufficient anxiety and political unrest that hindered constitutional changes towards self-government. After the assassination of the second Governor, Duncan Stewart, in December 1949, this movement lost ground so that by 1952, there was an ensuing

very real since the early 1950s, but was considerably weakened by the end of colonial rule, though it lingered on into the mid-1970s.[71]

The colonial authorities viewed Christian missions favourably, as their work of providing education was seen as a bulwark against communist influence. Despite having different agendas, the colonial government and the mission bodies used each other for their own ends.[72] The colonial government encouraged increasing thc number of primary schools in both rural and urban areas. The establishment of mission schools and government schools especially in rural areas helped contain the communist threat, confining it mainly to the Chinese schools in the major urban centres. By the end of 1956, most schools had become government-aided and so, government-controlled.[73] The enforcement of a common curriculum and of English as a medium of instruction were the means of building a cohesive Sarawak society and of combating communist indoctrination[74] so that by 1963, the colonial government had achieved significant progress in its political objectives.

The schools which the Christian missions began in the rural areas from 1946 onwards were handed over to the District Councils in 1954 in line with government policy.[75] During these years, the colonial government condoned the BEM style of combining education with Bible teaching.[76] But the introduction of an integrated national school system with a common curriculum, common teaching material and common examinations in 1961 had the side-effect of practically restraining any evangelistic activity of the BEM in the schools it had established and after 1961, relegating Bible-teaching to chapel time. This was the beginning of the marginalization of Bible teaching in schools taken over by the government. Instead, the BEM focused on establishing Bible schools which continued to make the students literate and helped to promote the cause of the Christian faith.

Despite its primary focus on evangelism, the BEM's work also met social needs. The BEM helped to raise the social and educational standards of the people by providing basic medical care, establishing schools, teaching basic craft-work and sewing, and providing agricultural training, as well as

---

period of political stability and significant constitutional developments until the formation of Malaysia in 1963. Vernon L. Porritt, *British Colonial Rule in Sarawak, 1946-1963* (Kuala Lumpur: Oxford University Press, 1997), 7-19.

[71] Porritt, *British Colonial Rule*, 77-89.

[72] A.J.N. Richards' comment in an interview on 3 April 1992, quoted in Porritt, *British Colonial Rule*, 325, n. 42. 'The missionaries have been…the best eyes and ears for the administrative officers in the outstation'.

[73] It included Christian mission schools and some Chinese medium schools.

[74] Porritt, *British Colonial Rule*, 321. The colonial government used education for these two purposes.

[75] Southwell, *Uncharted Waters*, 270, 272, 318-19. The BEM began schools in the Fifth Division and the Upper Baram region, Fourth Division, until 1954.

[76] The primary aim of making the natives literate was fulfilled, but not in exactly the way the colonial administrators would have liked it.

responding to governmental requests where possible.[77] The BEM worked closely with the colonial government where their common interests overlapped.[78] Moreover, at the invitation of the government, Southwell was involved in a vocational school training programme, the Community Development Project (CDP) at Long Lama in the Baram from 1956 to 1963, providing not only practical skills for manual labour, construction and farming but also an avenue for the brighter students to go for higher education at the government secondary schools and later into teacher training colleges.[79]

The colonial government was duly impressed with the social and educational work of the BEM, which improved the lifestyle and standard of living of the Kayan,[80] and Winsome Southwell was decorated by Queen Elizabeth II for her work among the Baram people at Long Tebangan.[81] So, these achievements dovetailed well into the colonial government's political aims.

During the colonial period, the administrative changes in the immediate aftermath of WWII, coupled with differing attitudes to Christian missions within the colonial administration (due to the influx of new colonial officers from other parts of the British Commonwealth), allowed the Brooke policy of geographical segregation for Christian missions slowly to become obsolete. During this time, the BEM extended its area of work from the Fifth Division into the Fourth Division, to which the colonial administrators had mixed reactions. They reluctantly acknowledged this expansion of the BEM work, which they could neither prevent nor undo, as whole longhouses had already become Christians following the preaching of the BEM missionaries, whom they had invited.[82] From then on, the BEM was to work the Upper Baram area and down to Marudi, the base of the Roman Catholic mission. During this phase, the Brooke zoning policy lapsed for the town areas and became increasingly difficult to implement in the interior, though the colonial administration still wanted to assert a semblance of control over the interior. In reality, 'in the post-war missionary work in the Fourth and Fifth Division, … Christian missions of different persuasion, mainly Catholic and Evangelicals, worked side by side in the same area and in competition'.[83]

---

[77] *BEM Fifteenth Annual Report*, 31 December 1948, 4. Southwell was requested by the Resident of Fourth Division to bring aid to the Kelabit at Pa Mein, who had experienced a disastrous fire, which destroyed almost all their possessions in their longhouses.

[78] Southwell, *Uncharted Waters*, 311. Hudson Southwell cooperated with the Department of Lands and Survey in Kuching in 1952 to produce a map of north-central Borneo, which later became the official map for many years.

[79] Southwell, *Uncharted Waters*, 330-36.

[80] The Governor, Sir Anthony Abell visited Long Tebangan, the BEM base among the Kayan in 1950 and was duly impressed with the work. See *BEM NL* December 1950, 2.

[81] Southwell, *Uncharted Waters*, 313. Winsome was awarded the Queen's Coronation Medal on June 1953.

[82] The Kayan of Long Tebangan and the Badang Kenyah of Lio Matu had converted to Christianity.

[83] Rooney, *Khabar Gembira*, 205.

Missions in an Independent Malaysia (1963-1979)

The formation of Malaysia on 16 September 1963 was a milestone in colonial history, in which the British government voluntarily relinquished a massive territory comprising Singapore, Sarawak and Sabah to the Malayan government, which exercised firm political control over the new Federation of Malaysia. Opposition to the formation of Malaysia came from Indonesia and the Philippines, which coveted and laid claim on the East Malaysian states. In Sarawak, there was an unsettling effect on those living along the borders of Kalimantan and Sarawak; and the abortive 1962 Brunei rebellion was catalytic to a re-evaluation of the BEM mission priorities.[84]

Though the 1961 proposal for the formation of Malaysia to include Singapore, North Borneo, Brunei and Sarawak, came from the Prime Minister of Malaya, Tunku Abdul Rahman, it had on previous occasions been broached by the British government.[85] The various parties had their different agendas and fears about the proposal. In the relationship between Singapore and Malaya, the increasing domination by the communists and other radical groups in Singapore's politics since 1948 was a major cause of concern to the Tunku. Fearing the possibility that an independent Singapore in 1963 would be controlled by communists, who would then use Singapore as a base for their activities to support their compatriots in Malaya, the Tunku saw the Federation as a bulwark against the communists by working with the moderate faction in Singapore politics.[86] However, members of the Tunku's party, the United Malay National Organisation (UMNO), the dominant party within in the Malaysian Alliance coalition or Federal government, feared the formation of a Malaysia with a Chinese majority. This fear was allayed by the proposal to include North Borneo and Sarawak, which has a sizeable Malay and indigenous population, so as to restore the ethnic balance.[87] However, Singapore's stay within the Federation was short-lived, and it separated from Malaysia on

---

[84] See Chapter 6.

[85] Tham noted that among those who revived this idea was the British High Commissioner of Malaya and Singapore, Malcolm MacDonald, in the late 1940s. See David Tham, 'British Attitudes towards the Greater Malaysia Proposal', in Michael Leigh (ed.), *Borneo 2000: Proceedings of the Sixth Biennial Borneo Research Conference* (Kuching: Universiti Malaysia Sarawak, 2000), 313-37.

[86] As Andaya and Andaya noted, the communists were kept under control by the colonial administration. 'Even when Singapore was given internal self-government in 1958, the British retained the responsibility of internal security and defence. This transitional constitution was to expire in 1963 and it was expected that Singapore would then demand and obtain full independence with total charge of its own affairs'. Andaya and Andaya, *A History of Malaysia*, 270.

[87] Ethnic Chinese form the overwhelming majority of the population in Singapore. Andaya and Andaya, *A History of Malaysia*, 271. Tham explains that, in relation to the British government, the Tunku had insisted that the Borneo states be integrated with the Malaysian Federation before taking Singapore on board. See Tham, 'British Attitudes towards the Greater Malaysia Proposal', 317.

August 1965, which, in part, was a result of the intensifying political struggle between the ruling Malaysian Alliance party and the Singapore's People's Action Party (PAP).[88]

However, the major indigenous groups of Borneo saw their interests as different from those of the Malays. They were initially reluctant to join the Federation, as Andaya and Andaya put it, 'because of widespread fears about an unknown future without the paternalistic rule to which they had been accustomed'. This resulted in Malaya granting major concessions to the two Borneo states, which facilitated their entry into the Federation in 1963 and gave them greater autonomy than that exercised in the peninsular states. The safeguards included a) the Borneo states controlling their own immigration; b) the recognition of Malay as the national language but English would continue as a medium of instruction and as official language for the state until the State legislature decided otherwise; c) Islam would be the official religion but other religions could be propagated; and d) indigenous people of these two states (considered as bumiputra)[89] would enjoy the special privileges similar to those the Malays enjoyed in Malaya.[90]

For the future of the new Federation, the Malaysian government argued the need to forge a new Malaysian identity; that is, the loyalty of the 'new Malaysian' was to the nation and not to any particular state or ethnic group. But the interpretation of the 'new Malaysian' became a highly contentious issue. The UMNO-dominated Alliance government viewed Malay language and culture as the basis of the Malaysian identity. The other ethnic groups argued that the Malaysian identity should reflect Malaysia's multi-ethnic diversity.[91]

The policies of the Federal government also became policies of the Borneo states. First, when Malaya achieved its independence on 31 August 1957, Islam was recognized as the official religion of the country. The consequent recognition of Islam as the official religion of Malaysia brought fears among Christians in the Borneo states that they would lose their religious freedom. The Islamic resurgence since the 1970s and later Islamization of the government machinery seemed to have reinforced these fears, dichotomizing the nation into Muslims and non-Muslims. Next, the implementation of Bahasa Melayu (or the Malay language) as the national language and in the educational system was crucial to the Federal government's intention in achieving national integration with Malay cultural traditions forming the basis. Its introduction of Bahasa Melayu as the medium of instruction in the education system had the positive effect of providing a common language, which the BEM and SIB were quick to use and promote in their work to their advantage. Also, the replacing of expatriates with local people in the civil service and other fields under the

---

[88] Andaya and Andaya, *A History of Malaysia*, 276.

[89] *Bumiputra* literally means 'son of the soil'.

[90] Andaya and Andaya, *A History of Malaysia*, 272.

[91] Andaya and Andaya, *A History of Malaysia*, 277.

Malayanisation policy of the Federal government led to the replacement of expatriate missionaries with local leadership after 1965, and this led to the ten-year rule for missionary residence in the country. By 1975, most Christian missions had their number of missionaries greatly reduced. Most BEM missionaries left the country with the result that the BEM ceased to function as a mission body when its last Field Director left in 1979.

The SIB continued its work unhindered despite the ten-year ruling, as the SIB from its inception had been established on the 'three-self' principle.[92] With the greater pace of urbanisation under Malaysian rule, the BEM shifted the focus of its work from the interior of Sarawak to the urban centres such as Kuching and Miri. Though the SIB was still predominantly a bumiputra church in 1979, the planting of SIB churches in the urban centres from the late 1960s onwards began to attract people of other ethnic backgrounds so that these urban churches were becoming like a microcosm of Sarawakian society. In anticipation of its closure, the BEM forged a partnership with the OMF in 1975, so that the OMF continued in an advisory role alongside SIB. Further, the special status of the bumiputras (i.e., the Malays and the indigenous people) benefited the SIB in no small way, since, as bumiputras, they enjoyed special privileges to economic and educational advancement.

The Ethnic, Cultural and Religious Context

In our treatment of the ethnic, cultural and religious context of Sarawak, the diversity and complexity of the indigenous Bornean people, in general, and the Orang Ulu, in particular, make it impossible to do justice to the subject within the constraints of space in this study. Hence, our discussion of this subject must necessarily be selective and confined to the main themes that have relevance to this study. Some of these themes include the role of the chiefs and their kinship network in the acceptance and spread of Christianity, aspects of their religion that provided contact-points with the Christian message, and the gradual movement towards greater egalitarianism in the less stratified societies.

The Ethnic Geography of Sarawak

Under Brooke rule, the three major ethnic groups of the Malays, Iban and Chinese were geographically segregated and played different roles in Sarawak. The Orang Ulu,[93] who inhabited the interior, lived in relative isolation from them, except for occasional visits by government officers or Chinese traders.

Geographically, the Malays were mostly distributed along the coastal and sub-coastal areas and in the urban centres. The Chinese were situated primarily in the towns and along the lower Rajang. The Iban mainly inhabited the sub-coastal areas along the rivers of the First and Second Divisions. Under Charles

[92] See Chapter 8. *BEM NL*, April 1955, 1.

[93] See Chapter 1.

Brooke's rule, they migrated to the Third Division and later, under Vyner's rule, to the Fourth and Fifth Divisions. But they were not allowed to live in close proximity with the Orang Ulu, who lived further into the interior, as a result of fierce battles with the Kayan after they had made their entry into the region of the Balleh, upper Rajang, of the Third Division around 1874.[94]

The Orang Ulu occupied the interior along the mountain spine near and across the Indonesian border, near the headwaters and upper reaches of the rivers of the Third, Fourth and Fifth Divisions. The Kayan were spread generally across the middle and upper reaches of the Balleh River, Third Division, and the Baram River, Fourth Division. Their neighbours, the Kenyah, were located across the upper reaches of the Balui River, Third Division, and the Baram River. The Lun Bawang were found along the upper Baram and Tutoh, the middle Limbang, the entire Trusan valley, the Lawas Damit basin and the Lawas area. In Sabah, they spread across the Ulu Padas, the entire Mengalong river valley down to Sindumin town. The Kelabit lived even further inland at the headwaters of the Rajang, Baram and Limbang. The Penan were a nomadic people living in the jungles and spread across the same area as the Kelabit, Kayan and Kenyah. During the time of the BEM's work, the Orang Ulu living over the Indonesian border accounted for between two-thirds (in the case of the Lun Bawang and Kelabit) and four-fifths (in the case of the Kayan and Kenyah) of the total population of each tribe.[95]

Islam and the Coastal People

The coastal people of Sarawak consist mainly of the Melanaus and the Malays. The Melanaus, who form about six per cent of the total population, live in the coastal area extending from the mouth of the Rajang to the mouth of the Baram. The majority of them are Muslims, a minority are Christians, and the rest are described by census reports as either of no religion or believing in tribal/folk religion.[96]

The Sarawak Malays, who form about twenty per cent of the total population, live along the coastal areas, being concentrated mostly in the First and Fifth Division. They are a very mixed people, who have since the fifteenth century been assimilated into the race as a result of embracing Islam and

[94] See Pringle, *Rajahs and Rebels*, 252-57. In the Rajang, they were not allowed beyond Kapit.

[95] Victor King (ed.), *The World Within: The Ethnic Groups of Borneo* (Kuala Lumpur: S.A. Majeed, 1994 [1978]). Tom Harrisson (ed.), *The Peoples of Sarawak* (Kuching: Borneo Literature Bureau, 1959).

[96] According to the 1980 census, there were 77 per cent of Muslim Melanaus, 12 per cent of Christian Melanaus, and the rest with either no religion or believing in tribal/folk religion. See *Population and Housing Census of Malaysia, 1980: State Population Report Sarawak Part I* (Kuala Lumpur: Department of Statistics, Malaysia, 1983), 227. R.G. Aikman, 'The Melanaus', in Tom Harrisson (ed.), *The Peoples of Sarawak*, 85-94.

following Malay culture.[97] Islam has been the basic defining factor and uniting force among the Malays. A distinguishing mark of the Malays has been their involvement in politics and in governing the state, first during the time of the Brunei sultanate, then under Brooke rule and presently under the Malaysian government; the Malay language has been the language of the State. The Malays were not in active contact with the Orang Ulu except when they came downriver to the coastal towns. The early contacts in the interior between Muslim traders and the Orang Ulu had long since been replaced by the coming of the more enterprising Chinese traders into the interior,[98] so that when the BEM started work among the Lun Bawang, the mission's fear of a race between Islam and Christianity for their allegiance proved to be unfounded.

The Orang Ulu and their Constituent People

The indigenous societies of Borneo can be described as either stratified or non-stratified communities.[99] The stratified societies like the Kayan and Kenyah may be distinguished from those like the Iban that exhibit more egalitarian tendencies by their clearly defined ranking systems with named hereditary ranks. These more stratified societies have greater mutual similarities, especially in their social stratification, than differences. Most of these societies traditionally possessed an aristocratic class, commoners, and slaves. In this system, only the aristocratic class could own slaves, who would either be part of the household or form a distinct household. Slaves performed the economic function of cultivating their master's farms. But slavery had traditionally been hereditary with apparently no provision for the slave to be free. The slaves had normally been war-captives, but with the abolition of slavery, they became included in the category of commoner.[100]

Lun Bawang society has a less stratified structure comprising two distinct classes. The lun dat include the lun demulun or slaves, normally those captured

---

[97] The Sarawak Malays consist of converted Dyak, Melanau, Malay proper from Sumatra and the Malay Peninsula, Bugis, Banjanrese and Javanese, and they also assimilated women through inter-marriage from other tribes or races. John Groatly, 'The Malays', in Tom Harrisson (ed.), *The Peoples of Sarawak*, 103-13. Victor T. King (ed.), 'Introduction', in *The World Within: The Ethnic Groups of Borneo* (Kuala Lumpur: S.A. Majeed, 1994 [1978]), 2-4.

[98] Chew, *Chinese Pioneers*. Trade into the interior of Sarawak had been taken over by the Chinese traders.

[99] King, 'Introduction', 34-42. But care must be taken not to make too sharp a distinction between them.

[100] Jerome Rousseau, 'The Kayan', and H.L. Whittier, 'The Kenyah', in King (ed.), *World Within*, 111-12, 142-43 respectively. The Kayan have a four-strata structure: *maren*, *hipuy* (both aristocrats), *pinyin* (commoner) and *dipen* (slave). The Kenyah have five classes: *deta'u bio* (big aristocrats), *deta'u dumit* (small aristocrats), *panyin* tiga (good commoners), *panyin* ja'at (bad commoners) and *panyin lamin* (slaves). Only the *maren* and *deta'u bio* (and their families) of each community were leaders of the village and longhouses.

in warfare or their descendants, and the lun petabpar or those who cannot provide sufficiently to feed their families and must sell their labour to others to make ends meet. The second class, the lun do', claim Lun Bawang ancestry without any social blemish of having a slave ancestor in their genealogy. From the lun do come the lun mebala or those who are famous through achievement; that is, those who have excelled in hunting, farming, and public speaking.[101] The abolition of slavery by the Brooke administration in 1928 thus moved Lun Bawang society towards an egalitarian basis, a development which was of some significance for the work of the BEM.

In the organisation of these indigenous societies, the highest authority was normally vested in the high chiefs (or temenggong) of particular river systems. In pre-Brooke times, their authority had been based on hereditary military strength and support from alliances with powerful families in other river systems. During the Brooke and colonial eras, they were answerable to the Residents or District Officers. In Sarawak, each of the major river valleys has a temenggong and several penghulu, who have charge over several villages each. Each village with a tua kampong (village headman) may consist of one or more longhouses and each longhouse also has its own headman.

The aristocrats had maintained their rank and status through the strategic role they had played in intercommunity relations with other chiefs,[102] their practice of finding spouses of their rank in other communities, thereby strengthening and widening their kinship networks, and their ability to host irau (feasts), usually after each harvest, and maintain a large family and the possession of prized family heirlooms. These chiefs play important roles in the initial acceptance or rejection of Christianity among their villages. Their acceptance of the Christian faith also means the facilitation of its spread through their kinship network. For instance, the conversion of Penghulu Tama Paya Anyi of Long Atip to Christianity through the effort of Southwell also saw the turning of three villages to Christianity.[103]

Both stratified and non-stratified societies gradually became more egalitarian following the abolition of slavery in 1928 by the Brooke administration.[104] Other factors tending towards egalitarianism in later years have been: a) government policies promoting democratic village political life, especially since the colonial period; b) the role of education and the choice of literate village elders; c) the introduction of money as the medium of exchange and the replacement of traditional heirlooms by consumer goods as symbols of

[101] Jayl Langub, 'Ethnic Self Labelling of the Muruts or Lun Bawang of Sarawak', *SG*, December 1987, 30-35 (31). See also J.L. Deegan, 'Some Lun Bawang Spirit Chants', *SMJ* 18.36-37 (1970), 266. The Kelabit are viewed as having a common origin and ancestry with the Lun Bawang. F.H. Pollard, 'Some Comparative Notes on Muruts and Kelabits', *SMJ* 4.14 (1935), 223-27. Pollard's view has been supported by J.L. Deegan.

[102] Rousseau, 'The Kayan', 113.

[103] Southwell, *Uncharted Waters*, 273-74.

[104] King, 'Introduction', 35.

prestige, rank and importance; and also d) the spread of Christian influence. This movement towards a more egalitarian society reinforced BEM's democratic church policy of encouraging every-member participation. Though it helped pave the way, in principle, for any Orang Ulu to take on leadership positions within the indigenous church, the SIB, it was a gradual development.

Despite the hierarchical structure of these societies, their village decision-making process has always been consensual. Both the Kenyah and the Kayan have an informal council of male elders, who make decisions on behalf of the village. The decision-making process begins with the tua kampong calling for a meeting which anyone, including women, may attend. Prior to and during the meeting proper, all may voice their opinions, though often the voices of the aristocrats carry more weight in the matter. At the end of the discussion, the tua kampong will seek a consensual decision, failing which the discussion continues for another round and another until it is resolved. By skilful rhetoric and words of wisdom, a tua kampong may often lead a group to consensus.[105] Similarly, the local church elder or pastor could by his wisdom and rhetorical skill lead the local church after much discussion on an issue to a consensual decision.

The ritual dimensions of every important human activity (for example, child-birth, naming of a child, going on a journey, building a longhouse, rice farming ritual, marriage and death and burial), enhanced the role of the chiefs and aristocrats, and those with a prominent place in these activities. The chief often held the prerogative of choosing and burning the land and the timing of planting and harvest.[106]

Social relationships were based on agricultural activities, as rice cultivation was performed by work teams on the basis of their geographical proximity and availability. The same work team usually consisted of ten to twenty members working together through the whole planting process from clearing the forest to harvesting. Each team has a form of rotating leadership.

Sometimes there have been conflicts in social relationships, which have resulted in a movement of a household to another longhouse or to the formation of separate longhouses or villages.[107] Other factors causing the fragmentation of villages may have been due to the demographic pressure on the land or land scarcity, disagreements about migration, rivalry between chiefs and also change of religion to Christianity.

When the BEM arrived in Sarawak, the Orang Ulu societies were relatively isolated from the outside world except for the minimal contact with the Brooke

---

[105] Whittier, 'The Kenyah', 129.

[106] Jerome Rousseau, *Central Borneo: Ethnic Identity and Social Life in a Stratified Society* (Oxford: Clarendon Press, 1990), 127, 184-86. Rousseau noted that in one instance, the chief delayed the firing of the fields for several weeks, while everyone else wanted to go ahead with it.

[107] James L. Deegan, 'Community Fragmentation among the Lun Bawang', *SMJ* 22.43 (January-December 1974), 229-47.

administrative officers. Their self-contained and self-sufficient communities and their considerable distance from other societies made it easier for the BEM to work among them unhindered even into the early years of independent Malaysia.

The Worldview of the Orang Ulu

Despite their distinct identities, Bornean traditional societies show much commonality in their rituals and beliefs.[108] Victor King notes that all Dyak groups do not perceive their creator deity[109] as playing a central role in their everyday religious life, nor is this deity perceived as omnipotent.[110] The daily affairs of the Bornean people are affected by their beliefs in ancestor spirits and all kinds of spiritual entities inhabiting the cosmos. They perceive some of these spirits as benevolent, others as malicious, and others again as both, depending on their mood and actions on humans. For instance, when disasters (such as flooding waters which are believed to be inhabited by spirits), cause destruction, these spirits have to be appeased with offerings from time to time.[111] It is well known that the fear of the spirits loomed large in the minds of the Bornean people.

The spiritual realm is believed to be intimately intertwined with the world of human beings but separate from it. For the Bornean people, communication from the spirit realm comes through the appearance of supernatural beings through dreams or through their incarnation as birds or animals. The sighting of particular birds is believed to be 'a pronouncement by the gods, either commending or cautioning against a proposed course of action'.[112] Observing these omens strictly would avert any disaster. On the other hand, human contacts with the spirits occur most commonly for cases of sickness or soul

[108] Rousseau, *Central Borneo*, 27. 'From our current ethnographic knowledge, no ritual or belief appears to be specific to central Borneo as a whole. Ritual, headhunting, animal omens, and a large number of taboos are found throughout Borneo.…Of course, specific religious beliefs and rituals can be differentiated between various central Borneo groups'.

[109] Victor T. King, *The Peoples of Borneo* (Oxford: Blackwell, 1993), 232-33. Jerome Rousseau, *Kayan Beliefs: Ritual Life and Religious Change in Central Borneo* (Leiden: KITLV Press, 1998), 91. Rousseau notes that all Dyak groups have a religious cosmology that had two tiers, a higher level of a supreme god or gods and a lower level of local spirits. These lesser spirits are concerned with the affairs of the local communities and environment.

[110] King, *The Peoples of Borneo*, 233. 'Its position and status may vary between different ethnic groups'.

[111] King, *The Peoples of Borneo*, 233-34. It was believed that in ancient times, the ancestor spirits were once living among them, but are now separate and live in the spiritual realm.

[112] Derek Freeman, *The Iban of Borneo* (Kuala Lumpur: S.A. Majeed, 1992[1955]), 118.

loss.[113] The dayong or shamans play an important role, often entering into 'relations with the spirits through trance, and send their souls out to contact the supernatural'[114] to seek the help of the spirits for a cure to the ailment. Consequently, it was an ever-present reality in their daily affairs to be constantly in touch with the supernatural, so that they had to be mindful of the relations between this world and the spiritual realm. Their fear of the spirits provided a point of contact for BEM missionaries in their presentation of the Christian message.[115]

The performance of numerous rituals and strict observance of taboos, which exhibited some variation among the indigenous groups, permeated every important human activity (see above). The rituals associated with the rice farming cycle were performed on behalf of the whole village by a ritual specialist, and were intended to ensure a plentiful harvest.[116] Among the Kayan, as Rousseau observes, the occasional sighting of bad omens in the morning of the first day of farm work has led to the cancellation of rice cultivation for a whole year, and people have had to resort to scarcity crops.[117] In other situations, the strict observance of these ritual prohibitions and taboos, if occurring during harvest time lasting for a month at a time or longer, usually resulted in great losses of crops. These crops were ravaged by wild animals and consequently, caused much hunger and hardship among them.[118] The BEM missionaries met with such situations and other ritual prohibitions particularly among the Lun Bawang before WWII and the Kayan and Kenyah in the immediate post-war period.[119]

In the building of a new longhouse, the ritual specialist is charged with choosing an auspicious site, determining it by the taking of auguries, and the sighting of a particular omen bird. Into the hole, where the pole of the new house is set, the blood of a sacrificial cock is poured. At the completion of the

---

113 Soul loss is believed to happen when during sleep, one's soul strays too far or gets lost, and is captured by spirits. This then directly explains human sickness because the body is deprived of its spiritual essence or energy. If the soul cannot be recovered, then death will inevitably result. King, *The Peoples of Borneo*, 235.

114 King, *The Peoples of Borneo*, 235.

115 Lees, *Drunk before Dawn*, 89-91. See Chapter 5 for further discussion.

116 The rice farming cycle has a central role in *Orang Ulu* societies. Freeman, *The Iban of Borneo*, 172-73. For the Iban, these are conducted by the *tuai burong* or the augur of the longhouse.

117 Rousseau, *Central Borneo*, 133. Rousseau disputes Banks' assertion that observance of Kayan omens and taboos has generally precluded farm work for 117 days in a year.

118 C.H. Southwell, 'The Kayans and Kenyahs', in Tom Harrisson (ed.), *The Peoples of Sarawak*, 43.

119 Freeman, *The Iban of Borneo*, 122-23. Ritual prohibitions are very common. For example, on the completion of a longhouse or when a death occurs, prohibitions on the whole community leaving its immediate precinct for a period of time come into force. Numerous mourning prohibitions, immediately after the burial, in the case of the Iban, usually last for about one or two weeks.

longhouse, a cock is also sacrificed and its blood smeared on the foreheads of all the men, women and children in the community.[120] Similarly, when a longhouse is afflicted with diseases and unwarranted deaths, it is believed to have been brought about by a serious transgression of ritual prohibition. The averting of this danger, if the breach is a grave one, will involve the sacrifice of a fowl or a pig as an expiatory offering.[121] This practice of blood sacrifice to appease the spirits was to provide another point of contact for the BEM missionaries, facilitating their presentation of the message of Christ's death as a propitiatory sacrifice.[122]

The relation of the Orang Ulu to the spirit world, as Freeman notes, was not only that of appeasing the spirits but also of manipulating them to their own advantage.[123] For example, for a good harvest, friendly relations have to be maintained with the spirits and deities responsible for the earth, forest and rice. Offence is avoided by following certain prescriptions and prohibitions and by presenting offerings and being ever-mindful of omens.[124] Also, they can avoid misfortune on a long journey by watching for signs presented by the spirits, and by having a series of propitiatory offerings to be presented to the gods.[125] However, as Rousseau acknowledges, careful attention to omens has been known to cause considerable delay to a simple journey,[126] a phenomenon which did not escape the attention of the BEM missionaries.[127]

Among the Orang Ulu, the strict observance of these taboos and the number of sacrifices that were required came under increasing question in the light of their increasing contact with the outside world, education and Christian influence, particularly in the immediate post-war period. When the Orang Ulu, especially whole longhouses, converted to Christianity through the work of the BEM, their attitude toward traditional practices changed and some of these

---

[120] Freeman, *The Iban of Borneo*, 122. Conley notes a similar practice among the Kenyah; that of blood being poured into the hole, where the largest post of the new longhouse is set. William Conley, *Kalimantan Kenyah: A Study of Tribal Conversion in Terms of Dynamic Cultural Themes* (Nutley: Presbyterian and Reformed Publishing, 1976), 62.

[121] Freeman, *The Iban of Borneo*, 123.

[122] See Chapter 5.

[123] Rousseau, *Kayan Beliefs*, 118. 'An Iban's attitude towards his gods is far from passive, rather he is constantly concerned with the ritual manipulation of magical and supernatural forces, so that they will combine to work to his advantage'. See Freeman, *The Iban of Borneo*, 119.

[124] King, *The Peoples of Borneo*, 245. Rousseau explains that in the old Kayan religion, 'people had some control over omens: if they saw an omen bird about to cross their path in an auspicious way, they turned the boat around and made it into a good omen'. Rousseau, *Kayan Beliefs*, 118.

[125] Freeman, *The Iban of Borneo*, 119.

[126] Rousseau, *Central Borneo*, 221.

[127] Lees, *Drunk before Dawn*, 55-56.

practices either fell into disuse, or were modified or replaced by Christian ceremonies. Similarly, their worldview also experienced a significant change.[128]

Headhunting was an important longstanding institution in the social, cultural and religious life of the Orang Ulu.[129] Its formal cessation in Sarawak in 1924 left a great void in their lives which may have had an important bearing on their receptivity to Christianity, as in the case of the Kalimantan Kenyah,[130] or led to adverse physical and psychological effects, resulting in a state of depopulation, as in the case of the Murut.[131] This was the situation when the BEM missionaries first found them. When mass conversion happened within Murut society in 1933, it had the effect of slowing the population decline and increasing productivity for their rice agricultural activities. We shall examine later the factors that made the Murut receptive to the Christian message.[132]

The Inroads of Modernity

James Brooke's vision of bringing civilization to Sarawak was a first step toward the inroads of modernity, but its pace during Charles Brooke's era was rather slow as result of his ad hoc action and his ambivalent attitude towards Western civilization, believing that the Englishmen of industrial Britain were no better than his Dyak subjects. As for Vyner Brooke, he felt the dilemma of isolating his people and exposing them to the rapid changes in the world. Being sensitive to the charge that earlier Brooke policy had been anachronistic[133] and aware that the opening up of British Malaya had enjoyed much success, Vyner worked toward a cautious adaptation of Sarawak to the modern world.[134]

Politically, steps towards modern governance in Sarawak began under Charles Brooke with the formation of the Supreme Council, consisting mostly of indigenous chiefs, and then the Sarawak General Council, later known as the Council Negeri.[135] The climax to this process was the introduction of a new written constitution by Vyner Brooke in 1941 which was to replace the absolute

---

[128] See Chapter 5 for further discussion.

[129] Rousseau, *Central Borneo*, 275-76. According to Rousseau, 'heads are imbued with power; they were both beneficial and dangerous, and this was the justification for placing them in the chief's care, because he was endowed with sufficient supernatural force to withstand their ill-effects.... Headhunting renewed the vitality of the longhouse and the land'.

[130] Conley, *Kalimantan Kenyah*, 65-88, 347-48

[131] W.H.R. Rivers, *Essays on the Depopulation of Melanesia* (Cambridge: Cambridge University Press, 1922). Chapter 8 attributed the depopulation of the Melanesian society to the cessation of headhunting.

[132] See Chapter 4 for further discussion.

[133] See *SG*, 1 December 1936.

[134] See *SG*, 1 May 137; Rajah's Speech to Council Negeri, 25th meeting, 29 April 1937.

[135] The first Council Negeri meeting was held in Bintulu in 1867 with five Europeans and sixteen native leaders, most of whom were Malays.

rule of the Brooke Rajah with a democratic form of government.[136] After WWII, the British colonial government introduced the 1957 Constitution and then, the 1963 Constitution that prepared Sarawak for self-government.[137] A result of colonial rule in the administrative structure was the recruiting of more Orang Ulu into the government machinery and the streamlining of the indigenous chieftainship so that there was greater intervention in the running of their villages through government-appointed indigenous chiefs; a practice that is continued under the Malaysian government.

The immigration of Foochow Chinese Methodists and the arrival of James Hoover of the American Methodist Episcopal Mission led to the introduction of many modern amenities and facilities for farming and daily living.[138] The effects of modernization under Brooke rule such as the building of roads, a railway and the town's water supply in Kuching, were first felt in the coastal towns, then found their way slowly up the riverine systems into the interior, or conversely when those in the interior went downriver to the coast. Under colonial rule, there was an accelerated pace of modernization with improved development schemes and communication systems,[139] which laid the foundational infrastructure for the development of a modern state.

The contact of the Orang Ulu with modernization had been sporadic during Brooke rule, but this accelerated under the British colonial and Malaysian governments. From the early 1950s, the transition from barter trade to a cash economy began to affect Orang Ulu society. The rubber boom of the 1950s, which resulted from the Korean War, and the growth of logging industries in the 1970s and 1980s, accelerated their participation into the cash economy. This resulted in many Orang Ulu frequently travelling downriver to coastal towns to acquire modern goods for their homes and new ideas from the outside world.[140] Further, the process of urbanisation since the 1960s witnessed

---

[136] See the text of Rajah Vyner Brooke's address in *SG*, 1 April 1941, 61; *SG*, 1 December 1941, 259-60. Runciman, *The White Rajahs*, 248-49 shows the text of the Nine Cardinal Principles of the new Constitution.

[137] The 1957 Constitution provided for 24 elected members and 18 official and nominated members of the Council Negeri. The 1963 Constitution increased the elected members to 36 and reduced the official and nominated members to 6 so that it became a government that was more representative of the people.

[138] See Chapter 2.

[139] New roads, ports, an airfield, schools, teacher training colleges, hospitals and improved healthcare services, government offices, radio service and agricultural schemes, were funded by the Colonial Development and Welfare Fund (CD&W), a fund from the taxes paid by the British people to help rehabilitate British colonies after WWII. Joan Rawlins, *Sarawak 1839 to 1968*, 2nd ed. (Basingstoke/London: Macmillan, 1969), 147-48.

[140] Ding Seling and Jayl Langub, 'The Orang Ulu: An Overview', *SMJ* 60.61 (December 1989), 23-29. By the mid-1960s, sophisticated items such as radios, tape recorders, sewing machines, outboard motors, rice mills, electricity generators and later television sets found their way into some of the longhouses.

increasing numbers of Orang Ulu going downriver for employment and higher education, but returning to the interior, mostly for vacation and during festival seasons. As will be discussed in Chapter 8, modernization had an impact on the spirituality of Orang Ulu Christian youths. Church and mission leaders felt that the spiritual fervour which their young people once had in their tightly-knit interior communities was being lost as a result of the pressures and temptations of life in the towns, a problem which the BEM and SIB addressed by starting churches in the towns.[141]

In the villages that became Christian, the BEM provided basic medical care and promoted basic health education. At Lawas, the BEM ran a dispensary with a fully qualified medical doctor at a time when qualified doctors were rare.[142] The BEM pioneered successful air-flights into the interior, after acquiring an aeroplane in August 1949.[143] Initially, there were grave doubts by the colonial administrators about its safe and effective use into the interior of Sarawak. After approval was granted by the colonial government in December 1950, the BEM opened up many airstrips in the Third, Fourth and Fifth Divisions of Sarawak and in British North Borneo. This air service facilitated faster travel, better medical attention and closer ties between the BEM and the Orang Ulu.[144] In short, as a mission, the BEM played its partly unintentional role as an agent of modernization, introducing modern amenities to the Orang Ulu society, which have been further improved under the British colonial and Malaysian governments.

The Coming of Literacy and Education

The introduction of western-style education into Sarawak came through the efforts of the Christian missions under Brooke rule after 1849.[145] But the early mission schools, which offered English-medium primary education and were open to all races, attracted predominantly Chinese urban dwellers and catered generally for those in towns so that education was not readily available to the rural areas. The first two Rajahs had serious misgivings about western-style education for the indigenous people and tried to shield the indigenous people from education as long as possible and so left education in the hands of Christian missions. But under Vyner Brooke, the establishment of primary schools in longhouses and villages began after the recommendations made by the Hammond report of 1937. By 1941 some progress had been made in

---

[141] A possible reason for the loss of spiritual fervour by the young people could be their inability to see the relevance of their Christian faith in an urban and more sophisticated society of the towns.

[142] L. Edwards and P.W. Stevens, *Short Histories of the Lawas and Kanowit Districts* (Kuching: Borneo Literature Bureau, 1971), 70-72.

[143] The aeroplane was donated by Stafford Young, a BEM missionary in the late 1930s. *BEM NL*, August 1949, 1. It arrived at Lawas in June 1950. *BEM NL*, August 1950, 1.

[144] Edwards & Stevens, *Short Histories*, 72. Lees, *Drunk before Dawn*, 120.

[145] See this chapter for further details.

education for the rural population, which was briefly disrupted during the WWII years of 1942 to 1945. The colonial administration increased the number of the new outstation mission schools that led to a steady growth of Lun Bawang, Kelabit, Kayan and Kenyah students.[146] Since the mid-1960s, the opportunities opened to them as bumiputras saw the trickle of these Orang Ulu students going to study at the post-secondary training colleges,[147] giving way to a torrent of students in the 1970s who gained admission into local universities and returned as professionals to take up important positions in the civil service and the private sector.[148] These effects of modernization and urbanisation on the Orang Ulu were to have implications on BEM policies, which we shall examine later.[149]

The response to literacy among the Orang Ulu has been mixed. Most Christians have valued education highly, as it provided them with a means of upward social and economic mobility and facilitated their integration into the national economy under independent Malaysia. Although education did not impel a movement into Christianity, it had an ambiguous effect on the Orang Ulu Christians, strengthening some in their Christian faith and causing scepticism in others.[150]

The Missionary Context: Other Christian Missions in Sarawak

The Society for the Propagation of the Gospel (SPG)

The work of the Anglican Church began with its first missionary, Francis McDougall, in Sarawak in June 1848. With great optimism, he dreamt of converting the whole of Borneo, starting missions on every river alongside the government resident and training and sending children from his school to convert their fellow countrymen.[151] His vision fitted into James Brooke's policy of civilization, commerce and Christianity, though he gave greatest priority to Christianity.

The first five years (1848-53) under McDougall were foundational to the Church in setting the range of its future work. As a medical doctor by training, McDougall provided medical services in addition to establishing schools and starting missions to the major people groups, namely, Malay, Chinese and

---

[146] Porritt, *British Colonial Rule*, 297-98.

[147] The Training Colleges then included Teacher Training Colleges, the Agricultural Training School, Kuching, Police Centres throughout Malaysia and Medical Headquarters, Kuching.

[148] Seling and Langub, 'The Orang Ulu', 26-28.

[149] See Chapter 8.

[150] See Chapters 6 and 8.

[151] Peter Varney, 'The Anglican Church in Sarawak from 1848 to 1852', *SMJ* 16.32-33 (1968), 380.

Dyak.[152] The medical services, which grew to a hospital with twenty-four beds by 1851, were closed as a result of a lack of medical personnel in 1915. As Saunders notes, the hospital had the full support of James, but not of the SPG, as it was perceived that the hospital was distracting McDougall from his spiritual duties.[153]

The beginning of the day-school was a political necessity and had financial assistance from the government, but McDougall knew, as Saunders observes,[154] that results in a missionary sense would take a long time. From McDougall's experience of the schools in Singapore, Penang and Malacca, no converts were made. Instead, the school children became 'practical infidels', despising the religion of their fathers without accepting Christianity. However, it was a way of reaching out to the Chinese community. But the success of school work later led to two new schools, a boys' school and a girls' school under Bishop Hose in 1886. These two schools have become St. Thomas' School and St. Mary's School, Kuching and they have contributed significantly to the rise of literacy and also upward social mobility among the Dyak.

The original purpose of the SPG mission to evangelize the Dyak was diverted by its early attention towards Malay and Chinese work in Kuching.[155] Its work among the Dyak began in September 1851 when William Chambers was sent to the Skrang, but later moved to establish a church at Banting.[156] From Banting, the missionaries moved in all directions up the River Strap, the Batang Lupar and beyond into Simmanggang and the Rivers Krian and Saribas. With the arrival of five new missionaries in 1862, the work reached its peak by the time McDougall retired in 1868; thus, with their long service, stations were established at every principal river in the Second Division. With the later migration of the Dyak Anglican members into the other Divisions, the SPG mission set up work among them in the Third to Fifth Divisions from the time of Vyner. This work expanded greatly with the development of the indigenous ministry so that the Anglican Church in Sarawak today is predominantly a Dyak church. But none of its work came into any close contact with the BEM

---

152 McDougall first established a school and dispensary in 1848, a mission house in August 1850 and a church in 1851.

153 Saunders, *Bishops and Brookes*, 50-51. According to Saunders, McDougall differed pointing out that the hospital took less of his time than his dispensary, cost the Mission nothing because the Government fully supported it, and provided opportunities for missionary work.

154 Saunders, *Bishops and Brookes*, 51.

155 H.P. Thompson, *Into All Lands: The History of the Society for the Propagation of the Gospel in Foreign Parts 1701-1950* (London: Society for Promoting Christian Knowledge, 1951), 399.

156 Chambers was the first missionary to reduce the Dyak language into writing and to begin translation of the Gospels, the Prayer Book and a number of hymns. See Saunders, *Bishops and Brookes*, 37-38, 41-42.

or SIB even in the early years of Malaysia, as the BEM did not begin significant work among the Dyak until the 1960s.

Mission work among the Malays was short-lived,[157] and it was abandoned in 1852 when McDougall went on leave, as not only was there little progress but also James had wanted no proselytization of the Malays for political reasons. Other factors included suspicion, resistance and an Islamic revival among the Malays in 1850.[158] Though the SPG mission continued to provide education for the Malays, proselytization among the Malays became prohibited, and this prohibition was later more strictly enforced upon every Mission body including the Roman Catholics and BEM.

By 1881, the Brooke zoning policy had allocated the Anglican mission to the First and Second Divisions, and the Roman Catholic Mill Hill mission to the Third Division. As a result, the SPG mission was prohibited from working in Sibu and Miri during Charles' rule, but under Vyner's rule, the SPG mission was allowed to extend its work there. Its inability even to sustain, let alone expand its work during the period of the second and third bishops from 1869 to 1908[159] was partly responsible for the Second Rajah's decisions to restrict its work and, more importantly, to allow the Mill Hill mission into the Third Division for political reasons. Other factors behind the decline of the work till its lowest ebb in 1908[160] were the retirement of long-serving clergy, the lack of new clergy and funds, a long interregnum between the second and third bishops from 1879 to 1881, and the bishops' inability to cope with the increased demands of their bishoprics, which then also included Singapore and British Malaya.[161]

The mission's ultimate aim to train 'a succession of native churches and pastors in Borneo'[162] did not begin to materialize until Bishop Logie Danson's bishopric (1916-1931).[163] The trickle of new clergy,[164] the problems of

---

[157] McDougall was initially over-optimistic about the Malays converting to Christianity, once they were provided with education.

[158] Saint, *Twenty Years*, 26.

[159] William Chambers was the second bishop from 1869-1879 and George F. Hose, the third bishop from 1881-1908.

[160] Thompson, *Into All Lands*, 402.

[161] The bishops, Chambers and Hose, had to spend about half the time each year away in Singapore, rendering them less effective in Sarawak.

[162] See *Statement* printed by the Borneo Church Mission Institution, 16 July 1850.

[163] From 1869-1908, the Diocese of Labuan and Sarawak was re-organized to become the Diocese of Labuan, Sarawak and Singapore. From 1908, the Diocese separated into two – Singapore, and Labuan and Sarawak. From 1916 to 1922, there were only 3 new missionaries, and Danson turned his attention to 'training an Asiatic ministry'. See Thompson, *Into All Lands*, 656-57.

[164] 'In 1900, the Bishop wrote in great distress of his lack of men and the Society commented that never in its history had there been such a dearth of clergymen offering themselves for missionary work'. When Bishop Hose resigned in 1908, there were only 3 European and 2 Chinese clergy. See Thompson, *Into All Lands*, 402.

manpower brought by the First World War and the lack of funds necessitated the training of Asian clergy. This development was espoused almost as a last resort, almost eighty years after the idea was first mooted. It was a fruitful initiative, for by 1931 sixty per cent of the clergy were Asians,[165] and a firm transition to Asian leadership in the Anglican Church in Borneo had been made with positive results. This development was further strengthened with the establishment of the House of Epiphany in 1952 for the training of local people for priesthood. By 1928, when the BEM started work in Sarawak, the Anglican Church had begun to nurture Asian leadership for the church.

The Anglican mission policy was accommodative of traditional cultural and religious practices so that Christian practices often co-existed with their traditional Dyak practices. This situation raised the issue of the inculturation of the Christian gospel within a culture, which we shall examine in a later chapter.[166]

The Mill Hill Fathers

When the Roman Catholic Mill Hill Mission was given permission to work in Sarawak by Charles in 1881, three conditions were applied to its work: firstly, it was to work in an area where the SPG mission was not operating; secondly, there was to be no conversion of Muslims; and thirdly, there was a preference for a non-Anglo-Saxon priest to start the Mission.[167]

The first three missionaries were directed to work in upper Sarawak and the Rajang, Third Division and permission was granted to establish Kuching as their headquarters.[168] The Mission focused on the Dyak and combined literacy work, new farming methods and agricultural self-sufficiency with their missionary work, which became the pattern of their work.[169]

In literacy work, the mission pioneered education establishing the St. Joseph's Institution, Kuching, a premier school in Sarawak today, and St. Paul's Institution, Kanowit. Generally, the Catholic schools grew and outstripped the Anglican schools mainly because the Catholic mission had more funds and long-serving staff. By the end of the century, a few Dyak were beginning to attend schools in Kuching, which catered mainly for the Chinese while the outstation schools were mainly for the Dyak, Kayan and Kenyah. By 1940, schooling had become widely accepted, not only producing leaders for the church but also society.

---

[165] *Fitly Framed: Diocese of Borneo, 1855-1955* (Kuching: Centenary Committee of the Diocese of Borneo), 2. Twelve of the twenty priests were Asians in 1931. The first Asian bishop, Basil Temengong, was consecrated on 6 December 1968 and was bishop for 16 years until 1984.

[166] See Chapter 5.

[167] Runciman, *The White Rajahs*, 213.

[168] The three missionaries were Fr. Jackson and Fr. Goosens at Kuching and Fr. Dunn at Kapit and later Kanowit.

[169] Edwards and Stevens, *Short Histories*, 128.

The work of the Mill Hill Mission among the Dyak grew rapidly with outstations in the surrounding areas of Kanowit and Kuching. Further, the opening of the work among the Chinese in Sibu in 1902 was in response to the mass immigration of Chinese into Sibu in 1901. This work was to spread downriver towards Binatang (now known as Bintagor).

The success of the Kanowit work persuaded the Brooke government to allow the Catholics to work in Marudi and the upper or ulu Baram area, Fourth Division, in 1901; but this work, which faced many difficulties from the beginning, bore little result. The Miri station, which was started in 1914, was originally envisaged as a staging post for the work in the ulu Baram area. But with the discovery of oil in the 1920s, Miri became an important mission on its own. In the immediate post-war period, the conversion of the Kenyah to Christianity in the ulu Baram was to bring the Roman Catholic mission into contest with the BEM, which had recently moved into the ulu Baram area and had experienced a mass conversion among the Kayan.[170]

The work of the Catholic mission attained a sharper focus during the long Prefecture from 1897 to 1933 of Fr. Dunn, who was instrumental for providing stable leadership, teamwork among the missionaries, expansion of the mission and a sustained implementation of his vision.[171] By 1930, the work in Sarawak was concentrated in three major areas, Kuching/First Division, Rajang and Baram/Labuan, with the work in Kuching and the Rajang becoming very well established.

The subsequent entry of various Roman Catholic orders helped supplement and strengthen the work of the Mill Hill Fathers. The lay brothers looked after the schools and relieved the missionaries to do much travelling to start new work especially in the outstations. The Franciscan Sisters of St. Joseph (popularly known as the White Sisters) contributed much to establishing convents, girls' schools and medical services in Kanowit, Kuching, Sibu and Mukah.[172] They played an important social role in their work in education until 1940, initially breaking the prejudice against schooling for girls and then training the young women in the domestic arts to equip them to be suitable

---

[170] Southwell, *Uncharted Waters*, 244-45.

[171] Fr. Dunn initiated a Provincial Chapter in 1897, which met to deal with problems among the missionaries and gave opportunity to review regularly the Mission's activities and priorities. Further, Dunn developed a twofold objective of having common policies for the Mission and of expanding work into new areas. A result was the expansion of the work among the Melanau in Mukah, which experienced much success due to the faithful service of a long-serving missionary. The Mukah mission, first began by Fr. Stotter in 1899, was taken over by Fr. A. Mulder, who was its Rector from 1908 for a long period of forty years until his retirement. See Rooney, *Khabar Gembira*, 42-44.

[172] The Franciscan Sisters of St. Joseph initially came in two batches: the first in 1885 and another in 1889.

wives to the young men converts with the aim of creating a Christian community, thereby sustaining their gains of missionary work.[173]

The move to establish an indigenous diocesan clergy began as early as in 1888, but difficulties in providing the candidates with a suitable standard of education, an extremely high drop-out rate,[174] the length of training, the prospect of a celibate life, and the ascetic lifestyle of the clergy were often discouraging factors. Of greater success was the founding of the indigenous Little Sisters (officially known as Sisters of Sarawak) in 1926. These Little Sisters were an extension of the White Sisters and worked alongside them in both school and medical work in Sibu, Kanowit and Mukah.[175]

Internal migration had a positive effect on the spread and growth of the Catholic mission. First, there was migration for employment purposes to the towns. The more well-educated Roman Catholics were normally regarded with some sense of local importance, which had an indirect influence on the indigenous people. Second, the Iban tendency to travel, which earlier had the effect of causing tribal friction, became in later times a means of spreading Catholicism. There were two effects of the 1924 peace-making at Kapit. The Catholic families which were moved from Kanowit to River Pila became the spearhead of Catholic influence in remote upper Rajang, especially with their example of a more productive and peaceful farming life. Also, the peace-making deflected Iban migration from Belaga into Bintulu, so that the Catholic mission followed on the heels of this migration into the upper Rajang, then across into the country to Tatau, Bintulu, Batu Niah, into the Tinjar and even into Limbang.[176]

The steady growth of the Catholic mission had been sustained through a combination of factors. These included an adequate supply of manpower, the complementary work of the Sisters and lay brothers in schools and medical services, the presence of long-serving staff at a station or school, common policies that encouraged some measure of understanding of the overall priorities of the Mission and teamwork, and prudent financial management. Another factor was the willingness of the |Mission to follow the Catholic Dyak as they migrated from the Third Divison (Belaga) into the Fourth (Bintulu) and Fifth (Limbang) Divisions.

---

[173] In this matter, the White Sisters acted as marriage brokers between the young women and prospective young men converts. Rooney, *Khabar Gembira*, 152-53.

[174] Of the five pre-1930 candidates, only one actually reached priesthood. In one case in 1896, when the candidate had completed his academic studies, he was instructed to go to Canton for further Chinese studies, at which point he decided that he had no vocation for the ministry. Rooney, *Khabar Gembira*, 122.

[175] Rooney, *Khabar Gembira*, 95.

[176] Rooney, *Khabar Gembira*, 114.

The Methodist Episcopal Mission and the Foochow Chinese

As mentioned on page 17, the beginning of the Methodist Church in Sarawak resulted from a mass immigration of Foochow Chinese under the leadership of a Methodist pastor, Wong Nai Siong, in 1901.[177] The Foochows were quick to organize themselves into seven congregations, (where they started a church and a school, which usually occupied the same premise), at different places in 1902.

The American Methodist Episcopal Mission, which sent James Hoover to Sarawak in 1903, took charge of the mission work after the return of Wong Nai Siong to China. His style of mission work during his long tenure in Sarawak (1903-1935) incorporated both spiritual and temporal objectives.[178] His more significant contributions were mainly in the achievement of temporal aims. He encouraged the planting of rubber among the immigrants, which contributed to the economic development of Sibu in general and to the prosperity of the Foochow Christians in particular, thereby gaining much respect and fame for himself and the Methodist mission. In short, the Methodist mission stood for education, civilization, progress and modernity.

During Charles' rule, the Foochow Christians were strictly confined to the lower Rajang basin. But from the time of Vyner, especially from 1917 to 1925, migration out of the lower Rajang began, spreading to Sarikei,[179] Binatang, Kapit, Bintulu, and the Baram, Fourth Division.[180] By the end of colonial times, the Foochows had spread to all the major coastal towns in Sarawak, bringing along with them their churches.[181]

The growth of the Sarawak Chinese Methodist Church (SCMC) had generally been remarkable despite having only a few missionaries before WWII, but its work had largely been confined to the Foochow community.[182] The Foochow settlements expanded greatly in the third decade (the 1920s) with increased immigration from China as a result of the rubber boom. With the establishment of each Foochow Christian community, churches and schools were built wherever they went. They supported their own pastors who doubled up as teachers in the schools through a self-imposed system of tax on the produce (like rubber, pepper and sago) of their land which were sold. Pastors were either imported from or trained in China. The local Foochow churches were self-propagating and self-supporting from their inception, except for a

---

[177] They came in two batches to settle in Tanah Merah near Sibu in 1901 and 1902.

[178] James Hoover acted more like a town planner, engineer and contractor, introducing some of the latest modern inventions that brought modernity to Sarawak.

[179] Work in Sarikei first began in 1917, forty miles downriver from Sibu.

[180] The Foochows were often involved in planting vegetables, rubber and sawing timber.

[181] The work in Kuching started in 1955 under Rev. Yu Tek Soi.

[182] Liong, 'A Historical Inquiry', 148, 153. By 1935, SCMC had only one missionary couple, 35 pastors in 43 churches with some 5,500 members and 40 schools with an enrolment of 2,500 pupils. By 1940, they had 3 missionary couples, 2 district superintendents, 44 pastors and 76 local preachers in 58 churches with some 7,000 members and 53 schools with some 4,000 pupils.

short period between 1919 and 1921, when there was a severe economic crisis caused by the slump in rubber price coupled with a soaring local inflation.[183] The Foochow Christians for that brief period had some aid from the Mission. As conditions improved, the churches grew in tandem with the establishment of the various village settlements. Further, the establishment of the Methodist Theological School (MTS) in 1954 had the effect of training future leaders for the Sarawak Methodist church.[184] In short, the SCMC was functioning as a 'Three-Self' church in Sarawak.

As Daniel Chew noted, there was some social impact of the Foochow Church particularly before WWII. Church leaders were also prominent community leaders. The Church became a rallying point and refuge for the Foochows in the Rajang and also acted as a pillar of communal life in the absence of other Foochow social community organizations.[185] Moreover, the close relationship between the Church and the growth of the Foochow colonies had the effect of encouraging others to embrace the Methodist faith.

Until the late 1930s, no work had been done among the other Chinese groups such as the Hakka or the Cantonese or among the Dyak. This insularity of the Foochow Christians' outlook was due to the need to survive as a migrant race in a foreign land and to preserve the family. Clannish and traditional bonds gave way to a more outward outlook as they became successful farmers, cultivators and businessmen. Further, the revival resulting from Dr John Sung's public meetings among the Foochows in 1936 had a significant impetus on the SCMC towards greater evangelistic efforts to other groups.

The first sustained Methodist work among the Dyak began at Kapit in 1939 under the direction of Paul Schmucker, with the assistance of Lucius Mamora, a Sumatran Batak trained pastor.[186] The work progressed slowly through education, evangelism, personal contact and visitation.[187] Despite the Japanese Occupation, the work among the Dyak continued under Mamora, but was taken over by an American missionary after WWII.[188] Subsequently, a great influx of American missionaries and funds led to the opening of new mission centres, schools, agricultural training centres and medical and mobile clinics along the Rajang particularly in the 1960s.[189] This period saw rapid growth in terms of

---

[183] The Foochow church became autonomous as the Sarawak Chinese Annual Conference (SCAC) in 1962.

[184] MTS trained both Chinese and Dyak pastors. In 1961, there were 24 students: 12 Chinese and 12 Dyak students.

[185] Chew, *Chinese Pioneers*, 151-52.

[186] Lucius Mamora was a seconded worker from Sumatra by the Malayan Mission.

[187] Liong, 'A Historical Inquiry', 152-53. B.A. St. J. Hepburn, *The Handbook of Sarawak* (Singapore: Malaya Publishing House, 1949), 140-41.

[188] Burr Baughmann was sent to head the work among the Dyak in Kapit.

[189] Christ Hospital, Kapit, was opened in 1957, reaching its peak in the 1960s as a 60 bed hospital. The hospital has been bought by the Malaysian government. Liong, 'A

numbers of indigenous pastors trained at MTS, increase in church membership, indigenous leadership taking charge of strategic mission centres along the Rajang and the establishment of an autonomous indigenous church, the Sarawak Iban Annual Conference (SIAC) in 1968. Unlike the Chinese Methodist Church, however, this church was not financially self-supporting. The withdrawal of the American mission in the mid-1970s left a vacuum in the work, which the SIAC was unable to sustain and fund. The gradual reduction of American funds over a decade since the grant of autonomy in 1968,[190] with the aim of weaning the indigenous church, SIAC, from its dependency on the parent mission failed to achieve its purpose. Further, the American mission, which was theologically liberal, was highly accommodative of traditional culture and religion so that, when whole longhouses became Christians, traditional religious practices continued alongside those of their new-found Christian faith. In this respect the religious beliefs and practices of the Methodist Dyak resembled those of the Anglican Dyak.

The Christian and Missionary Alliance and the First People Movements

The Christian and Missionary Alliance (C&MA), an evangelical, inter-denominational American mission body, was founded by Dr A.B. Simpson (1843-91) in 1897.[191] Its roots lay within the Holiness movement. Simpson espoused a premillennial eschatology, and a firm commitment to fulfill the Great Commission by urgently making known the gospel in yet unreached areas. [192] At the turn of the twentieth century, the C&MA worked enthusiastically in global missions and in expectation of the imminent return of Christ.

The C&MA regarded mission as the responsibility of the whole church, and believed in the creation of indigenous churches based on 'three-self' principles. With its vision to plant churches in 'unoccupied' areas, the C&MA work spread from South China and Vietnam and then to Indonesia.[193] Through the initiative of Robert A. Jaffray,[194] the work began in Indonesia at Makassar and East

---

Historical Inquiry', 159-65, 170-73. By 1960, there were 23 missionaries working among the Iban.

[190] The gradual reduction of funds was ten per cent each year for a decade from 1968.

[191] C&MA was an amalgamation of the Evangelical Missionary Alliance and the International Christian Alliance, which was set up in 1887. John Roxborogh, 'Christian and Missionary Alliance', in Scott Sunquist, David C.S. Wu, and John H.C. Chew (eds.), *Dictionary of Asian Christianity* (Grand Rapids: Eerdmans, 2001), 160.

[192] A.B. Simpson, *The Challenge of Missions* (New York: Christian Publishing, 1926), 42-56. Joel Carpenter and W.R. Shenk (eds.), *Earthen Vessels: American Evangelicals and Foreign Missions, 1880-1980* (Grand Rapids: Eerdmans, 1990), and Gerald H. Anderson (ed.), *Mission Legacies* (Maryknoll: Orbis Books, 1994), 37-47.

[193] John Roxborogh, 'Christian and Missionary Alliance', 160.

[194] R.A. Torrey, *Let My People Go: The Life of Robert A. Jaffray* (Camp Hill: Christian Publications, 1990).

Kalimantan in 1929 and 1930 respectively.[195] Its rapid growth resulted in the C&MA sponsoring the formal constitution of the indigenous church, Kemah-Injil Gereja Masehi Indonesia (KINGMI) in Kalimantan and Makassar in 1946 and 1951 respectively. KINGMI was first organized in 1946 and legally incorporated in 1956 with three KINGMI regions (East and West Kalimantan and East Indonesia). By 1965, it had become a national indigenous church, Gereja Kemah Injil Indonesia (GKII) with work throughout the whole of Indonesia.[196]

The pattern of C&MA work in Indonesia followed Jaffray's three-fold priority of a) promoting literature, colportage and publications, b) stressing Bible school education for the indigenous Christians and c) planting churches. As local Bible schools were basic to their strategy, the founding of the Sekolah Alkitab Makassar (SAM) in Makassar in 1932 was instrumental in providing indigenous leadership for KINGMI, who would work alongside C&MA missionaries to strengthen existing work as in East Kalimantan and in supplying evangelists to reach new areas.[197]

Work in the interior of East Kalimantan, particularly among the Kenyah and Kayan of the Bulungan, and the Murut of the Sesayap districts, which was adjacent to the BEM work in Sarawak,[198] was pioneered by George Fisk and W. Ernest Presswood in 1930 and 1932 respectively, and resulted in great success, leading to the first Bornean people movements into Christianity. The conversion among the Murut in the Sesayap in 1932 triggered a similar mass movement across adjacent Sarawak, where the BEM missionaries had their work.

The mission approach that emerged began with missionaries first stationing themselves at a base in a coastal town (e.g. Presswood in Samarinda and Fisk in Tanjungselur) from which they made preaching trips into the Sesayap and Bulungan areas. Later, they started settled work in the areas where mass conversions had occurred with Fisk stationed at Long Punjungan in 1932 and Presswood at Long Berang in 1937. From these interior bases, they moved into new areas with Fisk making visits to the Apau Kayan in 1933. Both Presswood and Fisk were the only missionaries in these areas till 1939 and 1940 respectively; but Presswood was joined by John Willfinger in 1938, who later continued his work until WWII.

The mass conversions in the two areas occurred differently. That at Sesayap occurred in the context of the Muruts being in a state of depopulation. It

[195] Makassar was headquarters for the C&MA work in Indonesia from September 1930. Rodger Lewis, *Karya Kristus di Indonesia: Sejarah Gereja Kemah Injil Indonesia sejak 1930* (Bandung: Yayasan Kalam Hidup, 1995), 23-26, 482.
[196] Lewis, *Karya Kristus*, 469-71. Conley, *Kalimantan Kenyah*, 336.
[197] Lewis, *Karya Kristus*, 38-51, 55-61.
[198] The Murut in the Sesayap also occupy the Limbang, Fifth Division, in Sarawak. The Kenyah and Kayan of the Bulungan similarly extend across to the upper Baram, Fourth Division, and upper Balleh and Balui, Third Division.

resulted from the millenarian emphasis of Presswood's presentation of the Christian message, which the Muruts interpreted as a means of escape from their present state of misery so that they gladly responded and many left their farms immediately to await the return of Christ. This mass conversion resulted in many baptisms, including those who were to become leaders of the church.[199]

In the Punjungan area, the mass conversion which happened during Fisk's initial trip to Long Metep in 1931 was preceded by the prior conversion of the paramount Kenyah chief, Jalong Ipoy, who had earlier visited Fisk in Tanjungselor.[200] The decision to convert was made consensually by the elders, the leading men and the whole community.[201] Together with the conversion of the kudung man, it resulted in more people movements within the area and the establishment of three churches at Long Metep, Long Punjungan and Long Ketaman.[202]

At Nahakeramo in Apau Kayan, an adjacent area to Punjungan, in 1933, another mass conversion of over half the village occurred, partly due to the receptivity of the young chief, PeBaya' Jalong. According to Conley, one motive behind his conversion may have been the hope that Christianity would prove a means of advancement of his people through education. But, after Fisk's departure, the adat chiefs and leaders began their opposition towards Christianity. A more intense persecution of Kenyah Christians about six years later led to the burning down of a Christian longhouse, which was rebuilt further downriver from the main village.[203]

In contrast to the Murut, the conversion of the Kenyah occurred mainly through the combination of the ministry of the missionaries with indigenous initiatives and was aided by a number of factors: firstly, by the conversion of a chief or other leaders such as a kudung man or an adat chief among the people; secondly, by village migration and the Kenyah propensity to travel; and also, by some kind of event perceived as supernatural, as in an incident when a

[199] Lewis, *Karya Kristus*, 159, 164. Those who became leaders included T. Daniel Tebay, Sakai Laban and Martin Rining Laban.

[200] Conley, *Kalimantan Kenyah*, 284-86.

[201] It resulted in 221 baptisms with the chief as the first candidate.

[202] Conley, *Kalimantan Kenyah*, 288-91 (290). The *kudung* man or the rice ritual man, as he was called in Indonesian terms, performs the necessary rituals to ensure a good rice harvest. See also Lewis, *Karya Kristus*, 116-17. Silwanus Laeng was the *kudung* man, who joined SAM in 1932 and became superintendent of Punjungan district, KINGMI.

[203] Conley, *Kalimantan Kenyah*, 293, 304-305. Earlier, the people had asked the Dutch controller from Tanjungselur who had visited them for a schoolteacher for the village. But the promise of the Dutch controller did not materialize. So, when Fisk stationed an Ambonese Bible school student, Yohanes Sahitapi there, he found ready listeners and willing disciples and this resulted in 200 baptisms.

person who publicly opposed the missionary and his message died the next day (i.e., a form of power encounter).[204]

The theological stance of the C&MA missionaries, like those of the BEM, was less accommodative of indigenous religious traditions, so that their practices and ritual symbols and paraphernalia (such as sacred charms and human head trophies) were often swept away and destroyed, a practice that became the norm among converts.

Starting Bible schools was an important means of consolidating the work. At Long Berang, Presswood's short-term Bible school for a month in 1935 was assisted by students from Sekolah Alkitab Makassar on their practical field assignment. This work, which was aimed at promoting literacy for the sake of reading the Bible and for preaching, grew, became upgraded to a basic Bible School, and later shifted to Long Sepayang, at the confluence of the Sepayang and Krayan Rivers.[205]

As C&MA prescribed no clear policy for the structure of the indigenous church, it was left to the individual missionary to shape the organisation and management of a local church. At Pujungan, Fisk appointed seven elders to each of the three churches in Long Ketaman, Long Punjungan and Long Metep, and taught them about internal matters of church life. Hence from the beginning, each local KINGMI congregation managed their own church affairs and their steady multiplication reflected the self-propagating character of the Kenyah church.[206] In short, Fisk encouraged a self-governing church, and a leadership model which was patterned initially after that of the village council of elders.

In the Sesayap, Presswood appointed twenty leaders for the various churches and taught them to manage the activities of the Murut churches in 1938.[207] Willfinger further enhanced their organisational skills by initiating the first celebration of Easter in 1941 at Long Berang. One thousand people attended, among them some Murut Christians from Sarawak.

The C&MA support policy toward indigenous workers, in contrast to the BEM, was initially to hire national pastors and evangelists. But in January 1956, the mission stopped this practice on realising the need for KINGMI to be financially independent. KINGMI in Kalimantan had to embark on a self-support policy for national pastors from the local congregations, encouraging the principle of tithing among church members.[208]

---

[204] Conley, *Kalimantan Kenyah*, 318, 327. The term 'power encounter' is a commonly-understood term in evangelical mission circle, but is less well-known in other circles.

[205] Lewis, *Karya Kristus*, 38, 42-43. In 1940, the Bible School had 68 students.

[206] Seventeen churches were organized and grew steadily from nearly 3,800 baptised adults in 1936 to some 4,300 baptised members in 1940. The pattern of management was adapted from the North American C&MA (like conducting Sunday and weekday meetings). Conley, *Kalimantan Kenyah*, 291, 296-97.

[207] Lewis, *Karya Kristus*, 169-71.

[208] Conley, *Kalimantan Kenyah*, 332.

An effect of conversion among the Kenyah has been a spontaneous indigenous initiative in propagating their new religion. One converted village headman, Panai Raub at Long Nuat, travelled over to Sarawak to share the Christian message with his Murut relatives between 1936 and 1937, when there was already a mass movement of Lun Bawang into Christianity in neighbouring Sarawak.[209]

Indigenous initiative came to the fore during the Japanese Occupation. In the Sesayap, Aris Doemat, a SAM graduate, was instrumental in consolidating and even expanding the work there,[210] and had a strong influence among the Christians in the Kelabit Highlands in Sarawak, an area of BEM work.[211] But the KINGMI work in the Sesayap, which expanded rapidly, began to stagnate from the 1950s. The reasons cited included converts not being properly discipled, a lack of understanding of a committed Christian lifestyle, and the incapacity to deal with moral issues within the churches, so that by 1956 the problems of charging excessive bride-price,[212] frequent quarrels, divorce, and adultery became rampant and remained unresolved. Further, the low educational standard among the pastors and evangelists was insufficient to help them meet the rising needs of a more literate community.[213] Moreover, KINGMI had problems fully funding their work; a result of its dependence on the parent mission body for finances. All these challenges of planting and developing an indigenous church were similarly faced by the SIB.

The practice of having annual and district conferences served both spiritual and organisational purposes. In 1949, the first district conference in Sesayap was organized at Long Sepayang with 153 indigenous delegates from 23 churches. They adopted a constitution and elected a full board of office bearers; thus began the formation of KINGMI, Kalimantan.[214]

The C&MA work illustrates one possible pathway to establishing an indigenous 'Three-Self' church. The remainder of this book will examine the route that the BEM took to achieve a similar goal.[215]

The study of the political, cultural and religious context of the BEM in this chapter shows the manner in which the BEM has functioned in a mix of circumstances, where its work (in particular, the implementation of its mission polices) was moderated and fashioned by a dynamic interplay between governmental (first Brooke, then colonial and Malaysian) policies, and

---

[209] Lewis, *Karya Kristus*, 165-67.

[210] Lewis, *Karya Kristus*, 174. Aris Doemat was appointed the district head/elder of the churches in the Sesayap district in 1941.

[211] Harrisson, *World Within*, 254-56.

[212] The issue of high bride price was also an issue faced by the SIB in the 1950s.

[213] Lewis, *Karya Kristus*, 179-81. Most of the pastors had their training only at the local Bible school (i.e., at Long Sepayang).

[214] Lewis, *Karya Kristus*, 178.

[215] See Chapter 6.

indigenous societal aspirations and practices in the face of modernization and life within a new nation state, Malaysia.

Having sketched the background context of the BEM, I will next examine the characteristics of the Christian tradition that shaped the BEM.

Chapter 3

Australian Christianity and the BEM

The BEM began as an Australian missionary society in 1928 mainly through the initiative of Charles Hudson Southwell, a student of the Melbourne Bible Institute (MBI), with the encouragement and counsel of its principal, the Rev. C.H. Nash. The three pioneering missionaries of the BEM, Southwell, Frank Davidson and Carey Tolley, who went out to Sarawak in 1928 were all graduates of MBI in 1928, as were the majority of Australian missionaries who subsequently served the BEM from 1928 till 1975. However, from 1950 onwards, there was a small stream of BEM missionaries from the United Kingdom, among whom were Dr Bill and Shirley Lees and Dr Bill Hawes, who became the third BEM Field Director in 1968.

In character, the BEM was an inter-denominational, evangelical mission body from its inception. Its three pioneering missionaries came from three different denominations: Southwell was Baptist, Davidson was Anglican and Tolley was a member of the Christian Brethren.[1] Similarly, the ten founding BEM Council members were evangelicals from three major denominations (Anglican, Baptist and Brethren) in Melbourne.[2] Much of the ethos and purpose of the BEM was shaped by the nature of evangelical Christianity in Australia in general and in Melbourne in particular. This chapter will examine the nature of the Australian evangelical Christianity from which the pioneering missionaries of the BEM came, and its influence on the BEM and its missionaries.

The evangelical movement from the 1730s to the 1980s, despite its diversity and a variety of self-definition, displays certain common characteristics. These David Bebbington has identified as crucicentrism, biblicism, conversionism and activism.[3] Additionally, evangelicalism was both a movement 'with

---

[1] Lees, *Drunk before Dawn*, 27.

[2] Minutes of the Borneo Fellowship meeting dated 31 August 1928. See Southwell, *Uncharted Waters*, 63. Details of the ten founding members in terms of their denominations and occupations are as follows: C.H. Nash (Anglican, Principal, MBI), R.S. Tregaskis (Superintendent of Men Students, MBI), C.H. Perrin (Chief Engineer of Victorian Railways), E. Stafford Young (a member of the wealthy Young family who owned the Colonial Sugar Refinery in Queensland, Brethren), Mabel Heath, Harold Jeffrey, Alexander Henderson, Southwell (Baptist), Davidson (Anglican), and Tolley (Brethren).

[3] David Bebbington, *Evangelicalism in Modern England: A History from the 1730s to the 1980s* (London: Routledge, 1993), 2-3. The beliefs are a) the centrality and

common heritages, common tendencies, influences and an identity', and a conscious fellowship 'with a network or coalition of friends, family and community with a strong sense of belonging, that is inter-denominational; sometimes functioning almost like a denomination'.[4] Not only did Australian evangelical Christianity from the mid-nineteenth century share these characteristics of its counterpart in Britain, but it also had to cope with the perceived threats of modernism, liberal theology and ritualism.

Australian evangelicalism was shaped by various influences which made it in some respects similar to and in other respects distinctive from its British parent. Firstly, the Church Act of 1836 created the situation whereby the Anglican Church in Australia was never 'in law established',[5] so that no one denomination was more favoured than the other as had been the case in England and Scotland.[6] This move opened the field for any denomination or Christian group to assert its influence. As a result, evangelicalism, by virtue of its activism and inter-denominational character, continued as a steady force within Australian Protestantism through the network of individuals, both clergy and lay, across the denominations and voluntary organisations.

Secondly, the Australian churches had to create their own institutions, which led to a large importation of clerical staff from England and Ireland until the early twentieth century,[7] giving rise to a significant proportion of Church of Ireland clergymen in Australia, who were predominantly evangelical. Notable among them were H.B. McCartney and his son in Melbourne,[8] John MacCullagh, long-time dean of Bendigo,[9] and later T.C. Hammond in Sydney. The Irish clergy migrants, especially after the disestablishment of the Irish Church in 1869, brought with them their pattern of active evangelism among the Roman Catholics in their own country. In Brian Dickey's estimate, they brought a convinced evangelical stance, a suspicion of ritualism and

sufficiency of Christ's sacrifice on the cross for the Christian life, b) the divine inspiration and final authority of Scripture for Christian faith and life, c) the need to be changed with a personal conversion experience to Christ, and d) the propagation of the gospel through evangelism and missions.

4 George Marsden (ed.), 'The Evangelical Denomination', in *Evangelicalism and Modern America* (Grand Rapids: Eerdmans, 1984), x-xvi.

5 Brian Dickey, 'Evangelical Anglicans Compared', in George A. Rawlyk and Mark Noll (eds.), *Amazing Grace*: *Evangelicalism in Australia, Britain, Canada and the United States* (Grand Rapids: Baker Books, 1993), 216.

6 Roger C. Thompson, *Religion in Australia: A History* (Melbourne: Oxford University Press, 1994), 9; David Parker, '"The Evangelical Heritage of Australian Protestantism": Towards An Historical Perspective', *The History Teacher*, May 1981, 21.

7 Dickey, 'Evangelical Anglicans Compared', 219. It is only to be expected as there was the obvious social difference between the settled societies in the United Kingdom and the settling communities in Australia.

8 Brian Dickey, *The Australian Dictionary of Evangelical Biography* (*ADEB*) (Sydney: Evangelical History Association, 1994), 227-28.

9 Dickey, *ADEB*, 229-30.

Romanism, combined with activism, dedication, missionary fervour, and a willingness to work with or without diocesan approval as self-starters, which constituted 'a major factor in making the Australian case different from the English model'.[10]

As for the Baptists, the first Baptist ministers were graduates of the strongly evangelical Spurgeon's College, which 'in its first three generations sent a hundred and six young ministers to New Zealand and Australia.... Among them were Dr F.W. Boreham and Dr C.J. Tinsley'.[11] Also, Thomas Spurgeon, Charles Spurgeon's son, spent sixteen years in Australia and New Zealand before he returned to the Metropolitan Tabernacle to succeed his father. The Methodists, in addition to their pastoral ministers, had itinerant evangelists like Rev. William G. Taylor who, on the model of its founder, John Wesley, preached throughout the country, resulting in large numbers of conversions.[12] In short, evangelical Christianity exercised an important influence in Australian religious life for some two hundred years.

Thirdly, another characteristic of Australian evangelicalism, which Stuart Piggin has noted, is the hegemony of Anglicanism.[13] The first Anglican clergymen were evangelicals.[14] But the High Church tradition, which began to displace evangelicalism as the dominant influence in the Anglican Church from 1820 to 1860, came through the establishment of bishoprics,[15] except for Melbourne and Sydney, where evangelicals continued to have significant influence.[16] In Melbourne, despite having a convinced evangelical bishop in Charles Perry ans his successors, James Moorhouse (1876-1886) and Field Flower Goe (1886-1902), the evangelical tradition did not become entrenched with the result that Anglican evangelicalism became a minority party within the

---

[10] Dickey, 'Evangelical Anglicans Compared', 237.

[11] J. Edwin Orr, *Evangelical Awakenings in the South Seas* (Minneapolis: Bethany Fellowship, 1976), 61.

[12] Orr, *Evangelical Awakenings in the South Seas*, 62. Parker, '"The Evangelical Heritage of Australian Protestantism"', 17.

[13] Stuart Piggin, 'The American and British Contributions to Evangelicalism in Australia', in Mark Noll, David Bebbington and George A. Rawlyk (eds.), *Evangelicalism: Comparative Studies of Popular Protestantism in North America, the British Isles, and Beyond, 1700-1990* (New York: Oxford University Press, 1994), 291.

[14] The first clergyman, Rev Richard Johnson, chaplain to Port Jackson colony from 1787 to 1801 was an evangelical Anglican. His successor was another famous evangelical Anglican clergyman and magistrate, Samuel Marsden who served from 1794 until 1838.

[15] Dickey, 'Evangelical Anglicans Compared', 224-25. The establishment of the bishoprics portrayed High Church Anglicanism as the norm. William Broughton (Bishop 1835-1853) resisted evangelical influence and imported to Australia the High Church tradition which was fashionable in the first half of the nineteenth century among churchmen.

[16] The comparison between Anglican evangelicalism in Sydney and Melbourne has been a subject of much study. See Stuart Piggin's Perry Memorial Lecture, 'Pietism, Pluralism, and Provincialism: The Divergent Paths of Melbourne and Sydney Evangelicalism, 1848-1988', *Southern Cross* February 1991, 12-13.

Anglican Church. Except for a few notable clergy, Melbourne evangelicalism has generally been more laity-led as a movement. It often circumvented Anglican structures by frequently using lay inter-denominational agencies with evangelical charters.[17] Also, it has been more inter-denominational than its Sydney counterpart. As Darrell Paproth notes, 'during the last quarter of the nineteenth century and the first half of the twentieth century, three men dominated the cause of Australian missions: Rev. C.H. Nash (Anglican), Rev. William Lockhart Morton (Presbyterian) and Rev. Hussey Burgh MacCartney Jr (Anglican).[18] In contrast, Sydney had Bishop Frederic Barker (1854-1881), who helped entrench Anglican evangelicalism as the dominant influence, which has since been the dominant Christian style. Through the influence of T.C. Hammond, Sydney Anglicanism was characterized by its combativeness and militancy, and it was also clergy-dominated. Melbourne evangelical Anglicanism, on the other hand, was more moderate, mainly due to the irenic personalities of Melbourne evangelicals like Nash.[19]

Fourthly, Australian evangelicalism showed great similarity to British evangelicalism in its religious denominations, mission bodies and voluntary organizations and in its response to the perceived threats of liberalism, higher criticism and ritualism, particularly up till WWII. As in Britain and the United States of America, the evangelical-liberal tension emerged as a major inter-denominational issue after the First World War. With only a few cases of this controversy in Australia, chief among which involved Dr Samuel Angus of St. Andrew's Presbyterian (Theological) Hall, evangelical influence continued entrenched in Australian churches.[20] After WWII, the influence of American fundamentalism increased, bringing with it a slightly greater polarisation that began to be felt among evangelicals from the 1960s. But as David Parker rightly noted, Australian conservative Protestantism has not been marked by the militancy and controversy of the North American variety.[21]

---

[17] Dickey, 'Evangelical Anglicans Compared', 226. Stuart Piggin, *Evangelical Christianity in Australia: Spirit, Word and World* (Melbourne: Oxford University Press, 1996), 98-99, 107. Some of these prominent Anglican laity included the tea merchants, James and John Griffith, Horace and John Hannah and Edwin Lee Neil, and H.P. Smith, who started the Upwey Convention and jointly founded the Melbourne Bible Institute (MBI) with Dr James J. Kitchen.

[18] Darrell Paproth, 'Hussey Burgh MacCartney: Mission Enthusiast' (Unpublished Paper, 2004), 21.

[19] Dickey, 'Evangelical Anglicans Compared', 230-31.

[20] Piggin, *Evangelical Christianity*, 92-94. The Angus controversy did weaken the Methodist, Presbyterian and Congregationalists Churches. From this lesson, conservative evangelicalism was defended with greater determination by the Sydney evangelical Anglicans (e.g. D.J. Knox, R.B. Robinson and H.S. Begbie) and Baptists (e.g. G.H. Morling and C.J. Tinsley).

[21] David Parker, 'Fundamentalism and Conservative Protestantism in Australia, 1920-1980' (PhD thesis, University of Queensland, 1982), 473.

Within this matrix of Australian evangelicalism, the BEM was born through an inter-denominational network of friends and institutions in Melbourne. Melbourne evangelicalism was expressed through an interlocking network of key individuals. Chief among them was Nash, working cooperatively in conjunction with the other movements and organizations. For the rest of this chapter, I will examine a) the influence of C.H. Nash, b) the revivalistic and evangelistic movements, c) the missionary movement through the China Inland Mission (CIM), d) the Keswick Convention movement, and e) the Bible College movement through MBI.

The Influence of Rev. C.H. Nash

During the period from 1920 to 1942, the Rev. C.H. Nash, an evangelical Anglican clergyman and the first principal of the Melbourne Bible Institute (MBI), exercised a strong influence within Melbourne evangelical circles by providing the necessary leadership appropriate for its time and within an inter-denominational context. His leadership was exercised mainly through the MBI, the Upwey Convention, the Bible Union of Victoria, the City Men's Bible Class (CMBC), missionary and evangelistic organisations and individual laymen.[22] Through his personal qualities and the nature of his leadership, he gathered a group that formed a large part of the evangelical leadership in Melbourne.[23] Melbourne, at that time, had the strongest, best organized and most determined network of lay evangelicals.[24] Nash provided the necessary teaching, mentoring and leadership to focus their energies and activities. Many of these lay evangelicals were very able men who rose to the top of their professions.

The greatest influence that Nash had on the BEM was through MBI, which supplied BEM with most of its Australian missionaries. It is necessary to understand the kind of influence and theological training Nash underwent so as to understand the type of training he would have provided.

When Nash was a student at Corpus Christi College, Cambridge (1885-1889) and at Ridley Hall (1889-1890), Cambridge evangelicalism was still shaped and influenced by the legacy of Charles Simeon. As J.C. Bennett argues, no evangelical Anglican has exercised a greater strategic influence than

[22] Darrell Paproth, *Failure Is Not Final: A Life of C.H. Nash* (Sydney: Centre for the Study of Australian Christianity, 1997), 9. According to Piggin, C.H. Nash was 'arguably the most influential clergyman of his generation' in Melbourne. See Piggin, *Evangelical Christianity*, 99.

[23] He acted as a facilitator of people to work and develop their own gifts and to exercise their own initiative. See Paproth, *Failure Is Not Final*, 10.

[24] Some of these laymen traced their spiritual ancestry to R.A. Torrey's visit to Melbourne in 1902; others to the Geelong Convention in 1891 and still others to the Evangelization Society of Victoria founded in 1883. See Piggin, *Evangelical Christianity*, 98.

Charles Simeon on Anglican evangelicalism and the British missionary movement in the early nineteenth century.[25] Further, Simeon had the reputation of being a mentor of younger clergy[26] as well as being a committed 'Churchman' and a 'Gospel-man'.[27] As a churchman, he advocated submission to proper authority and adopted a conciliatory stance toward the bishop.[28] His influence was continued into the later nineteenth century by H.C.G. Moule, the first principal of Ridley Hall, who was regarded as his spiritual heir.[29] Part of the Cambridge evangelical tradition as expressed at Ridley Hall was its loyalty to the Anglican heritage; that is, these evangelicals were committed churchmen, and Nash was no different.[30] Nash's commitment to the 'church principle' and so to his church denomination was reflected in his advice as principal of MBI to his students and those who attended his City Men's Bible Class[31] to remain loyal within their denominations.[32]

Nash displayed an evangelical scholarship that was prepared to engage with doctrinal liberalism or modernism when necessary. As a powerful defender of the authority and inspiration of the Bible, Nash was not alone. There were others like the Very Rev. R.G. Macintyre, an elder statesman in the

---

[25] J.C. Bennett, 'Charles Simeon and the Evangelical Anglican Mission Movement: A Study of Voluntaryism and Church Mission Tensions' (PhD thesis, University of Edinburgh, 1992), 394.

[26] According to Bennett, the chief marks of character that Simeon desired to produce in those he mentored included personal humility, fidelity to God, confidence in proper ministerial authority, dependence on the Holy Spirit, a moderate temperament, hard work, practical trust in God and perseverance in the face of opposition and affliction. See J.C. Bennett, 'Charles Simeon and the Evangelical Anglican Mission Movement', 145.

[27] A.W. Brown, *Recollections of the Conversation Parties of the Rev. Charles Simeon* (1863), 60. Quoted in J.C. Bennett, 'Charles Simeon and the Evangelical Anglican Mission Movement', 6.

[28] Bennett, 'Charles Simeon and the Evangelical Anglican Mission Movement', 140.

[29] See Bishop J.R.S. Taylor's remark in his Foreword in H.C.G. Moule, *Charles Simeon* (London: Inter-Varsity Fellowship, 1952 reprint). 'Handley Moule himself inherited and adorned the great tradition which Simeon established. No one who knew him (Moule) could fail to recognize the similarities between the two men.... Less than fifty years after Simeon's death, Moule became his spiritual heir in more sense than one'.

[30] Paproth, *Failure Is Not Final*, 23. Paproth argues that Lightfoot and Westcott at Cambridge, who were conservative in their ecclesiology and were committed to the Church of England, certainly exercised an influence on Nash's churchmanship. More likely, the influence of Lightfoot and Westcott was to reinforce the church principle which was already held by Cambridge evangelicals.

[31] Paproth, *Failure Is Not Final*, 124. His ecclesiology, which emphasised the place of the established church in the kingdom of God, may have an influence on those who were only interested in evangelism and disliked denominational rivalries.

[32] D. Paproth, '"The Melbourne Bible Institute": Its Genesis, Ethos and Purpose', in G. Treloar (ed.), *The Furtherance of Religious Beliefs: Essays on the History of Theological Education in Australia* (Sydney: Centre for the Study for Australian Christianity, 1997), 135.

Presbyterian Church of New South Wales and 'a weighty defender of revealed religion' or Lionel Fletcher, an influential Congregational evangelist who provided a counter-balance to the liberal ethos of Australian Congregationalism.[33] Despite the influence of Rev. Frederick J. Williams in advocating liberal theology in Victoria, the Baptists in Victoria had remained generally conservative and closer to the Protestant mainstream without accepting the increasingly influential liberal theology among the Anglicans, Methodists and Presbyterians.[34]

This trait of Nash, as Darrell Paproth argues, was influenced by the commitment of B.F. Westcott and J.B. Lightfoot to a high standard of biblical scholarship, which maintained 'an attitude of moderation and toleration characteristic of Anglicanism at its best'.[35] In short, Cambridge evangelicalism found a ready ally in the biblical scholarship of Westcott and Lightfoot. By 1895, many British nonconformist evangelicals had come to accept historical and critical methods in the study of the Bible.[36] Evangelical Anglicans were slower to adopt advanced critical views, but were nonetheless prepared to employ moderate critical methods.

British evangelicals, of whom Nash was an example, were generally not militant, separatist, inerrantist or dispensational premillennialist like the American fundamentalists, though they did share a similar concern over 'destructive' biblical criticism.[37] Consequently, in the first few decades of the twentieth century, Australian evangelicals, of whom Nash was an outstanding example, commended a positive approach to the evangelical faith without becoming polemical or developing a narrow fundamentalism. They always believed that every Christian must be ready to give a reason for his faith.[38] In

[33] Ian Breward, *A History of the Churches in Australasia* (Oxford: Oxford University Press, 2001), 257-58. Though liberalism was influential, it was 'out of touch with the religious experience of a significant part of its constituency'.

[34] Ian Breward, *A History of the Australian Churches* (St. Leonards: Allen and Unwin, Australia, 1993), 94-95, 123. Rev. Frederick Williams had founded a network of 10 churches and 21 preaching points in Victoria. Though liberalism was influential, it was 'out of touch with the religious experience of a significant part of its constituency'.

[35] Paproth, *Failure Is Not Final*, 24.

[36] Willis B. Glover, *Evangelical Nonconformity and Higher Criticism in the Nineteenth Century* (London: Independent Press, 1954), 286. See Parker, 'The Evangelical Heritage', 17.

[37] Paproth, '"The Melbourne Bible Institute"', 129-33.

[38] Of note were two occasions where Nash defended the inspiration and authority of the Bible, first at the Melbourne Town Hall in 1907 and later, at the Bible Union in 1923. See David Chambers, *Tempest Tost: The Life and Teaching of the Rev. C.H. Nash, MA* (Melbourne: Church Press Publications, 1959), 173-81. David Parker, 'The Bible Union: A Case Study in Australian Fundamentalism', *Journal of Religious History* 14.1 (June 1986), 74-79. C.H. Nash was the first President of the Bible Union which was founded in Melbourne in 1923. It had two objectives: 'to promote the reverent study of the Holy Scriptures, and to resist the various attacks made upon their inspiration and authority as the written Word of God'. Paproth, *Failure Is Not Final*, 28. See F.W.B. Bullock, *The*

response to the liberal views of Samuel Angus, the Presbyterian Professor of New Testament at St Andrews College, University of Sydney, Nash gave an exposition of the evangelical understanding of 'The Efficacy of the Death of Christ' at the 1933-1934 Australian Keswick convention.[39] Moreover, the ethos of Ridley Hall and particularly that of Handley Moule, was influential in commending the evangelical faith in a positive spirit while maintaining respect for those who held contrary views.[40] Like his mentor Nash, Southwell, the BEM pioneer, followed a non-polemical approach to matters affecting the Christian faith. In one instance, Southwell spoke to a group at the Tanjong Lobak College in Miri on a Christian perspective on the subject 'Science and the Bible' and later gained a convert in the person of the Australian science teacher at the College.[41]

Nash showed his indebtedness to the influence of Handley C.G. Moule at Ridley Hall, who combined learning and scholarship with the pietistic Keswick tradition.[42] The impact of Handley Moule on his students was that of a mentor.[43] His daily exposition of the Greek text of the New Testament[44] became very much the pattern of Nash's teaching and preaching ministry in Melbourne. Nash would give Bible exposition using only the Greek text, speaking with a clarity and devotion that instilled an evangelical fervour in his hearers.[45]

Handley Moule himself had been closely aligned with the holiness teaching and ethos of the Keswick movement since 1884, becoming its frequent speaker and theologian.[46] This holiness emphasis was brought into the life of Ridley Hall through his experience, personality and teaching. Similarly, Nash was

---

History of Ridley Hall (Vol. 1; Cambridge: University Press, 1941), 334, 336. There was no doubt that Nash was a good scholar. When he was in Ridley Hall from 1889-1890, he was already a Scholar of Corpus Christi and he was awarded a First Class for the Preliminary Theological Examination of Cambridge in 1890.

39 *Keswick Quarterly*, February 1934, 25. Cited in Paproth, *Failure Is Not Final*, 121.

40 Chambers, *Tempest Tost*, 24. When Handley Moule was installed as the first Principal of Ridley Hall in 1881, he spoke briefly on the ethos of Ridley as having 'the spirit, namely of respect for the convictions of others, while yet of definite adherence to their own convictions of the Divine truth'.

41 Southwell, *Uncharted Waters*, 354-35. Ron Nugent is the Australian Science teacher, who later went to study at the Bible College of South Australia in 1976. See *BEM NL*, February 1977, 3.

42 Paproth, *Failure Is Not Final*, 26-29. Handley Moule, later Bishop of Durham, was a well known and respected evangelical leader and scholar and was deeply involved with the Keswick Convention.

43 Chambers, *Tempest Tost*, 25. Moule had regular meals with his students and while on walks, counselled and engaged them in deep discussion. Nash recalled Moule's help over his difficulty about the question of infant baptism during such a walk.

44 Bullock, *The History of Ridley Hall*, I, 230. Chambers, *Tempest Tost*, 24.

45 Paproth, *Failure Is Not Final*, 28.

46 Marcus Loane, 'The Keswick Convention and the Missionary Movement', *Southern Cross* 3 (Sydney: Diocese of Sydney, n.d.), vi-vii.

closely involved with the Upwey Convention, the Australian counterpart to the English Keswick Convention. He first took the Bible readings at the second convention and thereafter became its frequent and popular speaker for over twenty years.[47]

The holiness movement in Australia had two offshoots: Pentecostalism and sinless perfection. Australian Pentecostalism in the 1920s was a nascent movement on the fringe of mainstream evangelicalism. In 1925, A.C. Valdez Sr, an overseas visitor, started his ministry at Sunshine, a Melbourne suburb, promoting Pentecostal teaching and practices. Within a year, the Pentecostal mission had become a church.[48] At this time, Len Jones, an MBI student who had attended Pentecostal meetings, spoke in tongues and influenced eight other students. Nash promptly placed a ban on holding prayer meetings or such meetings to receive the 'baptism of the Spirit',[49] and discouraged any involvement with the Pentecostal movement.[50] The MBI Council, which met on 24 June 1925, unanimously supported Nash's action. It resulted in Len Jones and the other students later leaving MBI, despite attempts by Nash to dissuade them from doing so. Though he was committed to holiness teaching, Nash could not subscribe to any 'second blessing' theology.[51] He was instrumental in excluding Pentecostalism from MBI and this action influenced his students in subsequent years.

In 1939, a Miss Winnie C. Mills, who was a Pentecostal, applied to be a missionary candidate with the BEM. The Field Conference, comprising the missionaries in Borneo who met at Jesselton from 27 October to 7 November 1939 felt that 'provided her medical report is satisfactory and...that she is not actively involved with Pentecostalism', her application should 'be dealt with by the Home Council as it feels best'.[52] At the same time, the Home Council met in Melbourne on 2 November and decided that 'it would not be desirable for her to proceed with her application'.[53] Of the missionaries who served with BEM from 1928 to 1975, it is significant that none were Pentecostals.

In a similar way, Nash was instrumental in checking a strand of perfectionist teaching in Melbourne, which was promoted by Alan Neil, a former student of

---

[47] It was not simply because of his knowledge of the Greek or his eloquence as a speaker but also because of the impact of his personality. Paproth, *Failure Is Not Final*, 29, 112.

[48] Piggin, *Evangelical Christianity*, 102. Hundreds of people met at Sunshine Hall; some received the baptism, others healing and conversion. News of this Sunshine revival spread throughout Australia so that people came from around the country.

[49] Paproth, *Failure Is Not Final*, 102.

[50] Paproth, *Failure Is Not Final*, 228.

[51] Paproth, *Failure Is Not Final*, 103.

[52] *BEM Field Conference Minutes*, 27 October-7 November 1939, 2.

[53] *BEM Home Council Minutes*, 2 November 1939 (OMF), 1. There is no doubt the influence of Nash lingered among the Council members even though he had resigned from the Council then. See Chapter 4.

MBI from the mid-1930s.[54] In 1938, he wrote a series of articles rebutting Neil's views on sinless perfection,[55] and his views commanded great respect among the Melbourne evangelicals. Though the BEM did not face this problem, its Council members and missionaries would have been sufficiently influenced by his teaching and public arguments against sinless perfection to be cautious about this teaching.

Evangelical commitment to missions is well known. Nash's deep commitment to missions was influenced by James Hudson Taylor, the founder of the China Inland Mission (CIM).[56] Though Nash did not become a missionary,[57] he was a facilitator of many young men into the mission field through his ministry at MBI.[58] His strong link with the CIM was undoubted, since MBI was founded through initiatives from the CIM.[59] During his long association with the CIM, Nash had, at MBI, trained no fewer than eighty CIM missionaries.[60] At MBI, Nash first directed Southwell's attention to Borneo when he challenged the students to the unevangelized lands north of Australia in mid-1927.[61] Southwell's interest in Borneo grew when he came in contact with a fellow student, Ronald Grant, and together they began to pray for the evangelization of Borneo.[62]

At that stage, Nash functioned very much as an advisor to Southwell, suggesting to him that, as no evangelical Protestant mission body was working in Borneo at that time, he should write to the existing mission bodies to inquire whether any of them would consider extending their missionary outreach to

---

[54] Alan, who was the son of Lee Neil, a close friend of Nash, studied at MBI in 1926 and became a missionary to the Solomon Islands with the South Seas Evangelical Mission (SSEM). Alan Neil had a successful ministry for ten years in the Solomon Islands that had seen revivals. But, he was forced to resign because of his views on sinless perfection. In the mid-1930s, Alan spoke on the subject of perfectionism at MBI. After he left, Nash sought to correct what he thought was doctrinally unsound. Paproth, *Failure Is Not Final*, 114-15.

[55] Neil wrote an article in an evangelical paper, *The Edifier*, on 10 June 1938. Piggin, *Evangelical Christianity*, 111. Paproth, *Failure Is Not Final*, 115, 180.

[56] Hudson Taylor spoke at Cambridge when Nash was a student, and Nash had ever since closely followed the progress of the CIM. Chambers, *Tempest Tost*, 124.

[57] Paproth, *Failure Is Not Final*, 90-91. He had offered himself as a missionary candidate to the CIM in 1917, though he did not have a clear and insistent call.

[58] Marcus Loane, *The Story of the China Inland Mission in Australia and New Zealand, 1890-1964* (Sydney: CIM/OMF, 1965), 71. The first graduate of MBI, Theo Lowther, became a CIM missionary to China.

[59] Loane, *The Story of the China Inland Mission*, 73, 90, 92, 111. Nash was a CIM Council member of the Melbourne section from 1916 until 1937.

[60] Chambers, *Tempest Tost*, 124.

[61] Southwell, *Uncharted Waters*, 61.

[62] Ronald Grant later became a missionary to the Solomon Islands with the SSEM.

include Borneo. But all of them felt that they were unable to extend their mission to include Borneo.[63]

The impact of Nash on his students, especially those who became BEM missionaries, was through the force of his personality, the conviction of his scholarship and teaching, and the warmth of his piety.[64] In his farewell speech as the principal of MBI in 1942, Nash recalled his threefold vision for his ministry; firstly, a concern for biblical research and openness to all honest investigation and criticism of the Scriptures; secondly, a confidence in the potential of youth in the service for Christ and thirdly, a commitment to the Great Commission and the missionary enterprise. These three concerns of Nash were important formative influences on his students.[65]

Revivalistic and Evangelistic Movements

Revivals, such as those associated with George Whitefield, Jonathan Edwards, Charles Finney and John Wesley, have become a characteristic feature of evangelicalism. At this juncture, it is important to clarify the terms 'revivals' and 'revivalism' for our discussion.

A 'revival' may be defined as a distinct religious phenomenon within the Christian religion with the following traits: a) it usually exhibits a firm connection with the Pietistic or evangelical tradition; b) the participants anticipate a reviving and renewing act of God; c) it highlights some sort of dramatic conversion or intense experience of grace in individuals; d) it is also a communal event, involving the whole life of the Christian community; and e) the fact of spiritual declension is assumed, and hence 'revival' is prescribed as the remedy.[66]

The term 'revivalism', on the other hand, refers to the techniques and programmes designed to foster revival. It is usually traced back to Charles Finney's 'new measures', which he developed out of his own remarkable

---

[63] This issue will be discussed further in Chapter 4. Southwell, *Uncharted Waters*, 62. Lees, *Drunk before Dawn*, 24, 26.

[64] W.S. Clack, *We Will Go: The History of 70 years of Training Men and Women for World Missionary Ministry, 1920-1990* (Melbourne: Bible College of Victoria, 1990), 26-27. According to W.S. Clack, with sound scholarship, there was weightiness in his exposition of the sacred Scriptures and the Christian faith, which was coupled with a warm and emotional nature that was deeply concerned for the welfare of every student who came his way. Nash was more of a mentor in whom students found a patient listener, a qualified adviser and understanding friend. Two words 'warmth' and 'weight' aptly sum up his ministry.

[65] Chambers, *Tempest Tost*, 109-110.

[66] This definition of revival is adapted from the description given on the nature and definition of revival by Edith L. Blumhofer and Randall Balmer, *Modern Christian Revivals* (Urbana/Chicago: University of Illinois Press, 1993), xi-xii.

experience and success in the so-called 'Second Great Awakening' in New York State from 1789 to 1830.[67]

In his study on revival and revivalism, Stuart Piggin has identified four periods in the development of the revival tradition since the Great Awakening.[68] The spontaneous revivals of the eighteenth and early nineteenth centuries led to the development of the revivalistic tradition in the mid-nineteenth century, first in the United States and subsequently in Britain. Although it had its share of indigenous revivals from the mid-nineteenth to mid-twentieth century,[69] Australia became increasingly exposed to the international revivalistic and evangelistic tradition, especially when many well-known British and American evangelists visited Australia from 1890 to 1912.[70]

This revivalistic and evangelistic tradition that spread to Australia, particularly Melbourne and Sydney, became more organized with time.[71] From 1863, organized revivalistic meetings and evangelistic campaigns, involving particularly the Methodist and the Baptists, entered a new phase. The Methodists had their itinerant evangelists travelling around the country reaping fruitful results for some twenty years from 1860 to 1880. In contrast, the Baptists, including Thomas Spurgeon, the son of Charles Spurgeon, conducted their missions in the major cities with the aim of building great central

---

[67] Stuart Piggin, *Firestorm of the Lord: The History of and Prospects for Revival in the Church and the World* (Carlisle: Paternoster Press, 2000), 66-67. As Stuart Piggin noted, 'Revivalism has been described as an 'Americanisation of revival'.

[68] Piggin, *Firestorm of the Lord*, 63-64. The four periods are: a) the revivals experienced most frequently in Methodist churches after the death of John Wesley (1791), b) the age of revivalism from 1850 to 1950, usually associated with Charles Finney (1792-1875), c) overlapping with the age of revivalism since the beginning of the twentieth century, highly significant revivals occurred in places where Protestant missionaries had a significant presence and d) since the end of WWII, revivals broke out among people who are attempting to form their own national identity following the departure of the colonial powers, or among the marginalized minority peoples trying to cope with the onslaught of western materialism and secularism.

[69] See Stuart Piggin, '"Towards a Theoretical Understanding of Revival": Recent Developments in the Historiography of Revival', in M. Hutchinson, E. Campion and S. Piggin (eds.), *Reviving Australia: Essays on the History and Experience of Revival and Revivalism in Australian Christianity* (Sydney: Centre for the Study of Australian Christianity, 1994), 13-17.

[70] Among them were Hudson Taylor, founder of the CIM in 1890; George Grubb, the Church of Ireland evangelist in 1891; John Mott, the student leader in 1896; Dr Reuben Archer Torrey, Principal of Moody Bible Institute with Charles Alexander as his song leader in 1902; and Charles Alexander in 1907, 1909 and 1912, with Wilbur Chapman for the 1909 and 1912 evangelistic campaigns. Most of these evangelists, according to Piggin, 'drank deeply at the wells of revivalism'. See Piggin, *Firestorm of the Lord*, 68.

[71] See Orr, *Evangelical Awakenings in the South Seas*, 50. Prayer meetings were held in the Anglican, Baptist, Congregational, Methodist and Presbyterian churches, and in the YMCA.

congregations patterned after Spurgeon's Metropolitan Tabernacle.[72] By the end of the nineteenth century, two patterns of revivalistic and evangelistic meetings became popular: first, the holding of big evangelistic campaigns in cities; and, second, having itinerant evangelistic preachers travelling around the country and holding large tent-meetings.

From the late nineteenth century to the first half of the twentieth century, there were a series of important revivalistic and evangelistic campaigns that significantly shaped evangelical strategy in Australia. Firstly, the Church of Ireland evangelist, George Grubb, who visited Melbourne and Sydney in 1890 and later returned to speak at the first Australian Keswick in Geelong in 1891[73] was a highly successful speaker.[74] The impact of his meetings was such that there was an enduring atmosphere of revival at Geelong.[75] Later, there were the Torrey-Alexander and Chapman campaigns from 1902 to 1912,[76] the Gipsy Smith campaign in 1926,[77] and, three decades later, the Billy Graham campaign in 1959. With each mass evangelistic campaign, the pattern was a higher degree of organization and inter-denominational cooperation among the churches,[78] ranging from the use of local evangelists, the use of large buildings like the town hall or theatres, [79] the introduction of a song-leader and choir,[80] appeals

---

[72] Orr, *Evangelical Awakenings in the South Seas*, 56-57.

[73] D. Paproth, 'Revivalism in Melbourne from Federation to World War I', in Hutchinson, Campion, and Piggin (eds.), *Reviving Australia*, 149. Piggin, *Evangelical Christianity*, 58.

[74] Piggin, *Evangelical Christianity*, 58, 76. As a result of his meeting at Geelong, forty people offered themselves for missionary service. His message focused on the higher Christian life and missions. On the higher Christian life, he taught a 'second blessing' understanding of holiness; i.e., a person ought to be sanctified by a second experience of the Holy Spirit after conversion.

[75] Paproth, 'Revivalism in Melbourne', 149. The work of Grubb was viewed as being preparatory for the Torrey-Alexander missions.

[76] Orr, *Evangelical Awakenings in the South Seas*, 109-10, and Piggin, *Evangelical Christianity*, 59-60.

[77] Walter Phillips, '"Gipsy Smith in Australia in 1926": the Commonwealth Evangelistic Campaign', in Hutchinson, Campion, and Piggin (eds.), *Reviving Australia*, 185-201.

[78] Orr, *Evangelical Awakenings in the South Seas*, 106, 109-110. In the case of the Torrey-Alexander campaign in 1902, the level of cooperation among the churches in Melbourne was extremely good. See also Piggin, *Evangelical Christianity*, 59-60.

[79] In Melbourne, the city suburbs were divided into fifty mission centres with fifty local evangelists preaching in halls and large tents. In the city, the town hall, several theatres and the 7000-seat Exhibition Building were used. See Piggin, *Evangelical Christianity*, 59-60. The impact was great and in the words of a Melbourne doctor, Dr William Warren, 'The big revival has begun'.

[80] Paproth, 'Revivalism in Melbourne', 150.

for decisions and for re-dedication,[81] and in the 1959 Billy Graham Crusade in Melbourne, prayer support for three years prior to the event.[82]

By the time the BEM was founded, holding mass evangelistic meetings had become part of Australian evangelical activity. The BEM missionaries held evangelistic meetings in the pioneering Sarawakian situation on a similar pattern to the work of the early Australian Methodists and Baptists. This necessitated combining itinerant preaching and large evangelistic meetings in longhouses among the unevangelized tribes of the Lun Bawang, Kelabit, Kayan, Kenyah and Iban. The style of the BEM evangelistic meetings, though resembling the Australian large tent-meetings in the rural areas, was often ad hoc, depending on the permission of the longhouse chiefs to allow the BEM missionaries to preach; their evangelistic style was adapted to the local conditions, allowing for the community to meet on their own to decide whether they wished to embrace Christianity. There were often personal follow-up and Bible class sessions for converts as a norm. Further, the BEM missionaries longed, prayed and hoped for revival and large numbers of conversions.[83]

The China Inland Mission (CIM)

The CIM, founded in 1865 by Hudson Taylor, had by 1940 become the most well known missionary organization in Australia, and possibly in the world. The visit of Hudson Taylor to Australia in 1890 had created a considerable impact that not only aroused evangelical public interest but also led to the formation of a CIM Council in Melbourne[84] and a total of 50 missionaries from Australia going to China within five years.[85] The trickle of Australian and New

[81] Phillips, "'Gipsy Smith in Australia in 1926", 195. In addition, during the Gipsy Smith campaign in 1926, there was no penitent's bench or enquiry room for counselling new converts.

[82] Piggin, *Evangelical Christianity*, 154-71. Piggin argues that the six criteria for a revival were met in the 1959 Billy Graham Crusade. These six criteria include a deep expectation for revival, an unprecedented unity among the major Protestant churches and organisations, ardent prayerfulness, revitalization of churches, large numbers of conversion and a reduction in social vices and crime. A revitalized church meant among other things, increased numbers of churchgoers, theological students and missionaries. For example, in 1969, more than half of MBI's 160 students were products of the 1959 crusade.

[83] See Chapter 7 for further discussion.

[84] The Kitchen family became the backbone of the CIM in Melbourne. Dr John James Kitchen gave up his medical practice and devoted himself fully in the work of CIM and Upwey Convention. See Piggin, *Evangelical Christianity*, 72.

[85] Twenty-five of these candidates came from Victoria; its capital is Melbourne. Loane, *The Story of the China Inland Mission*, 11-13. The most famous of these missionaries was Florence Selina Harriet Young, who later returned to Australia and founded the South Sea Evangelical Mission in 1904. Piggin, *Evangelical Christianity*, 69-70.

Zealand missionaries serving in China with the CIM became a stream; in 1913, there were 176 missionaries, increasing to 213 in 1920 and 354 in 1942.[86]

The BEM, founded in 1928, patterned itself very much on the CIM, since the formative influences in Southwell's life and missionary thinking had been missionaries from the CIM.[87] Just as the CIM was founded to evangelize the interior of China, BEM was to evangelize the tribes in the interior of Borneo.[88] The BEM also adopted the 'faith principle' of the CIM: a radical dependence on God. This faith principle meant a sole reliance on God for every need of the mission.[89] According to Hudson Taylor, God will provide 'strength, grace, protection, enablement for every emergency as well as daily bread'.[90] Together with this principle, there were two other convictions that motivated their mission work. The first conviction was that all who do not know Christ are eternally lost and the second that the Second Coming of Christ would come when the gospel had been preached to all people. Similarly, the BEM professed to look 'to God alone for all the needs of its members, no appeals for financial aid or collections being made by or received for the Mission. No more is expended than is received by the Mission, going into debt being considered inconsistent with the principles of entire dependence on God'.[91]

The BEM adopted the CIM's form of government, which had a centralised leadership structure and was field-led. The General Director in the field was in charge of the whole organisation. But, as the three pioneer missionaries were young people, it was felt that BEM should initially be led by the BEM Council in Melbourne until such time as it could be directed from the field by the General Director, who would be assisted by an Advisory Council, and when it was judged desirable and practicable by a Council meeting with a 75 per cent majority of all existing members. The BEM Council's responsibility was then to 'direct and supervise all affairs of the Mission except so far as provision is made under its authority for local administration, receives and accounts for all moneys and gifts and is generally responsible for the well-being and progress of the Mission'.[92] In short, the BEM Council was the final decision-making body, although there was provision for local administration in the Field by the Field Secretary and an Executive Committee, which comprised those members of the Council located in the field.

---

[86] Loane, *The Story of the China Inland Mission*, 158, 163. Piggin, *Evangelical Christianity*, 72.
[87] Lees, *Drunk before Dawn*, 25. Southwell, *Uncharted Waters*, 52-56.
[88] Opening Statement of the BEM Constitution, September 1939.
[89] Dr & Mrs Howard Taylor, *Hudson Taylor and the China Inland Mission: The Growth of a Work of God* (London: CIM, 1918), 40-44, 52.
[90] Taylor, *Hudson Taylor and the CIM*, 41.
[91] Minutes of the Borneo Fellowship meeting dated 1 September 1928 with the agreed final draft of the Provisional Constitution of the BEM.
[92] Minutes of the Borneo Fellowship meeting dated 1 September 1928

Though the BEM adopted the 'faith principle' from the CIM, a crisis over its interpretation occurred in 1934, when Southwell was the Field Secretary. This crisis precipitated a change within the BEM so that full and final authority was transferred to the Field Conference with a Field Director. This crisis led to the resignation of most of the Home Council members, including C.H. Nash (Chairman), W.L. Wright (Secretary) and R.S. Tregaskis (Treasurer), and leaving behind only three members; Harold McCracken, a young lawyer, became the Chairman. It was at this period that the Constitution was amended by the Field Conference to make the faith principle unalterable and to give the Field Conference the final authority.[93]

There were other striking similarities between the CIM and the BEM: a) the BEM was inter-denominational and accepted all Protestant churches that subscribed to its evangelical statement of faith; b) the missionaries were all members of the Mission, irrespective of gender and whether or not they were ordained; c) missionaries of any type of training were equally welcomed; d) no distinction was made between ordained and un-ordained missionaries; e) single women were equally welcomed and could serve on their own as missionaries; f) missionaries were to identify as much with the local culture as possible; g) evangelistic work had the greatest priority and widespread evangelistic itineration was especially encouraged until a settled work began; h) converts were to be channelled into a local congregation and be used for evangelism; and i) missionaries had to be prepared to suffer and sacrifice for the Lord's sake.[94] However, in relation to point (e), it should be noted that the role of single women missionaries of the BEM was more restricted than in the CIM. Initially, the BEM sent out a woman missionary, Margaret Perrin, in 1930, but she subsequently returned to Australia without starting work in Sarawak. After that case, the single woman missionaries who were accepted were all fiancées of the BEM missionaries in Sarawak. The issue was re-opened in 1938, and it was agreed just prior to WWII that a single woman missionary could be employed to work under a married missionary couple or in a pair with another single woman, preferably a school teacher and a nurse, at a mission station.[95]

In the early years, the BEM operated with a head-station at Sungai Pranga, from which the missionaries travelled quite extensively throughout the Limbang valley, the region allotted for their work. When there was a mass conversion of the Lun Bawang in 1933 in the next river area, the Trusan valley, the BEM missionaries sought to start a settled work at Trusan. After repeated government refusal, permission was finally given in November 1937, and

---

[93] Letter of Harold McCracken to Dr Bill Hawes, 18 September 1969 (OMF). Minutes of the meetings dated 10 April 1934, 8 May 1934 and 12 June 1934. By May 1935, the switch had been completed as is evidenced in Letter of Harold McCracken to Rev. C.H. Nash, 10 May 1935 (OMF). See Chapter 4 for a fuller discussion.

[94] Fiedler, *The Story of Faith Missions*, 33.

[95] See Chapter 4 for further discussion. See *Home Council Minutes*, 7 March 1930, 1. *BEM Third Annual Report*, 31 March 1931, 2.

Frank and Enid Davidson started their task of teaching the converts in early 1940.[96] Again in the immediate post-war period, Southwell did extensive travelling into the interior of the Fifth Division, the Bario and Kelabit highlands and also across into the Baram. When mass conversions occurred among the Kayan and Kenyah from 1947 to 1948, it was followed by a settled work at Long Tebangan. Thus the BEM followed very much the CIM style of giving greatest priority to itinerant evangelism until a settled work within an area could begin. In short, BEM was almost a mini-version of the CIM working in Borneo.

The Keswick Convention Movement

The evangelicals of the late nineteenth century were also associated with the higher life or holiness movement, of which the Keswick Convention was the most visible expression. The Melbourne expression of Keswick was the Upwey Convention: formed in 1918, Upwey became an important part of evangelicalism in Melbourne. The first Keswick meeting was organized as an open air conference by Canon T.D. Harford-Battersby in 1885 at Keswick in the Lake District.[97] In time, Keswick became the focus for the higher life movement.

Despite initial suspicions, the Keswick movement became accepted as part of evangelical Anglicanism by the end of the nineteenth century. Its acceptance by Anglican evangelicals was due in large part to the influence of Handley C.G. Moule,[98] who had been careful to ensure that the Keswick influence did not go in any direction which he judged to be aberrant from orthodoxy.[99]

Although rooted in Evangelicalism, Keswick gave a new and more heightened emphasis on personal experience. It was this more experiential side of Keswick that, as David Bebbington argues, showed marked affinities with the culture of the contemporary Romantic Movement. Bebbington cites seven aspects of Keswick teaching, which showed indebtedness to the Romantic

---

[96] Southwell, *Uncharted Waters*, 98-99.

[97] The Keswick movement traced its indebtedness to the influence of American holiness preachers, Robert Pearsall Smith and his wife Hannah Whitall Smith, who promoted scriptural holiness at Oxford in 1874 and Brighton in 1875. See Bebbington, *Evangelicalism in Modern Britain*, 151.

[98] Moule had an experience similar to that taught by Keswick. After initial doubts about its influence, Moule concluded that it was free from the error of perfectionism and expressed his approval of Keswick in 1884, after reviewing Evan Hopkins' book, *The Law and Liberty of the Spiritual Life*. See Andrew Porter, 'Cambridge, Keswick, and late nineteenth century Attitudes to Africa', *Journal of Imperial and Commonwealth History* 5 (1976-77), 18; J.B. Harford and F.C. McDonald, *Handley Carr Glyn Moule, Bishop of Durham: A Biography* (London: Hodder & Stoughton, 1922), ch. 11.

[99] Bullock, *The History of Ridley Hall*, I, 354-55. According to Moule, 'I had to try to correct manifest aberrations from a sound faith and to guide a noble zeal where it seems to need guidance'.

culture or worldview. Firstly, 'several of those associated with Keswick had poetic inclinations', such as Francis Ridley Havergal and Charles Fox. Secondly, 'the Lake District, where the conventions were held, symbolized the appeal of nature for the movement'. Thirdly, there was 'an element of crisis in the Keswick teaching on sanctification. Dramatic moments were the stock in trade of Romantic literature. The narrow escapes of Scott's narratives were typical of the highly charged juncture, the kairos, that compelled attention of Romantic stories. A decisive point of change along these lines was near the centre of Keswick tradition'. Fourthly, 'faith was exalted by the movement'. Holiness was taught to have come by faith. Further, this 'idea of faith was given a broader application', so that Keswick did not make any appeal for money but subscribed to the 'faith principle' of resting on God for the means to carry on His work. Fifthly, there was also the stress on an internal sense of peace and rest following a full surrender of one's life to Christ. Sixthly, Keswick taught a constant struggle in the repression of sin in the believer's life, and that victory over sin is given through the experience of the power of the Holy Spirit. Finally, Keswick subscribed to a premillennial eschatology, which expected the return of Christ before the start of the millennium. That is, it believed in a heroic deliverer who would appear on the stage of the world to set everything right, which was a characteristic Romantic motif.[100]

The Keswick movement was a part of the larger Holiness movement and moderated by the cultural setting of Romanticism. It generally espoused one of two theological tendencies discernible in the holiness movement. Keswick speakers taught that sanctification suppresses, not eradicates, the sinful nature. They used terminology such as 'the higher Christian life', 'the deeper Christian life', or 'the victorious Christian life' to indicate the possibility of an exchanged life with victory over sin and power for service.[101] Nevertheless, the Keswick movement from the turn of the nineteenth and twentieth centuries increasingly rejected sinless perfectionism.[102] As shown earlier, the rejection of sinless perfectionism among Melbourne evangelicals was due mainly to the influence of Nash and later affirmed by the deputy chairman of the Upwey Convention, W.L. Wright.[103]

Keswick teaching had three major emphases.[104] First, the movement stressed full surrender to Christ for cleansing and consecration.[105] It is the decisive crisis

---

[100] David Bebbington, *Holiness in Nineteenth-Century England* (Carlisle: Paternoster Press, 2000), 77-85.
[101] Fiedler, *The Story of Faith Missions*, 213.
[102] Sinless perfectionism is the result of the other theological tendency, the eradicationist tendency. C.F. Harford (ed.), *The Keswick Convention* (London: Marshall, 1907), 107. See Piggin, *Evangelical Christianity*, 106.
[103] *New Life*, 21 December 1939, 2-3. *New Life*, first known as *The Edifier*, started since 10 June 1938. Quoted in Parker, 'Fundamentalism and Conservative Protestantism', 477.
[104] Fiedler, *The Story of Faith Missions*, 215.

experience after conversion that starts the Christian life on a higher plane. Second, the essence of this experience is to be 'filled with the Spirit of God' and receive the 'Baptism of the Spirit'.[106] Third, this experience results in power for service, which is the outcome of a Spirit-filled life marked by the 'rest of faith', power over sin, consciousness of communion with God and habitual prayer. This power for service makes one's efforts a joy and a privilege, not a chore or burden.[107]

The distinctive stress of Keswick teaching on experience struck a chord that was fundamental to evangelicalism, so that Keswick 'shaped the pattern of evangelical piety for much of the twentieth century'.[108] Its strength was in providing a spiritual undergirding for the evangelical movement. Keswick spirituality almost became evangelical spirituality. Melbourne evangelicals in particular were committed to Keswick spirituality.[109]

Since its beginnings, the Australian Keswick movement had generally adhered to this distinctive teaching. But by the 1960s, a change of emphasis became apparent and the Australian Keswick, like its British parent movement, became more like a Bible teaching convention, though it continued to offer a 'deeper life' teaching ministry.[110]

Keswick's emphasis on spiritual renewal, refreshment and power for service led to the formation of a strong partnership with the missionary movement and mission societies.[111] By 1907, the Keswick Convention was exercising a powerful influence on the missionary enterprise.[112] By the time BEM was

---

[105] A full surrender meant a giving up of all known sins and to fully surrender one's self to God, so that Christ became the Lord of all areas of one's life. Keswick also laid a distinctive stress on 'sanctification by faith'.

[106] This is a promise to be claimed by faith, irrespective of feelings and the consciousness of God's indwelling presence, which would be felt later. D.L. Pierson, *Arthur T. Pierson: A Biography by his Son* (London: Nisbet, 1912), 287-88.

[107] Fiedler, *The Story of Faith Missions*, 214-15. The term 'Baptism of the Spirit' was used by D.L. Moody to challenge believers to take a second step of faith to a deeper spiritual life. This second experience or blessing allowed believers access to all the riches of God's grace and power for service, and so to live a fulfilled life.

[108] Bebbington, *Evangelicalism in Modern Britain*, 151.

[109] Stuart Piggin observed that in Australia the encouragement of Keswick spirituality in the evangelical world resulted in 'something of a mini-revival in the 1930s'. Piggin, *Evangelical Christianity*, 99-100.

[110] Parker, 'Fundamentalism and Conservative Protestantism', 480-81.

[111] It is interesting to note that, prior to 1888, Keswick did not have a missions emphasis. Reginald Radcliffe was mainly responsible for its inclusion, so that Keswick was to later acknowledge that 'consecration and Evangelization of the world ought to go together'. See Harford (ed.), *The Keswick Convention*, 136.

[112] Keswick exercised a powerful influence on the missionary enterprise in three ways: a) by sending forth of 'missioners' and helping the societies (especially CIM and CMS) to send forth missionaries, b) by calling forth offers of missionary service at the Convention, and c) by its influence upon the minds and hearts of missionaries who have

formed, the Keswick Convention, especially the English Keswick, in the estimate of Eugene Stock, had influenced almost every missionary society.[113] Hence, in addition to giving a visible public focus to the higher life movement and promoting evangelical unity, Keswick's emphasis on missions dovetailed well with the rise of 'faith missions' during the late nineteenth century.[114]

In Melbourne, the Upwey Convention started under the leadership of Hervey Perceval Smith (better known as H.P. Smith) and the Melbourne Gospel Crusade (MGC) in 1918.[115] Nash became involved in the second Convention by taking the Bible readings and continued this involvement for over twenty years.[116] The Upwey Convention had an overlapping network of mainly lay people that made effective links with the CIM and MBI especially in Melbourne. From 1920, MBI became closely linked with Upwey.[117] The MBI had an afternoon session at every Upwey Convention to promote its work for nearly half a century.[118]

Upwey provided a focus for popular evangelical resurgence when evangelical theology was becoming marginalized in the churches, and facilitated the involvement of lay people. It networked symbiotically with the 'faith missions' and its missionaries. Keswick's threefold aim in relation to missionaries [119] certainly ministered to their felt needs. In return, the missionaries had a platform for sharing the work of their mission at Keswick, thereby providing an avenue for prayer support, finance and potential missionary candidates. At Upwey, many missionaries who were MBI graduates were farewelled or welcomed home with opportunities to speak about their mission work. Davidson of the BEM, an MBI graduate, when he returned on furlough in 1933-1934, was given such an opportunity to share the work of the

---

attended the Convention while on furlough. See Harford (ed.), *The Keswick Convention*, 139-40.

[113] 'There is not one mission field which is not indebted to Keswick for one or more of its labourers – in some cases for several of them'. Quoted by W.B. Sloan, 'The Influence of the Keswick Convention on Missionary Work', *IRM* 3.12 (October 1914), 708. Parker, 'Fundamentalism and Conservative Protestantism', 487. Loane, 'The Keswick Convention and the Missionary Movement', viii. The CMS and CIM were major beneficiaries of Keswick.

[114] Fiedler, *The Story of Faith Missions*, 110.

[115] Piggin, *Evangelical Christianity*, 98-99. Paproth, *Failure Is Not Final*, 111. The Upwey Convention later became known as the Belgrave Heights Convention since 1950. See Parker, 'Fundamentalism and Conservative Protestantism', 474.

[116] Chambers, *Tempest* Tost, 124; Paproth, *Failure Is Not Final*, 112.

[117] 'This symbiotic relationship between convention and Institute was a natural development given the missions emphasis of both MBI and Upwey, and because the same people were prominent in the leadership of the Institution and the convention'. See Paproth, *Failure Is Not Final*, 112.

[118] According to Paproth (personal communication), Upwey was the public face of MBI.

[119] That is, the promise of victory, rest in the heart and power for service. Harford (ed.), *The Keswick Convention*, 181.

BEM to a group of some six hundred people.[120] It was natural to expect BEM missionaries, many of whom were MBI graduates, to continue to forge links and build a symbiotic relationship with Upwey where BEM missionaries on furlough were given opportunities to speak. Even in regard to the choice of new Council members immediately after WWII, the Home Council deferred making decisions on new Council members until after the Upwey Convention, when Southwell had the opportunity to meet people who would be suitable to be invited to accept the positions,[121] indicating the similarity in the theological ethos of Upwey, MBI and BEM.

The BEM took the convention model to Borneo, organizing its first convention or irau before WWII among the Lun Bawang. The next big convention held at Lawas around Easter time in 1948 had between five and six hundred Lun Bawang, together with 68 out of the 75 church leaders, present.[122] Since then the Easter conventions or irau have been organized by each major people group among whom the BEM work had spread from the Limbang and Bario to the Upper Baram; first among the Lun Bawang, then Kelabit, Kayan and Kenyah. It is interesting that the BEM described this convention movement as 'Jungle Keswick'.[123] At these conventions, Bible readings or teaching were given by specially invited speakers from overseas, missionaries or local pastors. The outward form of the Keswick Convention has been adopted for these Easter conventions or irau but in reality, these have become Bible teaching conventions. At times, speakers like Dr Del Rees in 1952 and Geoff Bingham in 1964 taught the distinctive teaching of Keswick. Bingham's ministry resulted in frank confession of sin, restoration of fellowship and a deepening sense of unity among the BEM missionaries, and also a renewed sense of anticipation that God would build his church in Borneo in proportion as the missionary team were 'filled with the Spirit'.[124] Despite the general lack of emphasis on the distinctive teaching of Keswick, though this was not totally absent, the Easter conventions continued to serve the purpose of renewing the faltering spirit of participants, both pastors and laypeople, with the aim of enabling them to live a victorious Christian life.[125]

Melbourne Bible Institute (MBI)

The establishment of MBI should be understood in the larger context of the growth of the Bible College movement which grew out of the revival and

---

[120] *BEM Home Council Minutes*, 14 February 1933, 1. He spoke again at Upwey the next year.
See *BEM Home Council Minutes*, 13 February 1934, 1.
[121] *BEM Home Council Minutes*, 17 December 1945, 1.
[122] Lees, *Drunk before Dawn*, 85. See *BEM NL*, June 1948, 3; August 1979, 1.
[123] 'Jungle Keswick at Pa Matang', *BEM NL*, August 1953, 1.
[124] *BEM NL*, October 1964, 4.
[125] *BEM NL*, April 1970, 3.

missionary movements and which was closely related to the Keswick Convention movement at the turn of the century. The Bible College movement grew on both sides of the Atlantic toward the end of the nineteenth and early twentieth centuries.[126] The Bible colleges aimed at training lay people, who had a definite conversion experience and a sense of divine call to be missionaries and evangelists, and their approach was practical and biblical.[127] The defence of conservative evangelical or fundamentalist beliefs also formed an integral part of the movement. The centrality of the Bible as inspired Scripture shaped the objectives, method and curriculum of these Bible Colleges. The Bible Colleges were something of a populist protest against the mainline churches, their theological colleges and professional ministry, which were seen as not meeting the challenges of the age.[128] The success of this populist movement meant that, in the estimate of E.R. Sandeen, 'fundamentalism owed its survival to the Bible Institute'.[129]

The Bible College movement in Australia exhibited the same basic features as in Britain and America, with a strong missionary and evangelistic emphasis.

According to David Parker, there were four impulses or characteristics that gave rise to the founding of the Bible Colleges in Australia and these included a) the training of 'faith' missionaries for overseas mission, b) training for evangelism, c) training in the knowledge of the Bible as the prime requisite for any Christian worker and d) the anti-modernist intentions of its founders and promoters.[130] In regard to MBI, all four of these characteristics were present, though the first three seemed to have been given higher priority.

The MBI was formed through the express initiative of the CIM with Nash as its first principal in 1920.[131] The founding motive of MBI was to train missionaries to fulfil the Great Commission at home and abroad. Since its inception till 1970, the MBI had a good track record of sending its students out as missionaries.[132] Its commitment to foreign missions was a hallmark of MBI.

---

[126] In England, the East London Institute for Home and Foreign Missions (later known as Harley House) was founded in 1873. In North America, the Nyack Missionary Training College was founded in 1882. Moody Bible Institute, the most famous of these colleges, was established in 1889.

[127] In contrast, the theological colleges trained men for the ordained ministry, and were academic in approach.

[128] Paproth, '"The Melbourne Bible Institute"', 134.

[129] E.R. Sandeen, *The Roots of Fundamentalism* (Chicago: University of Chicago Press, 1970), 183.

[130] David Parker, 'The Bible College Movement in Australia' (Paper presented to the 9th SPABC Conference 22-27 August 1980), 3-4.

[131] Piggin, *Evangelical Christianity*, 91. Paproth, *Failure Is Not Final*, 92-93.

[132] The first batch of four students from the first year of its inception all became missionaries, three to China as CIM missionaries and one to Nigeria as a Sudan Inland Mission (SIM) missionary. See Paproth, *Failure Is Not Final*, 95. Many students have, since its inception till 1970, gone out as missionaries to Borneo, Papua New Guinea, Egypt, Ethiopia, Africa, Jordan (Middle East), India, Nepal, Bangladesh, Laos, Japan,

Moreover, the MBI gave rise to a number of Australian mission bodies, including the BEM in 1928.[133] The missionary emphasis of MBI was not only the result of Nash's commitment to missions but also of the MBI Council members, some of whom took an active interest in missionary bodies. Dr J.J. Kitchen, a council member was actively involved with the CIM as its Home Director. Mr Richard Stanley Tregaskis had been a missionary with the SSEM before becoming Secretary of MBI[134] and was closely associated with Nash for a long time. The next few principals, spanning the years from 1942 to 1980, were all former missionaries. J.W. Searle had been a founding member of the Unevangelized Fields Mission and had served in Papua New Guinea.[135] J. Graham Miller was with the Presbyterian mission in New Hebrides and N.P. Andersen with the Baptist mission in Bengal. Under Nash, MBI outgrew the older Bible colleges both in influence and numbers to become the premier evangelical Bible College in Australia.[136]

The BEM grew out of MBI, being founded by three MBI students who later became BEM's pioneer missionaries in 1928. Subsequent Australian BEM missionaries were also recommended to study at MBI prior to going to Borneo. In the pre-war period (1928-1941), these included George Aitken[137] and Roland Bewsher, who worked among the Bisayas at Limpasong, and Winsome Howell[138] and Enid Gray[139] who married Hudson Southwell and Frank Davidson respectively. In the early years of BEM's history from 1928 to 1935, those involved as foundation members of the BEM Council were also key personnel in MBI: C.H. Nash (Principal), R.S. Tregaskis (Secretary) and W.L. Wright (Council member). Also, in the initial years, when there was no field leader, Tregaskis was sent to act as Field Director of the Mission for a period of

---

Taiwan, Indonesia, Irian Jaya, the Solomon Islands and the Philippines. See Clack (ed.), *We Will Go*, 113-216.

[133] Others included the Unevangelized Fields Mission in 1931, which was later renamed Asia Pacific Christian Mission, and the Missionary Aviation Fellowship in 1947. See Clack (ed.), *We Will Go*, 88-89, 96, 98, 104-105.

[134] R.S. Tregaskis was also Treasurer of BEM Home Council until the end of 1934. See *Home Council Minutes*, 11 December 1934 (BCV), 1.

[135] Clack (ed.), *We Will Go*, 29, 96, 105.

[136] The other older Bible colleges were Angas College which was founded in 1893, the Chapman-Alexander Institute in 1914, and the Sydney Missionary and Bible College in 1916.

[137] Lees, *Drunk before Dawn*, 37. Southwell, *Uncharted Waters*, 46-47. George Aitken, who went out in 1931 and returned to Australia in 1934 due to ill health, consented to become the Chairman of the BEM Sydney Council in 1945. See *Home Council Minutes*, 17 December 1945 (BCV), 2.

[138] Winsome Howell (later Mrs Southwell) trained in midwifery, general nursing training and at MBI before she got married to Hudson Southwell. See Southwell, *Uncharted Waters*, 65-66.

[139] Enid Gray (later Mrs Davidson) spent six months in training at MBI. See *Home Council Minutes*, 10 April 1934 and 8 May 1934 (BCV).

six months from May to December 1930 and to study the situation in the field and make recommendation to the Home Council for action.[140] With such close links between MBI and BEM, the ethos and method of training at MBI clearly influenced the philosophy and missionary practices of these BEM missionaries.

MBI was inter-denominational and independent in sponsorship, training any person who had a conversion experience and sensed a call to serve as a missionary and evangelist. The objective of the training, according to Nash, was twofold: a) the acquisition of a thorough working knowledge of the Bible and b) the practical application of that knowledge into life situations.[141] The method of training was to focus on the Bible as the centre of all their teaching. The method of study was to use no other textbook for the study of the Bible than the Bible itself. It entailed a systematic study of the Bible aimed at giving the students a firm grasp of the Scriptures. Study of the Bible usually covered sequentially as many books of the Bible as possible. Doctrine and apologetics were taught with practical subjects like evangelism, Sunday school teaching, practical living skills and tropical medicine. Students were required to learn extensively from practical ministry like street or factory evangelism, religious education classes in schools, evangelistic campaigns and hospital visitation.[142] The course on basic medicine was first provided by Dr Norman Griffiths from 1925 and later by Melbourne General Hospital from the early 1940s for prospective missionaries.[143] The main aim of MBI training was to ensure that its graduates could exercise a strong evangelistic and Bible teaching ministry, be able to survive in the primitive conditions of missionary work and serve the needs of the local people in terms of hygiene, agriculture, building construction and education.[144]

Bible colleges espoused an evangelical understanding of the nature of the Christian life, stressing the need for a conversion experience and a daily devotion or 'walk' with God. The aim was progressive sanctification and training in personal holiness. This clear evangelical tradition equated progressive sanctification with growing spiritual maturity, authority and strength for life and ministry.[145] The method of fostering this kind of spiritual development was through lectures and the communal lifestyle of the college. Nash himself provided the principal role model as lecturer and mentor to the

---

[140] See *Home Council Minutes*, 4 April 1930 (BCV), 1-2, which sets forth the terms of the Borneo Commission under Mr Tregaskis. See *Home Council Minutes*, 3 January, 1; 6 February 1931 (BCV), 1 which recorded Tregaskis' return and report on the work in Borneo.

[141] It was spelt out by Nash in his inaugural speech at MBI. Clack (ed.), *We Will Go*, 14-15.

[142] David Parker, 'Theological and Bible Colleges in Australia: An Evangelical Perspective', *Journal of Christian Education* Paper 86 (July 1986), 10-11.

[143] Paproth, *Failure Is Not Final*, 99.

[144] Parker, 'Fundamentalism and Conservative Protestantism', 551.

[145] Paproth, *Failure Is Not Final*, 99.

students for two decades from 1920. The communal lifestyle of the college was fashioned in order to promote holiness through living together in a closely knit community.

The communal life experience within MBI was considered as an essential aspect of good missionary training, helping to improve the students' relational skills and general manners and etiquette, though their lifestyle and manners often reflected the middle-class values of Nash and the Council. Often the Mission bodies, for example the CIM, regarded the Bible College as a 'missionary training home' especially in the pre-WW II period. They took it for granted that the two years' residential requirement of learning to relate to one another in a communal setting was sufficient basic training for missionary work.[146] The communal life experience helped students to better discover their own strengths and weaknesses, and provided a sense of family spirit and belonging to the community.[147] The result was a fostering of an identity and a sense of belonging to the family at MBI and with its graduates dispersed throughout the world as missionaries.

This sense of community was particularly strong during Nash's time, when former students would return to MBI either as lecturers[148] or to speak about their work in the mission field, in order to recruit missionaries and muster prayer support.[149] The next MBI principal, J.W. Searle, continued this tradition of keeping this sense of identity with MBI among its graduates in general and with BEM in particular. Beyond the link through correspondence, MBI personnel and graduates were always welcome as visitors to the BEM work. Some were invited to speak at BEM meetings, as was the case with Principal J.W. Searle[150] and with Dr Del Rees, a CIM missionary, who spoke at the BEM Field Conferences in 1948 and 1952 respectively.

When BEM was given a two-seater Aeronca aircraft in 1949 by Stafford Young who had been a BEM missionary from 1934-1940, Missionary Aviation Fellowship Australia, which had been very closely associated with MBI, was helpful in seconding Brian Morton, an ex-serviceman who had flown over Borneo during WWII, to work with BEM.[151] This event indicates the extent to

[146] The results of a 'sanctified' lifestyle were reflected through tight discipline, modesty in clothing, abstinence from alcohol, gambling and other similar requirements. Parker, 'Fundamentalism and Conservative Protestantism', 549-50.

[147] This family spirit was continued, even after the students had graduated when they were serving in the mission field or in Australia, through the *Fellowship of Intercession* (a kind of prayer diary) and the Graduates Association. Paproth, *Failure Is Not Final*, 100.

[148] J.W Searle became successor to C.H. Nash as the next Principal of MBI.

[149] The sense of community is always strong where the Principal or lecturer knows every of its graduates.

[150] *BEM NL*, June 1948, 3; August 1979, 1.

[151] Lees, *Drunk before Dawn*, 96. See *BEM NL*, November 1979, 1. The aircraft had been used by the Flying Doctor Service in outback New South Wales, a service operated by Stafford Young's brother. It was reconditioned for use in Borneo.

which missionaries used the MBI network of friends and organizations to help each other in the mission field. In the course of grooming indigenous leadership for the SIB, it was natural for BEM to select leaders who showed promise and potential and to send them to MBI for further training, as was the case with Udan Rangat, Iki and Balan Seling in 1959[152] and with Gerawat Maran in 1978.

The Bible schools which BEM started were often patterned on similar lines to MBI in providing training in evangelism, grounding in the Scriptures and spiritual training within the context of a residential community. This was true of the first Bible school at Budok Ngeri, begun in 1947 and which later shifted to Lawas to become the central Bible school.[153] The Bible itself was the textbook for Bible knowledge and doctrine. For their practical training, the students often accompanied the missionaries on evangelistic trips to tribes other than their own.[154] This became a regular feature of their training. The overall aim of the BEM Bible schools reflected very much the same ethos and practice as MBI, though modified to local conditions. Their focus was on the training of missionaries and evangelists, (who also assumed the roles of pastors and teachers), to plant, build, serve and strengthen the church.

Conclusion

The BEM was an inter-denominational Australian evangelical mission body that showed a strong indebtedness to Melbourne evangelicalism and especially to Nash and the MBI. Besides the close links of personal friends and informal organisational cooperation, the network of MBI, CIM and Keswick movement played a significant role in the character of the BEM.

Nash provided the necessary mentoring and counsel that led to the formation of the BEM. In Nash, there stood a model of a gifted Bible expositor and teacher, and mission facilitator undergirded by Keswick spirituality. His example as a teacher, mentor and friend and the training at MBI in the residential communal life of a Bible college were to be later reproduced, whether consciously or unconsciously, by BEM missionaries who were training the indigenous people in the first BEM Bible school at Budok Ngeri in 1947.

The close link with MBI continued through the first two principals and MBI graduates who subsequently became BEM missionaries. When the indigenous leaders of the SIB were to be trained at a higher level than the BEM Bible schools could provide at that time, BEM naturally sent them to MBI.

As a missions organisation, BEM was a miniature mirror image of the CIM, mainly because the formative influences on Southwell's missionary thinking had been from the CIM. BEM was structured very much like CIM both in

---

[152] *BEM NL*, April-May 1959, 2.

[153] Lees, *Drunk before Dawn*, 84. The first students were 12 Lun Bawang couples. See *BEM NL*, August, 1954, 1; February 1980, 1.

[154] Lees, *Drunk before Dawn*, 101.

policy and practice. In its founding intention and later practice, BEM was led by the Field Director as head of the Mission, though for the first six years of its existence until 1935, it was led by the Home Council. Also, the highest priority was given to the evangelization of the indigenous people of Borneo and to explicit commitment to evangelical doctrine and the 'faith principle' of complete dependence on God through prayer for provision of all needs. In the evangelization of the indigenous people, BEM followed the CIM practice of itineration so that there was 'a widespread dissemination of saving truth to be followed by settled work as the way should open'.[155] Following the mass conversion of the Lun Bawang in the Trusan, Davidson began settled work among them just prior to WWII. Moreover, BEM emulated the CIM practice of regular General Conferences which also included local pastors and evangelists. However, BEM's policy toward women missionaries was more restrictive than that of the CIM, so that instead of treating single women missionaries as equal to the men, they had to work under a married couple or in pairs at a mission station. The distinctive Keswick tradition of spirituality was deeply formative for the pioneer BEM missionaries; but in later years, the BEM Conferences, termed 'Jungle Keswick', leaned more towards Bible teaching conventions, though from time to time the distinctive themes of Keswick teaching were re-emphasised.

In short, the evangelical mix of Australian Keswick spirituality, MBI Bible and missionary training, and CIM missionary philosophy and practice became the matrix from which the BEM was initially shaped and influenced as it began work in Sarawak.

Frank Davidson, Carey Tolley, Hudson Southwell
Alexander Henderson December 1928

[155] Taylor, *Hudson Taylor and the CIM*, 288.

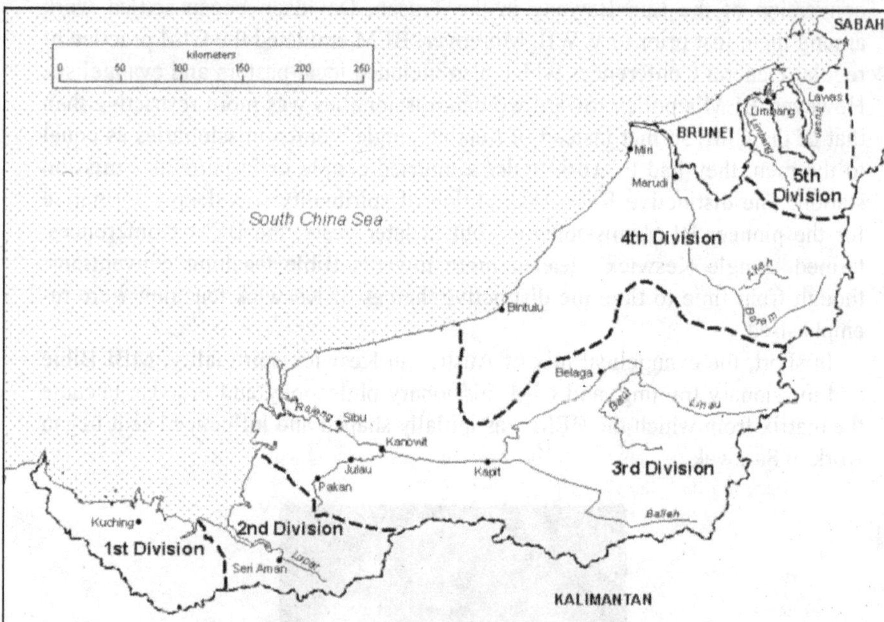

Map 3: Sarawak and its Divisions
during Brooke and British colonial rule

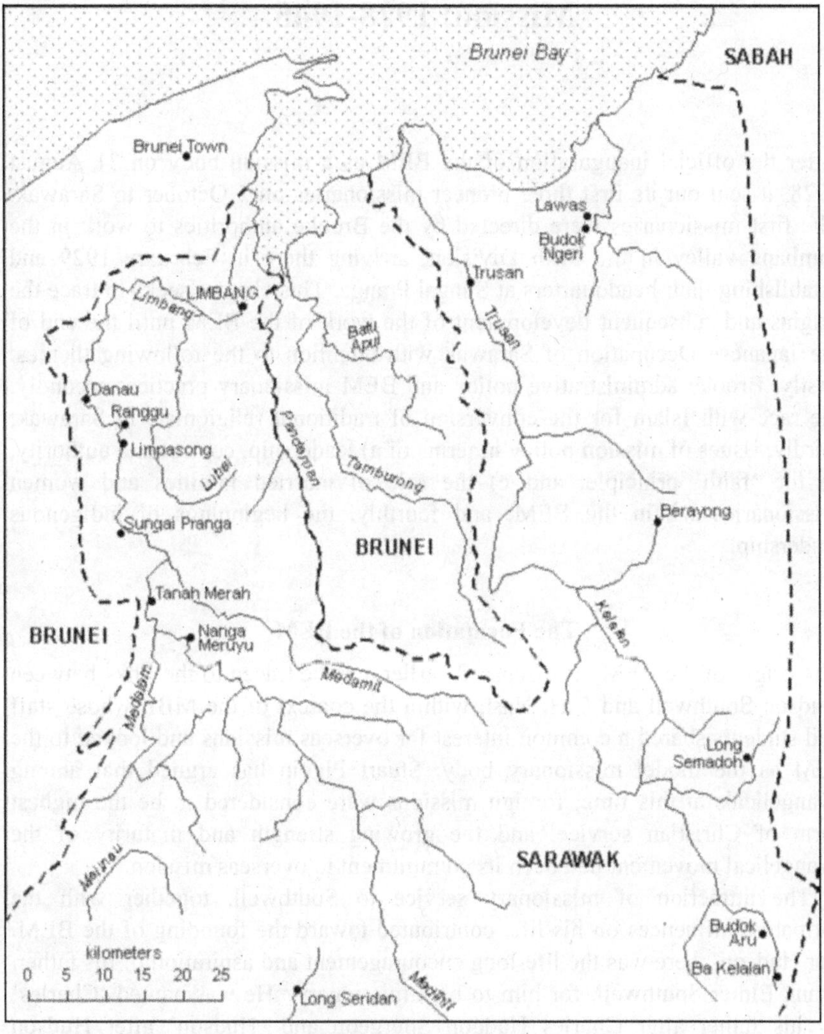

Map 4: Work of the BEM in the
Limbang District before WWII

Chapter 4

The Early History of the Borneo Evangelical Mission: 1928-1945

After the official inauguration of the BEM as a mission body on 31 August 1928, it sent out its first three pioneer missionaries on 5 October to Sarawak. The first missionaries were directed by the Brooke authorities to work in the Limbang valley in the Fifth Division, arriving there in February 1929 and establishing their headquarters at Sungai Pranga. This chapter seeks to trace the origins and subsequent development of the work of the BEM until the end of the Japanese Occupation of Sarawak with attention to the following themes: firstly, Brooke administrative policy and BEM missionary practice; secondly, the race with Islam for the conversion of traditional religionists in Sarawak; thirdly, issues of mission policy in terms of a) leadership, control and authority, b) the 'faith' principle, and c) the role of married families and women missionaries within the BEM; and fourthly, the beginnings of indigenous leadership.

The Formation of the BEM

The origin of the BEM, as discussed earlier, can be traced to the links between Hudson Southwell and C.H. Nash within the context of the MBI, whose staff and students shared a common interest for overseas missions and looked to the CIM as the model missionary body. Stuart Piggin has argued that among evangelicals at this time, foreign missions were considered to be the highest form of Christian service, and the growing strength and maturity of the evangelical movement had been its commitment to overseas mission.[1]

The attraction of missionary service to Southwell, together with the formative influences on his life, contributed toward the founding of the BEM. For Hudson, there was the life-long encouragement and aspiration of his father, Frank Elmer Southwell, for him to be a missionary.[2] He was named 'Charles' by his father after Charles Haddon Spurgeon and 'Hudson' after Hudson

---

[1] Piggin, *Evangelical Christianity in Australia*, 66. See also Stuart Piggin, *Making Evangelical Missionaries, 1789-1858* (Appleford, Oxford: Sutton Courtenay Press, 1984), 133-35.

[2] Southwell, *Uncharted Waters*, 52-54.

Taylor. His father would make known his aspirations for him at each birthday, giving him a note to that effect. At his fifteenth birthday, his father wrote: 'You know that our greatest desire is that you will strengthen the purpose of your will to serve our God.... D.L. Moody said (when he was) about your age: "I want to be the best man God can make," and from that moment he tried to please Him in everything and succeeded too!... That is what we expect from our firstborn'.[3] Even in 1921, his father's dying words to him served as an encouragement for missionary and evangelistic work.[4] There was an undoubted, strong underlying influence of his father inclining Hudson towards a missionary vocation. Further, through his contacts with CIM missionaries in Melbourne, Southwell was challenged to commit his life to God for his service at a CIM annual meeting in 1917. However, he was only free to pursue his calling in August 1926 when he finally entered MBI.[5]

At MBI, Southwell's missionary concern initially focused on China was re-directed to Borneo. He later became more convinced about his calling after reading a report by the C&MA missionary pioneer Rev. R.A. Jaffray that the people of the interior of Borneo had not heard about Christ.[6] The move toward the formation of a Borneo Fellowship and eventually the Borneo Evangelical Mission involved a few significant events. Firstly, in 1927, Davidson and Tolley, both students at MBI, joined Southwell in his missionary interest and prayer for Borneo. Secondly, on 17 May 1928, the gift of fifty pounds received from Stafford Young for the specific purpose of sending a missionary to Borneo was perceived as divine confirmation of their call to Borneo.[7] Thirdly, through the initiatives of the three young men and the availability of an elderly Scotsman, Alexander Henderson, who agreed to help them make initial contacts and settle them into Borneo, a pioneering team was in place.[8]

The Borneo Fellowship, formed on 4 July 1928, was to act 'as a focus for prayer, for sharing information and as a centre to which gifts to support this forward movement could be sent'.[9] The Fellowship produced a statement focusing on missionary work among Borneo's aboriginal inhabitants, the Dyak.

---

[3] Southwell, *Uncharted Waters*, 52-54.

[4] Southwell, *Uncharted Waters*, 53-54.

[5] Southwell, *Uncharted Waters*, 55-57. Southwell served out his nine years' contract with the Department of Technical Education in Victoria before finally entered MBI in August 1926 to pursue his calling.

[6] Meanwhile, Southwell visited the public library of Melbourne, collecting books and maps of Borneo and reading whatever was available.

[7] Southwell, *Uncharted Waters*, 62.

[8] Southwell, *Uncharted Waters*, 63. In early June 1928, Southwell, Davidson and Tolley went to Yallourn to make initial contact with Henderson. Henderson had, at one time, been a timber trader for seven years on the Kapuas River in Dutch Borneo (now known as Kalimantan) and was familiar with the area and colloquial Malay.

[9] Southwell, *Uncharted Waters*, 63. See 'An Outline of Events leading to the Formation of a Borneo Fellowship' in the Minute Book of the BEM Home Council (1928) located in BCV Library/Archive. See Appendix 3.

It issued an urgent call for prayer whose main points were that a) the field was near Australia and was therefore the special responsibility of the Church of Australia, and b) definite offers for immediate service were available.[10]

Then, to obviate the need to start another missionary organization, as Shirley Lees noted in her book, Drunk before Dawn, the three young men 'explored the possibilities of going out under the auspices of other missions'.[11] But the formation of the BEM was necessitated by the inability and unwillingness of the existing mission organizations they approached the Worldwide Evangelization Crusade (WEC),[12] the SSEM[13] and the CIM[14] to extend their sphere of work to Borneo.[15] The reasons for their refusal were twofold: firstly, this was a time of depression in the global economy, and secondly, the three mission societies were unable to second any senior missionaries to oversee a new work. The BEM was in fact originally envisaged as the Borneo branch of WEC, but affiliation with WEC never materialized. The reason, according to Norman Percy Grubb, the then General Secretary of WEC,[16] was the difficulty

---

[10] 'An Outline of Events Leading to the Formation of a Borneo Fellowship' in BEM Home Council Minute Book, 1928 (BCV).

[11] Lees, *Drunk before Dawn*, 26.

[12] WEC was founded by Charles Thomas Studd (1860-1931) in 1911. As one of the Cambridge Seven, he went to China under the CIM in 1885. Returning from China in 1894 because of poor health, he continued to serve the Student Volunteer Movement for six years, then moving on to serve in an English-speaking church in Ootacamund, India but he returned from India due to poor health again. In 1910, he left for Africa to establish the Heart of Africa Mission, which later became WEC. From 1913, C.T. Studd spent the rest of his missionary life (18 years) in Belgian Congo (Zaire). He was succeeded by Norman Percy Grubb, his son-in-law, as General Secretary of WEC in 1931. See Gerald H. Anderson, (ed.), *Biographical Dictionary of Christian Missions* (New York: Simon & Schuster Macmillan, 1998), 649.

[13] In 1868, the demand for cheap labour for the Queensland sugar plantations led to the immigration of 62,000 Pacific Islanders known as Kanakas. But in 1901, the Australian government adopted a white policy that decreed that all Kanakas had to return to their home islands by 1906. The immigration of the islanders led to the formation of the Queensland Kanaka Mission and their deportation resulted in the formation of the SSEM. Both these Missions were started by Florence Selina Harriet Young (1856-1940). The SSEM (first known as Solomon Islands Mission), which was founded in 1904, was an Australian non-denominational overseas missionary society, working among the South Pacific islanders. See Piggin, *Evangelical Christianity in Australia*, 69-70.

[14] Southwell, *Uncharted Waters*, 61-62. Lees, *Drunk before Dawn*, 26-27.

[15] Originally, the Borneo Fellowship was meant to be 'eventually related to some existing missionary organisation of an inter-denominational character, to obviate the addition of yet another to the many existing societies'.

[16] Grubb was General Secretary of WEC from 1931 to 1965. As a missionary, he had earlier served in northern Belgian Congo (Zaire) from 1920-1927 and helped to translate the New Testament into Bangala. Under his able leadership, WEC grew to 800 missionaries, working in 20 countries by the time of his retirement in 1965. See Anderson (ed.), *Biographical Dictionary of Christian Missions*, 265.

the BEM founders had with WEC's open-door policy to all Christians including Pentecostals. Grubb noted that the pioneers of the BEM viewed WEC with some concern, believing that some of its members tended towards over-emotionalism,[17] and certain of its Pentecostal emphases and practices were regarded as doctrinally unsound.[18] The establishment of the BEM thus resulted from the urgency of circumstance with the immediate availability of three young men who had offered themselves for service in Borneo, and the unwillingness of any existing missionary organization to extend their work to Borneo.

The BEM was thus formally established on 31 August 1928 with a council of ten founding members.[19] The BEM First Annual Report noted that having interviewed and ascertained the calling of Southwell, Davidson and Tolley, the BEM Home Council later held a commissioning service on 1 October to send them to Borneo, with Henderson as team leader and Southwell as the field secretary.[20]

Brooke Administrative Policies and their Impact on BEM Work

As was demonstrated in Chapter 2, Brooke policy had been to restrict and shape the work of earlier Christian missions in Sarawak, and the BEM faced similar restrictions within the Limbang valley, Fifth Division, for the initial five years.[21] The unusual means of the BEM gaining entry to Sarawak conformed to none of the usual formalities either an invitation by James or Charles Brooke, as was the case with the Anglican SPG and the Methodist mission, or prior government approval, as with the Roman Catholic mission. Hence, it raised

---

[17] Grubb wrote that 'the first founders...had in mind being the Borneo branch of the WEC, but that some difficulty in the WEC at that time made them feel it better to found an independent mission'. He also wrote that 'so many adverse rumours have gone about concerning the WEC these past years' in Australia. See Letter of Norman Grubb to Stafford Young, 4 January 1938 (OMF). He wrote that 'the sympathies of the WEC with a movement such as the Holiness movement or perhaps with Paget Wilkes' teaching were regarded with a certain amount of misgivings. So, also might be included the more ebullient, shall I say explosive spirit in the WEC (the misgivings here are due to the experience of seeming over-emotionalism in past)'. The Pentecostals were viewed not only with some suspicion about their doctrinal position especially relating to tongues but also their tendency towards emotionalism. See Letter of Stafford Young to Norman Grubb, 11 May 1938 (OMF).

[18] It is especially so in regard to the teachings on the Baptism of the Holy Spirit as a post-conversion experience and speaking in tongues as the initial physical evidence of the Baptism of the Holy Spirit.

[19] On the next day (1 September 1928), the inaugural meeting was held at MBI, when the final draft of the constitution was adopted. It was ratified at the next Council meeting.

[20] *BEM First Annual Report*, 30 June 1929, 2.

[21] The BEM missionaries were allowed to visit the next river, the Trusan, in 1935 but not to establish a base there until permission was finally given in November 1937.

suspicion in the minds of the Brooke government as to the genuineness of BEM's real motives.[22] This was partly aggravated by Henderson's previous involvement as a trader in Dutch Borneo. According to the BEM annual reports, government approval was given only after much careful scrutiny,[23] and the missionaries were directed to Sungai Pranga, the farthest outpost upriver along the Limbang.[24]

The main reason for directing the BEM to the Limbang valley may have been political, though for the mission itself the obvious reason was that the Fifth Division was still an unevangelized area untouched by any Christian mission.[25]

In view of the cautious attitude of the Brooke government to the BEM, there existed a paradoxical relationship between them. On the one hand, the government regarded the missionaries as its 'eyes and ears',[26] but, on the other, it monitored their activities through regular visits by its officers. The official government view was that it was dangerous and unsafe for the missionaries to venture too far into the interior. During the missionaries' visit to him in Miri on November 1933, the Resident, J.B. Archer, refused permission for them to work outside the Limbang valley.[27] Furthermore, he threatened them with

---

[22] When the four BEM missionaries arrived at Singapore, Davidson and Tolley stayed behind, while Henderson and Southwell journeyed on to Sarawak to gain permission to work there. Despite the fact that they carried two letters of introduction, one from the government of the state of Victoria, certifying that they were Australian citizens and requesting the protection of the government of Sarawak, and the other from the Chairman of the BEM Council in Melbourne, they came under great suspicion.

[23] See Southwell, *Uncharted Waters*, 26. *BEM First Annual Report*, 30 June 1929, 2. Henderson and Southwell were interrogated over three days by the Rajah's private secretary, Gerald McBryan and the Rajah's cousin and legal advisor, Charles Willes Johnson, presumably over the genuineness of their intentions.

[24] *BEM Second Annual Report*, 30 June 1930, 2. Southwell, *Uncharted Waters*, 29-30, 34-35. Davidson and Tolley joined Southwell and Henderson at Batu Danau, staying at the government bungalow house for three months before the Sungai Pranga site was found.

[25] During the last two decades of the century, Limbang had been a scene of social unrest: first, with the local revolt against the Sultan of Brunei which led to its acquisition by Sarawak in 1890; second, with the rivalry between the aggressive migrant Iban and the local Murut and between the upper Trusan Murut and outsiders, including that of the Brooke government. Robert Payne, *White Rajahs* (London: Robert Hale, 1960), 151. There had been two immigrations of the Skrang Iban from Second Division, first in 1931 and later in 1934 to the areas nearby the mission station. Politically, the Brooke government populated the area with loyal Iban, ensuring a firmer control over the Limbang valley area. It also relieved the Second Division of the pressure for land caused by the Iban practice of shifting cultivation.

[26] See Chapter 2, footnote 72 for Richards' comment about missionaries.

[27] Edwards and Stevens, *Short Histories*, 38. Earlier in October 1929, Davidson had gone to the upper reaches of the Limbang and continued overland to the Kelabit in the Medihit. The Chief Secretary visited them in August 1930 and prohibited the missionaries from working inland. Lees, *Drunk before Dawn*, 37.

expulsion from the country if they disobeyed.[28] A result of this prohibition was that the missionaries had to redirect and focus their work downriver among the Bisaya.

One consequence of the government's restriction on the missionaries' freedom to operate was ironically a sharpening of the focus of their work among the indigenous people in Limbang. Initially, all the BEM missionaries were based at Sungai Pranga, each doing itinerant evangelism in different directions to reach the sparse population of about three thousand Iban, Lun Bawang and Bisaya who lived within an area of about forty square miles. This work showed little result during the first five years. In time, the understanding developed that each missionary would work with a specific people group. By 1935, four areas of work had become more clearly defined: a) Bewsher concentrated on the Bisaya at Limpasong, b) Southwell on the Iban at Sungai Pranga and later at Tanah Merah and Nanga Meruyu, c) Tolley on the Iban on the Lubai, and d) Davidson on the Kelabit in the Medihit.

The mission philosophy of the BEM led to the emergence of a pattern of work familiar to students of missionary history in which evangelism and literacy dovetailed, as literacy was required of new converts in order to read the Scriptures for their spiritual nurture and witness to their people. Consequently, the preparation of reading primers and the translation of the Scriptures (especially the Gospels) became a necessity. Rudimentary medical services were also provided on a need basis, which was very beneficial, as sickness and ill-health were rife owing to poor hygiene, unhealthy lifestyles and a lack of immunity to the diseases which outsiders brought to the region.

At this juncture, it needs to be admitted that there is a heavy reliance on the BEM literature regarding its work in the pre-war years, as hardly any oral evidence from this period has been uncovered. However, oral surveys through personal interviews have provided accounts of the BEM work from the late 1950s and early 1960s.

We will now consider the work done by each of the four missionaries in their respective areas, as they were free to work within the confines of the Limbang valley.

At Limpasong, Bewsher's work among the Bisaya bore fruit when Itai and Lallang, his language teachers, became his first converts in 1936 and formed the nucleus of the Bisaya church.[29] Through their witness, the church grew to thirty members. By 1939, the church at Ranggu was responsible for its own affairs with four officer-bearers. As has been the case with most Protestant mission societies, the BEM placed great emphasis on having native evangelists to strengthen the church and to reach out to new fields.[30] The training of young

---

[28] Edwards and Stevens, *Short Histories*, 38.

[29] *BEM Tenth Annual Report*, 31 March 1939, 3; Lees, *Drunk before Dawn*, 38-41.

[30] *BEM Prayer Notes*, February 1940 and May 1941, prepared on 27 March 1941.

men (such as Punan[31] and his brother-in-law, George, at the school for Christian ministry),[32] in Bewsher's view, presented great opportunities for the spread of Christianity.[33]

Roland Bewsher at Limpasong

Limpasong School 1935

[31] Letter of R.A. Bewsher to Field Conference, 12 December 1940 (OMF). Punan was the young secretary of the Ranggu church who had indicated 'his full-time call to the ministry of the Gospel'.

[32] *BEM Prayer Notes*, 26 June 1941; *BEM NL*, January 1942, 5. Both Punan and George, his brother-in-law, had each opened a school at Ranggu and Danau respectively.

[33] *BEM Prayer Notes*, June 1941, prepared on 24 April 1941. 'The spiritual possibilities of such schools would be great if all the teachers were live Christian witnesses'.

There were no literate Bisaya in the upper Limbang valley at that time. According to Vernon Porritt, Bewsher's work of providing schooling, promoting health through hygiene and simple medical treatment, and improving methods of agriculture earned him in September 1940 a visit from the Resident of the Fifth Division, Fred Pollard, and subsequently an appointment to the new Council Negeri, the Sarawak State Legislature, to represent the people of Limbang in September 1941.[34] It is likely that Bewsher viewed his educational, medical and agricultural activities as preparatory to his evangelizing work. After WWII, he left the BEM and joined the Sarawak Administrative Service.

It is interesting to note that Porritt, a former colonial officer, highlighted an aspect of the work and achievement of Bewsher which is omitted in the mission sources, which focused almost exclusively on evangelistic and church-planting activities.[35] Of significance is Bewsher's appointment to the Council Negeri, which indicates favourable recognition of the work of the BEM in the eyes of the Brooke government. Perhaps, the invasion of Sarawak soon afterward and Bewsher's resignation from the BEM after WWII negated the need to publicise this appointment.

As for the work at Sungai Pranga, Southwell himself was more inclined towards an itinerant ministry, but the Home Council recommended that he should start 'a school for the training of young converts as evangelists, and that itinerant evangelism should be left at present to the other missionaries'.[36] However, without the help of an additional resident worker, Southwell found difficulty in meeting the demands of starting a school while doing district mission work and visitation. By April 1934, the school at Sungai Pranga had not even started. The Home Council seemed displeased enough for Nash to write to Southwell about the matter.[37] As it was also a pre-requisite of the Brooke administration before consideration could be given to the BEM's request to work in the Trusan, Southwell had little choice but to start the school. When it eventually opened, it operated as a Bible school on an ad hoc basis. After an initial abortive start, it began again with several Iban and Lun Bawang students, providing elementary education, and using the Gospels as

---

[34] Vernon L. Porritt, *Bapak Guru Orang Bisaya: A Pioneer in Social Experimentation in Sarawak, Ro Bewsher, 1910-1998* (Hull: Department of South-East Asian Studies, University of Hull, 1999), 2-4. As Porritt notes, 'Bewsher's philosophy was to be self-effacing, to prompt and suggest rather than organize and direct, and to encourage indigenous experimentation and discovery'. In his literacy work, his aim had been 'to achieve a hundred per cent literacy rate amongst the local Bisaya by training Bisaya teachers using phonic orthography'.

[35] Mission sources tended to focus mainly on matters relating to the Christian life, faith and spirituality. Other matters such as their literacy programme took a secondary place.

[36] In *Home Council Minutes*, 8 August 1933, 2, there was mention of the need for another worker to be in residence at Sungai Pranga in Southwell's letter to Davidson so that a regular school could be started.

[37] *Home Council Minutes*, 10 April 1934, 2.

textbook.[38] However, the Iban students left school whenever the farming season started. The first converts were Southwell's two Iban 'houseboys', Undi in November 1934 and later, Rompang,[39] as a result of attending the morning sessions of the school, where the Gospels were read and taught. This pattern of the first converts being domestic servants of the missionaries was also common in African missions in the late nineteenth century. The Lun Bawang students, who stayed on during the farming season, later wrote in their compositions what amounted to a statement of belief in the Christian faith to the delight of the Southwells; among them was Lawai, who became a leader in the Lun Bawang church in the lower Trusan during the Japanese Occupation.[40]

Lawai and his wife, Lua. Lawai was the first Lun Bawang believer to be baptised. He came from Limbang. The marriage of Lawai and Lua was the first Christian marriage in the early days of the BEM. They were married by Mr Frank Davidson. Lawai is a retired pastor.

The process of Christianization attracted important visitors to Sungai Pranga. Among them were Raut and Lupong, two Lun Bawang village headmen from the Trusan, whose conversions led to others in the Trusan,[41] and also that of Balang Imat, a Kelabit village headman from the Medihit in 1933. In 1939, Balang Imat himself was instrumental in leading Frank Davidson to bring about the conversion of Tama Kulin, the Penghulu of the Kelabit in the upper Limbang.[42] Here, we note the crucial role of indigenous initiative in

[38] The students ranged from ten to fifteen years of age.
[39] Southwell, *Uncharted Waters*, 73-74. The 'houseboys' were young adults rather than boys. Later, when Rompang, the second of Southwell's houseboys became a Christian, he admitted, 'It was not so much what you people said. But, I could not resist that Book!'
[40] *BEM NL*, September 1946, 5.
[41] *BEM Fifth Annual Report*, 30 June 1933, 2. Southwell, *Uncharted Waters*, 81.
[42] *BEM Eleventh Annual Report*, 31 March 1940, 5.

proclaiming the Christian message prior to the BEM missionaries working among them in the Trusan.

Though the BEM Annual Reports and missionary accounts gave greater prominence to the work of their missionaries, the short, almost incidental accounts of these village headmen facilitating the spread of Christianity among other village headmen are deeply significant. It can be argued that in the above cases the BEM accounts were often conscious about the need to provide short narratives of the work of the indigenous leaders.

The work among the Iban at Sungai Pranga involved visitations of the surrounding areas, Sunday worship and daily prayers, but it drew little response, except for their curious interest in the presence of a white woman, Winsome Southwell, who joined Southwell at Sungai Pranga after their marriage in 1932. The lack of receptivity by the Iban to Christianity, according to Southwell's unpublished memoirs, was in part due to their achievements as good farmers. Understandably, there was no reason for the Iban to change their religion when they appeared to be enjoying the favour of the spirits as shown by their good harvests. Another reason was that the older people, particularly the shamans, were strongly opposed to the Christian message.[43] Further, the Iban as a migratory people presented special problems to any sustained work. After Southwell returned from furlough in 1936, he had to relocate a day's journey upriver to Nanga Meruyu, where the Iban had moved. At Nanga Meruyu, he started a school for young people and did medical work. But the Iban continued to be generally unresponsive. The BEM Tenth Annual Report of 1939 mentioned this: 'The stay of the Southwells amongst the people has only served to emphasise the hardness of the Iban heart'.[44] The use of this kind of language common among evangelicals seems to be a way of rationalizing the lack of success in the work. Furthermore, it was a way of justifying to the BEM constituency the need for Southwell to move on to another area of work, which resulted in the shifting of the headquarters to Jesselton, British North Borneo (now Kota Kinabalu, Sabah), in 1939.

Tolley's work among the Iban on the Lubai from 1935 was equally discouraging and not very different from Southwell's work at Sungai Pranga among the Iban. It showed little result except for one convert. Later, Tolley resigned from the mission in 1938. The lack of results may have been a factor in his resignation, but a more likely reason was Tolley's fear of being marginalized by the other two pioneers when the Field Conference assumed ultimate control over the Mission.[45]

---

[43] Southwell's Unpublished Memoirs (Manning, West Australia: ca. 1988), 38.

[44] *BEM Tenth Annual Report*, 31 March 1939, 3. Lees, *Drunk before Dawn*, 49-50.

[45] *BEM Field Conference Minutes*, 27 October-4 November 1938, 2. In the Field Conference Discussion, 9 March 1938, 4, it noted Tolley's fear that 'Conference was taking too much control over individual members'. He further 'feared that the majority of strong personal convictions amongst members…would win the day'. He advocated 'greater importance be given to individual guidance'.

A dilemma was created for Davidson when the Brooke government gave permission to the BEM in late 1937 to start work at Trusan. The minutes of the September 1939 Field Conference recorded that 'Davidson expressed a disinclination to leave the Medihit and said that he did not perceive the move as the will of God. He admitted that he had not visited the Trusan and that only such a visit might influence him, as it had the rest of the Conference'. However, the Field Conference was unanimous in requesting 'Davidson to make a round trip to the Trusan with an open mind, and then reconsider the request of the Conference'.[46] But the great need in the Trusan did not leave the Davidsons with much of a choice.[47]

Though Davidson's work among the Kelabit in the Medihit from 1935 to 1938 did not bring much response,[48] he found the community responsive to Christianity on his return from furlough in 1939 as a result of the witness and the changed lives of the Lun Bawang Christians,[49] and his visit to the Medihit led to the conversion of Tama Kulin, the Penghulu of the Kelabit in the upper Limbang.[50]

The Davidsons and the Kelabits

---

[46] *BEM Field Conference Minutes*, 27 October-4 November 1938 and 25 August-5 September 1939, 2-3. The situation at Trusan had been made more urgent when Tolley sent in his letter of resignation on 28 July 1938.

[47] Davidson married Enid Gray in 1935 and they proceeded to work in the Medihit.

[48] *BEM Ninth Annual Report*, 31 March 1938, 5-7. Lees, *Drunk before Dawn*, 50-52, 57.

[49] *BEM NL*, April 1964, 2. According to Joan Cooper, 'the Kelabit Church discarded their animistic beliefs and customs through the Christian witness of their Murut neighbours', especially during WWII.

[50] *BEM Eleventh Annual Report*, 31 March 1940, 5.

When government permission was granted in 1937 to start a BEM base at Trusan, it necessitated the Davidsons' move to Trusan, as they were the only missionaries available to be relocated. After their return from furlough in 1939, they first spent three to four months teaching the Kelabit before they moved on to the Lun Bawang at Trusan in April 1940.[51] The work at Trusan was more fruitful and the Davidsons met a constant stream of visitors daily. The Davidsons taught them the basic tenets of the Christian faith and discussed matters relating to practical Christian living, such as how to pray before meals and for mundane matters like farming, going on a journey, and sickness. With local initiative, the first Lun Bawang church building was built in August 1941.

It is to be noted that at Trusan, the Davidsons felt that they and the Lun Bawang Christians had begun to learn about the power of God to heal and overcome shamanistic powers. There is no doubt that this experience was something very new to the Davidsons and beyond what they were accustomed to as Christians in Australia. It was recorded that the majority of prayer requests concerned sickness[52] and a great number of 'those prayed for were present the next Sunday to offer their praise'.[53] The natural practice of the BEM missionaries had been to prescribe medication for the sick but also to pray for their healing.[54] As the level of hygiene among the Lun Bawang had been extremely low, many common infectious diseases, which were rife, could be cured through western medication. From an indigenous worldview, sickness was understood to be caused by the spirits, so healing was often solely attributed to spiritual powers. From the missionaries' perspective, healing could be a result of both medicine and prayer.

In Lun Bawang society, the use of shamanistic powers to get rid of one's enemies was common. At Trusan, it was reported that 'at least one heathen had paid considerable sums to have a Christian cursed', but without the desired results.[55] It can be argued that the indigenous Christians learnt in practice that their God was more powerful than the spirits of their 'old religion', thereby emboldening them to witness to God as their all-sufficient protector.

It seems that one of the key aims of the BEM was beginning to be fulfilled at Trusan; it became the centre for training indigenous Christians for the upper Trusan churches, and for translating the Scriptures. The Davidsons were able to give Bible teaching and training to selected leaders of the Kelabit from the Medihit[56] and a few Lun Bawang from the interior Trusan church.[57] They

---

[51] Lees, *Drunk before Dawn*, 66.

[52] Tuberculosis and other infectious diseases were rife among the Murut.

[53] *BEM Prayer Notes* for August prepared on 26 June 1941. An item of praise noted that the Sunday services were overcrowded with people.

[54] Personal correspondence with Enid Davidson, 29 December 1992.

[55] *BEM Prayer Notes* for August 1941 prepared on 26 April 1941.

[56] Letter of F.T. Davidson to R.A. Bewsher, 1 October 1940 (OMF). See *BEM Prayer Notes* for May 1941 prepared on 17 February 1941. Tama Weng, a Kelabit from the Medihit, and two others stayed five months with the Davidsons.

stayed with the Davidsons for an extended period of time. With their help, a translation of some chapters of the Gospel of Luke in Lun Bawang were copied and used in the interior churches.

Further, local leaders from one interior church were beginning to reach out on their own initiative to help other churches, probably by imitating the example of the missionaries. In one instance, Davidson had desired to make a teaching trip to the Medihit Kelabit. But his trip was cancelled when he heard that some leaders from the interior Trusan church had visited the Medihit, and instructed their fellow believers there. He further noted that 'this is a practical beginning of the Interior churches showing concern for other untaught Christians, and is one result of (our) last visit to the interior'.[58] Davidson seemed delighted that the indigenous leaders were taking the initiative in teaching their own people; an outcome for which Davidson had hoped.

In order to comply with Brooke policy, the BEM's policy of widespread itinerant evangelism necessarily became somewhat curtailed so that it functioned in many ways like the earlier Christian missions in Borneo; that is starting churches and schools, and doing medical work. On the other hand, this policy fostered an outlook of aggressive evangelism among the pioneers, who were constantly looking for opportunities to expand its work.[59] The opportunity to expand came when the beginnings of a mass conversion movement developed among the Lun Bawang of the Trusan, the next river to the Limbang, in early 1933 as a result of the work of a C&MA native evangelist who crossed over from Kalimantan into the Trusan. The BEM missionaries established contact with this group of Lun Bawang when a headman and two men from the lower Trusan visited Southwell at Sungai Pranga inquiring about the Christian faith.[60] Later the BEM gained official permission to start a base among them in 1937 and helped consolidate the gains of this mass movement.

What prompted this mass conversion and why were the Lun Bawang so receptive to the Christian message?

This mass conversion of the Lun Bawang in the region needs to be understood in the context of their depopulation, which was first highlighted in 1922 by Ivor H. N. Evans and has since been the subject of scholarly study.[61]

---

[57] Notes for BEM Newsletter prepared on 21 May 1941. A couple, Labor Upai and Gadong, who were one of the few literate leaders among the interior church, stayed with the Davidsons for three weeks.

[58] Notes for BEM Newsletter prepared on 17 February 1941.

[59] It was this trait that was to gain them entry into the Baram, Fourth Division, in the immediate post-war period.

[60] Lees, *Drunk before Dawn*, 46.

[61] Explanations of this problem have ranged from suggestions of the psychological effects of culture contact on the Lun Bawang, malaria, gonorrhea, acute infectious diseases, malnutrition and inbreeding to excessive consumption of wine. See Ivor H.N. Evans, *Among Primitive Peoples in Borneo* (London: Seeley Service, 1922), 33-34; Owen Rutter, *The Pagans of North Borneo* (London: Hutchinson, 1929), 47-48; F.H.

Most likely, it was the result of a combination of factors. Firstly, the prohibition on headhunting among these people had deprived them of an activity that was an integral part of their religious, social and cultural life without providing them with an adequate substitute.[62] Such a deprivation may have caused such social and cultural disorientation in their lives that its psychological effects continued to linger without proper resolution. Secondly, this void was most probably filled by their excessive drinking of locally produced rice wine, about which Brooke administrators were able to attest that they were about a hundred days drunk in a year.[63] Thirdly, in their state of drunkenness, a neglect of personal hygiene and poor or non-existent medical care inevitably led to different kinds of infectious diseases that slowly decimated the population. Fourthly, their contact with outsiders exposed them to diseases that were alien to them and to which they had little immunity.

Religious conversions have been the subject of much recent scholarly debate, and Chapter 5 will return to this theme at greater length in relation to the later conversion movements among the Kayan. It is often suggested that conversion to Christianity among traditional people occurs because the change of religious allegiance offers the converts a wider and more secure identity in the larger and superior units of social, political and economic power created by modernization.[64] But in the case of the Lun Bawang, this explanation is perhaps unlikely as they were in a serious state of depopulation and also their contact with the outside world had been minimal, since they were prevented by the Brooke government from having such contact. In his anthropological study of religious change among the Lun Bawang, James L. Deegan argues that Christianity provided them with a new sense of meaning and worth after their experience of cultural disorientation resulting from the cessation of headhunting.[65] In a different study of the impact of Christianity on this same group of people in neighbouring Sabah, Sue Russell maintains that conversion was perceived as a change in allegiance from one supernatural power to another, which resulted from a spiritual encounter and from the quest for

---

Pollard, 'The Muruts of Sarawak', *SMJ* 4.13 (July 1933), 139-55 (148-49). Lindsay T. Ride, 'The Problem of Depopulation with Special Reference to British North Borneo', *The Caduceus* 13 (1934), 169-84; J.B. Crain, 'Murut Depopulation and the Sipitang Lun Dayeh', *JMBRAS* 45.2 (1972), 109-21.

[62] See Rivers, *Essays on the Depopulation of Melanesia*, which similarly proposes that the cessation of headhunting was a major psychological factor in the depopulation in Melanesia.

[63] Pollard, 'The Muruts of Sarawak', 148-49. 'The average Murut remained drunk one day out of every three'. See Edwards and Stevens, *Short Histories*, 36. See G.C. Davis, 'A Hundred Days Drunk', *Frontier* 6.1 (Spring 1963), 51. 'The Muruts were, by Government report, drunk a hundred days in the year.'

[64] Robert W. Hefner (ed.), *Conversion to Christianity: Historical and Anthropological Perspectives on a Great Transformation* (Berkeley: University of California Press, 1973), 14-25, 166.

[65] Deegan, 'Change Among the Lun Bawang', 288.

superior spiritual resources.[66] Both perspectives are useful to understand the complex nature of the conversion of the Lun Bawang.

Deegan enables us to understand the state of depopulation among the Lun Bawang, which had been going on for more than a decade. The Lun Bawang had experienced a deep sense of desperation and hopelessness about their condition, and also a sense of inferiority as they had become the object of scorn and rejection by the other tribes and the Brooke government. However, their receptivity toward Christianity may have been due to an inter-play of other factors. Firstly, the pre-millennial teaching about the imminent return of Christ preached by C&MA missionary Presswood in Kalimantan had been re-interpreted by native evangelists. The native evangelists came over to Sarawak, presenting the message of Christianity as a way of escape to heaven from present misery. As a result, the people left their farms untended and thought that they did not need to pay any further taxes to the government if they were going to be taken up into heaven shortly.[67] Tolley went to investigate this mass conversion of the Lun Bawang of the upper Trusan and he corrected this misinterpretation and presented a message of Jesus as their Saviour from the powers of the spirits, which was nevertheless understood as a message of hope. Further, when a man who had tried to persuade them to return to their old ways, died shortly afterwards, this was perceived as a spiritual encounter in which Christianity was seen as the more powerful religion.[68] Here, Russell sheds light on the conversion of the Lun Bawang. She argues that conversion is not only a power encounter but also a means to access supernatural resources, and in return, the believer gives allegiance to the supernatural power.[69] Hence, conversion to Christianity appeared to provide the Lun Bawang with a religion of superior transcendent power through a spiritual encounter and also spiritual re-orientation that gave meaning back to their shattered world after the cessation of headhunting. The change of religious allegiance helped the Lun Bawang gain a new sense of identity and worth.

The initial governmental refusal to allow the BEM to start a base at Trusan, with permission granted only for occasional visits from February 1934, had two underlying reasons: firstly, the teachings of the C&MA-trained native evangelists were perceived as extreme and subversive,[70] and secondly, the BEM was not allowed to begin any permanent work there until they had started a regular school at Limbang.[71]

---

[66] Russell, *Conversion, Identity and Power*, 151-54.

[67] Lees, *Drunk before Dawn*, 44. Southwell, *Uncharted Waters*, 76.

[68] Lees, *Drunk before Dawn*, 45.

[69] Russell, *Conversion, Identity and Power*, 151-54.

[70] *BEM NL*, June 1950, 4. It involved a misunderstanding of their teaching by the hearers about the Second Coming of Christ, which led the listeners not to plant any more rice.

[71] Lees, *Drunk before Dawn*, 48. Further requests to have a settled work in the Trusan were repeatedly turned down, first by the District Officer, Mr Bruce at Limbang, then by

The repeated refusal of the Brooke government to allow the BEM to expand its activities into the Trusan led to a re-evaluation of its strategy and sphere of work.[72] Southwell felt that since all the people in the area allotted to them had heard the Christian message, other areas needed to be reached. An exploratory trip by Southwell and Young into British North Borneo in April 1937 resulted in a decision shortly afterward to move the BEM headquarters to Jesselton and also start work at Ranau.[73] This latter decision, according to Lily Chan, prompted the Brooke government to review its position and grant the BEM permission to start a base at Trusan in November 1937.[74] By this time, news of the mass conversion of the Lun Bawang of the upper Trusan could not be easily contained and in July 1939 Edward Banks, the Curator of the Sarawak Museum, visited the Trusan to investigate reports of this change. He was amazed at what had taken place and later wrote about it in the Sarawak Gazette:

> The Trusan Murut house from being the foulest in Sarawak ... is now quite the cleanest and best kept…removal of the pigs (under the house), abstinence from alcohol and tobacco, at the same time teaching the Muruts to pray and sing Christian hymns in their own language, the results being now apparent thanks to …the Borneo Evangelical Mission… These are not isolated instances, whole houses and rivers full of people follow suit without an exception or a backslider anywhere.[75]

As a result of this movement among the Lun Bawang, the Davidsons were relocated from the Medihit to Trusan. As noted in Chapter 2, the BEM Twelfth Annual Report of 1941 recorded the visit to Trusan in November 1940 of the Rajah himself, who expressed surprise at the success of this work.[76] By 1940, the vast majority of the Lun Bawang in the entire Lawas District had been converted to Christianity.[77]

---

the Resident, Mr J.B. Archer at Miri, and later by the Rajah himself who visited Limbang in September 1935. The government's position on the decline of Lun Bawang population over the years was to allow the Lun Bawang to die out and be replaced by another group of people, most likely the Iban. See Edwards and Stevens, *Short Histories*, 36-37.

[72] See Chapter 2.

[73] The move to Jesselton, British North Borneo, took place in February 1939.

[74] Lily Chan, 'Christian Missions and the Ibans of Sarawak', 25. Lees, *Drunk before Dawn*, 61. Hepburn, *The Handbook of Sarawak*, 141.

[75] Edward Banks, 'Murut Morons', *SG* 31 July 1939, 107. See also J.C. Pollock, *Earth's Remotest End* (London: Hodder & Stoughton, 1960), 257-58.

[76] See Chapter 2. Southwell, *Uncharted Waters*, 101-102. Lees, *Drunk before Dawn*, 67. See McCracken, *Summing Up*, 178.

[77] 'From 1934 to 1938, almost every Lun Bawang in the Lawas District was converted to Christianity'. Edwards and Stevens, *Short Histories*, 37. There were about 3,524 Murut in the Lawas District in 1947 (11.8 per cent of a total population of 29,867 Murut in Sarawak). See Joseph T.H. Ko, 'Changing Patterns of Sub-National Ethnic Distribution in Sarawak, 1939-1980', *SMJ* 36.57 (December 1986), 1-11.

In short, not only did Brooke policy affect the work of the BEM, but the work of the BEM missionaries affected and changed the Brooke administrators' perception of the mission.

Mission Policy and Practice

BEM Policy on the Planting of an Indigenous Church

The 1928 provisional constitution of the Mission stated the purpose of the BEM as 'the giving of the Gospel to the natives in Borneo with a view of the formation of a Christian church from among them'.[78] In 1939 the Mission defined the character of this Christian church in terms of a 'Three-Self' indigenous church for the first time. The 1939 'Statement on the Character, Principle and Practices of the BEM' spelt out the object of the Mission as 'the speediest possible evangelization of the native tribes of Borneo, with the building up of a self-supporting and self-propagating indigenous church'.[79] The idea of this indigenous church, which would clearly also be invested with 'self-governing powers', was expressed as follows:

> ...the teaching of the New Testament indicates that there should be local individual churches with powers of self-government, and that when these increase in number they should be organized in a larger body, a Conference, which should exercise authority over the local churches.... The raising of self-supporting and self-extending Churches must ever be kept in view.[80]

At this juncture, it is necessary to raise the question of the possible sources of the BEM's use of the idea and language of the 'Three-Self' in the 1939 Statement. The BEM mission sources from 1928 to 1939 themselves do not provide an obvious answer to this question. No reference in BEM mission sources is made to the writings or theories either of Henry Venn (1796-1873) or of Rufus Anderson (1796-1880), the well-known British and American proponents respectively of the 'Three-Self' church concept in the nineteenth century. Neither do BEM sources refer to the principles of John L. Nevius (1829-1893), who placed particular emphasis on ending the 'old plan' of supporting national workers out of mission funds, and applying his 'new plan' of independence and self-reliance to indigenous churches from the beginning.[81]

---

[78] 'Provisional Constitution of the BEM' (1928). See Appendix 4.

[79] 'Statement of the Character, Principles and Practice of the BEM' (September 1939), 1. See Appendix 5.

[80] 'Statement of the Character, Principles and Practice of the BEM' (September 1939), 5. See Appendix 5.

[81] See John L. Nevius, *The Planting and Development of Missionary Churches*, Studies in the World Church and Missions 4 (Nutley, NJ: Presbyterian a Reformed Publishing, 1958), 8. Hunt Jr., 'The Legacy of John Livingston Nevius', 120-24.

Neither is there any reference to the principles and practices of the CIM as a possible source.

A conceivable indirect source of the BEM's commitment to 'Three-Self' principles is the discussions at the meetings of the International Missionary Council (IMC) held at Jerusalem in 1928 and at Tambaram in 1938. At the Jerusalem meeting, though secularism was acknowledged as going beyond geographical boundaries and involved all Christians in their missionary encounters, another major emphasis was on the relations between the older churches and the younger ones. It was clearly affirmed that the younger churches needed to be 'Three-Self'. A preliminary document prepared for the Jerusalem meeting quoted Venn's idea of a 'Three-Self' indigenous church with approval.[82] Correspondingly, voices were raised from the younger churches urging the adoption of a re-organized ecclesial structure to reflect that goal.[83] In particular, as Timothy Yates states, 'the thrust, already noticed at the Jerusalem meeting, towards an indigenous Chinese church, freed from the stigma of appearing to be a foreign religion, and accepting full responsibility for its own life, was strongly presented'.[84] There was no doubt that the ideal of the 'Three-Self' church was endorsed in Jerusalem.Though self-support was recognized as a vital element of this independent indigenous church, it was noted that in particular this area was one in which some younger churches had problems.[85]

At the Tambaram meeting of 1938, however, discussion of the 'Three-Self' principles was less prominent. Although in Volume 2 of the Tambaram reports, entitled 'The Growing Church', references were made to 'Three-Self'

---

[82] The 'ultimate object of a mission' was 'the settlement of a native Church under native pastors upon a self supporting system…the progress of a mission mainly depends upon the training up and the location of native pastors; and that…the euthanasia of a mission takes place when a missionary, surrounded by well-trained native congregations under native pastors, is able to resign all pastoral work into their hands, and gradually relax his superintendence over the pastors themselves…and so the mission passes into a settled Christian community. Then the missionary and all missionary agency should be transferred to all the regions beyond'. See 'Major Issues in the Relations of the Younger and Older Churches', *Jerusalem Meeting of the IMC, 1928* (London/Oxford: Humphrey Milford/Oxford University Press, 1928), III, 31.

[83] See 'Major Issues in the Relations of the Younger and Older Churches', *Jerusalem Meeting of the IMC, 1928*, III, 12-13. The Chinese leadership through S.C. Leung, a leading figure in the Church of Christ in China, argued that the Chinese church must be the 'centre of responsibility', and that missions must function through the church, and individual missionaries to act as officers of it rather than as representatives of the mission boards. See Yates, *Christian Mission in the Twentieth Century*, 67.

[84] Timothy Yates, *Christian Mission in the Twentieth Century* (Cambridge: Cambridge University Press, 1994), 67-69, 80.

[85] See P.O. Philip, 'The Indigenous Church', *Jerusalem Meeting of the IMC, 1928*, III, 195-204, citing the example of the Indian church.

principles in some reports on the various missions around the world,[86] it seems that the primary focus of attention had shifted to other issues such as the importance and centrality of the local church in mission and the relation between the Christian message and other religions.

It must, moreover, be emphasised that even before 1928, the faith missions had withdrawn from all involvement in the ecumenical missionary movement as represented since 1921 by the IMC: the lists of delegates at Jerusalem and Tambaram included no representative of either the CIM or the BEM.[87] Any direct indebtedness of the 1939 BEM Statement of 'Three-Self' principles to official IMC sources seems in principle unlikely.

Another possible source is Sidney J.W. Clark's work, The Indigenous Church, written in 1928 at the request of the Chinese and foreign secretaries of the National Christian Council of China. The extent of the influence of this document on the Chinese delegates to the 1928 meeting is uncertain, as they dealt with a different aspect of the issue at Jerusalem. The focus of Clark's paper was on the 'construction' (that is, the opening of new work in unworked areas) of an indigenous church on 'Three-Self' principles.[88] The Chinese delegates to Jerusalem dealt on the other hand with the manner in which the mission and missionaries should relate to the established Chinese church, advocating that the time for two parallel organizations, the mission and the indigenous church, was past. Missionaries should work as members of the church rather than representatives of the mission boards. Property held in trust should be handed over to the complete control of the Chinese church.[89]

The extent of the correspondence between the key ideas of Clark's booklet and the policy followed by the BEM from 1939 is certainly interesting and warrants close study. Clark insists that the key objective of any mission should be the pursuit of a single purpose, which he defined as the establishment of 'Native Churches', and all other mission agencies or activities, that is, education and medicine, were to be coordinated to achieve this goal.[90] He urges that the indigenous church should be prepared for independence from the very beginning.[91] He warns that no cumbersome institutions should be created that

---

[86] *Tambaram Meeting of the IMC*, II (London/Oxford: Humphrey Milford/Oxford University Press, 1939), 4-34.

[87] *Jerusalem Meeting of the IMC, 1928*, VIII, 5-16; *Tambaram Meeting of the IMC*, VII, 181-202.

[88] Clark was a wealthy Congregationalist layman who was Roland Allen's patron and friend and recruited him to work for the proposed Survey Application Trust and its publishing arm, the World Dominion Press. Sidney J.W. Clark, *The Indigenous Church* (London: World Dominion Press, 1928), 17. See Long and Rowthorn, 'The Legacy of Roland Allen', 65-68.

[89] Yates, *Christian Mission in the Twentieth Century*, 67.

[90] Clark, *The Indigenous Church*, 12-14; 33-36. See Chapter 6.

[91] Clark, *The Indigenous Church*, 15-16. See Chapter 6. The intention was that BEM tried to organize the indigenous church for independence as early and as quickly as possible.

would either absorb the time of the missionaries or be difficult to transfer to the church when the missionaries leave.[92] He recommends that mission policy should ensure that all Christian communities, however small, should have no lack of leaders, and should have the necessary resources to stand on their own feet.[93] The missionary's main task, according to Clark, was to distinguish natural leaders, give them the fullest opportunities to lead, encourage and support them in their leadership; conversely, the most difficult challenge for the missionary was to get out of the way of the indigenous leaders.[94] Clark also argues that church buildings should never incur any charge on the foreign mission.[95] Finally he insists that the relation between the mission and the Church is one of inter-dependence, not dependence or independence.[96] The close resemblance of Clark's ideas to Roland Allen's may mean that the former were either overshadowed by or filtered through the latter's ideas to the BEM. This may be one explanation of the failure of the BEM literature to make any reference to Clark.

The BEM may have been directly influenced by Allen's writings, notably his Missionary Methods: St. Paul's or Ours? (1912), his Pentecost and the World (1917), which was later reprinted as The Ministry of the Spirit, and his The Spontaneous Expansion of the Church (1927). However, there is no mention of his works in BEM literature prior to WWII. The first clear reference appeared in the BEM newsletter of December 1953, where Young advocated Allen's exposition of the Apostle Paul's church-planting methods: 'He (Paul) planted local churches, which became self-governing, self-supporting and self-extending'.[97]

There is still another and rather more plausible possibility: the influence of Nash. According to Alan Belcher, the second Field Director of the BEM, 'Nash was teaching Roland Allen's ideas in MBI'.[98] If Belcher is right, it is probable that Nash was familiar with Allen's ideas during the 1920s, but the issue of when he started teaching these ideas at MBI is uncertain. No further evidence has been uncovered to resolve this question. Also, as an evangelical Anglican clergyman, Nash would certainly have known of Venn's theory of the 'Three-

---

[92] Clark, *The Indigenous Church*, 14-15. See Chapter 6, and *BEM NL*, October 1952, 2.
[93] Clark, *The Indigenous Church*, 13, 19-24, 27-32. 'Steps should be taken to see that local churches make provision for themselves to take financial responsibility'. See *BEM NL*, October 1952, 2.
[94] Clark, *The Indigenous Church*, 28-30, 40. See Chapter 5 and Chapter 6.
[95] Clark, *The Indigenous Church*, 30. The BEM provided no funds for local church buildings. See Chapter 8.
[96] Clark, *The Indigenous Church*, 20-21. See Chapter 6.
[97] *BEM NL*, December 1953, 1. See Chapter 6 for further discussion on Allen.
[98] Interview with Alan Belcher, 29-30 October 2004. Belcher was the Field Director of the BEM from 1948 to 1968. Prior to joining the BEM, he was an active member of the Crusader Union of Victoria, of which he was a Committee member, and as a faithful helper of Nash at St. Martin's Mission, Melbourne. See *BEM NL*, April 1940, 5.

Self' church. He could have understood that Allen's principles represented a development and modification of Venn's theory. This possibility makes good sense and is worthy of further investigation.

However, if Nash had been teaching Allen's ideas at MBI in the 1920s, why is it that the 1928 provisional constitution of the BEM made no mention of the formation of a 'Three-Self' church as its objective instead of the more general 'formation of a Christian church from among them'? It needs to be remembered that the BEM was rather hastily formed in 1928, and even the organization had not been fully worked out.[99] As its constitution was meant to be provisional, it is to be expected that details of the organization of the indigenous church were to be spelt out as the situation demanded. It is quite possible that the idea of the 'Three-Self' was implicit in their stated original objective, but was only given fuller exposition in the 1939 statement. By 1939, the occasion demanded specific provision for the organization and structure of the indigenous church. Only from that date does the evidence permit us to speak with certainty of a mission that was explicitly committed to 'Three-Self' principles.

It is significant that the period between late 1920s and late 1930s was a time when the idea of establishing indigenous 'Three-Self' churches was mediated globally through the IMC meeting of Jerusalem. Within this milieu, it seems most likely that the notion of the 'Three-Self' church came through Allen's ideas, adopted by the BEM through Nash's influence and later expounded by Young.

The BEM's objective was to be fulfilled through the kind of Christianity that characterized it (see Chapter 3), namely, an evangelical basis of faith combining Keswick spirituality with a missionary ethos which closely resembled that of the CIM. In the following section, we will explore issues relating to a) the leadership, control and authority of the BEM, b) the faith principle, and c) the role of married couples and women missionaries.

Leadership, Control and Authority

At the time of its establishment on 31st August 1928, the BEM consciously patterned itself on the CIM, then the most successful evangelical missionary organization in the world, adopting its faith principle,[100] form of government and conservative evangelical doctrinal basis. Though adapted from that of the

[99] 'July 14. After much prayer, the feeling was unanimous that we must quietly follow the Lord's leading step by step rather than develop any complete organization at present'. See 'An Outline of Events leading up to the Formation of a Borneo Fellowship' in BEM Home Council Minute Book, 1928.

[100] The clause on Support in the BEM Constitution stated that, 'The Mission looks to God alone for the supply of all its needs, no appeals for financial aid or collections being made by or authorized by the Mission. No more is to be expended than is received by the Mission, going into debt being considered inconsistent with the principle of entire dependence on God'.

CIM,[101] the doctrinal basis was in reality closer to that of MBI, a CIM-sponsored Bible college.[102] It was almost identical to that of MBI, both in structure and wording. The MBI doctrinal basis has been attributed to C.H. Nash.[103]

The organizational structure of the BEM as originally envisaged was to place home members under the Home Council and missionaries under the authority of the Field Conference. The role of the home members was to build a sufficiently strong base among those who had a desire to pray for Borneo and support the missionaries sent there.[104] The suggested leadership structure of the Mission was that there should be a Field Director and a Home Director, each with an Advisory Council. Decisions were to be consensual with the intention of attaining unanimity and the Field Director (who would be the General Director) held the final decision.[105] This reflected very much the CIM model of control by the General Director in the field, but realising that it was premature 'to develop a complete organization at present', the 4 July meeting of the Borneo Fellowship agreed that, as a temporary measure, the Home Council should be supreme.[106] Subsequently, Henderson was appointed as leader of the pioneering team, a decision that was understandable as the three pioneer missionaries were regarded as young and inexperienced.

---

[101] See Southwell, *Uncharted Waters*, 62-63. 'This original constitution was a simple document based on the principles and practices of the China Inland Mission, but adapted to our start-up situation'.

[102] Members had to subscribe to a) the divine inspiration and supreme authority of all the Scripture of the Old and New Testaments; b) the Triune Godhead, Father, Son and Holy Spirit; c) the twofold nature of our Lord Jesus, God and Man, His Virgin Birth, vicarious death and bodily resurrection, His eternal Deity, His present Majesty, his future coming in Glory; and d) the fall of man and his consequent moral depravity and need of regeneration. Justification by faith through the substitutionary death of Christ. Sanctification by the Holy Spirit. Resurrection of the body, both of the just and unjust. Eternal life of true believers and eternal punishment of disbelievers. See *Minutes of Borneo Fellowship meeting*, 1 September 1928.

[103] See Bible College of Victoria (BCV) Faculty Handbook 2002, 12. The note in the Faculty Handbook on the Statement of Faith reads, 'The...Statement of Faith...is included in the College Articles of Association and was drafted by the founding Principal C.H. Nash'. MBI has been renamed BCV.

[104] There would be two types of members—field members and home members—in the ratio of one field member to every ten home members so as to make the home base sufficiently strong.

[105] 'Around each Director, there would be Advisory Councils and decisions would be made by the Director without formal motions, the desire being to attain unanimity, the final decision however would lie with the Field Director, who would be the General Director'. See 'An Outline of Events Leading to the Formation of a Borneo Fellowship' in Minute Book of the BEM Home Council 1928 (BCV).

[106] No clear decision was made regarding the role of the Home Director. At the 4 July meeting, those present included Nash, Tregaskis, Tolley, Southwell and Davidson. See Southwell, *Unpublished Memoirs*, 14.

This difference from CIM practice meant that the BEM was to be initially home-led.[107] The Home Council was responsible 'to direct and supervise all affairs of the Mission except so far as provision is made under its authority for local administration', to 'receive and account for all moneys and gifts' and to be 'generally responsible for the well being and progress of the Mission'. The daily administration in the Field was in the hands of the Field Executive, comprising the Field Secretary and an Executive Committee,[108] and answerable to the Field Conference, whose consent was required 'for all operations on the Field'.[109] The Council was to appoint a Field Secretary, who under the direction of the Executive Committee would report fully the progress of affairs on the field. There was clear provision for the subsequent transfer of final control and government to the General Director, assisted by an Advisory Council at a time judged desirable and practicable by a Council meeting with a three-fourths majority of all existing members.[110]

The original understanding of the supremacy of the Home Council as a temporary measure, with no time-frame for the transfer of power, was a recipe for later conflict between the Home Council and the Field Conference. This conflict began five years after the beginning of the mission. At this time, there was some personal unhappiness at the unsympathetic way in which the Council had handled a few matters: there was a marriage request from Davidson.[111] Also, the Council was perceived to be unable to fulfill its promise to advise on Young's trip back to Australia after he went to Sarawak in October 1934.[112] Moreover, the missionaries perceived an 'increase of authority from the home end' and Nash's letter to Southwell 'indicates a very real recognition of that and desires that such (that is, Nash's authority) should be recognized on the

---

[107] The BEM Home Council consisted originally of 'ten foundation members' and 'no less than five members shall be resident in Australia'.

[108] As an interim measure, the Field Secretary functioned more as a coordinator between the Field Conference and the Home Council, and he did not have the same powers as the Field Director.

[109] In the pre-war years, the Field Executive and Field Conference was one and the same body owing to the small number of missionaries in the field. The post-war years saw the separation of the two bodies.

[110] *Minutes of Borneo Fellowship Meeting*, 1 September 1928 (BCV).

[111] *BEM Home Council Minutes*, 28 February 1934, 2-3. Davidson made his special request to be married to Enid Gray and to go out together on 8 April 1934. Special meetings of Council with Davidson took place on 13 and 20 March 1934, but his request was turned down. At the 20 March 1934 meeting, when asked about the relationship between him and the Council, he was honest enough to say that though he agreed to comply with their decision, he could not affirm that he had entire confidence in the Council. He had not much of a choice but to comply; otherwise the Council would 'not accept responsibility for recommending his return to Borneo'. This was a beginning of his unhappiness with the Council.

[112] *BEM Field Conference Minutes*, 28-29 June 1935, 2. In the view of the missionaries, the Home Council failed to keep its promise to give its advice through cable by 27 April 1935.

Field'.[113] These feelings among the missionaries were generally directed particularly at Nash and Tregaskis.

The tussle for the control of the Mission rested on a mismatch of perspectives. For the missionaries, it related to trust in, and proper recognition of their abilities by the Home Council, especially its senior members. The missionaries felt that their maturity and ability to lead were not duly recognized, nor were they treated as equals, hence, the perception that the Council was strengthening its authority rather than relinquishing it to the field. The Field Conference also felt that they were in a better position than Home Council members, who had no experience or exposure to the field, to appraise the 'conditions, needs and problems of the Mission sufficiently (so as) to govern the Mission well', and also that, 'nine tenths of the work and problems … are at its seat of operations'. For the work to expand and grow, they argued, the government of the Mission must be focused in and around the scene of action. On the other hand, the Home Council felt that it was still premature for the BEM to be fully field-directed, particularly when the missionaries themselves had great difficulties in working cooperatively in the field.[114]

The missionaries' fear that the Home Council under Nash's control did not seem to show any intention to relinquish or transfer control to the field in the foreseeable future meant that the Field Conference had to make as strong a demand for control as possible. It is common for pioneer missionaries with strong character to want greater control in order to chart the direction of their work. Their unsaid view was that the more the BEM approximated to the CIM, the more successful it would be. But owing to the democratic style of the Field Conference, field control in the pre-war years did not fully materialize in the way the pioneers envisaged, that is, to have a field leader whom all could respect. The missionaries were all strong-willed individuals, and every one saw himself as no less capable than his peers in leadership quality.[115]

The precipitating incident that resulted in hastening this process of the transfer of power was the question raised by Tregaskis, the Treasurer, at the Home Council meeting on 10 April 1934. It related to the nature and

---

113 'Notes on Statement on Financial Methods', *BEM Home Council*, 8 May 1934. According to the minutes, Tolley made this comment to Nash in his letter to Southwell. That letter is untraceable.

114 Responding to the Field Conference Memorandum for Home Council meeting, 11 February 1936, Nash and other senior members of the Council felt that the move for the Mission to be fully field directed was still premature. See Lees, *Drunk before Dawn*, 77. Also, they felt that the missionaries were still unable to make clear consensual decisions. Even after three years, Mrs Hopkins in the 6 July 1939 Home Council meeting commented: 'I have been troubled by the fact that there has been no proper control. It seemed that each one (missionary) wanted to do what he wished and to work where he wished. There has been much moving about. The Conference has had its own views, but the individual has determined his field'.

115 See below in this chapter.

implementation of the 'faith principle', which will be discussed later in this chapter.[116] The issue at stake was whether, in making known the needs of the mission to their home constituency, the BEM could still be said to affirm the 'faith principle'. The Field Conference felt that the Home Council had departed from the principle on which BEM was founded by wanting to make their needs known. Hence, the Conference took a unanimous decision in October 1934 which amounted to a vote of no confidence in the leadership of Nash. It called for a change in the Council especially in the control of the Council, which they perceived to rest primarily with Nash and Tregaskis. The Conference further implied that Tregaskis was not fully content with the faith policy of the mission, even though Tregaskis' view was that making needs known did not contravene the faith principle. Further, the Field Conference asserted that it should have final authority and the Council should only act as an Advisory Council.[117] Its unilateral action of appointing Home Representatives to coordinate the prayer fellowships, handle money and act as representatives, and Southwell as the Administrative Head on the field for the interim period,[118] was, in effect, an ultimatum to the Home Council to dissolve and approve the transfer of power to the field, which, in principle, the Council did on 11 December 1934.[119] However, it was only on 11 February 1936 that the Home Council resolved to transfer final authority to the Field Conference for a probationary period of three years, after which 'final authority shall pass from the Council to the Field Conference at the end of the term'.[120]

The unilateral decision by the field resulted in all the members of the Council resigning except for three younger members, (McCracken, Trinham and Grice). This crisis paved the way for a set of younger leaders in the Home Council under the leadership of McCracken, a young lawyer from Melbourne, who had been able to relate much better as a peer with the field missionaries and was to provide the much needed discussion and on-going advice on matters relating to the Mission and support for the field.[121]

The final transfer occurred when the Home Council at its 6 July 1939 meeting vested the Field Conference with final authority, after the three-year probationary period had expired.[122] In fact the Conference had already

---

[116] See below in this chapter.

[117] *BEM Field Conference Minutes*, 25-27 October 1934, 3.

[118] *BEM Field Conference Minutes*, 25-27 October 1934, 9-10.

[119] *BEM Field Conference Minutes*, 26 January 1935, 1. The Home Council on 11 December 1934 agreed to hand over control to the field.

[120] Memorandum Letter for Frank Davidson regarding Council and Home matters, 28 July 1938.

[121] McCracken, *Summing Up*, 145-47. His regular correspondence with the various Field Directors was a hallmark of his role as Chairman of the Council through his long service.

[122] *BEM Home Council Minutes*, 6 July 1939, 1. In the words of McCracken, the Chairman, 'Personally, I cannot see how we can do anything else but to give the Field

recognized that the governance of the Mission was clumsy and indecisive[123] with the result that, by December 1937, an executive committee comprising Southwell, Young and Bewsher had been formed to take decisions between conferences, though these decisions needed to be ratified by the next conference.[124] Under the new Constitution drawn up in 1939, the Field Conference was supreme. It was to meet once in every two years and elect from its members an executive committee and a chairman or alternatively delegate the election of its chairman to such a committee.[125] The Home Council 'was to direct and supervise all affairs of the Mission in so far as they relate to Australia and New Zealand'.[126]

Mr. Harold McCracken, President of the BEM Home Council (left) and Dr. Bill Lees

The transfer of authority to the field, a process under way since December 1935, did not, however, lessen the problems that existed in the field among the pioneer missionaries. Earlier differences in opinion concerned field administration and distribution of funds among the missionaries. With regard to

control'. In the new Constitution, Clauses 3 and 4 were written to ensure that the doctrinal basis and faith principle of support became 'unalterable'. Despite McCracken expressing doubts as to whether this was legally possible, there was no objection to its inclusion.

[123] *BEM Field Conference Minutes*, 30 August 1937, 6-7. There was discussion on whether to scrap the Conference and have a leader who could make the necessary decisions or to have a Committee if there was no leader. In Field Conference Memorandum Letter to Frank Davidson regarding Council and Home matters, 28 July 1938, an executive committee and a Chairman who would manage the Mission were advocated.

[124] See *Field Conference Minutes*, 31 December 1937, 1.

[125] See 'Statement of the Character, Principles and Practice of the BEM' (1939).

[126] *Home Council Minutes*, 6 July 1939, 2.

field administration, there were two opposing views: Tolley held that every worker had 'complete independence' to 'look to God for guidance in service and be responsible only to Him', whereas Davidson and Southwell maintained that 'in a mission, such independence is not the best method, but that final responsibility for the work must rest elsewhere, both for coordination and control'. There was unanimity in decision about field administration among the missionaries only after Tolley resigned in 1938.

With regard to distribution of funds, two methods were discussed. The first was to distribute funds following a definite system of allowances according to the needs of each station and worker.[127] The second method was to divide all funds equally among all in the field, regardless of the needs or the work undertaken, reserving only a margin for expenses which belonged to the Mission as whole. The former method, that is, the existing practice, was supported by Southwell,[128] and the Home Council,[129] but the Field went ahead with the latter method of equal distribution so that it became the established practice.[130]

The most difficult problem was the selection of a permanent leader. This problem was recognized early by Young, who as vice-president suggested to the Home Council on 31 December 1934 that there should be a rotating system until a permanent leader was recognized.[131] After the transfer of final authority to the Conference in 1939, the understanding was that the office of field chairman or director was to be rotated among the missionaries once every two years.

But without a field director who was able to make final decisions on any matter, and given that any decision in the field according to the Constitution had to be made by consensus, it was only a matter of time before the decision-making process faced serious problems. Problems which had surfaced early in the work continued even after the transfer of authority, as the field missionaries held differing views of their work. Southwell had seen itinerant work as essential for extending the work further afield and advocated the identification of sites near the villages where missionaries could stay during short visits so

---

[127] That is, for rations, servants, itinerant work and maintenance among others.

[128] Field Report by C.H. Southwell, 5 July 1933. Southwell argued that 'if these modifications became permanent, it would mean some radical changes in the mission'. But it did not come true.

[129] *Home Council Minutes*, 12 December 1933, 2. The Home Council left the decision to those in the field since 'the adoption of any plans must be left to those in authority in the field as they alone are fully conversant with local needs and conditions which may vary from time to time'. In effect, the Home Council merely referred the problem back to the field, even though it expressed a contrary opinion.

[130] Letter of C.H. Southwell to Field Executive, 8 May 1941. Southwell's view did not always prevail and his perceived repercussions on the Mission were exaggerated.

[131] *Home Council Minutes*, 12 February 1935, 1.

that sustained contact could be made.[132] Davidson, on the other hand, felt that as time proceeded, the role of the missionaries should be a settled one with native evangelists bringing the Christian message to the people.[133] The differing approaches reflected their different temperaments and experiences. Southwell, with an outgoing personality, was not one to be confined to work in one station only. His love for adventure and his missionary philosophy gave greater importance to itinerant evangelism than settled work. Moreover, despite his work with the Iban at the head station, Southwell had been unable to start a settled work or a regular school at his station. On the other hand, Davidson had begun to experience the beginnings of a settled work among the Kelabit before he moved to Trusan. At Trusan, he saw the great value of a settled ministry as the centre for training indigenous workers for that region.

When final authority was transferred to the Field Conference in July 1939, Southwell had assumed the position of Field Chairman.[134] In late 1940, while on furlough in Melbourne, he wrote back to ask the other missionaries about his continuing as Chairman after detecting some unhappiness about his leadership.[135] Davidson replied in the negative.

> The Constitution provides for, and I understood that we expected, a change in Chairmanship at least every two years, till such time as the Lord brought us all to one mind about the Chairman being suitable as a permanent leader and/or director. Frankly, I do not think we have reached that stage yet.... To be frank again, if when you return, you found and established a permanent work, more or less as R.A. Bewsher has had at Limpasong, my views of you as being suitable as permanent leader might change.[136]

The implied thrust of Davidson's point was that Southwell was still unable to establish 'a permanent work' so as to achieve the mission objective of starting an indigenous church. On the other hand, Davidson's work was beginning to bear fruit in that direction. Also, given his background as the second son of the managing director of Morgan and Scott, the publishers,[137] Davidson would not have thought of himself as any less a leader than Southwell.

---

[132] Southwell's Field Report to Home Council, 26 April 1933 as attachment to *BEM Home Council Minutes*, 9 May 1933.
[133] *Home Council Minutes*, 13 June 1933, 1.
[134] *Field Conference Minutes*, 23 March 1939, 1. The position of Field Secretary had been rotated among Southwell, Young and Bewsher. Letter of Stafford Young to Field Conference members, 28 March 1939 (OMF). With Southwell at Jesselton, Young was released for the Dusun work at Ranau, Sabah.
[135] Letter of C.H. Southwell to Field Conference, 4 November 1940 (OMF).
[136] Letter of F.T. Davidson to Field Conference, 4 December 1940 (OMF). Enid Davidson wrote an earlier letter on 3 December 1940: 'I think that different ones should hold this position as provided for in the Constitution'.
[137] Lees, *Drunk before Dawn*, 24.

Southwell generally assumed that he would continue as Chairman and leader of the Mission, working from headquarters but being 'mobile', visiting all parts of the work. His priority of work was as follows: firstly, his responsibility for the administrative work of the mission also meant a measure of freedom of movement; secondly, he had wanted to make itinerant visitations to the Iban; thirdly, there was to be local ministry wherever he might reside.[138] However, the Davidsons believed that the Chairman, like any other field missionary, needed to establish a permanent base, and assumed that a settled work for the Chairman would be the priority. Their over-riding concern, as expressed by Enid Davidson, was that a steady settled ministry should give rise to trained native evangelists and teachers.

> There is the work for which we chiefly came here - the training of native evangelists and teachers. Until we have a house, school and church built, and another worker, we cannot fulfill all these tasks efficiently.[139]

Though Southwell returned to assume the chairmanship, there was an uneasy tension. At the crux of the matter was the decision-making process of the Mission itself. The final locus of decision rested with the Field Conference, in which every field member had an equal voice. As decisions had to be by consensus, it proved a very difficult task for a Chairman whose decision could be overturned. To overcome this problem, Young proposed a trial period of five years for Southwell to have a free hand to govern the Mission. He knew that without a leader who had final decision-making powers, the situation often reached an impasse with 'each one voicing his conviction from time to time and voting in Conference'.[140] This issue remained a thorny and unresolved one among the pre-war missionaries, which was only shelved by the interruption of WWII. In the post-war era, Belcher was elected the second Field Director in 1948 and remained in that position for twenty years, while Southwell subsequently resigned from the BEM in 1955.

The Faith Principle

Since the BEM's inception, the faith principle of solely depending on God without making financial needs known, had been held as a sacred given.[141] When funds were low, it could not be assumed that there would not be a re-evaluation of the principle or mounting pressure on the missionaries to share their needs. When there was an inadvertent sharing of needs (that is, the

---

[138] Letter of C.H. Southwell to Field Conference, 24 April 1941 (OMF).

[139] Letter of Enid Davidson to Field Executive, 6 August 1940 (OMF).

[140] Letter of Stafford Young to Field Conference, 23 June 1941 (OMF). Commenting on the existing situation, Young said 'Conference governs and unfortunately quite often with a divided vote. There is no mandate for any one member'.

[141] See Fiedler, *The Story of Faith Missions*, 55, for the origin of the faith principle in faith missions.

cancellation of the missionaries' return passage due to a lack of funds) in 1958,[142] a public apology was made with a strong affirmation in the faith principle. Any departure from this policy, according to Belcher, was tantamount to saying, 'God is not faithful'.[143]

It has been mentioned in the last section that there were two understandings of this faith principle. The Field Conference held that depending solely on God meant not making their needs known publicly, that is affirming the 'pure' faith principle. The Home Council, however, did not view making needs known as contravening the faith principle. Since BEM started in 1928, it had generally been short of the budgeted funds. At the Council meeting of 10 April 1934, Tregaskis, a missionary with the SSEM before becoming Secretary of MBI, expressed the view that sharing of needs with a large circle of prayer partners was not contrary to the faith principle.[144] Further, he pointed out that since the inception of the BEM, nearly two-thirds of the financial needs of the Mission had been given by members of the Council because they knew the needs. Though he advocated that specific needs of the missionaries and the Mission be made known,[145] he also felt that even when needs were shared, God could still withhold the supply.[146] His concern stemmed from the few situations where the constituency may have been given the wrong impression that the needs of the missionaries had been adequately supplied, when it was not. For example, in the case of the return fare for Tolley's furlough, there was a shortfall of £24. Further, both Aitken and Bewsher at Limpasong had taken £40 from their personal allowances to defray the cost of the new building with the indication that a further £25 was still needed.[147] As for contributions sent directly to the

---

142 *BEM NL* August-September, 1958, 1. Earlier in 1940, the possibility of purchasing a bungalow in Jesselton as headquarters was published in the newsletter, and the Field Conference admitted its mistake, promising not to repeat it.

143 *BEM NL*, April-May, 1959, 4.

144 Statement by Treasurer at BEM Home Council meeting, 10 April 1934. On the Council meeting of 10 April 1934, Tregaskis expressed dissatisfaction that 'no statement of financial needs of the Mission was made in the Annual Report, the monthly circulars or to the members of the Prayer Bands'. He further strongly suggested that mention should be made in the next newsletter of the amount still needed to reimburse the Transport Fund for Tolley's passage, a statement every month of receipts and expenditure towards the needs in the field and a statement of any special expenses that may arise from time to time.

145 'Notes on Discussion on Financial Methods', *BEM Home Council Minutes*, 8 May 1934.

146 Tregaskis argued: 'I feel that if the amounts are stated—what we need every month and what has gone forth—if we pray and tell people, God can still withhold it'. It was pointed out to him that if this was done, it would change the original intention of the Mission to be based on faith lines, and a constitutional change would be required. See 'Notes on Discussion on Financial Methods', 8 May 1934.

147 Statement by Treasurer at Home Council meeting 10 April 1934. At the Home Council meeting of 8/5/1934, it was reported that in the past four months, only £73 were sent to Borneo whereas the lowest possible amount required for effective work was

missionaries by supporters, Tregaskis received reports that 'the amounts some have received have been very small indeed, almost negligible'. Thus, contrary to what many might expect, the objections to the 'pure' faith principle approach came from those who knew the needs and had repeatedly supplied the funds. But the suggestion by Tregaskis to make financial needs known was understood by the missionaries as a departure from the original intention of the Mission to operate along faith lines.[148]

The Council was seemingly faced with two options, either to maintain absolute silence in relation to the needs of the Mission and take no responsibility for the full support of the missionaries on the field, or to view the Mission as contractually obliged to support the missionaries on the field. But the Council was itself divided, with the more senior members, who formed the majority, opting for making needs known.

Surprisingly, the missionaries unanimously maintained in 1934 that there should be absolute silence on financial needs and an entire dependence on God, affirming the 'pure' faith principle. For them, it was a question of reviewing the spiritual state of the Mission not their financial practice.[149] The suggestion that the shortage of funds was God's indictment on the Mission to set its house in order, and that even the Home Council should not know the details of the finances, was offensive to the Council members. The subsequent decisions taken by the Field Conference, as discussed earlier, served to provoke their resignation.

The implementation of this principle must be understood within the framework of the social background of missionaries and the local lifestyle in Sarawak. Generally, the early missionaries had come from, or were connected to well-to-do families, and had access to some personal private means.[150] In addition, having adapted to the lifestyle in Sarawak, they could live off the land and, from time to time, would receive gifts of agricultural produce from the

£160. 'Prior to this, the amounts had been a little better, but never in the history of the Mission (with the exception of the first two years) had they been able to send forward the full amount of £10 per missionary per month'.

[148] This issue was raised about two years earlier and the faith principle was reaffirmed. See *Home Council Minutes*, 14 March 1933, 2. But, when this was raised again in 1934, it was perceived by the missionaries that some Council members, particularly Nash and Tregaskis were unhappy with the faith principle of the Mission. See *Field Conference Minutes*, 25-27 October 1934, 2.

[149] In response to Tregaskis' Statement of 10 April 1934, Young wrote to the Home Council saying that their present predicament of low funds was God's way of telling them: 'Set your house in order'. He also said: 'My *preference* would be rather to keep back the knowledge from 100% of the people'. In the discussion, Council members were led to the perception that the field missionaries did not even want them to know of the financial situation of the Mission. See *Home Council Minutes*, 6 July 1939, 2.

[150] Young had offered a generous sum to purchase a bungalow in Jesselton as the BEM headquarters in 1940. He was able to fly home on furlough in 1940. See *Field Conference Minutes*, 28-31 December 1940, 5.

indigenous people among whom they worked and also food parcels from friends in Australia.[151] Conversely, the Home Council members who functioned in a cash-based economy would have difficulty appreciating the fact that the missionaries could live reasonably well on a rather low budget in rural Sarawak, except for capital expenditures of the Mission and larger sums of money needed for return passages for missionaries going on furlough.[152]

After the transfer of final control to the Field Conference in 1939, there had been a dire shortage of funds, and a sum of eight hundred dollars was placed in the Reserve Fund.[153] Realising the need for funds in case of sickness and furlough, the missionaries agreed to contribute ten per cent of their monthly allowance to the Sickness and Furlough Fund.[154] So when a missionary went on furlough after four years, there would be sufficient money. Also, there was a monthly allocation from the General Fund (when it had an excess of two hundred dollars) to the Sickness and Furlough Fund. This practice became the norm and was given high priority.[155] In effect, a subtle change in the thinking of the Field Conference had taken place which was not seen as contradictory to the 'pure' faith principle. Earlier, the missionaries had looked to God alone 'for all and every specific need but by 1939, the shift had been to look to God alone to supply 'all that was needed for the work generally', and the Mission did the necessary allocation towards the needs.

A further shift took place in 1959 when adherence to the faith principle did not preclude imparting news about the faithfulness of God in providing for capital expenditure on new Bible school lecture rooms, the gift of a new generator, and a generous gift toward the purchase of a new aircraft. The newsletter also mentioned the priority given to allocating funds for the Sickness and Furlough Fund, and gave testimony of answered prayer to two specific gifts that met the cost of a new block of Bible school accommodation.[156] Nor earlier in 1941, was it felt wrong to mention the rising cost of living on the field as a

---

[151] It was a BEM practice to send off new missionaries with the necessary essentials and food parcels, which continued with individual missionaries receiving food parcels on occasions. Canned foods like ham and jams were the usual items sent to them.

[152] The monthly living allowance of $60 in 1941 was enough to sustain an indigenous family of at least three people, and it did not include child allowance, which was a quarter of the paid allowance to each missionary. A couple was paid as two missionaries.

[153] *Field Conference Minutes*, 27 December 1939, 3. Other funds included the General Fund and the Transport Fund which had a healthy credit balance of $908.00 at 26 December 1936.

[154] *Field Conference Minutes*, 28-31 December 1940, 1. The idea of a 'Sickness and Furlough Fund' was first mooted in the December Field Conference meeting of 1936.

[155] The rationale was that 'there is never the possibility of a sick missionary not being able to travel home immediately or for a family on early leave'. See 'Our Financial Policy', *BEM NL*, April-May 1959, 4.

[156] *BEM NL*, April-May 1959, 4.

result of WWII.[157] So the shift in understanding meant that it was not wrong to provide factual information so long as no specific need was mentioned.

Single Men, Single Women and Families

In the initial years at Sungai Pranga, much of the missionaries' time was engaged in constructing a more permanent home for themselves, language learning and befriending the neighbouring people. The advantage of having single young men in constructing houses at the base or outstations was obvious. During the years when the pioneers were all single men, people came to them out of curiosity, as they had not seen any white man living among their midst, or they came to get medical help, as there were no government clinics then in the interior.[158] Beyond that, there was little response. There were disadvantages for single men. Since they were without wives, the host society could not interpret the intentions of the missionaries as being genuine and peaceful; hence, a certain amount of cautiousness. Such an attitude was reflected in Southwell's words when Winsome Howell joined him after their marriage:

> I was happy beyond words to have Winsome with me at last, and her presence also had a positive effect upon others. Her arrival in Sungai Pranga was an indication to the people that we had come to live among them permanently.[159]

Moreover, single men could have been exposed to the risk of sexual temptation and moral impropriety.[160] It was no secret that many officers in the Rajah's administrative service had mistresses. Even the Resident of the Fourth Division, who was also in charge of the Fifth Division, had two local mistresses. He fathered a son from one and he married the second later.[161] Viewed from this angle, the Home Council's encouragement of the pioneer missionaries to get married was a prudent one; hence Southwell returned to Australia to marry Winsome and came back to head the mission base at Sungai Pranga in 1932.[162]

---

[157] *Field Conference Minutes*, 3 December 1941, 1. 'Costs of essential foods and services have risen considerably…some items have risen two, some three, or even four times the pre-war prices. So, the present cost of living and travelling is much higher than it was before the war'.

[158] Southwell, *Uncharted Waters*, 37.

[159] Southwell, *Uncharted Waters*, 68.

[160] See Deborah Kirkwood, '"Protestant Missionary Women": Wives and Spinsters', in Fiona Bowie, D. Kirkwood, and S. Ardener (eds.), *Women and Missions: Past and Present* (Oxford: Berg Publishers, 1993), 26.

[161] J.B. Archer, *Glimpses of Sarawak between 1916 and 1946* (Hull: Department of SEA Studies, University of Hull, 1997), xv.

[162] Southwell, *Uncharted Waters*, 65-67. Southwell was engaged to Winsome Howell just before he left for Sarawak. His recall in December 1931 to be married was obviously a delight to him. They were married in April 1932 and returned to Borneo in June 1932.

In the initial stages, it seemed impractical to have single women working in a context where there were three single men living in rather cramped and difficult conditions for over a year before they could move into their more permanent house.[163] The acceptance of single women missionaries required the work of the Mission to have expanded sufficiently to accommodate them in a proper base with appropriate accommodation and to give them a clear idea of their sphere of work; all three requirements were still unfulfilled. As a result, two applications from single women (Miss Bicker and Miss Wilson) in 1930 were turned down with the reply that there was no present likelihood of single women candidates in the field, other than 'those with special qualifications'.[164]

What did the Home Council mean by saying that women with special qualifications were required in the field? Basically, the Home Council gave priority and encouragement to the missionaries to be married to their fiancées first before any further consideration could be given to single women missionaries. Not only would their presence among single men in the field present difficulties, but there was also the issue of their safety and protection.[165] The preference was for husband-and-wife teams. Each person was to have a sphere of ministry that complemented the other's. This model was later adopted by the indigenous workers. By mid-1934, the Home Council envisaged that the work should have five missionaries, four of whom should be married and occupy outposts.[166] This decision subsequently resulted in all the pioneer missionaries, Southwell, Davidson, Tolley as well as Bewsher, getting married and concentrating on different geographical locations of the Limbang valley, with Southwell at the head-station in Sungai Pranga.[167]

---

[163] Lees, *Drunk before Dawn*, 35. The three missionaries shared a small palm-leaf shelter, measuring ten feet by twelve.

[164] *Home Council Minutes*, 1 August 1930, 1 (Miss Bicker); 2 March 1931, 1 (Miss Wilson).

[165] There were objections to sending single women missionaries to the field. Peter Williams in 'The Recruitment of Women Missionaries' in *Women and Missions: Past and Present*, 43-69, lists the following: a) women tempted the men missionaries (49); b) it was unbiblical to use women to convert and teach men (52); c) women missionaries needed European male protection in a hostile indigenous country, where they would be exposed to excessive danger (52-53); and d) some women missionaries might have looked forward to forging marriage relationships, which they were unable to do at home (62).

[166] *Home Council Minutes*, 10 July 1934, 1-2. Also, the Council would not place any barrier in the way of either Davidson or Tolley to be married and have their wives in the field.

[167] All the single women missionaries accepted by the Mission before 1940 became wives of the field missionaries; first Winsome Howell was married to Southwell (1932), then Enid Gray to Davidson (1935), Florence Thomson to Tolley (1935) and Mary Black to Bewsher (1939).

In regard to missionary wives, the BEM adopted the CIM principle that they were full missionaries, sharing the work alongside their husbands.[168] This meant that missionary wives were generally expected to undergo similar training as the men. Subsequently, the women candidates, such as Winsome Howell and Enid Gray, went for training at MBI before they were allowed to get married. Hence, when Davidson was on furlough in Melbourne, his request to marry Enid without her going for any training and leave for Borneo by April 1934, was not acceptable to the Council.[169]

Until 1938, the BEM did not seriously consider recruiting single women, except for those who were fiancées of serving missionaries.[170] This issue was raised again by the Home Council in early 1938. The Field Conference discussed the matter and recognized that (a) two single women would be better than one, (b) single women were cited as some of the most valuable workers in other missionary fields, but that (c) their present difficulty was a proper place for their training. The Field Conference agreed that it would accept applicants from single women for consideration, even though there appeared no immediate sphere of service for them.[171] Shortly afterwards, Mary Black's application was approved and she worked alongside the Davidsons before subsequently marrying Bewsher.[172] Despite showing much promise, the next female applicant, Winnie C. Mills,[173] was rejected because of her active association with Pentecostalism.[174] Though recognising that there was a need

---

[168] A.J. Broomhall, *Hudson Taylor and China's Open Century* (Sevenoaks: Hodder & Stoughton, 1988), IV, 234. Taylor had written to missionary candidates with this advice: 'Unless you intend your wife to be a *true* missionary, not merely a wife, home-maker and friend, do not join us'.

[169] *Home Council Minutes*, 28 February 1934, 1-2.

[170] The decision after Perrin's case was not to accept any single unmarried woman. *BEM Home Council Minutes*, 9 February 1932. See Letter of BEM Home Council to M. Perrin, 16 March 1932 (OMF). 'But as experience has accumulated it has been needful from time to time to alter and amend our methods, and there is...no one either on the Home Council or in the field who favours the attempt to maintain *unmarried* women in the work at the present time or foresees any early prospect of their useful employment there'.

[171] *Field Conference Minutes*, 9 March 1938, 4.

[172] *Field Conference Minutes*, 25-28 July 1938, 3; 27 October-4 November 1938, 1; and 11 January 1939, 2. By this time, the Tolleys had resigned, which meant that she had to be with either the Southwells or the Davidsons. Black had met Bewsher in Newcastle, N.S.W., when he was on furlough in late 1936 and a romance had begun then. See Letter of the Bewshers to BEM, 8 January 1940. Quoted in Porritt, *Bapak Guru Orang Bisaya*, 30.

[173] *Home Council Minutes*, 6 July 1939, 7.

[174] *Home Council Minutes*, 2 November 1939, 1. Letter of Winnie C. Mills to Harold McCracken, 12 October 1939 (OMF), setting forth her Pentecostal convictions. See also *Field Executive (Inaugural Meeting) Minutes*, 27 December 1939, 1. The Field Conference concurred with the Home Council's decision, though with 'great regret at losing the prospect of one who seemed likely to be a promising and valuable worker'.

for a single woman worker working alongside a married couple, the preference was still for a man, especially when the work at Trusan necessitated an additional worker in 1940 to relieve Frank Davidson's work in the interior.[175] The general view was that there was limited scope for single women missionaries. In September 1940, the issue of single woman was kept very much alive with another application from a Miss Bowd. Bewsher was prepared to have a single woman missionary at Limpasong.[176] The Mission's understanding of the issue broadened to allow for two single women occupying a station. Davidson expressed his view as follows:

> As units, there seems to be little scope for them with the Mission's present outlook and method of working. But, in pairs they could exert a very special ministry, more especially if one could be an experienced nurse and the other a school teacher. In Lawas or Trusan they could have a big ministry without the need of much travelling. Such a pair could occupy Limpasong if R.A.B (i.e. Bewsher) should go to the Tutong to open a station there. They could take over here (i.e. Trusan) if in the future we move to Lawas to start the Tagal work and to be more central.[177]

The general agreement was that while there was limited scope for a single woman, she could work under a senior married couple at a station, at a central Bible school, or as part of a pair at a settled outstation. With this understanding, Miss Bowd was accepted, but was prevented from going to Borneo because of WWII.[178] Subsequently, this understanding of the role of single women missionaries became the accepted mission policy in the post-war years.

---

[175] Letter of F.T. Davidson to Field Executive, 3 August 1940 (OMF). A decision was made by October 1940. See Letter of R.A. Bewsher to F.T. Davidson, 28 October 1940 (OMF). 'It is decided that your station is to be staffed with another European worker, *preferably a male*, and a likely candidate is under consideration by Home Council'. The male candidate was Brian Morcombe. See Letter of C.H. Southwell to F.T. Davidson and Field Executive, 17 September 1940 (OMF).

[176] Letter of R.A. Bewsher to Field Conference, 12 December 1940 (OMF). He was willing to have Miss Bowd.

[177] Letter of F.T. Davidson to Field Conference, 4 December 1940 (OMF).

[178] Letter of Strafford Young to Field Conference, 1 October 1941 (OMF). 'Now the war looks as if it will prevent her from coming out for some time'. By August 1941, the BEM Field headquarters received a notification from the Chief Secretary advising the evacuation of all European women and children from Sarawak. See Letter of R.A. Bewsher to C.H. Southwell, 16 August 1941 (OMF). In view of the slowness in communications and not knowing the situation in Sarawak, Miss Bowd had indicated that she was ready to leave for Sarawak by end September 1941. See *Home Council Minutes*, 22 September 1941, 1.

The Japanese Occupation and the Rise of Indigenous Leaders

The Japanese Occupation of Sarawak, which began in December 1941, disrupted the work of the BEM missionaries, who were forced to withdraw into the interior, where they continued their work until they were captured or forced to surrender. Despite this difficulty, there were positive long-term effects for the BEM. Close ties were forged with the Europeans from both the public and private sectors. The BEM missionaries were instrumental in evacuating some of them into the interior. Mr McLaren of Lawas Rubber Estates joined the group under Davidson and Brian Morcombe and withdrew into the interior of the Trusan.[179] The other group under the Southwells had Mrs Anderson, the wife of Jim Anderson, the Resident of Limbang, and several European planters with them. They withdrew upriver along the Limbang and arrived at Long Semadoh, where they were warmly welcomed by the locals, much to the disbelief of the accompanying Europeans.[180] The help given to the Europeans and the impressions of their work with the Lun Bawang were not forgotten. After WWII, Anderson was reappointed Resident of Limbang, and was positively predisposed towards the work of the BEM.[181] The Lawas Rubber Estates through the efforts of Mr McLaren gave land to the BEM to build their headquarters at Lawas.[182]

The urgency of the times necessitated intensive teaching of the indigenous leaders in the Christian faith. At the base and school which Davidson hastily set up, representatives of each of the interior churches came and were taught. They copied for themselves the Gospel of Luke, which Davidson had translated for use in their churches.[183]

Further, cooperation between Southwell and John Willfinger of the C&MA resulted in the establishment of a school at Punang Trusan, the translation of the Gospels of Mark and Matthew, the conducting of weekly services and teaching tours among the believers along the upper Matang River. With the demand for the surrender of the BEM missionaries by the Japanese authorities, the Southwells journeyed down, meeting with many Murut believers and conducting farewell services and baptisms for several hundreds of people. Together with the Davidsons, they finally surrendered in September 1942 at Sundar and were taken to Batu Lintang in Kuching.[184]

---

[179] Southwell, *Uncharted Waters*, 112. Edwards and Stevens, *Short Histories*, 50-51.

[180] Southwell, *Uncharted Waters*, 105-16. From the Medihit, they had help in their journey from thirty Lun Bawang Christians from the upper Trusan.

[181] *BEM NL*, May 1947, 6. Brian Morcombe reported a warm welcome by the Andersons at Limbang. See Southwell, *Uncharted Waters*, 184.

[182] *BEM NL*, October 1955, 2. Lees, *Drunk before Dawn*, 107. The land consisted of twenty acres of flat land on which no rubber had been planted. In 1950, the BEM headquarters was sited on this piece of land in Lawas.

[183] *BEM Thirteenth Annual Report*, 31 December 1946, 2. Lees, *Drunk before Dawn*, 68.

[184] *BEM Thirteenth Annual Report*, 31 December 1946, 2. *BEM NL*, November, 1946, 3. Southwell, *Uncharted Waters*, 117-27, 131-34.

The internment of the BEM missionaries at the Batu Lintang Camp meant that the young indigenous churches in the Trusan and Bario had to fend for themselves. This situation was similar to the aftermath of the communist takeover of China in 1949, when the Chinese churches had to continue on their own. The fact that after WWII, the BEM missionaries discovered that these Lun Bawang and Kelabit churches, especially in the upper Trusan and Kelabit Highlands, were thriving implied that indigenous leaders must have arisen to manage the affairs of their churches. In the Trusan, the Lun Bawang village headmen and the deacons, who were generally the more senior men, kept faithful watch over the church members[185] together with those who were trained at the Bible school by Davidson.[186] Among them was Racha Umong, who later became a headman and the first President of the SIB.[187] In the lower Trusan, leaders included headmen Raut and Kading Telau, Lawai and Guru Riong.[188] Also, Selutan, Balang who had trained in the C&MA Bible school in Kalimantan was invited to pastor an interior Lun Bawang church.[189] The remoteness and relative inaccessibility of the interior protected them from harassment by the Japanese authorities.

In the Kelabit Highlands, leaders arose to hold the churches together. The community leaders, such as Penghulu Tama Kulin at Medihit in upper Limbang and headman Tama Bulan at Pa Tarap, played important roles in the churches. According to Southwell, Tama Bulan, having embraced Christianity just prior to WWII, took the initiative to invite Aris Doemat, an Indonesian C&MA pastor from Sulawesi in charge of the interior KINGMI church during the Japanese Occupation to teach the Kelabits the way of the Christian faith.[190] However, according to Robert Lian Saging, in 1940 three young Kelabit, Galih Balang, Balang Riwat and Tama Ingan, who went to study at the C&MA school in Belawit in Dutch Borneo, were converted and returned to teach the Kelabit about Christianity. Galih Balang is said to have then invited his teacher Aris to Pa Tarap, a move which led to the conversion of the Kelabit in Pa Tarap.[191]

---

185 *BEM NL*, April 1964, 2. There were 10 Lun Bawang churches in existence. Some leaders included headmen Raut and Kading Telau, Lawai and Guru Riong in the Trusan. Interview with Stephen Upai Rining at Lawas (22 September 2004). According to Stephen, most of the headmen were the first converts and they both led and taught in the churches in the Lawas district.

186 Interview with Lawai Asi, 21 September 2004. Lawai was the first convert among the schoolboys at Sungai Pranga. He was among those subsequently trained by Davidson, and he moved to Rumah Kading at Long Tukon, Trusan during the Japanese occupation. Both headman Kading Telau and Lawai were leaders and teachers at the church there.

187 Urud, *Datuk Racha Umong*, 44. See Chapter 6.

188 Headman Raut was converted through his visit to Southwell at Sungai Pranga.

189 *BEM NL*, October 1963, 4. Selutan, Balang was later to become the vice-president of the SIB.

190 Southwell, *Uncharted Waters*, 190-91.

191 Saging, 'An Ethno-History of the Kelabit Tribe of Sarawak', 249-50, 279.

Both Southwell and Saging's accounts may well be true as the headman still had to give permission for the invitation to be given to Aris. Major Tom Harrison, the commanding officer of the 'Z' Special Unit forces, acknowledged that 'Aris had continued his work of proselytism throughout the Occupation and with some conspicuous successes...not only consolidated the small beginnings...but powerfully extended it'. Generally, the influence of Aris's brand of American fundamentalism was felt in the indigenous church, which adhered to a very strict Christian ethic.[192] The steadfastness and stability of the Kelabit church at Pa Mein was attributed to the leadership of Mein Ribu, aided by schoolteacher Guru Paul, forming a partnership of a local leader and a teacher.[193] Another person of influence was Guru Pantalusang. As a teacher in the government school in Bario, he also acted as pastor. He later moved to Long Beluyu in the Upper Trusan, preaching and counselling on Sundays and training a choir.[194] With congregations spread over a reasonably large area, indigenous leaders, who were community leaders, pastors or teachers played the vital role of maintaining the communal life of the churches during this period.

The closing years of WWII saw British forces operating from the highlands of the interior among the Orang Ulu of the Fourth and Fifth Divisions to liberate Sarawak from the Japanese. Their style of operation, which was carried out in complete disregard of traditional beliefs and customs, may have had a profound impact on the people. Despite the infringement of customary taboos the Allied Forces won and this may have called into question their indigenous cosmology, caused a re-examination of their lifestyle, and triggered a subsequent mass conversion into Christianity which affected several Christian denominations.[195] The BEM was particularly successful in harnessing these gains in the immediate post-war period.[196]

Conclusion

The early history of the BEM work in Sarawak was characterized mainly by the interaction between Brooke policy and BEM philosophy and practice. The Brooke policy did in fact modify BEM practice so that instead of widespread itinerant evangelism across the region, the mission had little choice but to be content with saturating its assigned area, the Limbang valley, with the Christian

---

[192] Harrisson, *World Within*, 255. Southwell, *Uncharted Waters*, 180. Aris was based at Belawit in Kalimantan when Indonesia declared independence from Netherlands after WWII. Harrisson, who kept a watchful and critical eye on the activities of the BEM, was later to become the Curator of the Sarawak Museum. See also *BEM NL*, November 1946, 3.

[193] *BEM NL*, December 1953, 2-3.

[194] Southwell, *Uncharted Waters*, 179. Lees, *Drunk before Dawn*, 86.

[195] See Chapter 2.

[196] See Chapter 5.

message. In other words, Brooke policy tended to minimize the distinctiveness of the CIM pattern of widespread evangelism, and made the BEM approximate more closely to the other missions than it had originally wished.

The restriction of mission work to a specific area not only sharpened focus of work and strategy, but resulted in a re-evaluation of strategy and sphere of work. The BEM's decision to move its headquarters to Jesselton and start new work in Ranau, British North Borneo, which had been interpreted as moving its sphere of work as well, had the effect of influencing the Brooke government to re-evaluate its position and allow the BEM to set up a base at Trusan. The aggressive approach of BEM's itinerant evangelism, which fostered an outlook that constantly sought for opportunities for the expansion of its work, was to press governmental permission to the limit, a characteristic which will be examined later. This approach continued into the immediate post-war years with positive results for the Mission.[197]

The mission policy of the BEM as first enunciated in 1928 was stated in terms of the establishment of an indigenous church. However, only from 1939 had there been clear evidence that the BEM was explicitly committed to 'Three-Self' principles. As shown, it is impossible to establish conclusively the sources from which the BEM drew its statement of 'Three-Self' principles. The most likely hypothesis is that the BEM's adoption of the 'Three-Self' principles came from the ideas of Roland Allen. Allen's teachings were first mediated, most probably, through the teaching of C.H. Nash at MBI in the 1920s and through Stafford Young in the post-war period. The hasty formation of the BEM in 1928, where the organizational structure was not fully worked out and where the constitution was only provisional meant that there was the expectation to have a fuller constitution when the occasion demanded it. Though it is quite possible that the idea of the 'Three-Self' may be implicit in the 1928 Constitution, it was only in 1939 that the BEM was clearly explicit in its commitment to the 'Three-Self' principles.

The implementation of BEM policies in the field and the resultant experience deriving from it helped to shape BEM practice for the future. First, there was the assignment of, preferably, a married couple to focus work on one people group at a specific geographical location. Then, the pattern that emerged from settled work, which was guided by BEM's original goal of setting up an indigenous church, gave much higher priority to evangelism, Bible school teaching, the selection and training of indigenous leaders and the translation of the Scriptures than medical work and promotion of hygiene, though these were not neglected or absent. Also, the understanding on the use of single women missionaries to aid the existing work of the married couple at a station or to teach at a central Bible school or to work in pairs functioning as a nurse and schoolteacher became the accepted practice in the post-war years.

---

197 See Chapter 5.

The training of indigenous workers, particularly by Bewsher and Davidson, was but a small beginning toward fulfilling the expressed aim of the BEM to establish an indigenous church in Borneo. Further, the small size of the Mission meant that the missionaries had to entrust the work to indigenous leadership. Events such as the Japanese Occupation that threatened the lives of the missionaries or the work of the Mission further impressed upon the missionaries the urgency of the need to train indigenous leaders to establish self-governing, self-supporting and self-propagating churches. Other similar events in the future like the communist takeover of China in 1949 had the effect of urging the BEM in 1950 to formulate the fifteen-year policy. The Brunei revolt and the Indonesian confrontation in the early 1960s began the process of re-evaluation of their policies among a section of the BEM missionaries.[198]

During the Japanese Occupation, indigenous leaders, pastors and teachers took the initiative of holding the churches together. The urgency of the times and the task drew cooperative efforts from indigenous pastors -Aris Doemat, Guru Paul, Guru Pantalusang, and Balan Selutan-trained under the C&MA in Kalimantan. The style in which the indigenous churches operated during the Japanese Occupation was the result of a combination of influences: from the BEM missionaries, there was their model of evangelising, teaching and training; from the KINGMI pastors, there was the model of a laity oriented church and a strict ethical code; and from their own Lun Bawang and Kelabit cultures, there developed an indigenous style of governance as observed in the leadership of men of seniority in the community, often community heads themselves, who had become Christians.

Outside western influence on the Lun Bawang, Kelabit, Kayan and Kenyah during the Japanese Occupation had an impact on their cultures, religions and lifestyles that prepared them to re-examine their own way of life, adjust themselves to the outside world and later embrace Christianity.[199]

The manner of managing the results of mass conversions through the setting up of a settled base for the training of selected indigenous leaders, empowering them for ministry among their people, providing literacy classes, starting Bible schools and translating the Scriptures became the pattern for later BEM practice.

As an evangelical 'faith mission', the BEM was consciously modelled after the CIM, but displayed some modifications from the CIM pattern, whereby the BEM Home Council became the decision-making body as a temporary measure. The transfer of final authority took place in 1939, but not without some upheaval within the Mission. The egalitarian nature of mission membership and the locus of final authority being vested in the Field Conference meant that the field director did not have final decision-making powers, as was the case with the CIM. As a result, the difficulties experienced

---

198 See Chapter 6 for further discussion.

199 See Chapter 5.

in the Field Conference included the inability of accepting one another's view and also accepting Southwell as the permanent leader as there was the appealing idea of a rotating field director. These issues remained largely unresolved, but there was a measure of resolution with the intervention of war and, later, a change of field director in 1948. The BEM practice of having a governing Field Conference with a field director working with the members of the Executive Committee as the first among equals became the established norm. This practice was later to have some influence on the leadership structure and style of the indigenous SIB church.[200]

Madge and Alan Belcher, Second Field Director of BEM

[200] See Chapter 6.

The issue of control and transfer of final authority to the field, which loomed large in the relationship between the Home Council and the Field Conference, resulted from a mixture of factors. These included personal grievances against the Council, the impatience of the missionaries to plot the destiny of the Mission, and the perceived unwillingness of the Council under Nash, even after five years of existence, to transfer control as provided for in the provisional constitution. The significance of this transfer of control may have served as an important lesson to remind both the Field Conference and Home Council to avoid the same kind of difficulties, pain and hurt that could arise when establishing an indigenous church. Perhaps, the lesson learnt is that the Mission should facilitate the transfer of control to the indigenous church as soon as this was viable, without the church having to wrest power from the Mission. The change in the leadership of the Home Council paved the way for a better working relationship between the Home Council and the Field Conference so that, as will be seen later, the distinctive BEM fifteen-year policy was a result of this happy development.

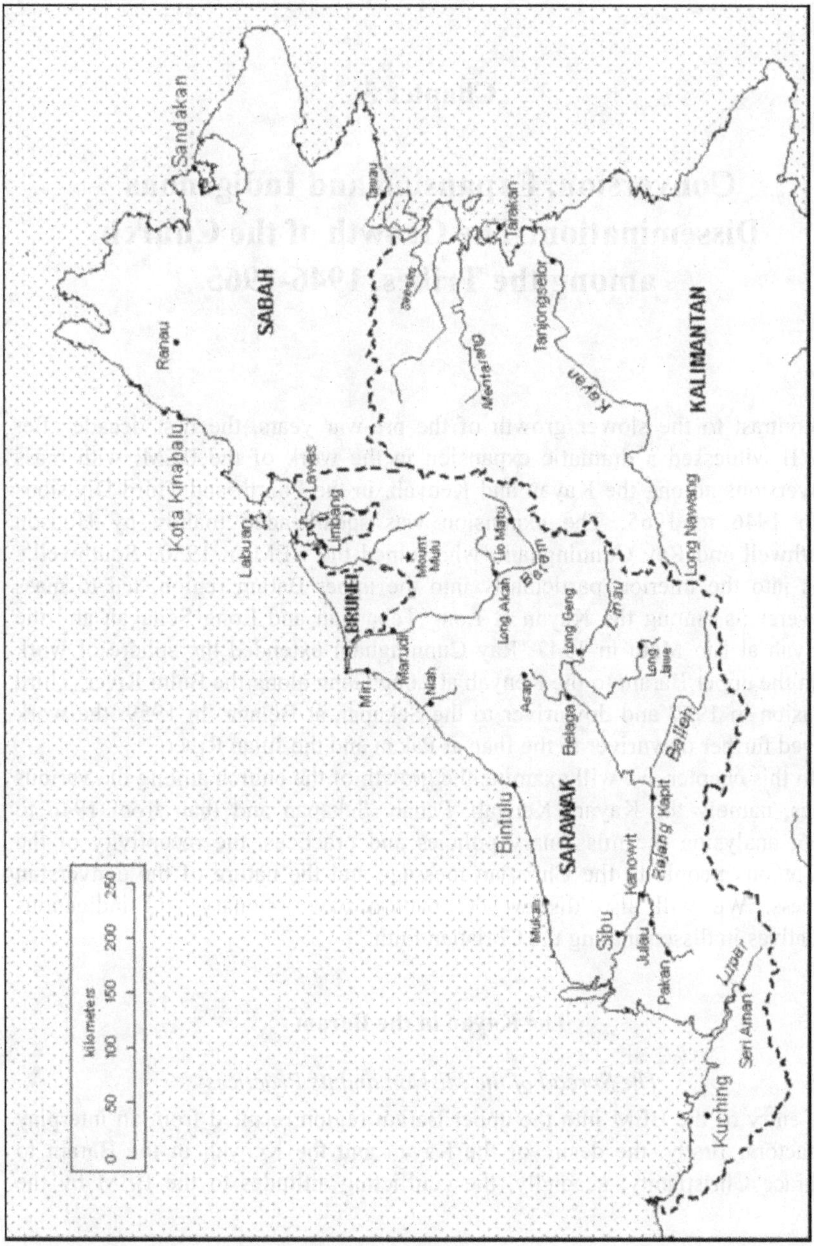

Map 5: Expansion of the BEM's work from the Baram to the Rajang

Chapter 5

Conversion, Expansion and Indigenous Dissemination: The Growth of the Church among the Tribes, 1946-1965

In contrast to the slower growth of the pre-war years, the first decade after WWII witnessed a dramatic expansion in the work of the BEM, with mass conversions among the Kayan and Kenyah, in the Fourth and Third Divisions from 1946 to 1965. The expansion was spearheaded mainly by Hudson Southwell and Ray Cunningham, who joined the BEM in 1950.[1] Southwell's trips into the interior, particularly into the upper Baram region, led to mass conversions among the Kayan at Long Tebangan and Long Senayan and the Kenyah at Lio Matu in 1947. Ray Cunningham extended the sphere of work from the upper Baram to the Kenyah at Long Geng along the Balui River, Third Division in 1957 and downriver to the Sekapan at Belaga. In 1959, the work moved further downriver to the Iban at Pakan and the Julau River.

In this chapter, we will examine the growth of the church among the various tribes, namely the Kayan, Kenyah, Penan, Sekapan and Iban from 1946 to 1965, analysing the missionary policies and practices, the receptivity of the indigenous people to the Christian message and the nature of the conversion process. We will also discuss the pattern of missionary and indigenous initiatives in disseminating the Christian faith.

The Kayan in the Baram

The Spread of the Mission and its Practices

The entry of the BEM into the upper Baram region resulted from an interplay of factors: firstly, the desire of the Kayan and the Kenyah in the Baram to embrace Christianity; secondly, the conflicting attitudes to the BEM by the

[1] Ray Cunningham was an Australian ex-serviceman who had been involved in the Pacific war and was in Borneo prior to the end of WWII. He went on to train at the Sydney Missionary and Bible College; after which he joined BEM as a missionary, arriving in Lawas in 1950. Ray Cunningham, *Longhouses Open Doors: God's Glory in Borneo* (Ormond: Hudson Press, 2002).

colonial administrators; thirdly, the increasing recognition of the BEM work by the government; and fourthly, the energetic initiatives of Southwell.

Ray Cunningham and Bruce Morton sailing for Borneo

According to Southwell's account, the Kenyah of Lio Matu had wanted to become Christians and issued an official invitation to the Mission, which was relayed to Southwell through W.H. Jacks, the district officer of Marudi.[2] Before Southwell visited the Upper Baram region, he had already been asked by Mr Meikle, the district officer of Lawas,[3] to investigate the case of a longhouse murder at Long Luping. In the Baram, Southwell found that Penghulu Tama Weng Ajang (also known as Temenggong Lawai Jau), the paramount chief of the Baram and also Kenyah chief, had converted to Roman Catholicism in May 1947, so Southwell moved on to visit the Kayan of Long Tebangan and the Kenyah of Lio Matu instead and led them to Christianity.[4] Complaints from Fr. Jansen, the Roman Catholic priest, that the Baram fell within the sphere of the Roman Catholic mission led to an openly critical attitude by John Orman Gilbert, the Resident of the Fourth Division at Miri, towards Southwell's entry into the area without his knowledge. Gilbert's stance softened after he realised that Southwell had visited the Baram on the invitation of both Jacks and

[2] *BEM NL*, February 1948, 1. Southwell, *Uncharted Waters*, 176-81. Jacks was visiting Lio Matu at that time.

[3] See Map 6.

[4] Southwell, *Uncharted Waters*, 213-19 & 228-32. See below in this chapter.

Meikle. Gilbert finally assured Southwell that he had no objections to visits to the area again, provided he was given advance notice.[5]

This watershed event was the beginning of a further relaxation of the governmental zoning policy for Christian missions. It also illustrates the variety in attitudes to the BEM among different colonial officials. In this case, a more sympathetic official was glad to accede to the specific request of the Kenyah of Lio Matu. Sometimes, officials in the interior, such as Jacks at Marudi, could on occasion exercise a measure of initiative independent of their senior officers.[6] Of significance was a later decision by the Governor of Sarawak who, after his visit to the BEM headquarters at Lawas in November 1947, was sufficiently impressed with the work that he permitted the BEM to work in the Baram, thereby over-ruling an earlier decision by the Resident to restrict the work to the shores of the Akah River in the Baram area.[7] Also, in his letter to Harold McCracken in April 1948, Southwell mentioned that he took care to cultivate good relationships with the Brooke, and later colonial, administrators, by visiting the District Officers and Residents regularly. He was often invited to stay with them, briefing them on the progress of the work of the BEM.[8] Further, the work of the energetic Southwell had spread so quickly in the Upper Baram area that it seemed futile for any colonial administrator to attempt to undo it.[9]

With two Christian missions in the Baram, the concern of the Resident was to maintain peace between them. The BEM newsletter of June 1948 reported that when a District Advisory Committee of all the penghulu or village chiefs in the Baram was assembled, the Roman Catholic priests and BEM missionaries were invited to be present when the subject of Christian missions was discussed. After outlining the sphere of influence that had been in force for the Christian missions, the Resident made it clear to them that all were free to

---

[5] Southwell, *Uncharted Waters*, 244-45.

[6] C.D. Cowan, *Nineteenth Century Malaya: The Origins of British Political Control* (London: Oxford University Press, 1961), 263. A parallel situation would be that in British Malaya, many actions taken by the Governors or other colonial officials were unauthorised actions which were either later approved by the British Colonial Office or even if disapproved could not be undone.

[7] *BEM NL*, June, 1948, 2. See Letter of Resident, Fourth Division, to Alan Belcher, 20 June 1952 (Ref. No. 24 in 0/7/50) which says the decision of Sir Charles Arden Clarke, Governor of Sarawak, that the area 'above Long Akah' on the Baram 'be open to any mission should stand'.

[8] Letter of C.H. Southwell to H. McCracken, 12 April 1948 (OMF). Southwell mentioned his visit to 'the Resident of Miri as a necessary preliminary to going up the Baram'.

[9] A later but parallel situation developed in British North Borneo (Sabah) in 1954 when the Resident Coombe proposed to enforce boundaries for Christian Missions so that the villages be distributed among the various Mission bodies. But, this proposal was objected to by the Seventh Day Adventist (SDA) and the BEM as being impractical and ill conceived, and the proposal was subsequently dropped. See Rooney, *Khabar Gembira*, 207.

follow whichever mission they wished.[10] In effect, this ruling meant that the unevangelized areas of the Baram were an open field for the missions, though the Resident's concern was for orderly and peaceful conversions decided freely by the Orang Ulu themselves and without acrimonious rivalry between the Christian missions.

From time to time, colonial administrators sought to assert some control over the Christian missions. When the BEM wanted to start work at Marudi, it had to apply for permission, which was subsequently granted. But the BEM Field Executive on 13 July 1956 decided on a policy that would circumvent future governmental restrictions, which was to use indigenous missionaries to spearhead entry into new areas, followed by intensive teaching sessions by composite missionary cum indigenous teams; and the new areas they had in mind included the Balui and the Rajang.[11]

The conversion of Tama Weng Ajang to Roman Catholicism[12] had the effect of spurring Southwell on a military-like campaign to wrest the Baram from Roman Catholic control, as was evidenced by some of the captions in the BEM newsletters from 1947 to 1949:

'Southwell forestalled by Roman Catholics',[13] 'Baram occupied', 'Position in the Baram still critical',[14] 'Outstanding spiritual victories' and 'Contest for the Baram'.[15]

The fear was that the Mill Hill Fathers, a larger body, would send more missionaries into the Baram;[16] hence the aim was to be the first mission body to get into these new areas. This sense of urgency and priority given to the work in the Baram resulted in many Kayan embracing evangelical Christianity by 1950.

---

[10] *BEM NL*, June 1948, 2-3. *BEM Fifteenth Annual Report*, 31 December 1948, 3-4. See also Letters from Resident, Fourth Division, to C.H. Southwell, 4 February 1948 (Ref. No. 14 in O/4/IV), and to Alan Belcher, 3 April & 20 June 1952 (Ref. No. 14 in 0/7/50 and 24 in 0/7/50 respectively). There was a parallel but separate development of a similar nature of two missions working side by side each other in Sarawak. See Alastair Morrison, *Fair Land Sarawak: Some Reflections of an Expatriate Official* (Studies on Southeast Asia Program: Ithaca: Cornell University, 1993), 77. 'In the Rajah's day, the spheres of influence of the two main missions were largely decreed by government – the Anglicans had the Second Division and the Catholics the Third Division. This practice had begun to be more loosely observed before WWII and after the war it was given up entirely'.

[11] *BEM Field Executive Minutes*, 13 July 1956, 2.

[12] See Malcolm MacDonald, *The Borneo People* (Singapore: Oxford University Press, 1985 [1956]), 267.

[13] *BEM NL*, October 1947, 2.

[14] *BEM NL*, April 1948, 1; August 1948, 1.

[15] *BEM NL*, April 1949, 1; October 1949, 2.

[16] Letter of C.H. Southwell to H. McCracken, 12 April 1948 (OMF). *BEM Fourteenth Annual Report*, 31 December 1947, 2.

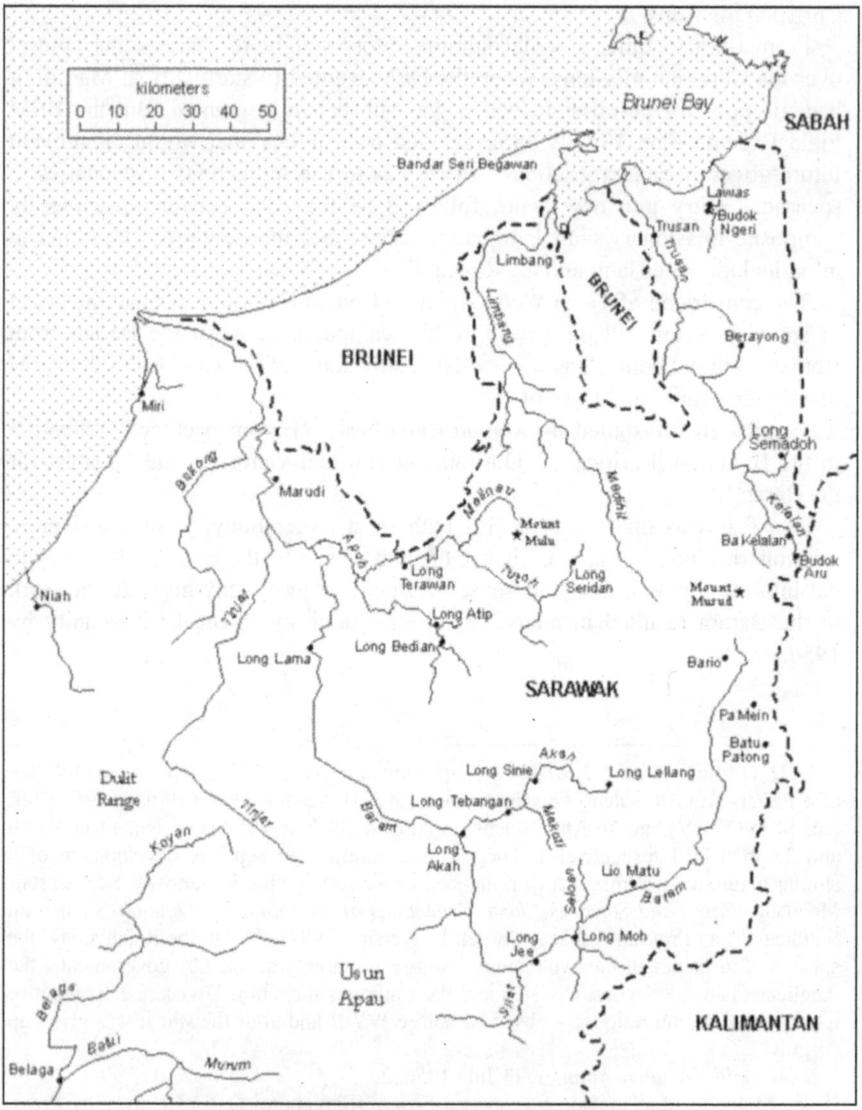

Map 6: Limbang and Baram Districts
(BEM work in the immediate post-WWII era)

The use of the first village in a tribe that had turned to Christianity as a missionary centre to reach others in that tribe and other tribes in the surrounding areas turned out to be a good strategy; Long Tebangan served that function for all the Kayan and Kenyah villages in the Baram[17] after the whole village embraced the Christian faith in 1947.[18] From early 1948, the BEM leadership followed an approach that covered the middle Baram region comprehensively, focusing on three areas, the Tutoh, Apoh and Tinjar Rivers (all tributaries of the Baram) with numerous visits by missionaries.[19] The result was that by 1965, the Kayan belonging to SIB were in a majority.[20] It is important to note that missionary activity alone would be insufficient to account for the rapid spread of Christianity among the Kayan. There would probably have been indigenous initiatives as with the earlier case of the Lun Bawang, even though there is a lack of evidence in this case.[21] Indigenous Christians, who accompanied BEM missionaries such as Southwell on their trips, also played important roles as interpreters, helpers and co-evangelists.[22]

The pattern of missionary strategy was first to approach the penghulu or headman, seeking his permission to speak to his people. If there was a refusal, there would be follow-up visits later. If the chief agreed to the request, Southwell would proceed to preach often in the open hall of the longhouse and challenge them to make a decision, but always leaving them to decide communally at their own pace and manner.[23] If they agreed to convert, they

---

[17] 'Encouraging News from Borneo', in *New Life*, 10 March 1949, 2.

[18] *BEM Fifteenth Annual Report,* 31 December 1948, 4; *Sixteenth Annual Report*, 31 December 1949, 4.

[19] Southwell, *Uncharted Waters*, 210-303.

[20] From a total population of 7,234 Kayan in the Baram in 1973, 4,042 (55.88%) belonged to the SIB, 2,379 (32.89%) Roman Catholics and 813 (11.23%) Bungan. Of a total of 21 longhouse villages, 13 were SIB, 6 Roman Catholic and 2 Bungan. See Peter Metcalf, 'The Baram District: A Survey of Kenyah, Kayan and Penan Peoples', *SMJ* 22.43 (1974), 29-40 (38).

[21] It is probable that there were Kayan individuals who on their own initiative walked from village to village to share the Christian message with their 'fellow tribesmen' just as what the ordinary Lun Bawang individuals such as Kasun and Lipang had done. Alternatively they could have shared the Gospel when they travelled down-river or visited their relatives. See BEM, *From Every Tribe* (Lawas, BEM, n.d.), 12 and Ken Nightingale, *Headhunter's Daughter* (Lawas: BEM, n.d.). The latter booklet was for sale in 1963. See *BEM NL*, February 1963, 1.

[22] See below in this chapter for further discussion.

[23] It has been observed that Southwell could not compel the Kayan to believe against their will. In response to Malcolm MacDonald's query about the activity of Southwell and the BEM, Rodney Needham, the Oxford anthropologist who was studying the Penan in the Baram, commented that 'Southwell does not preach in a house unless the leaders there invited him.... In any case, he couldn't compel changes in the people's faith unless they wished them, for the pagans are strong minded, self-respecting characters who don't abandon old beliefs against their will'. See MacDonald, *The Borneo People*, 302.

would be taken through the process of conversion in a manner consonant with the evangelical tradition of the BEM, even though the notion of communal conversion undertaken on the initiative of indigenous leaders was alien to this tradition. However, if a section of a longhouse wanted to convert against the wishes of the headman and the penghulu or chief of the clan, but was not prevented from doing so, Southwell would take them through the conversion process under his own leadership. This was the case at Long Sinie. Nevertheless, the missionaries' respect for the headmen, chiefs, and customary practices greatly helped to form a favourable impression of the missionaries, and softened initial suspicious and hostile attitudes toward the BEM. A notable example was Long Atip. The penghulu, initially hostile to Southwell, gave him a warm welcome a year later, and eventually announced his acceptance of Christianity, which was followed by a mass conversion of some three thousand from the surrounding three villages.[24] However, it did not necessarily follow that all of Southwell's evangelistic efforts were always effective.

The pattern of conversion among these Kayan villages was varied: there were conversions of whole longhouses, like Long Tebangan and Long Senayan, often led by the chief or headman;[25] conversion of a group within the longhouse, which led to the setting up of a separate Christian longhouse, as in Long Panai;[26] conversion of a group that continued to stay within the village or longhouse as in Long Sinie, despite strong opposition, which later led to more conversions;[27] and the conversion of three entire villages where the penghulu at Long Atip (who was himself a dayong), had initially opposed Southwell strongly, but converted subsequently.[28]

Mindful of its objective of the 'speediest evangelization of Borneo' and its goal of establishing an indigenous 'Three-Self' church, the Field Conference of 1948 saw the need to consolidate the Kayan work by stationing a missionary couple at the strategic centres that had been set up, a pattern that was to be the norm for other bases as well. At Long Tebangan, there were first the Belchers, then the Southwells, aided in 1948 by Ken Cooper and Horrie Hamer,[29] and later in 1950 by Cunningham.[30] With the rapid spread of the Kayan work, more stations were subsequently started, one at Long Atip in lower Baram in 1950,[31]

[24] *BEM NL*, June 1949, 4.

[25] *BEM NL*, October 1947, 4.

[26] Southwell, *Uncharted Waters*, 276-77.

[27] *BEM Fifteenth Annual Report*, 31 December 1948, 4. *BEM NL*, August 1948, 1; April 1949, 1.

[28] *BEM NL*, June 1949, 4; Southwell, *Uncharted Waters*, 273-74.

[29] *BEM Fifteenth Annual Report*, December 1948, 5-6. *New Life*, 10 March 1949, 2. With the presence of Cooper and Hamer, Southwell was freed to itinerate the surrounding country.

[30] *BEM Seventeenth Annual Report*, 31 December 1950, 8.

[31] *BEM Seventeenth Annual Report*, 31 December 1950, 8. *BEM NL*, December 1950, 2

and another at Long Lama in middle Baram in 1952.[32] From these centres, missionary visitations and outreach to the surrounding areas became a regular feature.

With the shortage of male missionaries, the Field Conference experimented with assigning two women, Winifred Burrows and Leah Cubitt, a nurse and teacher respectively, to take charge of Long Atip, (the base for the Tutoh and Apoh area).[33] This later became an accepted practice.[34] As in the past, the BEM continued the policy of having indigenous missionaries or pastors (preferably married couples) assist in the work among each ethnic group, so Balang Selutan and Muring were assigned to the Kayan at Long Atip, Upai Baru to the Kenyah in Upper Baram,[35] and Tebari and Layun to the Kenyah at Lio Matu.[36]

Women missionaries, such as Winsome Southwell, took on prominent roles as counsellors and guides to the Kayan women who were adjusting to their new-found faith, especially in relation to the fears of breaking numerous traditional restrictions and taboos. A specific contribution, although done unconsciously and informally at first, was to create alternative but informal Christian rituals associated with their daily life. They included saying prayers for new-born babies, those leaving the room in which they were born and those being bathed in the river. These rituals grew out of Kayan tradition, where it was forbidden to remove babies below a certain age from the room they were born in or to bathe them in a river without having made a sacrificial offering to the spirits. Furthermore, prayers were offered in the paddy huts near their farms for a good harvest, a supply of daily food and strength and protection for their work in the fields.[37]

The processes of consolidation and expansion went alongside each other. While Southwell concentrated mainly on reaching the other villages in the Baram until 1955,[38] the other missionaries focused on running primary schools, providing medical services and instruction on personal hygiene, translating the Scriptures and giving the Kayan language a written form.[39] The school which opened at Long Tebangan in January 1949 under the charge of Cooper had the

---

[32] *BEM NL*, February 1952, 4 and April 1952, 4.

[33] *BEM Seventeenth Annual Report*, 31 December 1950, 8. *BEM NL*, June 1951, 3; April 1952, 2. They started a school with 35 students.

[34] *BEM NL*, December 1958-January 1959, 4; September-October 1960, 2; and December 1961, 3. Following after them were Iris Greener and Jenny Dunn, then Dunn and Sybil Muir, and later Muir and Edna Bulpitt.

[35] *BEM Eighteenth Annual Report*, 31 December 1951, 10.

[36] *BEM NL*, February 1952, 4; June 1952, 4; April 1953, 1.

[37] *BEM NL*, October 1948, 3.

[38] Hudson Southwell left the BEM in early 1955 and started the Community Development Project (CDP), a Sarawak government project, at Long Lama in 1956. The CDP is basically a vocational training school. See Southwell, *Uncharted Waters*, 327-38. Also, *SG*, 29 February 1960, 31-33, *SG*, 30 April 1961, 58-59.

[39] *BEM NL*, August 1955, 4. Later, new techniques of wet farming were introduced which gave great yield to their crops.

aim of training its students for church responsibility and evangelism.[40] The promotion of literacy (through providing elementary education using the Bible as the basic text) was for the sake of reading the Bible and disseminating the Christian faith. In their model of training, the missionaries held to the firm conviction that an adherence to the New Testament pattern of church work and ministry would ensure success.[41] The school in effect became not only a centre of training for those in the upper Baram but also the centre of mission activity in Long Tebangan[42] until other stations were opened in the Baram. Like other outstation schools, the one at Long Tebangan was preparatory for the Bible school at Lawas, to which the best students were sent with the aim to train them to be pastors and teachers among their own people.[43]

The immediate effect of education was its novelty. Being able to read and write their Kayan language was an attraction for the young people, so that those who were married were keen on learning, resulting in night classes with many eager students.[44] In contrast to some other cultures such as the Yoruba,[45] pieces of writing were not regarded as having any magical properties among the Orang Ulu. It is not known whether the Bible was regarded as having magical properties among the Kayan. Nevertheless, the excitement of new Bible knowledge spurred the students to witness to the less frequently visited longhouses during their vacation. They returned to share their experiences as well as to seek answers for questions they encountered in their visits.[46]

The introduction of education was to have a long-term social effect on the Kayan. This first became evident at Long Atip, where the young people read and taught the New Testament to the older people, who were still illiterate.[47] This phenomenon created a division between the more literate young people and the illiterate older people, and also later a division between the literate leaders and illiterate leaders. Also, education provided an avenue to opportunities in further training and employment as in the government service, the police force or the teaching profession.[48] This led to a growing exodus of young people from the interior to the sub-coastal and coastal towns from the

[40] *BEM Sixteenth Annual Report*, 31 December 1949, 4-5. *BEM NL*, August 1949, 4; October 1949, 2.
[41] *BEM NL*, October 1949, 1. 'We must build on the New Testament pattern or the whole edifice will fall'.
[42] *BEM Seventeenth Annual Report*, 31 December 1949, 2. *BEM NL*, April, 1949, 1; August 1949, 4; December 1949, 2. The enrolment reached about fifty young people by the end of the year, consisting of six Kelabit boys from Long Lellang, six Kayan from Long Apoh and several from Long Sinie in addition to over thirty local boys and girls.
[43] *BEM NL*, August 1951, 2.
[44] *BEM NL*, April 1949, 1.
[45] J.D.Y. Peel, *Religious Encounter and the Making of the Yoruba* (Bloomington & Indianapolis: Indiana University Press, 2000), 223-25.
[46] *BEM NL*, December 1954, 3.
[47] *BEM NL*, December 1954, 3.
[48] *BEM NL*, October 1951, 3.

1960s, which, in turn, loosened them from their traditional values to adopt more western values, especially that of individualism.

Two matters relating to the work of the schools were to have wider implications for the BEM and SIB. Firstly, the Malay language was adopted as the main medium of instruction, since it was the lingua franca of the country, and the vernacular Kayan language was also used. This bilingualism enabled the Kayan to relate at once to those within their culture and those beyond; this practice was to have implications for the spread of Christianity to other tribes. This policy of using the Malay language contrasted sharply with the sole use of Iban as the medium of instruction and communication for the Sarawak Iban Methodist Church and also in their theological school, which has since been a limiting factor in its evangelistic outreach. Secondly, the handover of the primary schools to the government in the mid-1950s freed the missionaries to focus on the work of itinerant evangelism, short-term Bible schools and deacons' schools and Bible translation.

During the first couple of decades after WWII, the traditional leaders of Christian villages were generally elected to church office. Their functions included conducting Sunday services, managing church affairs and acting as spiritual advisors.[49] At Long Tebangan, the headman, Jok Ngau, and his deputy, Wan Jor, were both deacons in the church.[50] At Long Atip, among the deacons were Penghulu Tama Paya Anyi and his son-in-law, Avet.[51] At these outstation bases, while the local leaders took charge of their own church affairs, the missionaries played a facilitating role by providing them with training through short-term training schools or deacons' schools held at regular intervals. These schools provided intensive courses in Bible teaching, preaching and general church matters, including church management and basic public health. The aim of this training was to encourage literacy among church leaders so as to enable them to fulfill their church responsibilities more effectively[52] and to aid them in the task of translating the Scriptures into Kayan.[53] The emphasis of these leadership training sessions by the BEM missionaries focused on the development of a Christlike character and servant leadership in the church, though the acquisition of basic practical ministerial skills was in no way discounted.[54] In short, the missionaries acted as facilitators and advisors in the ministries of the indigenous churches on a need basis, working cooperatively with the local leaders.

---

[49] In case of Mein Ribu in Pa Mein, he served as pastor as well. *BEM NL*, December 1954, 1.

[50] *BEM NL* October 1951, 3.

[51] Avet, a Kenyah from Long Wat, married the daughter of Penghulu Tama Paya Anyi of Long Atip. *BEM NL*, June 1957, 1.

[52] *BEM NL*, February 1952, 2 and June 1953, 1.

[53] *BEM NL*, August 1953, 4. With assistance from Leah Cubitt, the deacons had translated portions of Scripture in Kayan.

[54] Cunningham, *Longhouses Open Doors*, 74.

Kayan Receptivity and Conversion

The subject of conversion is a complex one which has attracted a growing volume of scholarship from a variety of perspectives.[55] From a social scientific perspective, conversion may be regarded simply as the change from one religious allegiance to another. From such a perspective, scholars of Christian missionary encounters seek to identify the various motivations behind the indigenous appropriation of Christianity within the larger social, cultural and political context.

The BEM literature provides a reasonably detailed account of the conversion of the Kayan in terms of their change in religious allegiance to Christianity,[56] but gives particular emphasis to the Kayan's acceptance of Christianity as the outcome of an encounter between contesting spiritual powers. This stress is not surprising in view of the prominent place held by the fear of the spirits within Kayan culture. It must also be noted that the Kayan were not passive receptors of the Christian message. At Long Tebangan, the process of conversion began when Southwell presented them with the Christian message. It was followed by a stage of indecision, where there existed a division of opinion within the community, with strong opposition from nine dayong. The community was left to make their own decision. A second phase began when the dayong relented and agreed to embrace Christianity, and they later performed their customary rites for the final time. Then in a public gathering, the community renounced their old ways, which was first done by the dayong individually, followed by the whole gathered assembly. Next, they pledged their allegiance to Jesus Christ as Saviour and Lord. Afterwards, all the fetishes and charms in the longhouses and in the surrounding compounds were destroyed. Mission accounts report that the community experienced an intense sense of joy and relief in consequence. Events which followed shortly afterwards were perceived as further proof of God's protection and power over the spirits. Firstly, the chief dayong, who had fallen ill, recovered after being given medicine by Southwell followed by prayer. Then, on a hunting expedition, the

---

[55] Robin Horton, 'African Conversion', *Africa* 41 (1971), 85-108 and 'On the Rationality of Conversion, Parts 1 & 2', *Africa* 45 (1975), 219-35, 373-99. Humphrey Fisher, 'Conversion Reconsidered: Some Historical Aspects of Religious Conversion in Black Africa', *Africa* 43 (1973), 27-40 and 'The Juggernaut's Apologia: Conversion to Islam in Black Africa', *Africa* 55 (1985), 153-73. Cyril C. Okorocha, *The Meaning of Religious Conversion in Africa: The Case of the Igbo of Nigeria* (Aldershot: Groves Publishing, 1987). Lewis R. Rambo, *Understanding Religious Conversion* (New Haven, CT: Yale University Press, 1993). Hefner (ed.), *Conversion to Christianity.* Christopher Lamb and M. Darrol Bryant (eds.), *Religious Conversions: Contemporary Practices and Controversies* (London/New York: Cassell, 1999). Sebastian C.H. Kim, *In Search of Identity: Debates on Religious Conversion in India* (New Delhi: Oxford University Press, 2003).

[56] *BEM NL*, October 1947, 4. Lees, *Drunk before Dawn*, 89-91. Southwell, *Uncharted Waters*, 215-19.

men chased a sambhur deer, an animal taboo to the Kayan, which ran into a cemetery, a place where they greatly feared the spirits of the dead. The men experienced no harm, contrary to their former beliefs, and also enjoyed a treat of venison for dinner. At Long Senayan, a similar conversion experience was reported, with subsequent celebration expressed in dancing, but there was a marked difference from such practices in the past. The headman was reported to have said the following:

> On former occasions, whenever the dayongs danced, evil spirits would come into them and possess them. They would fall into a trance and utter sayings beyond their control. This time when the dayongs danced nothing of this sort happened to them.[57]

This was perceived as proof to the Kayan that the spirits had really gone. Thus, these specific incidents, where the power of Christ was perceived as tangibly superior to the power of the spirits, had the effect of firmly rooting the Kayan in Christianity.

It is instructive to note that the religious encounter between Southwell and the Kayan was not merely one-sided, that is from the missionary to the missionized. In fact, it also had implications for missionary theology. Though the presentation of the Christian message to the Kayan, as reported in the BEM newsletter of October 1947, reflected the evangelical tradition of the BEM, there was a significant modification of that tradition. Evangelicals have regarded the substitutionary atonement as the heart of the Christian message. However, Southwell appears to have adapted his message to make it relevant to Kayan beliefs in relation to the powers and malignity of spirits in human affairs and the need for appeasement and sacrifices, including blood sacrifices, to the spirits. Southwell's record suggests that the Christian message he preached had two predominant themes. The first and more traditional evangelical emphasis focused on the purpose of God in creation, the promise of the Redeemer, the life and sacrificial death of Christ, and the choice between two ways which faced all people.[58] This well-established evangelical emphasis enabled the Kayan to relate the propitiatory sacrifice of Christ for human sin to customary blood sacrifices of animals as a means of propitiating the evil spirits.[59]

---

[57] *BEM NL*, October 1947, 4.

[58] Southwell, *Unpublished Memoirs*, 169. Enid Davidson recorded that Southwell's Christian message to the Lun Bawang in 1933 was typically evangelical, which focused on the story of Jesus, especially his life, miracles, death and resurrection, including ideas about God and his creation, man's alienation from God, the origin of sin and the redemptive sacrifice of Christ. See Enid Davidson, *The Lun Bawang and the Gospel* (n.d.), 7.

[59] In a similar situation, where the Davidsons worked among the Kelabit prior to WWII, they noticed the 'prevalent practice of blood sacrifices and the smearing of blood on the arms and chests of the people'. Enid Davidson observed that 'the way was opened for us to talk about the significance of the power of blood. The Old Testament sacrifices were

The second predominant theme in Southwell's preaching emphasised the power of Christ over Satan and the spirit world, the origin of Satan, Satan as the enemy of God and of mankind whom God has created, the coming of Christ to deliver human beings from the power of the spirits, and the need to renounce Satan and all his works, which included the disposal of their fetishes and charms.[60] This latter emphasis of Southwell may be understood as incorporating some aspects of a Christus victor motif, and as such represents a significant theological development of a European evangelical tradition which had tended to underplay both the resurrection of Christ and the continuing relevance of the witness of the New Testament to the reality of invisible spiritual powers.[61] Southwell spoke in the following terms of the evangelistic encounter: 'I could sense there was a real battle … and I could feel the powers of evil strongly resisting any decision for action. So I read to them the gospel story about how Jesus cast out demons and how demons feared him.'[62] The evidence suggests that BEM missionaries working in the indigenous context in Sarawak began to revise their presentation of the atonement by giving much more emphasis to motifs of spiritual combat than they would have done in their western context. They did so because the context opened their minds to the reality of evil spirits and hence to the need to proclaim the victory of the Cross and resurrection. It may also be observed that in the earlier work of BEM among the Lun Bawang, the missionaries reported that 'generally a pagan will only be drawn to accept that which appeals to a need that is particularly felt… Some pagans, we find, are drawn by the news of God's mighty power over evil spirits'.[63]

It is important to note that not all western missionaries, including some evangelicals, were comfortable with presenting the Christian message in such terms, as they came with an Enlightenment mindset, which regarded belief in spirits and the rituals associated with them as superstitions. Within the Sarawakian context, both the American Methodists and the Roman Catholic missionaries appear to have regarded the indigenous beliefs, practices and rituals as harmless aspects of their cultural superstitions, allowing them to be

---

very meaningful to the Kelabit, and we were able to tell them about the sacrifice of Jesus and the power of His blood to wipe away our sins'. *Personal correspondence with Enid Davidson*, 29 December 1992.

[60] Southwell, *Unpublished Memoirs*, 176. 'I stressed the power of Christ over the spirit world, and I spoke about Satan, the enemy of God and enemy of mankind whom God had created'. See Southwell, *Uncharted Waters*, 209 & 215. 'I spoke…especially of the power of Christ over the spirits, the origin of Satan, and of sin in Eden'. *BEM NL*, October 1947, 4.

[61] Evangelicals of the nineteenth century and twentieth century subscribed mainly to the substitutionary idea of the atonement. The *Christus victor* motif is one of the theories of the atonement of the early Christian church and was most famously advocated by Gustaf Aulen, *Christus Victor* (London: Society for Promoting Christian Knowledge, 1975 [1960]).

[62] Southwell, *Uncharted Waters*, 230.

[63] Nightingale, *Headhunter's Daughter*, 7.

retained alongside the new Christian practices, hence their adherents were permitted to wear both their old religious charms and crosses.[64]

In the indigenous acceptance of Christianity, the Kayan experienced a significant change in their worldview, and appropriated for themselves a Christian dualism between God and Satan, identifying the spirits whom they had formerly revered and feared as emissaries of Satan, and Christ as the conquering Lord who had vanquished the spirits. The change of religious allegiance involved in conversion to Christianity represented in Kayan consciousness a liberation from the malignity of the spirits, but not a denial of their existence, as an acceptance of a western worldview in its entirety would have implied. Even after their acceptance of Christianity, the Kayan continued to believe in the reality and power of the spirits, but the former fear had been removed. Similar conclusions are reached by Sue Russell in her study of the Lun Bawang people in British North Borneo. Russell notes that the introduction of Christianity into a society involved a power encounter in which people trusted in God's power to protect them from other spirits; this power encounter shows the ability of Christianity to offer superior resources for protection and well-being. To obtain these resources, they had to give their allegiance to God.[65]

The BEM sources on the conversion of the Kayan suggest the presence of power encounters in similar terms to those described by Russell. In the case of Long Sinie, during the disposal of customary charms, two cases of 'demon possession' occurred, upon which Southwell proceeded to deliver the possessed persons in the name of Jesus. Southwell backed up his action at Long Sinie by preaching a sermon based on two stories about Jesus casting out spirits from the Gospel of Mark, chapters 5 and 9.[66] Gospel narratives which had long been familiar but of mainly theoretical value in the Australian environment now acquired new immediacy and relevance, and encouraged Southwell to introduce what was almost certainly for him the new practice of exorcism. It is significant that the incident at Long Sinie occurred after Tama Paya Anyi, the Penghulu of Long Atip, who was a dayong and reputed to have great occultic powers, had been summoned by the more resistant upper social class to try to stop the

---

[64] The Iban at Nanga Julau were reported to be surprised meeting the SIB Kenyah Christians who 'had no charms or talismans' on them. The Iban in the Rajang had been familiar with Roman Catholic Christianity and they 'were so used to the kind of Christians who wore crosses around their necks and Iban charms around their waists'. Similarly, in the Roman Catholic or Methodist Iban longhouses, it was not uncommon to see old religious practices existing alongside Christian rituals. See Cunningham, *Longhouses Open Doors*, 88.

[65] Russell, *Conversion, Identity and Power*, 151-52. Power encounter is defined as a 'confrontation between two or more spiritual powers'. Quoting Marguerite Kraft, 'Reaching Out for Spiritual Power: A Study in the Dynamics of Felt Needs and Spiritual Power' (PhD dissertation, Fuller Theological Seminary, 1990).

[66] Southwell, *Unpublished Memoirs*, 169.

community from throwing out one of their sacred charms. According to Southwell, this decisive event was a 'demonstration of the power of the name of Jesus'.[67] Penghulu Tama Paya Anyi himself was converted to Christ a year later, a noteworthy change of allegiance to serve a God of superior power which appears to have been triggered by the encounter at Long Sinie and the observable benefit that Christianity had brought to the Kayan people.

The message increasingly proclaimed by the BEM missionaries asserted that the power of Christ was superior to that of Satan and the spirits, and portrayed Christianity by rational persuasion to be a more powerful religion. This claim was experientially validated in the experience of the Kayan by events immediately following their conversion, as discussed earlier. Evangelical Christianity seems to have appeared to most Kayan as both intellectually more cogent and experientially more assuring than their old religion. The appropriation of a modified form of evangelical beliefs both undergirded and dovetailed with their conversion experience to provide the Kayan with a new sense of freedom, meaning and identity.

In this respect, it is interesting to note Peel's suggestion that in the making of a Christian community, missionaries and indigenous people (in his case, the Yoruba of Nigeria) faced each other with 'quite distinct objectives' and 'the story of their interaction is of the trade-offs they achieved over time between them'.[68] In the case of the Kayan, it can similarly be argued from the evidence presented earlier that the missionaries made substantial progress toward their objective by challenging the Kayan worldview and by presenting the biblical narrative of the purpose of creation, the fall, the promise of redemption in Christ and his propitiatory sacrifice, the dualism of God and Satan, and the power of Christ over Satan and the spirits in a form that could be easily understood by the Kayan. However, the missionaries also made substantial concessions to the Kayan objective, namely the desire for power or resources for living; these resources embraced control over the spirits and the enhancement of benefits which they believed would follow - fertility, safe childbirth, good health and good harvests. Thus, the gap between Kayan expectations and BEM intentions was not such a great mismatch. The Kayan had appropriated the Christian faith in a form that provided them with the freedom from their fear of the spirit world, and in so doing had reshaped both the gospel which the missionaries brought and their own worldview.

Horton famously suggested that people may convert to Christianity because it offers them a new macrocosmic identity in a world religion, founded on the acceptance of Christian beliefs.[69] Further, it has been suggested that this conversion is often a particular response to social and cultural changes that

---

[67] *BEM NL*, August 1948, 3. See Southwell, *Uncharted Waters*, 263.

[68] Peel, *Religious Encounter and the Making of the Yoruba*, 154.

[69] Horton, 'African Conversion', 85-108 and 'On the Rationality of Conversion', 219-35, 373-99; Hefner (ed.), *Conversion to Christianity*, 20-22.

create the need for a new and wider framework of social and cultural identity.[70] This view has an element of truth in regard to the conversion of the Kayan, since it was occasioned by their prolonged exposure to the presence of western military forces during WWII, which contributed to a predisposition toward western culture, education and Christianity. We should also take note of the fact that the Kayan, Kenyah and Iban of the interior of the Third and Fourth Divisions converted to Christianity irrespective of denominational affiliations, that is there was a mass movement of these indigenous people into whichever Christian church was working in their area. In addition to the BEM, mass movements took place into the other Christian denominations working in the interior of the Third and Fourth Divisions, which were the Roman Catholics[71] and the Methodists.[72] In recording this dramatic people movement into Christianity among the Iban, W.O. Phoon noted that 'since 1952, an Iban Methodist conference has been set up, with a current estimated membership of over sixteen thousand in sixty-two churches with thirty eight pastors ... The Iban conference is reputedly the most rapidly growing Methodist church in the world'.[73] Further, the receptiveness of the Kayan may be due to their relatively better treatment by the white man than by the Japanese during WWII and their wish to identify with the victors. In short, an aspect of their initial openness to Christianity was one of prudent calculation.

Any scholarly discussion of conversion to mission Christianity has now to come to terms with the influential work of Jean and John Comaroff on the conversion of the Tswana in nineteenth-century South Africa by the London Missionary Society (LMS).[74] The Comaroffs argue that the LMS missionaries engaged the Tswana in a 'long conversation' at two levels. First, there was 'the tangible attempt to convert the Africans, to overwhelm them with arguments of images and messages, thereby to establish the truth of Christianity'. Second, there was 'the effort to reform the indigenous world: to inculcate in it the hegemonic signs and practices ... of European culture'. The Comaroffs argue that though 'the colonized people frequently rejected the message of the colonizers', the Tswana were profoundly affected by the new hegemonies of the colonizing ideology and culture.[75] There is then a discontinuity between

[70] Pollock, 'Conversion and Community in Amazonia', in Hefner (ed.), *Conversion to Christianity*, 166.
[71] See Rooney, *Khabar Gembira*, 64, 117.
[72] See Terence Joseph, 'The Longhouse Church in Sarawak' (ThM thesis, Southern Methodist University, 1964), 131-32 and Jonathan Jelanding Munting, 'History of the Iban Church in Sarawak' (Research Paper, Trinity Theological College, Singapore 1979).
[73] W.O. Phoon, 'Malaysia-Singapore', in Donald Hoke (ed.), *The Church in Asia* (Chicago: Moody Press, 1975), 414.
[74] Jean Comaroff and John L. Comaroff, *Of Revelation and Revolution*, 2 vols. (Chicago/London: University of Chicago Press, 1991 & 1997)
[75] Comaroff, *Of Revelation and Revolution*, I, xi, 199-200, 311.

'conversion' and 'conversation', where 'the two modes of transformation did not occur together as intended'.[76] However, the missionaries through their intimate, daily long-term dealings with the Tswana, were effective agents of cultural colonialism, so that the Tswana were not only drawn into the western capitalist economy but they also had their cultural norms replaced with western ones. It is this contention in particular which has been generalized by other scholars analysing processes of mission-induced conversion.[77] The Comaroffs understand conversion mainly from a western materialist perspective. The idea of conversion as 'spiritual transformation' is marginal to their discussion in their chapter on 'Conversion and Conversation'.[78] Norman Etherington has, however, pointed out that materialist explanations alone cannot really explain the nature of conversion to mission Christianity in Africa.

> Some have assumed that attachment to a mission is the hallmark of conversion and that identifying the motivations that led individuals to reside at missions will tell us about conversion. The most common conclusion is that material incentives were most powerful in drawing people to missions. However, reasons for residence are not the same reasons for mental transformations and cannot really unlock the mysteries of conversion.[79]

Etherington's point seems equally valid for conversion among the Kayan. From the narrative of Kayan conversion discussed earlier,[80] it has been argued that the spiritual dimension predominated in the Kayan appropriation of Christianity, but this does not mean that other motives are to be precluded.

How far is the Comaroffs' contention that missionaries were agents of cultural colonialism applicable to the situation in Sarawak? Did the BEM missionaries consciously or unconsciously seek to propagate western ideology and cultural forms so as to change the local culture?

As we have noted earlier, the Brooke experiment in Sarawak was an oddity in colonial history. Under Brooke rule, there had been a reluctance to expose the indigenous people to western culture and modernity but Vyner Brooke eventually relented only because there seemed to be no other choice but to embrace modernity.[81] Just as the Brooke government had sought to protect as much indigenous culture as possible, likewise the BEM missionaries were highly selective in their programme for cultural change. The cultural changes which they advocated were those associated with indigenous religious practices, which inevitably led to a fundamental re-shaping of the cosmology,

---

[76] Comaroff, *Of Revelation and Revolution*, I, 311.
[77] Comaroff, *Of Revelation and Revolution*, I, 7-11
[78] Comaroff, *Of Revelation and Revolution*, I, 198-251.
[79] Norman Etherington, 'Recent Trends in the Historiography of Christianity in Southern Africa', *Journal of Southern African Studies* 22.2 (June 1996), 216.
[80] See above in this chapter.
[81] See Chapter 2.

as has been observed in the above narrative of indigenous conversion. However, any overt attempt to replace the indigenous culture with western cultural patterns was strongly opposed by Harrisson, the curator of the Sarawak Museum, who made his criticisms public in the Sarawak Gazette at the time when the Kayan were embracing Christianity through Southwell's efforts.[82] Harrisson's public criticism of the earlier work of the BEM among the Murut evoked a response from Southwell, who argued that far from destroying the indigenous culture, acceptance of Christianity had enhanced some aspects of their culture: he maintained that some of their arts and crafts, including indigenous songs, were being revived rather than destroyed as a result of the appropriation of Christianity by the Murut. He further contended that the observable changes in indigenous culture were due to the effects of modernization and these were already apparent before the advent of the BEM.[83] Southwell's case was supported by Rodney Needham, the Oxford anthropologist, who commended the work of the BEM to Malcolm MacDonald, the then Governor-General of Malaya and British Borneo, in 1947, saying that, contrary to the negative rumours about the Mission, Southwell and his colleagues 'do not force Christianity on the natives' nor sweep away all their customs destroying the good with the bad.[84] The public exchange between Harrisson and Southwell may have made the BEM missionaries more cautious about imposing their western values and culture on the indigenous people. In the later 1950s, there were no further criticisms from Harrisson, most probably because the influence of modernity and western education in the schools was already impacting the local cultures. The most marked changes to Kayan culture were the result, not of mission influence, but of economic and social contact with people in or from the coastal towns.[85]

The BEM missionaries in Sarawak did not consciously attempt to reshape the everyday material world of the Kayan to make it conform to western cultural forms. Rather the opposite was the case. The missionaries in the outstations usually adapted to the local culture and made some attempt to live

---

[82] 'The Muruts', *SG*, 1 December 1947, 225-26. Harrisson criticized the work of the BEM for earlier altering the customs and culture of the Muruts and warned that the same may happen in the Baram.

[83] Southwell's letter to the Editor, *SG*, 1 April 1948, 85-86. Southwell acknowledged that under modern influences whether from the Mission or increasing contact with coastal influences, 'the pattern of native life and culture is bound to change'. As for 'the change to wearing shorts and cutting the hair', it had already 'begun before the advent of the mission'.

[84] MacDonald, *The Borneo People*, 301-303. The Governor-General of Malaya and British Borneo made a visit to Sarawak in November 1947. See *BEM NL*, February 1948, 1 and Lees, *Drunk before Dawn*, 93.

[85] An example is the cutting of their hair and their long ear-lobes which they used to wear when they lived in the interior. See Seling and Langub, 'The Orang Ulu', 23-29, for the influence of modernity in the coastal towns on the Kayan.

on the same level as the local people.[86] Their conservative evangelical mission philosophy meant that their encounter with the Kayan focused primarily on spiritual matters, rather than on the visible trappings of 'civilization' which the nineteenth-century LMS missionaries of South Africa regarded as integral to their enterprise - remaking the everyday world of the Tswana through the building of houses, cultivation of farms with the plough and tilling the earth in straight lines. Furthermore, in contrast to missionaries in nineteenth-century South Africa, the agenda of the BEM missionaries did not consciously encourage the indigenous people in the interior to participate in the urban capitalist economy. The missionaries were, on the contrary, anxious that the indigenous people should be isolated from the influence of the town as long as possible. Their dictum was 'we are a jungle outfit; we wouldn't be happy in the towns'.[87] As will be noted in Chapter 6, it was the pressing trend of modernization and the rural-urban migration of indigenous people in Sarawak for employment or higher education that propelled the BEM missionaries to start work in the coastal towns, thereby embracing the cultural values of a cash economy in the process.[88] By then, it was a matter of necessity.

As a result of conversion to Christianity in a society where rituals played an important role in nearly every aspect of everyday life, the issue of replacement rituals among the Kayan inevitably arose though the BEM evangelical tradition was one in which prayers and hymns, much more than the sacraments, fulfilled 'ritual' functions. It was reported that the Kayan requested Southwell for advice regarding these replacement rituals. In response, he translated five prayers for them to use as models for prayers in the morning and in the evening, a grace for meals, a prayer for children's dedication and the Lord's Prayer.[89] Furthermore, hymns were also translated into the Kayan language and the singing of them became a popular feature of Kayan communal life. In addition, daily prayer meetings became a common practice for every church.[90] Although the missionaries would have given the initial advice as to how to conduct daily prayer meetings, it is probable that the local leaders improvised other prayers as and when the occasion demanded. A similar picture of missionary instruction followed by indigenous creativity and improvisation applied to the drafting of prayers for every aspect of their daily life, which included the various agricultural duties, making a journey, naming of children and dealing with

---

[86] In their search for meat, the missionaries hunted using local methods. See Southwell, *Uncharted Waters*, 38-39. The idea of living as closely to the local culture as possible is adapted from the CIM's practice in China.

[87] *BEM NL*, May 1980, 1. See also Pollock, *Earth's Remotest*, 253.

[88] See Chapter 6.

[89] *BEM NL*, October 1947, 4.

[90] *BEM NL*, June 1970, 3. Ted Hand, General Secretary of the BEM Australasian Home Council observed positively that the SIB churches were in reasonable shape, considering that many of them had been in existence for over thirty years and yet had a 50% attendance at their daily prayer meetings.

sickness.[91] For some of these situations, it is probable that the missionaries created new prayers when the practices were not present in their home country. As for one important aspect of Kayan social life, that of extending hospitality to guests, Southwell deliberately encouraged the drinking of coffee instead of borak (locally brewed rice wine), which in earlier days had led to frequent intoxication.[92] Hence the missionaries not only drew from their own western Christian tradition but also had to produce new prayers and rituals when faced with unfamiliar situations, for which they had not encountered before in their own home country, thus becoming affected or changed by the context in which they worked.

In short, the Comaroffs' contention that Christian evangelism was a means towards the end of integrating indigenous people in a colonial capitalist economy is of limited relevance to the context of twentieth-century Sarawak. It has been argued that neither the Brooke government nor the missionaries advocated that the indigenous people of the interior embrace a western capitalistic economy. It only became inevitable under the pressure of modernity, leading the people to accept new western cultural forms and lifestyle. As for the 'colonisation of the mind', so central to the Comaroffs' argument, the form of near-dualist 'power Christianity' which emerged from the conversion process was neither a characteristically western ideology nor native to the Bornean context.

It is, of course, unlikely that all were considered 'converted' according to the evangelical tradition of the BEM. In this mass movement into Christianity, Southwell was well aware that not every Kayan would have experienced authentic personal 'conversion' in the way the BEM missionaries understood it, and his dictum was 'mass movement into Christianity leading to individual salvation'.[93] For the children, some womenfolk and young adults, and a number among the older tribal folk, their conversion was a matter of communal solidarity within the longhouse. It is to be expected that some of those who embraced Christianity secretly accommodated more of their traditional religious practices than the evangelical tradition of the BEM would have allowed.[94] The frequent comment of the older folks that 'it is alright for you to

---

[91] This was often taught informally and these practices became a part of their new lifestyle.

[92] Southwell had earlier recommended this practice of coffee drinking as a substitute for *borak* to the Kelabit and then to the Kayan and Kenyah. Coffee was grown locally and was an inexpensive substitute. *BEM NL*, October 1947, 3. See also Southwell, *Uncharted Waters*, 198.

[93] Interview with Dr Bill Lees, 14 June 2004. Through teaching given at Bible schools, conventions and deacons' schools, the BEM missionaries sought to ensure personal conversions among the people.

[94] In his study of Christian mass movements in India, Waskom Pickett noted that in regard to the fear of evil spirits, there was a small proportion (almost 5%) of professing Christians who used additional protection, e.g. wearing an amulet wherever they went.

change but don't expect me to change'[95] was one way of expressing generational dissent and a preference for the old religion.

The Kenyah in the Baram and in the Balui and Upper Rajang

The Spread of the Mission and its Practices

The first mass conversion of the Kenyah to Roman Catholicism in the Baram came through the initiatives of the powerful and influential Penghulu Tama Weng. The approach of Southwell had been to keep close continual contact with the chief, and to focus on the areas that were not under his jurisdiction, while responding to invitations that came from longhouses and villages under his jurisdiction. Southwell's work in the upper Baram resulted in the first mass conversion of the Kenyah at Lio Matu in 1947.

The introduction of evangelical Christianity among the Kenyah had from the beginning faced strong resistance from the chiefs: from Penghulu Tama Weng, who did not allow his villages to embrace this form of Christianity, and from the Bungan Penghulu Mape Arang of Long Moh, who later showed a more favourable attitude. In 1951, Penghulu Mape called a council of all his village headmen, which decided that each village was to be given the freedom to decide on its own whether to embrace Christianity. Following this significant decision, the Lepu Aga Kenyah (a sub-group of the Kenyah) decided to convert immediately and half of the village called Southwell to throw out their indigenous religious objects.[96] Further, it was reported that if his people wanted to convert to Christianity, Penghulu Mape would allow them to choose only evangelical Christianity, though he himself did not convert.[97] As expected, Lio Matu became the centre of work among the Kenyah, with Ray and Evelyn Cunningham stationed there from 1953 to 1957. The Cunninghams consolidated the work among the Kenyah, by holding literacy classes for both young and old for the purpose of reading the Bible, providing their language with a written form, translating portions of Scriptures, and doing medical work.

See J. Waskom Pickett, *Christian Mass Movements in India* (New York: Abingdon, 1933), 185-87. Elizabeth Koepping, in her study of Anglican Christianity among the Kadazan in neigbouring Sabah, makes the observation that there was a small group of locals who had embraced Christianity but still continued 'to base their identity solidly' in their traditional religion, believing that the traditional religion should be respected on equal terms with Christianity. See Elizabeth Koepping, 'Hunting with the Head: Borneo Villagers Negotiating Exclusivist Religion', *Studies in World Christianity* 12.1 (2006), 59-78 (66-69). See the case of an indigenous pastor having charms in his house in Chapter 7.

[95] Cited in Cunningham, *Longhouses Open Doors*, 55. This kind of comment was common in longhouse conversions among both the Kayan and the Kenyah.

[96] *BEM NL*, June 1951, 3.

[97] *BEM NL*, October 1951, 2.

In addition, they made trips to the other Kenyah villages and also made contact with the Penan, a nomadic tribe, in Baram.[98]

In 1950, the BEM adopted a fifteen-year policy of establishing an indigenous 'Three-Self' church by 1965.[99] The urgency of building an indigenous church within nine years impelled the 1956 Field Conference to plan to expand its work among the Kayan and Kenyah of the upper Rajang area, Third Division.[100] The extension of the work among the Kenyah in Long Geng on the Balui River in the Third Division,[101] came in 1957 after an invitation by eight families there who had earlier turned to Christ and who wanted to be taught the Christian way. They had converted as a result of the witness of a relative from Lepu Aga, Baram, who had visited them.[102] From the beginning, the church elected their own leaders after having been taught about the qualifications of Christian leadership from the Bible.[103] The people were quite clear that only three were eligible to hold office and unanimously elected them.[104] To consolidate this work, Ray moved to stay at Long Geng in 1958.

When Ray began work in the Balui, there were three groups: one adhering to the old Kenyah customs, another to the Bungan cult[105] and finally the Christians, who had by then increased to twelve families.[106] By the mid-1960s, the Kenyah had left their old customs and had become either Bungan or

---

[98] Cunningham, *Longhouses Open Doors*, 56-64.

[99] *BEM Eighteenth Annual Report*, 31 December 1951, 12. See Chapter 6 for further discussion.

[100] *BEM NL*, October 1956, 1.

[101] After Belaga, the upper Rajang River is called Balui. Along the Balui from Belaga to the Indonesian border, there were some eighteen villages, varying in size from ten families to ninety families.

[102] Lees, *Drunk before Dawn*, 154. Shirley Lees, *Jungle Fire* (London: Oliphants, 1964), 51.

[103] Based on the teaching of 1 Timothy 3:1-12.

[104] *BEM NL*, August-September 1957, 3.

[105] The Bungan cult was the traditional Kayan religion in its simplified form. It had its origin with Juk Apui, a Kayan who lived in Uma Jalai, Long Abang in Kalimantan. In a dream in 1948, he was told by the goddess Bungan to do away with the restrictive practices and false beliefs of the Kayan religion and to follow her teachings, which were simple and will give him good fortune and bountiful crops. Bungan practices did away with the animal and bird omens, and the customs and procedures of observing omens before planting, building and journeying. But it retained observances relating to death taboos, visits to the grave and cemetery, ceremonies to celebrate padi planting and harvesting, and certain rites of general propitiation. The Bungan cult was brought over to Sarawak in the early 1950. Ian Prattis argues that the cult is a result of the pagan Kayan religion coming into contact with western Christianity. See Tom Harrisson, 'Ulu Problems—Zealots and Dreams', *SG*, 30 June 1956, 145-47; E. White, 'Bungan—A New Kayan Belief', *SMJ* 7.8 (December 1956), 472-75; Fr. P. Aichner, 'Adat Bungan', *SMJ* 7.8 (December 1956), 476-77, and Ian Prattis, 'The Kayan-Kenyah Bungan Cult in Sarawak', *SMJ* 11.21-22 (1963), 68.

[106] *BEM NL*, August-September 1957, 2-3; June-July 1958, 2.

Christians and even those who were Bungan were beginning to turn to Christianity.[107] By the time BEM ceased to function as a mission body, the majority of Kenyah in the Balui had become SIB Christians.

As reported in its newsletter, the BEM leadership had a comprehensive strategy of work, focusing on four key groups of people and areas: first, the Sekapan tribe under their chief, Penghulu Puso, in the district around Belaga; second, the Kayan under their chief, Hang Nyipa, who was Bungan, located at Long Murum; third, the Penan; and fourth, the Kenyah in Long Jawe, the most distant village up the Balui. The Kenyah at Long Jawe, who had recently migrated from Kalimantan, had become Christians under the KINGMI and had sent an invitation for someone to give them Christian instruction.[108] This missionary approach of having a base at each of these strategic areas was reasonably successful. The shortage of BEM missionary personnel meant that indigenous pastors took the initiative for the work in these bases, making the work of the BEM missionaries supplementary. By this time, the BEM missionary policy of 'missionaries without stations' was an entrenched policy.[109]

Kenyah Receptivity and Conversion

The receptivity of the Kenyah at Lio Matu to Christianity provoked an internal crisis among the Kenyah in relation to their traditional beliefs and customs. According to the headman, they had stopped following the omens in their farming ritual for two years when Southwell first met them, though they continued to make sacrifices and observed the pantang for fear of the malignity of the spirits.[110] Furthermore, they had found that their customs and rituals had become excessively burdensome.[111] Their crisis, like that of the Kayan, had been triggered by their contact with the western military forces, whose activities challenged their worldview and system of beliefs and exposed them to a new way of life.

Their conversion resembled closely that of the Kayan at Long Tebangan, exhibiting a similar interplay of factors as well as in their process of conversion. The impetus for change came first from the headman, then from the

---

[107] *BEM NL*, October 1967, 3. There was a general disillusionment with the Bungan cult as it had not been able to adapt to the sophistication of modern civilization and also the educated young people were openly critical and would have no part in their traditional practices. Moreover, the death of Juk Apui, the high priest of the cult, had left the movement without a leader. Most embarrassing to the cult was the conversion of several of his longhouses to Christianity.

[108] *BEM NL*, June-July 1958, 2.

[109] *BEM NL*, July 1960, 1.

[110] *BEM NL*, October 1947, 4. Southwell, *Uncharted Waters*, 231-34.

[111] According to the headman, in one farming season, the community had to sacrifice 40 fowls and several pigs to the spirits as well as a lot of *borak*. In addition, each family had to make its own sacrifices. Southwell, *Uncharted Waters*, 229-30.

the leading dayong, resulting in the renunciation of the old ways first by the other dayong and later by individuals, with the disposal of their charms and taboos. This was accompanied by the act of commitment to Christ, a prayer of protection from the spirits and an experience of intense relief, liberation and joy.[112]

The conversion of the Lepu Aga Kenyah came out of the decision of the 1951 council over which Penghulu Mape presided. The chief's change in attitude may be attributed to several factors. Firstly, the BEM missionaries, especially Southwell and Cunningham, had been careful to cultivate a close and cordial relationship with Penghulu Mape that included friendly discussion on religion. In their on-going interaction, the missionaries insisted that they had no intention to of changing Kenyah customs, nor did they interfere with, denigrate or ridicule Kenyah religious practices.[113] In one instance, arriving at Long Moh in 1949 during the initiation ceremony for children, Southwell stayed with the community till the end of the ceremony and left without any opportunity to share the Christian message.[114] The compliance, whether conscious or otherwise, with the Kenyah's etiquette that governed the social relationships and religious interactions augured well for the work of the BEM.

Secondly, their fellow Kenyah across the border in Kalimantan had become Christians through the work of the C&MA, so it appeared good to embrace evangelical Christianity for the sake of clan solidarity and unity. Further, Penghulu Mape had been interested in having a school and had asked the government several times for it but to no avail.[115] He doubtlessly hoped that the BEM could provide a school as it had done earlier at Long Tebangan and Lio Matu, if he allowed his people to embrace evangelical Christianity. It can be argued that the conversion of the Lepu Aga Kenyah was due largely to a desire for superior access to resources or power, whether spiritual or material, as by this time, the Lun Bawang, who had formerly been regarded as dirty, backward and ignorant by the Kayan and Kenyah had become most successful, having been the first to become Christians and receive the benefits of education.[116]

---

[112] *BEM NL*, October 1947, 4.
[113] Southwell, *Uncharted Waters*, 226.
[114] Southwell, *Uncharted Waters*, 283-85. The initiation ceremony of children into adulthood was a big festival. Once the festival started, the whole village was placed under a taboo. The sacrifice of a pig was required for each of the seventy-two children present at the ceremony. A prayer was whispered into the ears of the pigs and the blood of each pig was daubed on the head of the respective child. The liver of the pig was then taken out and put on a platter to be examined by the *dayongs* to see if the omens were good. Accompanying this festival were much entertainment, dancing in groups of thirty people, chanting in harmony and feasting.
[115] Southwell, *Unpublished Memoirs*, section 17.5. Cunningham, *Longhouses Open Doors*, 62-64
[116] *BEM NL*, October 1951, 2.

The Penan, the Nomadic tribe of the Baram

The Spread of the Mission and its Practices

When churches were started among the Kayan and Kenyah in the Baram, the Penan heard the Christian message as they came out to trade or barter with the various tribes, so some became Christians.[117] But it was only during the organized market days or 'tamu' that the missionaries approached the Penan of the Silat River directly with the Christian message and conducted Bible teaching sessions for them, for example, as Ray Cunningham did at Lepu Aga in 1951.[118] Because of their nomadic lifestyle, contact with them depended on their occasional visits to the BEM stations at Long Atip, Long Tebangan and Lio Matu, often for medicine, and they sometimes joined in the Sunday church service.[119] Encouraging responses came first at Long Atip in April 1952, after Win Burrows with a couple of Kayan deacons accompanied two Penan into the jungle to treat a sick woman. There followed a series of conversions, beginning with eighteen Penan.[120] Also at Lio Matu in 1954, a Penan family decided to stay for six weeks, learning to read and attending the Bible classes for the Kenyah.[121]

Visits made to them by missionaries led to a number of conversions among the Penan, including the chief of the Silat River.[122] His conversion is described as follows:

> It was a solemn occasion when Akam Lawing, the chief of the Silat Penan, declared he was going to trust Jesus. In front of his people he took a knife and cut off a small cane container tied around his waist, containing a sacred stone blackened with dried blood. It was believed that the stone had come from the gods and held supernatural powers.[123]

With each successive tamu or visit to them, there were more conversions among the Penan.[124] At other times, they would go to the BEM stations to ask to become Christians.[125] By 1957, there were three Penan boys joining the

---

[117] *BEM NL*, April 1949, 1. Some Penan had become Christians earlier because of the Kelabit from Long Lellang. Raja Maran, a deacon there, had two Penan helpers and he had assisted Southwell in his first visit to the Kayan in Baram. See Southwell, *Uncharted Waters*, 207.

[118] *BEM NL*, February 1952, 1.

[119] *BEM NL*, June 1954, 2.

[120] *BEM NL*, June 1952, 2.

[121] *BEM NL*, April 1954, 4.

[122] *BEM NL*, October 1952, 3. Cunningham's work was made easier as the Lepu Aga Christians had done some teaching among the Penan there. *BEM NL*, February 1953, 2. Cunningham was to spend some time with Tama Siba, the leader of the Penan.

[123] Cunningham, *Longhouses Open Doors*, 60.

[124] *BEM NL*, February 1955, 2 and October-November 1955, 2.

[125] *BEM NL*, October-November 1955, 2.

Kenyah in the school at Lio Matu,[126] and a set of reading primers in Penan was completed for them.[127]

In the light of this growing work, the 1957 Field Conference first decided to make Lio Matu the centre for the Penan work, with Phyllis Webster in charge. Short-term schools arranged for them catered for about five different groups of Penan; some from as far away as Long Akah and Apoh. When the school closed, they returned to the jungle until the next series of lessons.[128] In 1958, the BEM moved the centre to Long Bedian and started a school for the Penan.[129] Soon after, one Penan entered Lawas Bible School, followed by several more in April 1960.[130]

Miss Phylis Webster, Penan

The government's plan to encourage the Penan from as early as 1949 to settle into longhouses or villages so as to make it easier to provide amenities, educational and medical facilities for them,[131] also worked to the clear advantage of the BEM. The Penan communities that had responded included one at Silat River and another of twenty families at Long Lamai along the Balong River in upper Baram.[132] Extensive trips were made to this more easily accessible group,[133] with Webster and Leah Cubitt conducting a school that included reading, Bible study lessons, hygiene and other practical matters

[126] *BEM NL*, February-March 1957, 2.
[127] *BEM NL*, August-September 1957, 4.
[128] *BEM NL*, October-November 1957, 2-3; January-February 1960, 2.
[129] *BEM NL*, February-March 1959, 4. Dariu, Lehai, Pelutan and Ving were students of Webster.
[130] *BEM NL*, October-November 1957, 3 and March-April 1960, 4.
[131] *BEM NL*, April 1949, 1.
[132] *BEM NL*, November-December 1960, 4.
[133] *BEM NL*, April 1962, 4.

concerned with a settled lifestyle. An attendance of seventy was reported,[134] and by 1962, they had a government primary school.[135]

By 1963, the work among the Penan was reported as having the fastest growth in the Mission,[136] as more Penan were settling down to a cultivator rather than nomadic lifestyle.[137] The BEM had three concerns: firstly, the need for local pastors to consolidate the work; secondly, the need for the translation of the Scriptures into Penan; and thirdly, the need to integrate the Penan into the life and activities of the SIB, which had already been officially formed in 1959.[138] These aims were being fulfilled with the starting of a feeder Bible school at Long Bedian in July 1963, in which Pastor Dario and his wife, Lahai, (both Penan) took charge and also with the sending of ten Penan to the Lawas Bible School for training to be future leaders of the Penan church.[139]

Ray Cunningham at Pakan

Penan Receptivity and Conversion

The conversion of the first eighteen families in 1952, when Win Burrows went into the jungle to treat a sick Penan woman, took place in a manner that was similar to the pattern of the earlier Kayan and Kenyah conversions, including the disposal of their charms and fetishes. But the factors that contributed to their conversion were probably twofold. Firstly, the act of Burrows in accompanying the Penan into the jungle to treat a sick woman was surprising

---

[134] *BEM NL*, March-April 1961, 3; May-June 1961, 3.
[135] *BEM NL*, August 1962, 3.
[136] *BEM NL*, June 1963, 2.
[137] *BEM NL* February 1964, 3. Five groups of Penan were settling down to a farming life.
[138] *BEM NL*, August 1962, 3.
[139] *BEM NL*, August 1963, 3 and December 1963, 1.

and unthinkable for a white woman to do; it was an act that touched their hearts. Further, as the Kenyah, who were considered their 'masters', had begun to convert, the conversion of the Penan might be understood as an act of solidarity with the Kenyah. Finally the conversion of the Penan, as of other groups, had an explicitly spiritual dimension; it was remarked by a BEM missionary that 'their capacity for taking in deep spiritual truth has been notable'.[140]

The Sekapan of the Belaga

The conversion of Penghulu Puso of the Sekapan gave the work of the BEM a great moral encouragement.[141] This conversion was, however, a different story from the Kayan and Kenyah. The majority of his sixty-family community refused to convert with Puso and even absented themselves when he destroyed his fetishes and charms. Later, others were slowly won over when a Lun Bawang missionary couple came to live and work among them.[142] In a hierarchical society, it is to be expected that the conversion of a chief will be followed by a large number of his followers. But in the case of Penghulu Puso, only 'a few families turned to Christ'.[143] This unusual situation may be attributed to Puso's heavy addiction to opium. It is probable that his opium addiction had taken a toll on his mind, body and health and created for him a personal crisis and a desperate need. Further, despite possessing some of the most powerful charms in his tribe, it can be surmised that he had found his spirits powerless to deliver him from his opium addiction. If this was the situation, it would probably have created for him a 'dissonance' with his traditional belief system, so as to make him more receptive to the Christian message. The context of Puso's conversion resembled to some extent the situation of the Lun Bawang in the 1930s, but with a difference. His conversion was a change of allegiance driven by his quest for superior resources to deliver him from his personal predicament. After his conversion, he was subsequently but rather slowly delivered from his opium addiction.[144] The slow deliverance from his addiction may have made his people less inclined to embrace Christianity.

---

140 Lees, *Jungle Fire*, 76-77. *BEM NL* , April 1964, 2.

141 McDonald, *The Borneo People*, 222. Penghulu Puso of the Sekapan was acknowledged as one of the great leaders who had shown 'true courage, wisdom and vision' in their fight against the Japanese during WWII.

142 Cunningham, *Longhouses Open Doors*, 86. *BEM NL*, February-March 1959, 2. The Lun Bawang couple was Balang Selutan and Muring.

143 *BEM NL*, April 1964, 3.

144 Cunningham, *Longhouses Open Doors*, 86.

The Iban in Pakan and the Julau and Niah Rivers

The Spread of the Mission and its Practices

As the BEM began its work among the Iban in the Limbang and Lubai in 1928, but without much tangible result, the Mission was ever afterwards mindful of the need to work among the Iban, the largest of the indigenous groups in Sarawak.[145] In 1956, the Field Conference reflected on the need to re-start the work among the Iban of the Limbang.[146] During this time, the focus of work had shifted to the Baram and beyond, and the BEM missionaries were looking for opportunities to expand to any unreached group of people in the Third and Second Divisions. Opportunities came when there were invitations to visit Iban longhouses further south in the Rajang, first going to Nanga Julau to the home of Pengara Banyang, an Iban chief in 1959[147] and later establishing a base at Pakan around three longhouses, Rumah Empali, Rumah Dundang and Rumah Liman.[148] This beginning of the Iban church had eighteen families under headman Empali.

As it had been BEM policy to encourage local leadership, four men were elected as leaders or deacons of the church from among the founding members at Rumah Empali. They also asked for and received a Lun Bawang pastor and his wife to live among them.[149] To encourage their integration with the other Christian tribes, two of their leaders were sent to represent the Pakan church at the 1960 Inter-Tribal Conference held by the SIB.[150] But as Cunningham observed, a dilemma existed for the Iban church, which did not want its leaders to be away from them, while the BEM and SIB wished them to be more integrated with the other cultural groups.[151] Another factor was the distance between Pakan, the upper Rajang and Lawas. Part of this difficulty was solved by making the Inter-Tribal conference a biennial conference from 1961.[152]

---

[145] The 1947 census showed that Christians only formed about 2.9% (1,245 Roman Catholics, 4,135 Anglicans, 709 Methodists and 87 BEM Christians) of the total Iban population of 190,326 in Sarawak. See J.L. Noakes, 'Sarawak and Brunei: A Report on 1947 Population Census', *SMJ* 5.3 (November 1951), 628-44.

[146] *BEM NL*, October-November 1956, 1.

[147] *BEM NL*, August-September 1959, 3. He was warm and welcoming but did not convert, probably restrained by his Roman Catholic relatives. See also Cunningham, *Longhouse Open Doors*, 88-90.

[148] *BEM NL*, March-April 1960, 2. But government permission had to be sought from Kuching and was given by end January 1960. But government permission to work at Nanga Julau was refused.

[149] Cunningham, *Longhouses Open Doors*, 91-3. *BEM NL*, May-June 1960, 1 and January-February 1961, 2-3. Pastor Labo Tadam and his wife, Bau were not properly supported. Pastor Labo was given $5.00 per month instead of the pastor's allowance of $21.00. *BEM NL*, October 1961, 1.

[150] *BEM NL*, January-February 1961, 1. Empali and Tungkus were the representatives.

[151] Cunningham, *Longhouses Open Doors*, 102-103.

[152] *BEM NL*, December 1965, 2.

This work among the Iban, which had begun well, was followed by a declining interest in the Christian religion. When Cunningham moved to Pakan in October 1961 to consolidate the work there, he noted that the Iban had no real desire for spiritual growth; a week-long Bible school had to be reduced to one and a half days, and support for the pastor had been insufficient. Nevertheless, pressing opportunities came through many new invitations to visit and speak at the Iban longhouses, which bore slow but steady results of conversions of small groups within the longhouses.[153]

The most promising work was among the school children attending Cunningham's night meetings for singing and teaching, of whom a number were sons and daughters of chiefs and headmen from River Wak. During Cunningham's visit to the homes of two of these children, some young people decided to become Christians.[154] After the Cunninghams left Pakan in 1965, the work was continued by the Nappers, the Burtons and later the Colemans. They focused more on the young people, who became very responsive, and through them reached their family, relatives and new areas.[155] Contact was also made with the older Iban through literacy classes to enable them to read the Bible. By the time BEM officially ceased its work in Sarawak, more than eighty churches had been established in that area.[156]

However, according to Peter Varney, an Anglican priest, news of the rapid spread of the SIB from the Fifth Division to the Third and Second Divisions was viewed with some apprehension and fear by the Anglicans. They feared losing their members to the SIB, as the SIB members seemed very confident about their Christian faith. Moreover, the SIB was viewed more as a cult group with heretical teaching. Thus, the Anglicans were ill at ease with the impending spread of the SIB into their areas.[157]

Iban Receptivity and Conversion

Conversions among the Iban were of two kinds: the first among the older people in the longhouses and later among the young people, mainly schoolchildren. Conversions among these two groups exhibited different characteristics. During the 1960s, the interior of Sarawak was beginning to open up to the increasing effects of modernization and to a higher level of education. The impact of education created a social stratum of a more literate

---

[153] *BEM NL*, August 1964, 2. Often on every trip, there were conversions of eight to ten families.

[154] *BEM NL*, December 1962, 2. More young people from Wak River began to convert. See *BEM NL*, April 1963, 4.

[155] *BEM NL*, February 1965, 4.

[156] Cunningham, *Longhouses Open Doors*, 102-103.

[157] Interview with Peter Varney, 7 March 2006. Peter Varney is an Anglican priest who served in the Diocese of Kuching from 1967-1968. At that time, Varney was a doctoral anthropology student with the London School of Economics, University of London. He had earlier visited Labuan and Sarawak in 1959 when he did his National Service.

younger people in the midst of older illiterate people. These young people, who were exposed to western scientific thinking, were openly critical of their own traditional religions.[158] The influence of these young people was strengthened by the opening of new roads everywhere in the Rajang and leading to the Second Division, which greatly increased social interaction and mixing, and indirectly contributed to a waning interest in the local religions. The conversion of the older people, who were still strongly connected to their traditional way of life, was indirectly influenced by the young and educated people. They were also influenced by the different lifestyle of the Lun Bawang, especially the pastors among them, who exhibited a demeanour of confidence and a freedom from the restrictions of their local religion, as they had come from a group of people that was once most despised in Sarawak. The crux of their conversion was once again a desire for superior resources of power over the spirits.[159]

Missionary Initiatives and Indigenous Assistance

It was once common for western writers to attribute missionary initiatives as the main cause for the spread of Christianity among indigenous people, often neglecting and sometimes discounting the role of indigenous dissemination. There have certainly been increasing voices in recent years calling for correctives to this view.[160] In the work of the BEM, indigenous assistance and initiatives played a very important role.

In the post-war era, indigenous pastors or workers were always part of the team in every BEM mission trip. Their role not only augmented that of the BEM missionaries but at times made a substantial contribution. In the case of the Kayan at Long Tebangan, Guru Riong and Kading, the two Lun Bawang companions of Southwell, played no less important roles. At a crucial stage, Guru Riong was invited to join the sub-headmen to discuss whether the Kayan should convert, a privilege not granted to Southwell. There was no doubt about the importance of Riong's role as advisor and counsellor to them. Further, when the decision had been made, the Kayan requested Guru Riong and Kading to help them get rid of their charms,[161] a significant request from the

---

[158] *BEM NL*, October 1967, 3. By 1960, the Iban already had members of its community in tertiary education. See *BEM NL*, July-August 1960, 4.

[159] *BEM NL*, May 1960, 1.

[160] See, for example, M. Loiuse Pirouet, 'East African Christians and the World War I', *Journal of African History* 19.1 (1978), 117-30. Pirouet argues that missionary thinking in the aftermath of World War I had failed to recognize the role of indigenous initiatives in the dissemination of the Christian message, as their underlying assumption had been that African Christians deprived of European leadership would either lapse into heathenism or wander into wrong paths. A similar kind of missionary thinking was expressed during the fall of China to communism in 1949, that without European missionary leadership, the demise of Christianity would be inevitable in China.

[161] Southwell, *Uncharted Waters*, 214-18.

perspective of the indigenous people. If Guru Riong, considered as one of them, could get rid of the charms and have freedom from the fear of the spirits without any harmful consequences, then it served to confirm the rightness of their decision. Importantly, the prayer for protection over the whole village led by Guru Riong had a subtle and re-assuring effect in confirming the ability of an indigenous Christian's prayer to withstand the power of the spirits.

At Long Tebangan and Lio Matu, the two main centres of work among the Kayan and Kenyah respectively, indigenous pastors collaborated with the missionaries. For instance, the Lun Bawang couple, Tebari and Layun, who were stationed at Lio Matu in 1953,[162] started a school in Lepu Aga, the next village from Long Moh,[163] which became highly popular with the young people, and they had also prepared seven boys to attend school in Lio Matu, an idea opposed by a senior member in the community. Further, Tebari had taken a group of schoolboys on a trip to the Penan in the Silat River, resulting in one Penan leader going away to another area to find his relatives and to bring them to Silat to make them Christians.[164] Here, the indigenous work not only assisted and complemented, but also extended beyond that of the missionary.

Indigenous initiative was evidenced in the conversion of some eight families at Long Geng through visits by their Christian relatives from Lepu Aga, Baram, which later resulted in an invitation to BEM to begin work at Long Geng. Further, the new Christians showed some initiative in re-interpreting their Christian faith in relation to issues raised about their worldview. In one instance, when their relatives from Kalimantan had accused them of discarding too much of their Kenyah customs and not respecting the Kenyah gods, they reasoned that if they respected their Kenyah gods, they would come under their power; but since Jesus is more powerful than the Kenyah gods, they would affirm their faith in Jesus alone.[165]

The mass conversion of the Kayan, especially at Rumah Kahal (or the Uma Kahei village) in the Belaga in 1959, was not the direct result of BEM missionary work,[166] but of the indigenous ministry of Tama Pudun, a Kenyah deacon from Lio Matu. Further, the consolidation of the work in this village was first done by Pastors Anyi and Ngau, recent graduates from the Lawas Bible School, who were then stationed at Rumah Puso, and later by two deacons from the Baram churches, who spent a prolonged period of time with the locals to act temporarily as their spiritual leaders. This was much to the delight of the BEM, 'a particularly pleasing aspect of this work at Uma Kahei is that it is getting a consecutive ministry from its inception by Bornean men'.[167] Another situation of a similar kind, where the indigenous pastor had more

[162] *BEM NL*, February 1953, 2.
[163] *BEM NL*, August, 1953, 4.
[164] *BEM NL*, October 1953, 1, 4; December 1953, 3.
[165] Cunningham, *Longhouses Open Doors*, 76.
[166] Ray Cunningham had visited them but without any results.
[167] *BEM NL*, August-September 1959, 3; October-November 1959, 1.

success than the BEM missionary, was the case of the Iban of Bakong, a tributary of the lower Baram, who had shown some interest in the Christian faith and had a couple of visits by Ray Cunningham in 1961;[168] and the fruits of the conversion of fourteen families in a village along the Bakong came through the ministry of Pastor Wan Maring of Long Atip.[169] In short, the indigenous leaders and pastors had begun to show themselves to be competent in evangelism, were often more successful than the missionaries, and had shown initiative to plant and nurture a new church in their own way.

The major outreach towards the Iban had come from the indigenous people themselves, though the BEM missionaries initiated Iban work in a couple of cases as at Pakan and Niah. The Iban work at Rumah Empali, Pakan, was consolidated and expanded by the Lun Bawang pastor Labo Tadam and his wife, Bau, to the surrounding areas. The conversion of Adam, the headman of a village in the Sugai River area, while visiting his relative, Empali, the Iban headman, subsequently led to the conversion of four families from his village. Later visits by other indigenous pastors like Mamat and Ipui, helped them in their understanding of their new-found faith and the application of the Bible to their daily lives.[170] In short, the Iban outreach had expanded through the connecting network of families and friends in the surrounding areas and was facilitated by indigenous pastors.

The other area of promising work in Pakan involved an outreach to Iban schoolboys, which was first initiated by the missionaries. This had the spin-off effect of spurring schoolboys to engage actively in discussions about issues of life and the Bible among themselves, which not only served to strengthen their grasp of their Christian faith but also to witness to other schoolboys, displaying initiatives independent of the missionaries that led to further evangelistic efforts. A missionary reported approvingly on the initiative and keenness of an Iban schoolboy.

> It is interesting to note how they have caught on the idea of discussing the Word of God among themselves. One of the young men from this group took us along the track to spend a night at Rumah Boyong. Here we were given a splendid hearing. Clearly the general reaction was favourable.[171]

Another aspect of indigenous initiative may be seen in the work of gifted indigenous pastors who engaged in missionary outreach to the areas

---

[168] *BEM NL*, August 1961, 4. The Iban in this area had migrated from more crowded Second and Third Divisions. Though the Iban were forbidden by law to enter Kayan territory, they were allowed to do so if they were moving to join relatives who were already living there. As a result of this loophole, the lower Baram has some eight thousand Iban; of which three and a half thousand lived in the Bakong area.

[169] *BEM NL*, December 1961, 3.

[170] *BEM NL*, April 1963, 4. See Lees, *Drunk before Dawn*, 157.

[171] *BEM NL*, April 1963, 4.

surrounding their pastorates. Balang Selutan is a good example. When he was pastor at Long Atip, he made several trips to visit the unreached areas among the Kayan, Punan Ba, Iban and Penan. In his second pastorate at Trusan, he encouraged every church member to be an active witness for God, arranging for teams of pastors, deacons and church members to take part in evangelism to the surrounding areas. As a result, churches were established with local resident pastors in all except one of the areas visited.[172] The leadership style exhibited by Balang was one of example, encouragement and empowerment of his people in the common task of building the local churches.

Conclusion

In this study, we have shown the dramatic spread of the work of the BEM from 1946 to 1965 into the Baram, Fourth Division, and later into the Balui and Belaga, Third Division, through the interior overland routes and down to the major rivers, Baram and Rajang, toward the sub-coastal towns such as Pakan. This expansion had been motivated by the evangelistic outlook of the BEM missionaries, who sought every opportunity to evangelize the Orang Ulu, despite governmental restrictions. In the serial expansion of their work, BEM had a comprehensive strategy of outreach so that new areas were saturated with itinerant preaching trips with the aim of starting bases at strategic locations to consolidate their work where conversions had occurred. The BEM's preference for missionary couples at the various bases to develop the work within specified areas was a fruitful strategy.[173] Here, the BEM's mobilization of women in mission had initially been through married women working alongside their husbands at their respective bases. Later, it was accomplished through the use of single women, working either singly under a married couple or in pairs at a station, as in Long Atip, and involved in educational, medical, Bible translation work and Bible school training. In turn, their work was reinforced by another far-sighted policy of placing indigenous pastors and their wives as married couples to work alongside the BEM missionaries. In addition, the success of the BEM work may be attributed to having composite local-missionary teams on every itinerant mission trip and possibly also to the adoption of a culturally sensitive missionary approach, whether done consciously in response to official criticisms, or unconsciously according to the dictates of the specific situation.

The response of the BEM to the colonial control of mission activities had been to circumvent or employ creative methods in overcoming such obstacles. The impossibility of establishing a base in an area did not preclude regular visits by itinerant composite teams of missionaries and indigenous workers

---

[172] *BEM NL*, October 1963, 4.

[173] Long Atip for the Kayan in the Tutoh and Apoh area, Long Tebangan for the Kayan in the middle Baram and Lio Matu for the Kenyah in the upper Baram,

until conversions occurred, which then justified the setting up of a base. Further, the creative use of indigenous workers as a spearhead into a new area met with no effective governmental response.

The mass movement into Christianity, though dramatic, did not mean that all were regarded as 'genuine' conversions by the standards of the evangelical tradition of the BEM. Aware of this phenomenon, the Mission emphasised teaching the Scriptures till everyone professed 'personal salvation' in Christ.

The conversions among the Orang Ulu showed a complex variety of causes and factors. The initial conversions among the Kayan and Kenyah, especially at Long Tebangan and Lio Matu respectively, exhibited a similar cause, that is, the impact of outside western influence during WWII on Orang Ulu religion and culture, which made them re-evaluate some of their own cultural practices. Other factors were no less important. In interaction with the biblical message, their worldview underwent a re-orientation so that a transition was made from their traditional beliefs to an indigenized Christian worldview. The presentation of Jesus Christ as the Lord with liberating power over the spirits and their attendant practices sounded attractive to them, as traditional religious rituals had apparently left them hungry and in abject poverty.[174] Also this Christian belief in the superiority of the power of Christ was experientially validated in the conversion process as taboos were now infringed with impunity. Thus, conversion, on the one hand, meant identification with a world religion that was associated with a more advanced culture, technology and civilization. On the other, it meant a change of allegiance to a superior power or resources based on evangelical beliefs in the authority of Christ over the spirits. Later conversions among the the Kayan and Kenyah, and also among the Penan, Sekapan and Iban, laid a greater emphasis on this latter category, for instance in the conversion of Penghulu Tama Paya Anyi of Long Atip, who was also a shaman. In short, a dynamic interplay of factors gave rise to the complexities of conversion among the Orang Ulu.

With the benefits of modernity and education introduced first by the mission and promoted later by the government since the mid-1950s, the more educated young people, who had become more responsive to Christianity, migrated to the sub-coastal and coastal towns, which in turn, later caused a re-evaluation of BEM mission policy, a theme that will be examined in the next chapter.

Despite subscribing to the relative priority of evangelism over education, the BEM played no small part in introducing literacy and education among the Orang Ulu in the villages that had converted to Christianity. Their purpose in promoting literacy, to a greater extent than in the other Christian missions in Sarawak, was to promote the reading of the Bible and zeal in the propagation of the Christian faith. When the BEM offered both Malay-medium and vernacular

[174] Southwell, 'The Kayan and Kenyah', 45. 'Within recent decades, this whole religious structure had become an increasing and an intolerable burden – more so among the Kayan than among the Kenyah'.

primary education in contrast to the English-medium education of the SPG and Roman Catholics, it was to have wider social implications. The use of both the vernacular and Malay language has been instrumental in preserving the Orang Ulu cultural traditions for the SIB and also in enabling them to move beyond their own culture to relate to the other cultures in Sarawak and in assimilating other tribes into the church, themes that will be explored further.[175] In contrast, the Sarawak Iban Annual Conference (SIAC) which uses predominantly the Dyak or Iban language experienced great difficulty in reaching out to the other tribes.

This study has also shown that indigenous dissemination of Christianity had not only complemented missionary efforts but in many instances shown creative indigenous initiatives that enhanced and extended the work well beyond those of the BEM missionaries. The dialectical relationship in their work, that is, missionary initiative with indigenous assistance and in turn, indigenous initiative with missionary assistance, was central to the success of the serial expansion of their work, which entailed constantly looking out for new opportunities of work, starting new bases and consolidating them and exploring further avenues of expansion. This manner of work contributed greatly to the establishment of a 'Three-Self' indigenous church, the SIB, which will be the subject of our next chapter.

Dr Bill and Shirley Lees

[175] See Chapter 6.

Chapter 6

The Relationship of the BEM and the SIB Church 1959-1979

Since the inception of its work in Sarawak in 1928, the BEM remained constantly mindful of its objective to plant 'an indigenous Christian church', which was later clarified as a 'Three-Self' church in 1939. This goal was realized through the formal establishment of the SIB in 1959 as a separate parallel entity from the parent missionary body. In the last two chapters, we have examined the expansion of the BEM work, which first focused its work on the Limbang and Trusan Rivers, Fifth Division, among the Lun Bawang and the Kelabit in the pre-war period. It later witnessed a dramatic expansion in the post-war era into the Baram area among the Kayan and Kenyah, spreading in two directions: one southward down the Baram to the sub-coastal town of Marudi and later to the coastal town of Miri, (also the administrative centre of the Fourth Division), and the other across the overland mountain range from the upper Baram to the Balui River, upper Rajang area, Third Division and down the Rajang River to Belaga and later to the sub-coastal town of Pakan on the Julau River. Churches which were established were generally encouraged to be 'Three-Self' from their inception.

In this chapter, we will examine the approach which the BEM took to planting a 'Three-Self' church, by analysing a) the establishment of the SIB in 1959 and the circumstances surrounding it; b) the policies and patterns of work which supported the establishment of the SIB, the formulation and implementation of the distinctive fifteen-year policy and the rise of indigenous leadership and response; and c) the subsequent relationship between the BEM and the SIB in cooperative ministry from 1959 to 1979.

The BEM and the Formation of the SIB

The policy of the 'Three-Self' church was widely propounded in the nineteenth century—Henry Venn (1796-1873) and Rufus Anderson (1796-1880) being the most prominent British and American advocates respectively. But the implementation of this policy had been compromised, for example in Sierra Leone and the Punjab by the end of the high imperialist era, where the missionaries continued to hold dominant power either in or behind the ecclesiastical structures created to provide for indigenous autonomy.[1] In other parts of Africa similar trends became apparent. For example, in Uganda or (later) the Eastern Congo, the Conservative Baptist Foreign Mission Society (CBFMS), which strongly advocated the indigenous policy, had 'the intent of the policy reversed in its implementation'. As a result, 'appeals to the principles of the policy became the means of legitimizing increased missionary control over development of the mission-church organization', which led to a frustration of African initiatives and eventually to a rebellion against missionary domination.[2] In the case of China, both British and American missions were forced to devolve authority to indigenous churches as a result of militant anti-Christian sentiments and actions from 1922 to 1927, followed by the subsequent exodus of some 5000 Protestant missionaries from the country. But these attempts at devolution were hasty and superficial.[3] Though there was no formal abandonment of this policy by mission bodies, the issue often lay with the timing and the means, not with the aim of policy.

As discussed in Chapter 3, the 1939 BEM Statement expressed the goal of the BEM as establishing an indigenous 'Three-Self' church. By 1939, when the formation of indigenous churches was becoming a reality, the BEM spelt out clearly 'the principle of a self-supporting church and opposed the principle of supporting native workers out of Mission funds'. Individual churches were to be self-governing, in accordance with New Testament teaching, and 'when these increase in number, they should be organized into a larger body, a Conference, which should exercise authority over the local churches'. There was a provision for the missionary who had responsibility for each tribe, in consultation with the Christians, to decide on the details of organization and government in that district or tribe.

> Converts must be stimulated and encouraged in the study of the Word of God; suitable opportunities should be afforded them for the manifestation of their spiritual gifts...be encouraged to help by material giving, according to their ability, in the work of God. Native helpers especially should be afforded all possible help and encouragement; as they become able they should be allowed to

---

[1] Andrew Walls, 'British Missions', and John Webster, 'British Missions in India', in Torben Christensen and W.R. Hutchinson (eds.), *Missionary Ideologies in the Imperialist Era.1880-1920* (Aarhus: Aros Publishers, 1982), 162-63 & 42-44 respectively.

[2] C. Peter Williams, *The Ideal of the Self-Governing Church: A Study in Victorian Missionary Strategy*, Studies in Christian Mission (Leiden: E.J. Brill, 1990), 243-57; Jack E. Nelson, 'The Indigenous Policy: Ideals and Realities', *Mission Studies* 11-1, 21 (1994), 27-28.

[3] Brian Stanley, *The Bible and the Flag: Protestant Missions and British Imperialism in the Nineteenth and Twentieth Centuries* (Leicester: Apollos/IVP, 1990), 144-45.

> bear responsibility, and the element of foreign teaching, pastoral care, and supervision, be gradually withdrawn.[4]

The seriousness of this intention was reflected thus: firstly, in regard to the choice of missionary candidates, it stated that 'candidates are expected to satisfy themselves as to the Principles and Practice of the Mission, and not offer themselves unless they cordially approve of them and heartily desire to carry them out'.[5] Secondly, there was the reminder to all missionaries of their reason for becoming a missionary with the BEM. 'All should be constantly mindful of their professed objective of leaving home—the speediest evangelization of all native tribes.'[6]

The key issue did not lie with the conceptualization of the 'Three-Self' church but whether in its implementation, the policy would be refined, compromised or even subtly undermined by the missionaries themselves when a differing set of principles was emphasised, as was the case in the history of the CMS where Eugene Stock's idealism stood in contradiction to Henry Venn's realism.[7]

It is therefore instructive to trace the implementation of this policy by the BEM. Until the time of the internment of the BEM missionaries in 1942, the churches were organized along the style of their village councils and meetings, and had their own church buildings and set of church leaders or deacons. But with the dramatic mass conversions of the Kayan in the Baram in 1947, the need for an ecclesial structure (that is, a Conference) to coordinate and exercise authority over the work of these indigenous churches, which had hitherto existed as independent churches, became more urgent. In implementing the policy set out in 1939, Southwell initiated the first annual Conference of Native Christians as an Easter Conference in 1948, where sixty-five churches and sixty-eight out of a total of seventy-five church elders attended with the view 'to form a Conference' so as 'to begin the process of self-government and self-support'.[8]

The subsequent series of events during the decade witnessed steady strides toward the formation of the SIB; especially after the adoption of the fifteen-year policy by the BEM in 1950. As will be examined later, the fifteen-year

---

[4] Statement of the Principles and Practice of the BEM, 1939.

[5] Statement of the Character, Principles and Practice of the BEM, September 1939, 2.

[6] Statement of the Character, Principles and Practice of the BEM, September 1939, 3.

[7] Williams, *The Ideal of the Self-Governing Church*, 259-61. Stock's idealism stressed the unity of the Church, arguing that as the background of the bishop was not an important factor, it was proper for an Englishman to be the bishop of the church. His idealism, that supported the idea of letting the best man emerge to the position of leadership and be acknowledged by others, was in effect a way of legitimizing white bishops. Venn's proposal included the formation of a separate episcopate for the Africans so that they may be allowed to express cultural and national differences without being under the control of the 'dominant' Anglo-Saxon.

[8] Letter of C.H. Southwell to H. McCracken, 8 March 1948 (OMF).

policy was formulated in an atmosphere of political uncertainty and anxiety due to the perceived communist threat to the region of Southeast Asia, so that this policy gave BEM a great impetus to its work in establishing a 'Three-Self' church.[9] The first Pastors' Conference which was held in 1952 with thirteen pastors, including two wives, became an annual event and later developed into the Inter-Tribal Conference of the SIB.[10] The year 1954 was significant on two counts: firstly, a big step forward was taken by including national representatives for the first time into the 1954 BEM Field Conference, where the issue of a 'Three-Self' church was discussed.[11] Secondly, the formation of a representative body to administer the Bornean churches took place at this first Inter-Tribal Conference in December 1954, when a committee was formed, comprising Racha Umong as secretary, a representative from each of the churches from the six tribes present, a representative from the Bible School, and the Belchers (Alan and Madge) representing the BEM. This event was proudly reported as follows:

> This is surely a significant step towards implementing the Mission plan of building an indigenous church in ten years and of handing over control for the whole of the work to the Bornean Church… A further significant feature is that only two of the ten members are white missionaries.[12]

In 1956, the Inter-Tribal Conference accepted the handing over of responsibility from the BEM for all matters relating to the Bornean churches. This significant step was reflected in the change of chairmanship of the church council to Racha Umong.[13] At that time, the BEM Executive agreed that 'the Bornean churches needed a uniform pattern of church government'.[14] In the 1960 BEM Field Conference, it was agreed that

> The pattern of organization and church government already established is roughly presbyterial with a) local churches governed by elders and in some cases a pastor who more or less fulfils the functions of a presiding elder; b) the 'presbytery' or group of churches in a given district whose representatives meet at the Annual convention in their particular area; c) the 'assembly', or the annual inter-tribal

---

[9] See below of this chapter.

[10] The Inter-Tribal Conference later became known as the SIB General Conference.

[11] *BEM NL*, October 1954, 1.

[12] *BEM NL*, April 1955, 1. The committee comprised representatives of the six tribal churches: Murut Church, Sia Tagko; Kenyah, Tama Pudun; Kayan, Baya; Dusun, Kentuni; Kelabit, Mein Ribu; Tagal, Ansaning; Bible School, Udan Rangat; Pastors' representative, Racha Umong and Mr and Mrs A. Belcher.

[13] *BEM NL*, February 1957, 2. Alan Belcher, the BEM Field Chairman was invited as the advisor and liaison between the Church and the BEM.

[14] *BEM Field Executive Minutes*, 13 July 1956, 1.

conference. It would seem obvious that a constitution should be framed to conform to this pattern.[15]

The formal establishment of the SIB became a reality in 1959 with a draft constitution, which was provisionally accepted in 1960[16] and finalized in 1961.[17] The course of events revealed a gradual but sustained momentum in the implementation of policy. The most important development was the creation of SIB as a separate entity from the parent mission body with an executive committee consisting of all indigenous office-bearers. No funding was provided by the BEM nor was there any direct missionary participation or control in its ecclesial structure, except that two BEM missionaries were on the SIB Executive by invitation. The fact, that the SIB has continued to grow even after 1979 bears testimony to some measure of success in the implementation of the indigenous policy.[18]

It is a pertinent point to ask whether the BEM members on the SIB Executive or the BEM missionaries have wielded any indirect dominating influence. Undoubtedly, there was a certain extent of continuing missionary influence. Prior to the formation of the SIB, it is not surprising to read reports in BEM newsletters on the discussion of pressing church matters, such as in the 1955 Inter-Tribal Conference, which pointed to the influence of the missionaries on the Conference.[19] Moreover, some influence may be expected to continue over the SIB as the key leaders and pastors had been students at Lawas Bible School (LBS) working in subordinate positions to the missionaries. So the formation of the SIB as a separate entity did not necessarily bring about an automatic paradigm shift in their mental attitude towards the missionaries. Further, within the Asian context, being indebted to the missionaries in their role as mentors and teachers, local leaders would have held them in high esteem; the missionaries' views were often heeded, and not contradicted. There is also the fact that the site of the SIB headquarters was in the same vicinity as that of the BEM may have prompted SIB leaders to seek advice more than was necessary from the many missionary personnel present at Lawas.[20]

---

[15] *BEM Field Conference Minutes*, 15-26 July 1960, 7.

[16] *BEM Field Executive Minutes*, 18-24 October 1961, 1. The final draft of the SIB Constitution was an appendix to the minutes.

[17] *BEM NL*, February 1962, 2.

[18] See Chapter 1, footnotes 2 and 3.

[19] *BEM NL*, February 1956, 1. 'It is interesting to note that whilst a missionary does not have a hand in any local church or its affairs, yet every session in these meetings was led by a missionary'.

[20] Paper by Dr Bill Lees, Deputy Field Chairman of the BEM, entitled 'Year of Decision' for the Field Executive Meeting on 24 January to 1 February 1963. He suggested that despite the fact that 'the SIB is in full and absolute control of the church and the BEM had no official voice' in the SIB, but with the presence of so many expatriate personnel, the SIB in 'a real sense' 'cannot be prominent in Lawas'. 'The

The danger of stifling indigenous creativity and initiative was undoubtedly present. But it would be presumptuous to assume that the indigenous leaders were passive listeners to the BEM missionaries in any discussion or that they did not display sufficient discernment regarding advice given to them. The crux is whether the SIB has been able to make contrary decisions in the face of opposing advice by the BEM. The answer has been in the affirmative. First, in relation to involvement in politics by office-bearers of the SIB, the BEM leadership discouraged such a move. But the SIB leaders expressed a contrary view, arguing that a) Christians needed to maintain a raised voice for religious liberty in the land, as there were fears that religious liberty might be restricted, as it was in Peninsular Malaysia; and b) only pastors and church leaders apart from government teachers had the adequate education and experience to be able to make a positive contribution in the parliamentary process. Further, while the BEM leaders favoured Balan Seling and Udan Rangat for nominations to the Local Council, the SIB leaders voted for Racha Umong, [21] who was subsequently appointed to the Local Council and elected to the Council Negeri, Sarawak. [22] Moreover, on another occasion in December 1970, the SIB Conference felt the need to have a secondary school to cater for the children of the SIB members and decided in its favour, despite the recommendation of BEM.[23] The fact that the BEM had 'no official voice' in the SIB meant that it could not exercise a dominating influence or expect its advice to be always heeded. Furthermore, the BEM Field Executive under Dr Bill Hawes, the new BEM Field Chairman, met the SIB leaders to re-examine the relationship between the BEM and SIB in 1968.[24] In response to the BEM's insistence on handing over full responsibilities as quickly as possible within a certain time-frame to SIB, the SIB leadership expressed the opinion that the constant talk of a time-limit by BEM was perceived as the BEM being 'weary of them', and further commented that they did not want to be pushed into assuming full responsibilities, but would assume them at their own pace.[25] The terms of the

Government...will find it virtually impossible to believe...that the five Bornean executive members of the SIB are not subordinate to the twenty Europeans at Lawas'. Here the concern was that a wrong impression might be given to the Malaysian government concerning the independence of the SIB from the BEM. But the fact that had been acknowledged was that the SIB was in full control of their church.

[21] *BEM NL*, June 1963, 1. The choice by the BEM is understandable as Balan and Udan were the most educated by western standards in the community then.

[22] *BEM NL*, October 1963, 1.

[23] *BEM NL*, February 1971, 1. The BEM had advised that 'the difficulties involved rather outweighed the benefits'.

[24] Bill Hawes was BEM Field Chairman from 1968-1979.

[25] In 1965, on the matter of SIB/BEM relations (cooperation) the Field Executive noted that 'we are cautioned to 'go slow' in the handing over process, e.g. the Bookroom had proved too much for a Bornean to handle at this stage'. See *BEM Field Executive Minutes*, 6-11 May 1965, Appendix A: Report to Home Conference, Melbourne beginning 14 May 1965. According to *BEM NL*, October 1968, 1, the SIB leaders were

handover were thus no longer dictated by BEM but by SIB. Further, SIB leaders reiterated the need to appreciate the indigenous culture and customs better, as there were 'some areas of missionary failure at cross-cultural communication' often done unawares, which was 'the tendency to barge ahead with plans and projects without proper consultation with SIB'.[26] This was a veiled way of saying that the new BEM Field Director might not have fully understood the SIB leaders' polite way of turning down the suggestions of a time-table for the handover of responsibilities.[27] However, the BEM surprisingly provided sufficient space for SIB to grow and assume responsibilities at their own pace, rather than force the issue. Furthermore, it shows that the BEM was keener to handover responsibilities to the SIB than the latter was willing to accept.

In the case of the move of the BEM headquarters to Miri in 1974, the BEM Field Director consulted the SIB President, who was agreeable to his idea. However, Hawes subsequently found that the SIB Council did not approve of the move.[28] Though the BEM would have made the move to Miri regardless of their objections, the BEM was sensitive enough to the feelings of the SIB and did whatever they could to strengthen the existing goodwill. Ralph Davis, a Home Council member,[29] who visited Lawas in March 1975 summarised succinctly the attitude of the BEM to the SIB.

> Thc SIB was not in full agreement with the administration of the Mission moving to Lawas. The task ahead of us now is to prove in every practical way our goodwill to the SIB...show them warm Christian understanding and love, and

quoted as saying that 'We are aware that God wants us to assume responsibility for our own affairs and we are endeavouring to do it. Please go gently and we will tell you when we are ready. But for the moment can't we move into this job together and work hard while it is day?'

[26] *BEM NL*, October 1968, 1.

[27] Even when the SIB leadership disagreed with the BEM, they would not generally say it directly. But they would make it known in their polite indigenous way, which the older missionaries such as Southwell and Belcher would have understood, but not the newer missionaries. Interview with George Ngo Epoi, 7 October 2004.

[28] According to Bill Hawes, Jok Wan, the SIB President, initially agreed with the idea, but later did not gain the approval of the SIB Council. But the BEM at this stage felt it necessary to move its headquarters to Miri, which was more central to their emphasis on coastal urban work and outreach to the Iban. Interview with Dr Bill Hawes, BEM Field Director/Chairman, 17 May 2004. Even after the BEM's move to Miri, the SIB considered Lawas as central to their work in both Sabah and Sarawak. See Jok Wan, 'Report from SIB' in *BEM/OMF Conference Reports*, March 1975, 4. With the separation of SIB Sabah and SIB Sarawak into two separate bodies in 1977, SIB Sarawak became more aware that Miri was more central to their work in Sarawak.

[29] Ralph Davis was a business executive, an active Methodist layman and Honorary Treasurer of Campaigners for Christ. He had joined the BEM Home Council as a member in 1947. In 1970, he became the President of MBI. See *BEM NL*, June 1970, 4.

prove in deeds rather than words that moving the Chairman and his staff to Miri will be of no disadvantage to the SIB.[30]

On the other hand, the SIB accepted the decisions of the BEM without creating any great fuss, but it had made its view clear enough.

A significant fact, sometimes overlooked, was that the SIB did not have to struggle to break free from BEM missionary control, a fact that speaks volumes for the implementation of the policy. It was observed by Winston Edip that the relationship between the BEM and SIB leaders were generally harmonious without any major friction between them.[31] Also, as will be noted later in this chapter, the close relationship between the two key leaders of the BEM and SIB in their decision-making process is another significant consideration. Neither was the relationship between the missionaries and the SIB church so strained that the missionaries were no longer welcome after they had to leave Sarawak. When most of the BEM missionaries had to leave by 1979, the SIB sadly accepted the reality of the situation according to Tagal Paran, a former SIB President, but continued to invite them back for teaching sessions as visitors.[32] Further, they continued to be invited back to their celebrative events, such as Hawes was invited to be the speaker at their 25th Anniversary celebrations in December 1985.[33]

Interestingly, even a former colonial officer, Mr Alastair Morrison, speaks approvingly of BEM's work in establishing an independent indigenous church as an example of remarkable foresight:

> Although I thought the BEM was a little bit over-strict in some of its ideas, in some ways it acted with a remarkable degree of foresight. Reliance on foreign missionaries was minimal; a truly local church was established.[34]

Underlying all mission practice was a theology of mission, whether consciously or unconsciously expressed. The theology of mission of the BEM

---

[30] Ralph Davis, *Report to BEM Home Council* on March 1975 Field Conference held in Miri, 16 April 1975. See *Area Director's Field Report to the Australian Conference*, April 1975, 6, 'The move was undertaken by BEM on the understanding that SIB had cordially approved. However, it was discovered subsequently that this was not wholly the case. I have no question that this was the right move and the proof of our continued desire for the closest relationship with our SIB brethren will be shown in our actually working, planning and praying together. We are confident that this move will later be seen to have been of very positive advantage to the overall development of the SIB'.

[31] Interview with Winston Edip, 15 September 2004. If problems existed, they were normally minor isolated cases.

[32] Interview with Tagal Paran, 22 September 2004.

[33] *BEM NL*, 1st Quarter 1985, 1. The other key leaders including Southwell, Belcher and Cunningham, had continued to be invited for their major celebrative events. Further, from time to time, BEM missionaries such as the Lees, the Reasbecks, and Alf Tharratt, have been warmly welcomed to Sarawak.

[34] Morrison, *Fair Land Sarawak*, 41. (Italics mine).

was informed by a literal reading of the early church model in the book of Acts, particularly that of the apostle Paul, and also by Roland Allen's two influential books, Missionary Methods: St. Paul's or Ours, and The Spontaneous Expansion of the Church. Stafford Young expounded Allen's theology of mission in his articles, 'The Church Stands on its Own Feet' in the BEM newsletters of December 1953 and February 1954 and the 'Spontaneous Expansion of the Church' in the BEM newsletter of April 1954. Allen was perceived to have spelt out most clearly the New Testament pattern of church planting and church growth, so that the BEM was willing to adopt Allen's ideas, even though the churchmanship of Allen (an Anglo-Catholic) was quite different from that of the BEM. The focus was on Allen's distinctive pneumatology and Paul's strategy of planting and organizing 'Three-Self' churches shortly after their inception and then to completely trust the Holy Spirit to guide them.[35] Further, in another article, Young urged that in matters regarding sound doctrine and moral standards, 'it is time we trusted the Holy Spirit to enlighten these young churches'.[36] Though the BEM did not follow the pattern in strict detail with regard to the SIB, the mission perceived itself to be faithful in adhering to the principles of the Pauline pattern.

The process of devolving authority from BEM to SIB effectively began in 1956, three years before the SIB was formally established. In the context of Sarawak, this step of devolution and formation of the SIB is significant from two perspectives: firstly, the political—it took place when Sarawak was still under colonial rule and before attaining political independence as part of Malaysia in 1963; and secondly, the religious—it took place before parallel developments in the other and older Christian missions. For the Anglicans, the first local bishop was appointed in 1968[37] and for the Roman Catholics, the first Asian bishop was appointed in 1970 and the first archbishop in 1976,[38] and for the Methodists, the Sarawak Iban Annual Conference was formed in 1968.[39] It is certainly of importance that BEM, the last of the Christian mission societies

---

[35] *BEM NL*, December 1953, 1; February 1954, 4. The apostle Paul went 'where the Spirit led, sought open doors, aimed at conversion (as opposed to preparing the ground for future conversion), and planted local 'three-self' churches'. 'In six months, Paul would form a church, teach converts the necessary elements of the faith, arrange for church officers and the two sacraments', then moved on, 'leaving the Holy Spirit to work', and Paul himself 'only visited or wrote as he was led', but 'never settling down to govern or to give elaborate teaching to the newly formed church'.

[36] *BEM NL*, April 1954, 2.

[37] Bishop Basil Temenggong was the first Dyak Bishop of Kuching (1968-1984).

[38] Rooney, *Khabar Gembira*, 70, 220-21. The Province of East Malaysia with Kuching as archbishopric and Kota Kinabalu and Miri as two suffragan sees was created in June 1976, with Peter Chung as the first Archbishop, who was earlier appointed as Bishop of Sabah in 1970.

[39] The Sarawak Iban Provisional Annual Conference (SIPAC) was formed earlier in 1962.

allowed to work in Sarawak under Brooke rule, was the first to establish a 'Three-Self' church, even though the other missions had a similar goal.

The ability of the BEM in fulfilling its objective may be attributed to a few factors, which we will examine next. Firstly, the policies and practices of the BEM provided the starting point from which the SIB formulated their own policies and practices, which led to the promotion of indigenous initiatives. Secondly, the fifteen-year policy adopted by the BEM was a primary motivating factor; it has 'given an impetus and application to the work that nothing else would have done'.[40] Thirdly, there was an emphasis on both grass-roots and leadership training and development that contributed toward preparing the people for 'Three-Self'. Fourthly, there was the rise of indigenous leadership and response to the challenge of being 'Three-Self'. All these factors dovetailed to put missionary intention into reality.

The Promotion of Indigenous Initiatives

Mission policies of the parent mission body are usually passed on to the indigenous church through teaching and the practical outworking of policies, though these may subsequently be refined, modified, assimilated or rejected by the indigenous church. Thus, the mission policies and practices of the BEM became the starting point for their assimilation or refinement into the SIB.

The primary approach of the BEM was aimed at converting rather than civilizing. Though recognising the role of elementary or primary education and medical services as civilizing activities of the Mission, the BEM regarded these as secondary, though playing an integral role in preparing people to listen to the Gospel.[41] Their guiding principle in relation to medical work was outlined thus:

> an integral part of our programme in all our spheres of work, as an expression of Christ's love and grace, thus involving every missionary as a mobile medical unit...secondary in importance to the preaching of the Gospel and separate from it, in so far as we do not demand acceptance of our message in return for what we do medically.[42]

The underlying theological assumption of the BEM was that mission is to be understood as evangelism, which takes precedence over any social work that might be done by the mission; that is, social work is not understood as part of Christian mission. Hence, social work is separable from the primary task of evangelism. Whatever view may be taken of the theological adequacy of this perspective, it is clear that such a strict definition of mission led the BEM to sit lightly on institutional commitments, which made the process of devolution to the indigenous church much more straightforward. By 1952, BEM had

---

[40] *BEM NL*, December 1958, 2.
[41] *BEM NL*, December 1948, 2.
[42] *BEM NL*, October 1952, 2.

anticipated that missionary medical work would soon be withdrawn as it was only a matter of time before colonial government schemes would cover all areas of public services, leading to the view that it would be 'inadvisable to have any highly organized institution which the local church was unable to maintain after the withdrawal of the missionaries'.[43] By 1954, the government had begun to take over primary schools in the rural areas, including those run by Christian missions so that instead of disrupting the work of the BEM, it helped them to focus on evangelism, church leadership and development without the competing demands of operating primary schools and administering medical services. Further, the implementation of the fifteen-year policy discouraged the BEM from further developing heavy institutional programmes such as schools, clinics and air-services, which the SIB would be unable to maintain.

The pattern of work that developed in the pioneering situation, as discussed in the last chapter, was that BEM missionaries were always expected to be 'mobile', pioneering new areas, saturating the area with preaching and visitations, consolidating the work among converts by setting up strategic bases at specific geographical locations with a missionary couple or a team of two single women missionaries. Composite teams of missionaries and indigenous pastors on visitation trips or on itinerant evangelistic trips, and also the stationing of indigenous pastors at newly opened stations (for instance, at Lio Matu among the Kenyah, at Long Tebangan among the Kayan, and at Long Bedian among the Penan) working under the supervision of the missionaries, provided opportunities of missionary tutelage, though the benefits might be more mutual rather than one-sided. Further, missionary practices that proved successful and beneficial were imbibed through practical field experience and observation. So these practices became part of the tradition of the SIB.

The larger established churches, particularly among the Lun Bawang in the Limbang and Trusan, had been operating on their own since the time of the Japanese Occupation. They were cared for mainly by indigenous pastors with minimal missionary supervision, prompting occasional visits from missionaries, which were made easier by their proximity to the BEM headquarters at Lawas.[44] In the Kelabit churches, where no missionary had ever resided among them due to the shortage of missionary personnel, some deacons in effect functioned as pastors of the churches, as in the case of Mein Ribu, Tama Galang and Guru Paul.[45] Though there had been an earlier expression of intent to station a missionary couple among the Kelabit, there was no attempt to do

---

[43] *BEM NL*, October 1952, 2. By 1954, the BEM had nine trained nurses and two doctors. See *BEM NL*, October 1954, 2.

[44] The early graduates of LBS were assigned to the Lun Bawang churches: Lawai and Tua to Long Tukon; Singha Achang and Putan to Long Luping; Balang and Rigo to Tang Lepadan and Libat and Rinai to Ba Kelalan. See *BEM NL*, June 1951, 3.

[45] *BEM NL*, December 1953, 2.

so, as the BEM leadership was able to recognize the pastoral capabilities of these deacons. Rather than placing a missionary couple there, the Mission encouraged the indigenous leaders to attend the short-term Bible schools and later Lawas Bible School to equip themselves further for their task. Later a Lun Bawang pastor, Selutan Arun, was assigned to work among them at Bario in 1953.[46] Another priority of the BEM was to help those churches that did not have resident missionaries and also those in newly evangelized areas, which were given priority in the assignment of indigenous pastors. These pastors, so assigned, often exercised a measure of independence and initiative in their pastoral work in the churches,[47] though they were first under the supervision of the missionaries and later under the care of the Inter-Tribal Conference after 1956.

Tama Galang, Senior Pastor of the Kelabit Field

The need for delegation to indigenous leaders and pastors was also a consequence of the BEM philosophy of being 'mobile', so that by 1960, the BEM could speak of 'missionaries without stations' as it believed that 'a stationary missionary apparently invariably encouraged a group of dependent local believers'.[48] This practice was in effect an outworking of the church planting principle advocated by Roland Allen.[49] The logical implication of this

[46] *SG*, January 1979, 4.

[47] See Chapter 5.

[48] *BEM NL*, July-August 1960, 1.

[49] Roland Allen, *The Spontaneous Expansion of the Church* (London: World Dominion, 1927), 103-105, 144-45. Allen attacks the practice of maintaining mission stations as

policy was a reduction in the number of stations which became the case. In 1950, there were five stations and in 1960, there was only one main base and three sub-bases, even though the work had greatly expanded. Further, the missionaries in charge of all the various tribes except for the Kayan were stationed at the headquarters at Lawas and the scattered churches got an equal share of the ministry from these visiting BEM missionaries.[50] The reality of a shortage of missionary personnel was an added factor in the promotion of indigenous initiatives and their physical absence from the bases allowed sufficient room for indigenous leadership to bloom.

For effective delegation and apprenticeship, there had to be a measure of confidence in indigenous ability in the mindset of the missionaries, which the key leaders in BEM expressed in a number of ways. In reporting on the few native leaders who had been trained at the LBS, the June 1950 newsletter mentioned Udan Rangat as 'exceptionally gifted with poise above the average ... showing real spiritual understanding'. It was also said of Racha Umong and Amat Lasong that 'both these men are able preachers of the gospel and have missionary vision. It is men like these that are realizing the time...not far distant when the Christian natives will not only able to care for their own churches but also take the responsibility in evangelization and teaching others'.[51] Furthermore, Alan Belcher who was accompanied by two native leaders, Balang Selutan and Jok Ngau, in an evangelistic trip to the Kayan of the Bintulu River, reported 'how more effective was the native Christian as an evangelist than the white missionary'.[52] Also, the Field Conference in 1958 expressed the confidence that by 1965, SIB would be a truly 'Three-Self' church.[53]

Significantly, in his thought-provoking booklet, Second Thoughts on Missions, Dr Bill Lees, the Deputy BEM Field Chairman, expressed confidence in and gave insightful ideas about the ability of indigenous Christians. He argued that, despite the outward appearance of minimal literacy, they could exhibit an equal if not greater spiritual potential and intellectual insight than their white missionary counterparts in exercising their spiritual gifts. As an example, Lees cited the successful planting, growth and management of the Tagal church in Sabah by a Lun Bawang missionary, Amat Lasong.[54] Such

---

they absorb a very large proportion of the missionary's energies that other vital work had to be set aside to maintain them. The larger the mission station, the more expensive and demanding it was on the missionaries. At the mission stations, indigenous Christians became immobilized and very dependent on the missionaries.

[50] *BEM NL*, July-August 1960, 1.

[51] *BEM NL*, June 1950, 2.

[52] *BEM NL*, December 1954, 4.

[53] *BEM NL*, December 1958, 2.

[54] William C. Lees, *Second Thoughts on Missions* (Dorset: The Overcomer Literature Trust, 1964), 5-12. Amat Lasong, trained at LBS, was a Murut missionary to the Tagal tribe in British North Borneo (Sabah). He had successfully planted and nurtured the

confidence lay behind the decision by BEM to send indigenous people as missionaries on their own to the various tribes from 1952: Udan Rangat to the Dusuns in North Borneo, Balang Selutan to the Kenyah in upper Baram[55] and Amat Lasong to the Tagal.[56]

A major problem in Christian missions has been the paternalistic attitude of white missionaries arising from an underlying sense of racial and cultural superiority, so that the missionaries have done too much for the indigenous people rather than doing it with them. It was certainly difficult for the BEM missionaries at times not to have a sense of cultural superiority; evidence of this attitude surfaced when a BEM missionary wanted to marry a local woman and had to resign to do so.[57] But the paternalism of the BEM seems to have been of a rather mild character that did not hinder or intrude into the implementation of their mission objective.[58] At the root of this confidence in the ability of the church leaders and the indigenous church as a whole to make the right decisions about their own future was a pneumatological emphasis on the promised guidance of the Spirit to the Church (a central emphasis of Roland Allen's Anglo-Catholic missiology).[59] For instance, with Racha Umong, the government had been 'pressing in its attempts to get him into the government service', and it was further reported that 'the missionaries are not influencing him either way as it may be God's will for him to do this work'. It would be naïve to think that Racha did not seek any advice from the missionaries, but the important issue was whether the Mission was willing and discerning enough to allow him to make his own decision, which it did. As Racha's main concern was the spiritual needs of his own community, he was reported to be 'reluctant to enter government employ',[60] and later decided not to join government service. Hence, the confidence that BEM had in indigenous ability under the guidance of the Spirit of God, allowed them to respect decisions of native leaders and to delegate responsibilities to them.

One Anglican observer has positively commended the BEM for their promotion of indigenous initiative and leadership, and their encouragement of a 'Three-Self' indigenous church. Despite the small number of BEM

---

church eighteen months before Dr and Mrs Bill Lees went to live among them to do orthographic work with the aim to translate the Scriptures into the Tagal language.

55 *BEM NL*, August 1952, 2.

56 *BEM NL*, April 1952, 1. Lees, *Drunk before Dawn*, 112.

57 *BEM NL*, February 1952, 3. It announced the resignation of Trevor White and also his marriage to Sia Wa Wing, a national of British North Borneo.

58 Though the missionaries were paternalistic, they nevertheless were more willing to hand over responsibilities to SIB than SIB was willing to accept. Interview with Winston Edip, 15 September 2004.

59 *BEM NL*, April 1954, 2. In disseminating Roland Allen's ideas, Stafford Young argued that 'it was time for us (the BEM) that we trusted the Holy Spirit to enlighten these young churches' in matters relating to doctrine and moral standards.

60 *BEM NL*, June 1950, 2. *BEM Seventeenth Annual Report*, 31 December 1950, 5.

missionaries, they were 'able to work with a large number of very dedicated and committed indigenous members to build them up in a much stronger way'. This was perceived from the way the SIB members 'aggressively promoted their Christian faith', much to the fear of the other denominations.[61]

In short, the mission policies of the BEM from 1945 to 1959 created a culture that promoted indigenous initiative and leadership.

Mission Policies, Decision-making Processes and Preparation for Devolution

The Fifteen-Year Policy and its Implications

The fifteen-year policy, which gave the objective of the BEM a specific focus and time-bound goal, was a bold and unique step for a Christian mission within the Asian context to attempt. The development of this policy should be understood in the light of the events surrounding it and the motivation behind it. As C.M. Turnbull observed, the spread of the Cold War to Asia with the fall of China to Communism in 1949 and the Korean War in 1950-51 grew in tandem with the rise of newly emerging nations. She argued that with regard to Southeast Asia, 'the British government was convinced of the roll-on effect of communist subversion, whereby the triumph of communism in one country would destabilize its neighbour, each falling in turn until the region was engulfed by Communism. This was crystallised as the 'domino theory' after President Eisenhower drew on this analogy in April 1954', which later justified American involvement in Vietnam.[62] The assumed veracity of this theory survived into the late 1960s, causing much anxiety in the non-communist nations of Southeast Asia regarding Communism.[63] Further, the mass exodus of missionaries from China in 1950-1951 fuelled the fear of the growing threat of

---

[61] Interview with Rev. Peter Varney, 7 March 2006.

[62] C.M. Turnbull, 'Regionalism and Nationalism', in Nicholas Tarling (ed.), *The Cambridge History of Southeast Asia*: *The Nineteenth and Twentieth Centuries* (Cambridge: Cambridge University Press, 1992), II, 597-98. In the article, 'Communist Strategy in Asia', *SG*, June 1957, 129-30, it highlighted Lenin's blueprint for world domination: 'We will take Eastern Europe, then the masses of Asia. Then we will surround America.... We shall not have to attack. She will fall into our lap like an over-ripe apple'. See also George Hood, *Neither Bang nor Whimper: The End of the Missionary Era in China* (Singapore: The Presbyterian Church in Singapore, 1991), 26-56.

[63] See 'Communist Strategy in Asia', 129-30. During the 1950s and 1960s, the domino theory was widely believed to be true of the communist threat to countries in Southeast Asia. Though it was being disputed in the mid-1970s by Adam Malik, Foreign Minister of Indonesia and Lee Kuan Yew, Prime Minister of Singapore, it was nevertheless still held in some regard till the mid-1970s as 'the success of communist soldiery in Indo-China may well encourage the communists in Southeast Asia to try yet harder to achieve their goals'. See 'Domino Theory', *SG* March 1975, 43.

Communism in Southeast Asia and its implication for Christian missions.[64] Some Christian commentators spoke of the fall of China to Communism as the judgment of God on Christian missions for their association with western imperialism and for reluctance to grant autonomy to the mission-founded churches.[65] Others predicted that the Church in Asia would suffer the same fate as Western imperialism.[66] However, according to George Hood, as Mission Boards 'reflected on the China experience' from 1949 to 1953, there was a willingness to admit failure in some areas of their work but not in the whole missionary enterprise. Some of the failures identified were a lack of adequate theological training, a lack of a church-centred mission policy that developed a strong sense of Church, a lack in providing the type of missionary and style of service required, and the imposition of church structures inappropriate to the needs and resources of the country.[67] There was also a rediscovery of the writings of Roland Allen which provided much discussion in their process of 'Rethinking Mission', acknowledging the need for indigenous churches to be characterized by 'Three-Self' principles. Denominations which had 'heavy' institutionalized structures found implementing Allen's ideas difficult.[68] In contrast, the fear resulting from the fall of China and the possibility of a closed door to missionary work in Sarawak in the near future motivated the BEM to consider its role in establishing the 'Three-Self' church as quickly as possible.[69] Consequently, two questions loomed large for the BEM: firstly, 'Would the indigenous churches stand if the missionaries had to withdraw, not just for three years as during WWII, but indefinitely as from China?' and secondly, 'Would they endure in the face of persecution?'[70] A further impetus was provided by its

---

[64] For the response of the British Mission Boards to communist rule in China from 1949 to 1953, see Hood, *Neither Bang nor Whimper*, 57-142. Their initial 'stay put' policy in 1949 later gave way to a complete withdrawal of all but twenty missionaries from China by the end of 1951.

[65] David. M. Paton, *Christian Missions and the Judgement of God* (London: SCM, 1953), 25.

[66] K.M. Pannikar, *Asia and Western Dominance: A Survey of the Vasco Da Gama Epoch of Asian History 1498-1945* (London: 1953), 293.

[67] See Hood, *Neither Bang nor Whimper*, 212-18.

[68] Hood, *Neither Bang nor Whimper*, 188, 204-11, 215. 'How significantly the time spent by Mission Board secretaries in discussing ideas of Roland Allen affected policies and actions of the missions in the years that followed is impossible to measure' (209).

[69] 'We are very conscious of the dark shadow that is being cast over the East.... The events of the past few months in Korea are an urgent reminder to us…that *we should be on our knees that God will keep the door open in our field*…let us not forget our obligation to pray for the CIM as it faces unprecedented problems in China…and also for the Church and Christians in Korea as they face persecution, suffering and death'. See *BEM NL*, February 1951, 1.

[70] Lees, *Drunk before Dawn*, 103.

premillennial outlook that sought to hasten the second coming of Christ through spreading the gospel to every nation.[71]

Dr Bill Hawes, Third Field Director of BEM

The initiative for the fifteen-year policy came from Ralph Davis, a Council member, through the Home Council[72] and was adopted at its Prayer Conference in July 1950 before a proposal was forwarded to the Field Conference. Not surprisingly, Ralph Davis, a businessman, proposed a policy that had a limited time-frame and financial implications, one that committed material resources for a particular period of time. The original proposal was for the task to be completed in ten years, because the area of work was limited both in geographical size and in terms of the number of people to be reached, unlike China or India. The BEM was 'to give the Gospel to the interior tribes of British Borneo, to raise a self-supporting Church with a trained ministry and with the Scriptures in the tongue of the people'. It also drew attention to the work of other missionary societies, without mentioning names that 'seem to ebb and flow over the years, often dragging on and petering out, never seeming to attain the goal'. After handing over responsibility to the native Church, the Mission would become 'more in the nature of a servant of that Church', working in 'a subsidiary capacity to supply the assistance they might ask for'. The call to the Prayer Conference was that 'we can pray in faith that that vision will be fulfilled in our generation'.[73] The Field Conference surprisingly

[71] *BEM NL*, October 1950, 1; February 1951, 1.
[72] Letter of McCracken to Belcher, 21 July 1950 (OMF). *BEM NL*, October 1947, 1.
[73] Paper prepared for the BEM Prayer Conference at 'Clevedon' from 28-30 July, 1950. However, Harold McCracken's letter to Belcher, 5 July 1950 (OMF), mentioned fifteen years as the span of time to finish the job of establishing an effective church, but in a

accepted the proposal but agreed on a fifteen-year policy instead, giving the reasons that most of the missionaries were young and inexperienced, with some still at the language learning stage. Nominalism in the churches was beginning to be a serious problem, due to lack of personnel and consequent lack of teaching. The field of work was expanding rapidly, while the time-consuming need for travelling and teaching and also the painstaking translation of Scriptures, of at least the New Testament, into each native tongue required more time; fifteen years was deemed the necessary time frame.[74] The unanimity of the Field Conference in endorsing the proposal is surprising, and may in part be attributed to the strict selection procedure of only accepting candidates into the BEM who fully agreed with their basic philosophy of establishing a 'Three-Self' church.

The conviction that the task could be completed in fifteen years (that is, by 1965) was well articulated,[75] so that reports in the BEM newsletters used the imagery of scaffolding that needed to be removed once the building was completed,[76] or spoke of 'the biblical justification of finishing the task'.[77] In 1952, the BEM articulated the possibility of 'finishing the task in thirteen years' when the native church will 'stand on its own two feet',[78] and later expressed rather optimistically in 1958 that 'in 1965, there should be a strong church with its own leaders, pastors, ...financial arrangements and with, at least the New Testament in each tribal tongue'.[79] Though it realized that delegating authority and responsibility to others was always difficult, especially when it was from an experienced person to a less experienced one, that step was deemed as necessary. Moreover, it had been observed by a missionary from the Missionary Aviation Fellowship seconded to the BEM that 'interestingly, as responsibility is given and accepted, there develops a greater sense of co-labouring and one-ness between the Borneans and Western Christians'.[80]

But was there any ambiguity in the fifteen-year policy that could have given room for the policy to be undermined? Most of the BEM missionaries, like most evangelical missionaries in 'faith missions', had the concept of their missionary calling as a lifelong calling, unless forced to return to their home country through ill-health or under extenuating circumstances. The unconscious and unarticulated question in the minds of the missionaries was what their role

---

later letter to Belcher, 21 July 1950 revised it to ten years noting that the field size was limited unlike China or India and the task could be completed within that time limit.

[74] *BEM NL*, December 1950, 1. Lees, *Drunk before Dawn*, 101-103.

[75] E. Mary Wright, '"Eleven More years to go": Challenge facing the Borneo Evangelical Mission', in *The Life of Faith* 26 August 1954, 575-76. See also *BEM Eighteenth Annual Report*, 31 December 1951, 12-13.

[76] *BEM NL*, October 1963, 1. See also Lees, *Second Thoughts*, 25-26.

[77] *BEM NL*, October 1952, 4.

[78] *BEM NL*, December 1953, 1; February 1954, 4.

[79] *BEM NL*, December 1958, 2.

[80] *BEM NL*, December 1963, 1.

in the country would be when the period of fifteen years had ended, more so, when some of them were not yet old enough to be retired. At the time of its formulation in 1950, the fifteen-year policy meant that 1965 was the year in which the BEM would complete its work, withdraw or support the SIB Church, when needed, in other specialized ministries.[81] But as work expanded into new areas, the translation work of the Scriptures lagged behind schedule for all the tribes, except the Lun Bawang. Further, as potential missionary candidates enquired about how the fifteen-year plan worked for the BEM, there was an uncertainty in interpretation as to whether the fifteen years applied to completing the work among every tribe or applied separately to each tribe. This latter understanding was the clarification given and accepted at the Field Conference in 1958: 'the vision was related to each tribe amongst whom God opens a door'.[82] This subtle change had, in effect, legitimized an indefinite prolongation of stay in Sarawak as long as new areas of work could be successfully pioneered. It revealed the unresolved question in the minds of the missionaries about the exact interpretation of the policy, and the possibility of stifling the implementation of the 'Three-Self' policy was now present as a result of this subtle change.

Though the idea of withdrawal, first conceived in 1950, was couched in language that assumed the continued presence of missionaries in Sarawak, playing a supportive servant role to the SIB and providing the help that SIB might require, there was again some uncertainty in its interpretation. What did withdrawal mean exactly? Did it require a physical shift of the Mission from Lawas to another location? Did it mean leaving behind or handing over the established areas of work to SIB and moving to new areas of work? By 1961, though the understanding of the BEM leadership was that 'SIB is not subject to the BEM, but they want us to work with them and make a contribution they are as yet unable to make alone',[83] the mission as yet had not resolved this issue.

There were two views on this matter. The predominant view generally assumed that the Mission from its location at Lawas would merely continue to give the assistance that SIB required, working mainly among those of the interior, as its maxim had been 'we are a jungle outfit; we wouldn't be happy in the towns'.[84] A second view came from Dr Bill Lees (who was deputizing for the Field Director, Alan Belcher, who was then on furlough) in 1963 when he

---

[81] *BEM Field Executive Minutes*, 2; 6 November 1967, 3. At this meeting, the Field Executive reviewed the role of the BEM and the 15-year policy and was conscious of the need to hand over responsibilities as soon as SIB was able to accept them. See *BEM Eighteenth Annual Report*, 31 December 1951, 12.

[82] *BEM Field Conference Minutes*, 29 September-10 October 1958, 7. This re-interpretation of the fifteen-year policy was re-affirmed in the 1960 Conference: 'ten years ago, we adopted a fifteen-year policy for *each given* tribal area'. *BEM Field Conference Minutes*, 15-20 July 1960, 6. *BEM NL*, September 1960, 2.

[83] *BEM NL*, January 1961, 2.

[84] *BEM NL*, May 1980, 1. See also Pollock, *Earth's Remotest*, 253.

presented a paper entitled 'Year of Decision' in the aftermath of the Brunei uprising in December 1962 when missionaries had to be evacuated from Lawas.[85] This event prompted a re-assessment of the work of the BEM, and Bill Lees suggested that the BEM should relocate its work from Lawas into another area, leaving the SIB to supervise the established indigenous work in the interior.[86] The BEM could then move forward to pioneer new areas of ministries, for instance, in the coastal towns where Christian work among secondary schools was beginning.[87] But it did not mean that BEM would abandon its interior or rural work altogether, as pioneering new areas of ministries might entail reaching out to new ethnic groups in rural areas. This proposal was seriously considered and unanimously adopted by the Field Executive.[88]

Unfortunately, a rift resulted between Bill Lees and Alan Belcher, and Lees' proposal, which showed foresight into the trends that were affecting the church, was withdrawn or rather set aside.[89] The irony of Belcher's leadership,

---

[85] 'WA Man in Perilous Save', in *Daily News* (Perth), 12 December 1962. Also, '"Pilot Outwits Rebels": Mission families flown to safety', in *The Herald*, 12 December 1962. Between 1959 and 1962, negotiations among the United Kingdom, Malaya, Singapore, Sabah and Sarawak towards the formation of the Federation of Malaysia were strongly opposed by Indonesia and Philippines. This opposition was supported by local anti-Federation sentiments in Brunei and Sarawak. The Brunei uprising of 8 December 1962 was an armed coordinated attack on the oil town of Seria, targeting oil installations, police stations and government facilities in Brunei. Lawas, the headquarters of the BEM, was a neighbouring town from Brunei.

[86] Alan Belcher himself did not think it was wise to move the headquarters to Miri. Interviews with Alan Belcher, 30 October 2004; and with Ken Coleman, 8 November 2004. See also Lees, *Drunk before Dawn*, 163-64. McCracken was initially resistant to Lees' proposal, but later conceded that a move away from Lawas would have to come over time. See Letters of H. McCracken to B. Lees, 26 March, 1963 and 28 May 1963 (OMF).

[87] Paper presented was attached as Appendix 2 to the Field Executive Minutes 24 January-1 February 1963. As for relocation, a few suggestions were given but Miri was understood to 'be more central if we remember the Second Division'. See also Bill and Shirley Lees, *Is It Sacrifice? Experiencing Mission and Revival in Borneo* (Leicester: IVP, 1987), 97-100.

[88] *BEM Field Executive Minutes*, 24 January-1 February 1963, 2. The paper was noted to be 'a summary of the way the Lord has led our thinking'. *BEM Field Executive Minutes*, March/April 1963, 4, noted that 'the December 1962 affair was God's way of reminding us of the NT pattern which clearly shows that missionaries are not fixtures and were often led by the Holy Spirit.... The Executive has only one strong conviction and that is the Holy Spirit is insisting that we explore the matter fully, recognizing that He may be causing the cloud to move'.

[89] Bill Lees' paper was withdrawn out of respect for the Field Chairman, Alan Belcher, who returned from furlough in 1964. Though his paper was withdrawn, 'it was too late. The Mission was divided. We all continued to work together but with underlying tensions. It took twelve years...for the next generation of leaders to complete the move to Miri.... Those of us on both sides of the disagreement felt battered and bruised'. See

according to Ken Coleman, was that 'the BEM textbook was Roland Allen, which advocated that we work ourselves out of a job. But we got into the situation where we could not see ourselves ever working ourselves out of those jobs'.[90] But it was the trend of the rural-urban drift of the SIB youths, who were facing difficulties adjusting to life in the towns, and the resultant situation of spiritual 'drop-outs' among SIB youths in the towns, that it became the critical factor in propelling the BEM to move forward, especially when it was reported that there was an urgent request for assistance from the SIB.[91] Another factor that prompted the move of the BEM toward the coastal towns was the batches of younger missionaries joining the BEM from both Australia and Britain from the 1960s, who had tertiary or theological education and had been exposed to ministry in the cities in their home country, that they were better able to appreciate the trends impacting Sarawak.[92] They were not hemmed in by the original philosophy of 'BEM as a jungle outfit' or an interior mission, which envisaged a move to the towns as taboo.

A move to the towns meant that new opportunities became available, such as work among the town inhabitants, mainly the Chinese, among tribal people from non-SIB villages, and also among villagers who lived in the vicinity of the towns.[93] In 1963, the BEM under Dr Bill Lees sponsored the entry of an OMF missionary couple to work among the Chinese in Miri.[94] By 1966, work among the coastal towns was not only inevitable but of strategic importance. Further, in his paper entitled 'Whither the BEM?' presented at the 1966 Field Conference, Harold McCracken, the BEM President, advocated ideas similar to those put forward by Bill Lees in 1963. He contended that serious consideration should be given to planting churches in the coastal towns, ministry among students and the Chinese, the promotion of Christian literature and also the desirability of moving the mission headquarters out of Lawas. He further argued that the trend of urban migration 'will increase over the next few years

Lees, *Is It Sacrifice?*, 99-100. According to Dr Bill Hawes, Bill Lees was 'a man ahead of his times' and he did much strategic thinking for the BEM, and Bill Lees' thinking had a strong influence on the British missionaries of the BEM. Personal Interview with Bill Hawes on 17 May 2004.

[90] Ken Coleman was an Australian missionary in Sarawak from 1964 to 1974 and had his theological training at Moore College, Sydney. Interview with Ken Coleman, 8 November 2004.

[91] In *BEM/OMF Conference Report*, March 1975, 22, see Colin Reasbeck's report on 'Town Ministry'.

[92] Those from the United Kingdom included Dr Bill Hawes, Ian and Beatrice Clayre, and Colin Reasbeck who had tertiary qualifications or theological degrees, and those from Australia included Robert N. Burton, George Jackson, Ken Coleman and Keith and Marion Baker. *BEM NL*, June 1964, 1, August 1965, 3, June 1967, 1.

[93] *BEM NL*, May, 1980, 1.

[94] *BEM Field Executive Minutes*, 24 January-1 February 1963, 4. Percy King first started work among the Chinese in Miri. But this Chinese work later became a separate church, the Miri Gospel Chapel, outside of the SIB structure.

.... However, up to the present, we have refused to accept responsibility for planting churches in these towns... If we do not commence work in the coastal towns, it will mean the members of SIB will find their Christian fellowship amongst other groups and so weaken and divide the National Church'.[95] Further, the younger BEM missionaries were advocating that the future of the work of the BEM and SIB lay in the towns and among students.[96] By 1968, the impact of urbanisation, development and westernization of Sarawak on the SIB, especially on those moving into the towns, helped to define a role for the missionaries. That role was 'not to lead the church but to help it adapt to these twentieth century developments to help cushion the impact as the clash between the old and new occurs' and 'to gear the church to the emerging national culture'.[97]

Belcher himself resisted this move despite the obvious current trends.[98] This resistance and that of the older generation of missionaries was understandable,[99] as there were strong reservations about urban mission within evangelical mission bodies at that time. Roger Greenway's book, Apostles to the City: Biblical Strategies for Urban Missions (1978) was, in fact, a biblical justification which attempted to prepare the way for evangelical missions to direct their work toward the city.[100] Further, those who had worked long in the

[95] Paper presented at the 1966 BEM Field Conference by J. Harold McCracken, *Whither the BEM? Constitutional Changes and New Objectives*, 15 June 1966, 5-7. The concern was the loss of talented young leaders who were emerging as the professional class from the SIB.

[96] See Marion Baker, 'What next – the Towns?', *BEM NL*, December 1967, 2, and also Viola Taeni, 'The Privileged Generation', *BEM NL*, December, 4 stressing the importance of student work especially in Sabah.

[97] *BEM NL*, June 1968, 1. In 'The Church in Changing Borneo', *New Life*, 26 June 1969, 1, reported the address of Dr Bill Hawes to the BEM Australasian Conference in Melbourne in April 1969, stating that 'The BEM remains in Borneo at the invitation of the SIB, 'and in view of the rapid radical changes that were taking place in Borneo, 'the task' remains 'unfinished'. There were still (a) other unreached tribes, (b) the necessity of training Bible teaching-evangelists, (c) the spiritual needs of the young people in the towns and (d) the necessity for SIB and BEM to establish churches in the towns.

[98] 'Alan Belcher was a one vision man; that is, his vision is interior work ... He would have been happy to stay focused in the interior.... He focused only on one aspect and anything else is a deviation'. Interview with Ken Coleman, 8 November 2004. At most, Alan Belcher was willing to consider 'encouraging other evangelical groups to enter the coastal towns under the sponsorship of the BEM'. Further, it was recognized that this work posed 'peculiar difficulties, expense, and qualifications required for those taking on this work', implying that the BEM lacked the missionaries with the requisite qualifications. See *BEM Field Executive Minutes*, 23-31 May 1967, 6.

[99] Personal correspondence with Bob Burton, 23 December 2004. According to Burton, 'it took quite some time before this was accepted. Initially there was quite some resistance to such a move'.

[100] Roger Greenway, *Apostles to the City: Biblical Strategies for Urban Missions* (Grand Rapids: Baker Book House, 1978).

interior were generally too out of touch with the national and global trends and did not realize that the process of urbanisation was irreversible,[101] and were perhaps themselves fearful of their ability to cope with urban ministry. Also by the mid-1960s, some missionaries perceived the leadership style of the Belchers to be too directive, and expressed the need for a more open leadership style,[102] preferably with a change in leadership.[103] It is not surprising that the Belchers could have become more authoritarian in the later years as the newer missionaries of the BEM were very much younger than they. It became clear that without any change in the Field Director, the BEM would not have been able to redirect its work towards the coastal towns.

The move to change the Field Director had the influence of Harold McCracken, the BEM Home President, behind the scenes.[104] The change of Field Director to Dr Bill Hawes came in 1968,[105] and from then onwards, the BEM began to direct its work toward the coastal towns, so that the decade of the seventies saw the establishment of SIB churches in the towns.[106] None of

---

[101] 'The SIB did not expect the children to stay in the towns, but expected them to return to the villages and government work, schools or as dressers in the interior. The realization that children of SIB parents were not returning to *ulu* came in the mid-1970s when those who went for further studies, graduated and began to return and settle in the towns'. Interview with Colin Reasbeck, 29 May 2004. Both the older generation of BEM missionaries and SIB leaders were unable to foresee this trend. Interviews with Gerawat Maran, 23 September 2004, and with George Ngo Epoi, 7 October 2004.

[102] Any opposing view to the BEM Field top leadership, that is, the Belchers, was often deemed as unspiritual. Further, missionaries were expected to go where the Field Executive directed them, despite their calling to some other work. In the case of the Colemans, they felt called to work among the Dusuns in North Borneo but were directed to work among the Iban in Pakan. This directive style of the BEM top leadership only affected the internal relationship with the missionaries. The SIB was unaffected by what went on in the BEM. Interviews with Beatrice Clayre, 16 May 2004; Dorothy Summerson, 31 October 2004; and Ken Coleman, 8 November 2004.

[103] Interview with Ken Coleman, 8 November 2004.

[104] Belcher had been on sick leave for a while and the pressure for Belcher to decline or resign as Field Director came from Harold McCracken, the Australian Home Council Chairman and John Smith, the British Home Council Secretary. Interview with Ken Coleman, 8 November 2004. Harold McCracken, John Smith and Bill Lees were present at the 1968 Field Conference. In the interview (30 November 2004), Belcher himself tacitly admitted that because of the general impression that he was too controlling of the BEM, he was pressurized to resign. Lees, *Drunk before Dawn*, 168-69 provides a spiritualised account of the event.

[105] Dr Bill Hawes was a new BEM missionary from England who had just completed his first term of work and returned to find himself elected as Field Director. *BEM NL*, August 1968, 1; June 1969, 1-2. As the Field Executive continued to have few of the 'old missionaries', the shift was slow but steady.

[106] *BEM NL*, May 1980, 2-4. Kuching (1969), Sibu (1974), Kapit (1977), Bintulu (1980). In 1965 at Marudi, where the Southwells had retired from the CDC project at Long Lama, they started an Inter School Christian Fellowship (ISCF) work in the secondary school, which expanded and later became the SIB church at Marudi.

the older Australian missionaries, except for Ray Cunningham, pastored any of the town churches. In its work in the towns, the BEM sponsored the entry of OMF missionaries to work among the Chinese in Miri in 1963[107] and Kuching in 1969.[108] In view of the imminent merger of the BEM with the OMF in 1975, the BEM headquarters shifted to Miri in 1974.[109] With this shift in location to Miri, the BEM surprisingly handed over the Mission properties at Lawas to the SIB in December 1976. Even more surprisingly, it is reported that the BEM agreed to pay SIB rental for the buildings still occupied by its remaining missionaries.[110]

Though the fifteen-year policy did not originally envisage a total withdrawal of missionaries, and though the work of the Mission did not in fact come to an end in 1965, (fifteen years after the adoption of the policy in 1950), it was instead reinterpreted in 1960 as applying to each new tribal area as work opened up separately. For instance, it meant that, as BEM work began with the Kayan and Kenyah among the Baram in 1947 and the Iban in the Julau-Pakan area in 1960, the BEM was to complete their task among the Kayan and Kenyah in 1965 and the Iban in 1975. As a result, the year 1965 passed without any mention by the BEM of its original significance, after which, the fifteen-year policy lapsed from the mission vocabulary of the BEM. In effect, fifteen years became twenty-nine, when the BEM finally ceased its work in Sarawak in 1979. Nevertheless during the first ten years of its implementation, the fifteen-year policy gave BEM a sense of urgency and time-bound impetus to 'finish the task'. Indeed, well within fifteen years, the BEM had substantially fulfilled its task by nurturing the indigenous churches for a decade and establishing the SIB as an indigenous 'Three-Self' church, which was properly constituted in 1959 with a finalised constitution in 1961 and full ecclesiastical independence of the BEM. Further, the task as originally envisaged was completed among the Lun Bawang, as the first copies of the printed Lun Bawang New Testament were

---

Southwell *Uncharted Waters*, 341-42. From 1968 to 1970, Southwell was the Principal of St. Aidan's (Anglican) School in Miri, where he became involved with ISCF work again.

[107] *BEM Field Executive Minutes*, 24 January-1 February 1963, 4. During 1963, Dr Bill Lees, the Deputy Chairman, was in charge of the Mission when Alan Belcher was on furlough. See also *BEM NL*, June 1963, 1.

[108] It was either the younger BEM or OMF missionaries who pastored the town churches; for example, Colin Reasbeck, Douglas Sadler and Tony Horsfall in Kuching, Colin Reasbeck and Ray Cunningham in Miri and Brian Newton in Sibu. When Bill Hawes became the new BEM Field Director in 1968, Alan Belcher moved to work in the interior in Long Semadoh.

[109] By this time, the influence of Donald McGavran's work was well known in the BEM. *BEM NL*, August 1971, 1. Two areas of work became prominent: work in the coastal towns and focus on youth work, for instance, Youth Conferences among the interior youths. *BEM NL*, August 1971, 1; October 1971, 4. Sylvia Webb and J. Thomas were involved in starting these conferences among the Kayan. *BEM NL*, October 1972, 3.

[110] *BEM NL*, February 1977, 1.

distributed on May 1962.[111] But the same could not be said for the Kayan and Kenyah in 1965 as they were still without their New Testaments.[112]

Discussion of this fifteen-year policy was mainly confined to the BEM missionaries and oral evidence suggests that the SIB leadership and pastors were quite ignorant of it. They only knew that the BEM had the intention to plant a 'Three-Self' indigenous church, which they generally agreed was a 'very good idea', even though 'their general educational level then was Standard Five or Six'.[113] They also knew that the BEM would withdraw when the BEM felt that SIB was able 'to stand on its own two feet', in the same way as the C&MA missionaries did to the indigenous KINGMI church in Kalimantan.[114]

Leadership Training and Development

One central implication of the fifteen-year policy was the need to train indigenous church leadership and ministry. The training of leaders for a 'native church to stand on its own feet independent of foreign missionaries' was perceived by the BEM as a matter of utmost priority.[115]

LAWAS BIBLE SCHOOL

In training future leaders or pastors of the SIB, the Lawas Bible School (LBS), (which opened on 5 May 1947 at Buduk Ngeri, Limbang and later shifted to Lawas), played a central role. Its student enrolment started modestly with two Lun Bawang students and increased to twenty students by the end of June 1947,[116] and it continued to increase steadily. There were fifty-five students from five tribes in 1951,[117] sixty students representing six tribes in 1953, a

[111] Lees, *Drunk before Dawn*, 138-39.

[112] The Kayan New Testament was printed in 1970, which is, *Jaji Masing: Dalun Kayan* (Edinburgh: Bible Society of Singapore, Malaysia and Brunei/R.R. Clarke, 1970). The Kenyah New Testament was partially completed and printed in 1971, which is *Injil Ngan Katuk: Palai surat dan KitapTuket Mading* (Edinburgh: Bible Society of Singapore, Malaysia and Brunei/R.R. Clarke, 1971). This partial New Testament has the Gospel of Luke, Gospel of John, Romans, Ephesians, Philippians, 1 and 2 Timothy, 1 and 2 Peter.

[113] Interviews with John Urud, 15 September 2004; with Jok Wan and Pengiran Gugkang, 16 September 2004; with Balang Anid, 17 September 2004; with Balan Engan 18 September 2004; with Sigar Bee, Udan Rangat and Satu Lakui, 21 September 2004; with Sara Mulang, 22 September 2004; with Tubu Padan, 24 September 2004 and with George Ngo Epoi, 7 October 2004. In interview with Winston Edip, 15 September 2004, he recalled that he did not know of the fifteen-year policy until he was in Australia for his further studies.

[114] Harold McCracken's unpublished address to BEM 1968 Rally in Melbourne.

[115] *BEM NL*, April 1953, 2.

[116] *BEM Fourteenth Annual Report*, 31 December 1947, 2-3. Lees, *Drunk before Dawn*, 85. These students consisted of ten married couples.

[117] *BEM Eighteenth Annual Report*, 31 December 1951, 9.

slight dip to fifty students representing seven tribes in 1954; eighty students in 1955 and one hundred and seventy in 1962.[118] As a result, LBS was able to increase its supply to meet the demand for pastors.[119]

During the first two decades, LBS trained students were regarded as the 'cream of the churches'.[120] This meant that the churches had the best possible people to lead and pastor them. Some contributory developments included firstly, the students were married and much older in age; some had been deacons or leaders in the churches or in community leadership positions already.[121] Secondly, the BEM devised a system whereby the most promising students from the outstation Bible schools were sent to LBS. There were two criteria in the selection process: (a) the character and maturity of the student and 'definite interest in spiritual things'; and (b) priority was given to students from the tribes where no missionary yet resided, such as the Kelabit.[122] Further, the curiosity, novelty and excitement of schooling whereby new knowledge and skills were acquired were an undoubted attraction. Also, the incentive for training as pastors provided better students with an avenue for upward mobility into leadership positions in the church which functioned as an alternative social power structure in the community. So, the selection and training of the students with the best potential provided capable leadership for the SIB, fulfilling a significant aim of the BEM.

The post-war era saw a rapid rise of educational opportunities and standards in the country to which the BEM responded by reviewing and upgrading Bible school standards.[123] The highest qualification of the students then was primary four. Raising the entry qualification of LBS in 1955,[124] reviewing and upgrading its curriculum, and preparing selected students for higher education and later sending them for further theological studies helped indigenous pastors to meet the challenge of ministering to their increasingly literate communities.

---

[118] *BEM NL*, February 1954; p. 2, August 1954; p. 1, April 1956, 2; February 1962, 1. Lees, *Jungle Fire*, 26.

[119] *BEM NL*, January 1961, 1; August 1970, 3. There were 186 churches in 1960 and 266 in 1970. *BEM Field Executive Minutes*, 14 May 1965, 1. There were about 110 pastors in 1965 and 221 pastors in 1970.

[120] *BEM NL*, February 1962, 1; February 1970, 2.

[121] Some of these students include those whom we have mentioned in earlier chapters; those like Balang Selutan, Udan Rangat, Lawai, Racha Umong, Riong Awa, Tebari, Balan Seling, Mein Ribu.

[122] *BEM NL*, August 1951, 2.

[123] It was noted that 'fifteen years ago, almost all the students were illiterate'. Currently, a higher primary school standard for student entry was the norm. Soon, 'we are moving towards a secondary school standard of entrance'. *BEM Field Executive Minutes*, 9-11 & 14-16 October 1963, 1. *BEM NL*, February 1962, 1.

[124] *BEM NL*, June 1955, 2.

Udan Rangat and Balan Seling were sent to MBI in 1959, [125] and Tubu and Layun were sent to New Zealand Bible Training Institute (NZBTI) in 1963)[126]

However, the BEM was not directly involved in providing secondary education, which was provided by the government. Secondary schools were first established among the *Orang Ulu* communities in Limbang in 1962, in Marudi in 1963, in Long Lama in 1965 and in Bario in 1967. The Malaysia Certificate of Education, the equivalent of an English 'O' level examination, was first introduced in Sarawak in 1967. From 1958 to 1972, the maximum intake into Form 1 was 30% of the enrolment in Primary 6. From 1975 onwards, secondary education became available to all school children.[127] From the late 1960s, the rising educational level of the community at large was beginning to outstrip the qualifications of those entering LBS and confronted LBS and both the BEM and SIB with the need for higher level Bible training. By 1968, 'the SIB was requesting help (from the BEM) for higher Bible training courses for men of suitable calibre to minister to the better educated communities'.[128] This request was understandable as those in the SIB leadership did not have any secondary education. When Miri Bible College (MBC) was established in 1972, the preferred entry qualification was a Secondary Five education but it also initially accepted those with a Secondary Three education.[129] Also, the need for more Bible courses for laymen suggested that the more educated people were entering the professions instead of the pastorate,[130] a phenomenon which continued with the best students within the community going for higher education in the tertiary colleges and universities in the country, so that a professional class of workers began to emerge.

The philosophy of training offered by LBS was more akin to vocational school training with a field placement module sandwiched between two study modules.[131] Teaching in the classroom was put into practice not just during the period of the field placement but also at the weekend assignments, where students were required to preach in the surrounding churches or make itinerant evangelistic trips accompanying the missionaries into the interior, as in the case of Singha Achang with two women missionaries, Dorothy Summerson and

---

[125] *BEM NL*, February 1959, 3. They returned in 1962. Balan Seling returned with a theological diploma and was appointed assistant head of LBS in 1962. See *BEM NL*, April 1962, 4; April 1963, 2; June 1963, 1.

[126] *BEM NL*, December 1962, 1 and February 1963, 1. *Field Executive Minutes*, 2 & 6 November 1967, 2 noted that Samuel Agong was studying at Singapore Bible College (SBC).

[127] See The Sarawak Education Department, 'Outline of the History of Education in Sarawak', *Journal of Malaysian Historical Society, Sarawak branch*, June 1980, 11-23. From 1975, all Primary 6 students were automatically promoted into Form 1.

[128] *BEM NL*, October 1968, 1.

[129] *BEM NL*, December 1972, 3.

[130] *BEM NL*, October 1968, 1.

[131] *BEM Seventeenth Annual Report*, 31 December 1950, 4-5. *BEM NL*, February 1949, 4.

Betty Johnstone.[132] The BEM philosophy of leadership development has been that of learning and leading through participatory involvement of indigenous people in ministry, a feature that was seen in every aspect of BEM activities.

Despite the establishment of the SIB in 1959, the process of handing over the management of LBS to the SIB seemed slower than expected, but progress was nevertheless made. Since its inception in 1947, LBS had been entirely staffed by missionaries;[133] but had its first local staff in 1954[134], and by 1962, it had largely Bornean staff, except for the principal.[135] Although the SIB had been asked to appoint an indigenous principal by the BEM Field Executive in 1967,[136] there was no such appointment until 1972, when Tagal Paran became the first national principal,[137] after which LBS had a fully Bornean staff. There were a few reasons for the difficulty of finding a suitable indigenous principal for LBS. Firstly, the two most promising indigenous pastors, Udan Rangat and Balan Seling, both of whom were capable of assuming the principalship of LBS, resigned from the SIB in 1954 and 1967 respectively.[138] Secondly, those who might have been able to assume the post of principal of LBS did not feel adequately qualified. According to Tagal Paran, most of the older SIB pastors had only a Primary Six education,[139] and the in-coming students had more formal school education than they. Even Sara Mulang, the third principal of LBS, expressed similar sentiments of inadequacy.[140] Further, Gerawat Maran

---

[132] *BEM NL*, August 1953, 2. Singha Achang was pastor at Long Luping.

[133] Brian Morcombe was the first Principal from 1947 to 1948; Madge Belcher was the second Principal from 1948 to 1967 (Lees, *Drunk before Dawn*, 84-85; *BEM NL*, December 1948, 2); Rev. R. N. Burton was the third Principal from 1968 to 1972 (*BEM NL*, August 1968, 2; October 1968, 4).

[134] Lees, *Jungle Fire*, 26. *BEM NL* August 1954, 1. Udan Rangat was the first national member of staff, but he left the SIB in 1964. In the 1953 Pastors' Conference, it was decided that as soon as possible, some of the pastors be made members of the teaching staff at LBS. See *BEM NL*, February 1954, 2.

[135] *BEM NL*, February 1962, 1. The local staff included Belawan, Jok Wan, Balang Selutan, Tama Galang, Kelasi Ating and later Balan Seling. Madge Belcher was the Principal from 1948 to 1967.

[136] In 1968, when both the BEM and SIB leadership met, the SIB said that they would like to assume responsibilities at their own pace and not be pushed into them. See *BEM Field Executive Minutes*, 27-30 Sept. & 5-7 October 1967, 1.

[137] *BEM NL*, August 1972, 2.

[138] Udan Rangat left to become headmaster of a primary school in Lawas. Balan Seling left to become a politician.

[139] They expressed that none of the SIB leaders felt adequate enough to take over the Principalship of LBS. Interviews with Tagal Paran, 22 September 2004 and with Jok Wan, 16 September 2004.

[140] Interview with Sara Mulang, 22 September 2004. Sara Mulang left the SIB in 1977. In a 1968 meeting of the BEM Executive and Representatives from Home Council with the SIB Executive, Selutan, Balang (SIB President) expressed that 'pastors are feeling that their present training is inadequate and does not fit them for dealing with people who have a higher education than themselves'. See 'Comments made by Members of

commented that he was 'forced' to become the second principal of LBS in 1974,[141] as it was not good to have the position revert to the missionaries and moreover the ten-year immigration ruling on missionary residence was about to take effect in 1975.[142]

Deacons' Schools, Short-term Bible Schools and Annual Conventions

Another aspect of training provided by the BEM was aimed at training those in the churches, not only the deacons but also ordinary members who showed potential and promise. These deacons' schools were conducted regionally among each tribe.[143] This training of local church leaders through the deacons' schools produced a variety of results. It helped to develop literate leaders of the churches through the short-term deacons' schools and Bible schools among the various tribes on a regular basis: for instance, in 1950, the literacy rate among the Lun Bawang was about 2%, with most deacons being illiterate and untaught.[144] By 1951, the deacons' school, which was held at Lawas, had 42 deacons attending out of 90 people; the courses taught included preaching, telling stories, reading, writing, church organization and hygiene. Both Udan Rangat and Iki were recruited to assist as teachers.[145] Beyond grounding them in a basic knowledge of the Scriptures and gaining their help in translating the Scriptures into their own language, the deacons were also helped through dealing with specific issues in their churches and also organizing matters relating to church life. Further, the deacons' schools became a place for identifying potential leaders and encouraging them toward further study at LBS, as in the case of Mein Ribu, the Kelabit leader at Pa Mein and Dario, the Penan from the headwaters of the Akah River.[146] In these short-term Bible schools, indigenous pastors or teachers had the opportunity to act, first, as helpers and co-workers alongside the missionaries, and finally as leaders without missionary supervision or as co-leaders by November 1957.[147] Also by 1954, almost all the primary schools in the outstations had been delegated to indigenous pastors.[148]

SIB Executive at Meeting with BEM Executive and Representative from Home Council'.

[141] Interview with Gerawat Maran, 23 September 2004.

[142] See Chapter 8 for further details.

[143] The Lun Bawang and Tagal deacons'schools were held separately for them at Lawas. *BEM NL*, December 1958, 4.

[144] See *BEM NL*, December 1949, 2.

[145] *BEM NL*, December 1951, 3. *BEM Eighteenth Annual Report*, 31 December 1951, 4.

[146] Lees, *Jungle Fire*, 63. Dario and his wife Lehai attended the Kelabit-Penan deacons' school at Long Lellang. His small group of less than twenty worked to send him to LBS.

[147] *BEM NL*, October 1957, 3. By end 1957, the deacons' schools were mainly conducted by indigenous pastors except for the one among the Penan at Long Bedian. The co-leadership continued at the deacons' schools held at the Lawas headquarters.

[148] *BEM NL*, October 1954, 2. The indigenous pastor was also the school teacher.

Learning to read

Racha Umong and Tebari Mulid at Kayan Conference 1958

The role of the annual conventions or irau played an important role in the training and grooming of indigenous leaders. These Keswick-type conventions were organized tribally, first among the Lun Bawang in 1948 and later among the Kelabit,[149] Kayan[150] and Kenyah[151] in Sarawak and the Dusun and Tagal in North Borneo, with specially invited speaker(s) to give the Bible teaching.[152] J.W. Searle, principal of MBI, was the speaker at the first Lun Bawang convention at Buduk Ngeri, Lawas, in 1948.[153] These conventions were organized separately by the church in each tribe and were hosted annually by a different church in that tribe.[154] In 1955, the first Inter-Tribal Convention was held at Pa Mein in the Kelabit Highlands.[155] It also provided the churches with an opportunity to make forward plans, so that among the Lun Bawang churches, notification was already made known about the host churches for the conventions for the next four years at the 1957 Convention.[156]

Though their original aims were to strengthen the faith of the Christian communities through concentrated Bible teaching and also to act as a forum for discussion between the missionaries and deacons on problems facing the church, the conventions had other attendant effects. Firstly, they became a substitute for the traditional harvest festival. In contrast to their pre-Christian days when they would feast and get drunk, believers now 'feasted on the Scriptures' as these conventions exhibited a celebrative mood with joyful singing and combined choirs as regular features.[157] Secondly, the conventions fostered cooperative participation between members of the host church, where the convention was held, and the BEM and SIB leadership. Also the LBS students were often assigned to help in the practical organization of the convention.[158] Thirdly, the conventions promoted a sense of solidarity and oneness among the churches within a tribe and also across the tribes, expelling old fears and promoting a reconciliatory attitude, as may be seen in 1951 at

---

149 BEM, *Commit Thou to Faithful Men* (Melbourne: Spectator Publishing, ca. 1957), 7. First Kelabit convention at Pa Mein in 1955.

150 First Baram convention for Kayan, Kenyah and Penan at Long Atip in 1957.

151 *BEM NL*, August 1958, 3. First Kenyah convention at Long Akah in 1958.

152 *BEM NL*, August 1959, 1.

153 *BEM Fifteenth Annual Report*, 31 December 1948, 2. *BEM NL*, June 1948, 3. It was well attended with 500 people and 65 church leaders, so that the local church building had to be renovated to double its size.

154 Among the Muruts, the conventions were held at Buduk, Ngeri, Lawas (Easter 1948), Long Semadoh (Christmas 1948), Trusan (1949), Long Lepadan (1950) Brayong (1951), Ba Kelalan (1952), Pa Matang (1953) and Tang Lepadan (1954), Mengalong (1957), Long Luping (1958), Lawas (1961) and Long Litong (1962).

155 BEM, *Commit Thou to Faithful Men*, 7. *BEM NL*, August 1955, 3.

156 *BEM NL*, June 1957, 3.

157 *BEM NL*, February 1950, 3; August 1950, 4. The Bible Conventions were normally held during Easter, which did not coincide with the traditional harvest festival in June.

158 *BEM NL*, February 1950, 3; June 1951, 1. At Trusan (1949), the LBS students took charge of an evening meeting. At Brayong (1951), two LBS students were responsible for preparations and planning including hospitality, food and hygiene and sanitation.

Brayong, with the presence of a hundred Tagals among the Muruts and also in 1955 at Pa Mein, with the presence of Kayan among the Kelabit, groups which were once traditional enemies.[159] Fourthly, the pastors and deacons were drawn closer together in their deliberation, discussion and prayer concerning church matters,[160] realizing the themes of 'All One in Christ'[161] and 'A United Church'.[162] Not only did the conventions function as embryonic church assemblies even before the formation of SIB in 1959, they also became a place for the encouragement of local participation and the recognition of potential and capable leaders, the provision of opportunities for counselling and pastoral advice, (for instance, with the Kenyah who had wanted to support a pastor).[163] In addition, there was an interchange of ideas among leaders on dealing with problems facing the churches, learning about the needs of the younger churches and developing a missionary vision for their non-Christian neighbours.[164]

In all these conventions, a characteristic feature was the sharing of ministry between the BEM and SIB leadership in the main sessions. At Long Atip, the first Kayan Easter convention in 1952 had twelve meetings, of which only three were taken by BEM missionaries, the rest by the deacons or LBS students.[165] At Long Litong in 1962, all the speakers were indigenous pastors, Racha Umong, Balang Selutan, and Udan Rangat.[166] Also, the attendance increased from year to year, starting with 500 (Buduk Ngeri, 1948), 500 (Trusan, 1949), 900 (Brayong, 1951), 900 (Pa Matang, 1953), 1,600 (Tang Lepadan, 1954), 1,200 (Pa Mein, 1955), 2,000 (Mengalong, 1957), 3,700 (Lawas, 1961) and 2,000 (Long Litong, 1962).[167] Further, these irau were big communal affairs which gave much prestige to the host village, church and its headman. The rotation system of one village at a time hosting these conventions enhanced the social status, prestige and identity of the Christian villages among the tribe and also the relationship with other non-Christian Orang Ulu.[168] All these factors taken

---

159 *BEM NL*, June 1954, 4; August 1955, 3. Amat Lasong, the Murut missionary to the Tagals led the 100 Tagals to the convention at Brayong.

160 *BEM NL*, May 1961, 3.

161 *BEM NL*, June 1954, 4. Theme for Pa Matang convention 1953.

162 BEM, *Commit Thou to Faithful Men*, 8. *BEM NL*, August 1955, 3. Theme for Pa Mein convention 1955.

163 *BEM NL*, August 1955, 3.

164 *BEM NL*, June 1956, 1.

165 *BEM NL*, June 1952, 4.

166 *BEM NL*, June 1962, 3.

167 *BEM NL*, June 1948, 3 (Buduk Ngeri); February 1950 (Trusan), 3; June 1951, 1 (Brayong); August 1953, 1 (Pa Matang); June 1954, 4 (Tang Lepadan); August 1955, 3 (Pa Mein); June-July 1957, 2 (Mengalong); May-June 1961, 1 (Lawas); June-July 1962, 3 (Long Litong).

168 Russell, *Conversion, Identity and Power*, 99-105, 112-13. The ability of the church to initiate and host feasts enhances its social status and prestige and also shifts the focus of prestige to the host church. See *BEM NL*, June 1952, 4. The Penghulu of Long Atip felt a sense of pride as it increased his prestige.

together invariably led to the promotion of indigenous initiatives, leadership skills and capabilities, social empowerment and confidence and the development of a greater sense of unity and cooperation among the Orang Ulu within SIB.[169]

Writing class for new students, Lawas Bible School

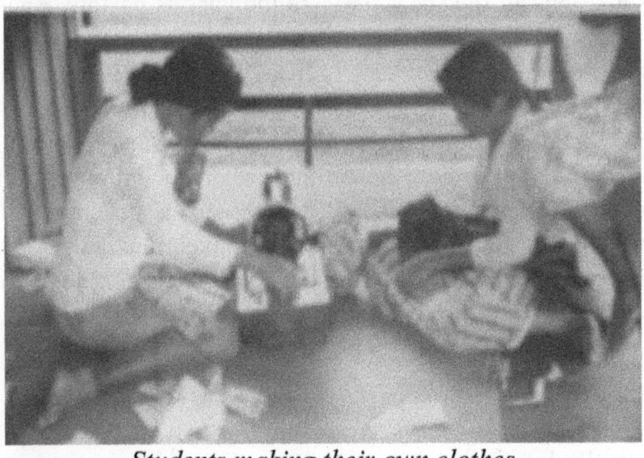

Students making their own clothes

Indigenous Leadership and Response

In the process of establishing a 'Three-Self' church, the indigenous church had to rise to accept the challenge. In Hendrik Kraemer's study of the East Javanese Church, he cited four reasons for the inability of the Javanese to attain self-government, which were mainly negative attitudes such as (a) fear among the

[169] Such inter-Orang Ulu meetings would have prepared the way for greater cooperation among the Orang Ulu within SIB and also beyond the SIB, resulting in their participation in the Orang Ulu National Association (OUNA), which was formally established on October 1966. See Seling and Langub, 'The Orang Ulu', 29-33 for the formation of OUNA and its activities. Balan Seling, formerly a SIB Deputy President, served as the President of OUNA from 1979 to 1988.

Javanese; (b) they were not in the mood for it, though they recognized the fairness of the idea and that they ought to be independent; (c) a self-depreciating attitude about their own abilities; and (d) their tendency to lean on supposedly stronger persons, in this case, the Dutch missionaries.[170] So it was perceived that, subjectively, they were not ripe for self-government because they were so strongly convinced about their own weaknesses and, objectively, because they were far removed from self-support, lacking in skills for self-administration and very hesitant in carrying out self-propagation.[171]

These negative attitudes were likely to occur whenever indigenous people were thrust into positions and structures of authority for which there had been no real precedent. The issue was whether they were given the chance to refute these negative attitudes by the evidence of their own competence, or whether the missionaries assumed that they were not yet ready for independence and self-government, and hence denied the indigenes the opportunity of proving their capabilities. The BEM missionaries, despite, no doubt, private reservations about indigenous capacity, were inclined, by their corporate ethos and policies, to encourage indigenous Christians to take responsibility.[172]

In the case of the SIB leaders, this chapter and the last have supplied evidence of the self-propagating initiatives and abilities of the SIB pastors and people. Further, during the 1958 Inter-Tribal Conference, a new possibility was raised of the SIB looking beyond Borneo for the expansion of its mission,[173] and also of SIB making links outside of East Malaysia.[174] This section will examine whether the SIB leadership possessed the required capabilities and skills for self-governance and self-support.

A self-governing SIB Church needed a central structure and a decision-making and implementation mechanism for it to be successful. Before the formal establishment of the SIB in 1959, there was a preparatory period of about five years from 1954, in which structural development kept pace with the gradual devolution of responsibilities to the future SIB leaders. As noted earlier, the creation of this structure in December 1954 saw the formation of a representative body for the administration of the indigenous Church. This representative body later became the Inter-Tribal Conference in 1956. Even in 1954, the representative body ventured to make two important decisions. The

---

[170] Hendrik Kraemer, *From Missionfield to Independent Church: Report on a decisive decade in the growth of indigenous churches in Indonesia* (London: SCM Press Ltd, 1958), 85. The missionaries viewed their self-depreciating attitude as follows, 'This widespread conviction of their own helpless condition is one of the greatest enemies of the Javanese people. It belongs to the vocabulary of self depreciation with which to honour the foreigners'. Though the Javanese lacked a sense of confidence and concord, they did show a solidarity among themselves.

[171] Kraemer, *From Missionfield to Independent Church*, 90.

[172] See above in this chapter.

[173] *BEM NL*, February 1959, 1.

[174] *BEM NL*, November 1976, 4.

first related to requesting the government to award marriage licences to Bornean pastors, as these had so far only been given to the missionaries. This situation had resulted in the great inconvenience of having to travel to Lawas for those in the interior who wanted to be married.

The second decision dealt with the issue of bride wealth, a complex and delicate question among the Lun Bawang churches.[175] The common practice of asking for very high bride wealth made it very difficult for any potential bridegroom or his family and relatives to raise the necessary amount. An initial ruling that pastors and deacons should set an example by not asking for any bride wealth for their daughters[176] was later confirmed by the Lun Bawang deacons in 1955,[177] but cultural realities later dictated the more pragmatic alternative of ruling that bride wealth should be kept within affordable limits.[178] The persistence with which the indigenous leadership persevered with its implementation of a policy of encouraging affordable bride wealth until it was generally accepted, (though its acceptance at times was difficult among some people), was commendable. The missionaries, on the other hand, wished that bride wealth be abolished completely. This attitude was reflected in the prayer request made in the BEM newsletter in 1956 that supporters should pray for a 'decision to have done with the giving and receiving of dowries (bride-wealth)'.[179] Nevertheless, in matters relating to indigenous socio-cultural practices, the missionaries were generally cautious about making decisions on behalf of the local Christians:

> How much better that these men should seek to discuss together and seek the mind of the Lord concerning the application of Christian principles to their own culture than that the missionaries super-impose their Western culture upon them.[180]

In the 1956 Inter-Tribal Conference, when responsibility for all church matters was first exercised by indigenous leadership, dealt with a wide range of relevant issues. Firstly, it assessed the situation of the churches in the different

---

[175] This problem did not affect the other ethnic groups such as Kelabit, Kayan or Iban. During the 1950s, the SIB leadership was predominately Lun Bawang.

[176] *BEM NL*, February 1955, 4 and April 1955, 1. It was difficult for young male students of LBS to find wives. The affected person, Uta, was head prefect at LBS who wanted to marry the daughter of a deacon in the Mengalong area but the bride wealth was too high, which was often £120.

[177] *BEM NL*, February-March 1956, 1.

[178] Interview with Udan Rangat, 21 September 2004. Pastors faced a dilemma; though they may be willing to forgo the bride wealth for their daughters, but when their sons got married, they have to help their sons pay for their bride wealth; for which they have little to give.

[179] *BEM NL*, February 1956, 1. The Newsletter was, of course, in error in describing bride wealth as a dowry.

[180] *BEM NL*, April 1955, 1.

areas, the number of pastors available and their designation, the support of the pastors by the churches, pastors' holidays and the length of time the pastor should serve in the church before returning to LBS for refresher courses. Secondly, it examined the role of the deacons, their gift of organization, their faithfulness to the work, their ability to read the Bible and their availability for itinerant evangelism. Thirdly, it considered the conditions within the churches, whether the villagers were all Christians, their church attendance, their desire for the Word of God and their witness to others both by life and word, and whether they were 'nominal, following Christian customs only'. Fourthly, it examined the different types of schools being held in the churches, such as day school, Sunday school, night school and deacons' school. Finally, it evaluated the attitude of the unbelievers in the area with regard to the gospel.[181]

By 1958, all local church management, church services and ordinances and church discipline were in the hands of the pastors and deacons. Only occasionally on matters of church discipline, did the leaders consult the missionaries and request Bible teaching on particular problems.[182] Thus even prior to its formal establishment in 1959, the future leadership of the SIB already had exposure to and experience of managing and coordinating church activities and church life at both local and inter-tribal levels, a task which they appeared to have accomplished reasonably competently. Further, the preference for a centralized structure for the BEM, according to Belcher, came from the church leadership who felt that they should be organized along a similar pattern as in the KINGMI church across the border in Kalimantan. As a result, two Indonesian pastors were invited to explain their ecclesial structure and constitution to the SIB leaders at the 1959 conference. The SIB leaders adapted KINGMI's structure which was presbyterian in form.[183] By 1961, the SIB Constitution was formally accepted so that the ecclesial structure was in place for them to function properly. The Inter-Tribal Conference, which was held biannually from 1961, functioned as the supreme decision-making body. Later it became the SIB General Conference.[184]

---

[181] *BEM NL*, February 1957, 2. Even before the SIB was formally formed in 1959, the indigenous leaders represented in the Inter-Tribal Conference were beginning to exercise their leadership role in 1956.

[182] *BEM NL*, December 1958, 2.

[183] Interview with Alan Belcher, 30 October 2004. Tagal Paran and Jok Wan acknowledged that the SIB constitution was modeled after that of KINGMI, Kalimantan, though they could not provide any further information about the event. In *BEM NL*, June 1960, 3, the two KINGMI representatives were two elders, Gugkang Tebari and Labo Tai.

[184] By 1980, the structure that was developed had a three tier structure: the church, district and State (i.e., Sarawak or Sabah) levels. The supreme body is the State General Conference. The State Central Council consisted of a Central Committee and other representatives of the regions and SIB ministries. There was a Combined Executive of both Sarawak and Sabah SIB (consisting of members of the two state Central Executive

Despite assuming substantial responsibilities from the BEM, there were still situations when the SIB would look to the BEM for advice. In the words of Tubu Padan, a former SIB President,

> The BEM allowed SIB leaders to organize as much as possible. But the SIB leaders did not feel confident to work alone and often asked for advice from BEM missionaries in areas of work which were not familiar to SIB leaders. As an example, SIB was often dependent on advice from the BEM missionaries as to how much people should give to the pastors.[185]

An interesting feature of the BEM-SIB relationship was the close relationship which the BEM Field Director and SIB President had with one another, for example, Alan Belcher with Racha Umong, and later Bill Hawes with Tagal Paran and Jok Wan.[186] According to Satu Lakui and Tagal Paran, the BEM did not make any decision that would affect the SIB without consultation with the SIB. The pattern of decision-making was that the two leaders (BEM Field Director and SIB President) would discuss the matter, and then their agreed decision was put forward to the SIB executive council for endorsement.[187] As Jok Wan puts it, the SIB did not seek advice from the BEM in every matter, but only in the matters where the SIB had been unable to manage without the help of the BEM.[188] Even when SIB leaders sought advice from the BEM leaders, they would not always heed the advice of the BEM Field Directors, as noted earlier in this chapter.[189] Another instance when the SIB diverged from BEM policy was the issue of receiving government grants for church buildings. As Tagal Paran puts it:

> BEM had the policy that SIB should not accept money from government for church projects or pastor's house.... But SIB agreed that it can accept money from the government, but churches cannot be used for political purposes. The BEM was afraid that if SIB accepted money from the government, the churches and/or its

---

Councils) for their joint projects. See *Sidang Injil Borneo (SIB) Handbook and Rules* (Kota Kinabalu/Miri: SIB Sabah/Sarawak, 1980).

[185] Interview with Tubu Padan, 24 September 2004.

[186] A factor facilitating this was that the BEM and SIB headquarters were in the same premises.

[187] Interview with Satu Lakui, 21 September 2004. Satu Lakui was Secretary of SIB from 1966 to 1971. Interview with Tagal Paran, 22 September 2004.

[188] Interview with Jok Wan, 16 September 2004. Jok Wan cited ministry in the towns as the help which SIB needed from the BEM. According to Winston Edip, the older SIB leaders were generally more dependent on the missionaries. 'In the past, when there was problem, the attitude was to wait till Pendita Meripa (Alan Belcher) come and then to seek his advice'. Interview with Winston Edip, 15 September 2004.

[189] It is unlikely for Racha Umong who is described by Alastair Morrison as a 'notable personality' and 'prominent leader' among the Lun Bawang to be always heeding the advice of Alan Belcher. See Morrison, *Fair Land Sarawak*, 53. Interviews with Satu Lakui, 21 September 2004 and with Tagal Paran, 22 September 2004.

buildings may be used for political campaigning. When Racha Umong was a politician, he had allocated some government funds for church buildings.[190]

Initially, the SIB Executive had decided not to accept any government money for building SIB churches, as they did not want to be obligated to the government or allow any opportunity for the government to interfere into their affairs. This decision was made out of deference to Alan Belcher.[191] However, Balan Seling also noted that this 'issue was not really clear from Scripture, different churches in different countries might well come to different decisions, according to their consciences'. Furthermore, there was a view among SIB members that 'as they gave taxes to the government, it would be right to receive money in return, for their churches'.[192] It was only after both Racha Umong and Balan Seling became politicians that the SIB began to change its view. To the credit of the BEM, there was no compulsion on the SIB to conform to its policy on this matter,[193] as the BEM realized the impracticability of doing so, even if it had the intention. In reality, the SIB was already independent of the BEM, except for situations which the SIB found so unfamiliar or difficult. By establishing SIB as a separate ecclesial body, the BEM had started a process of devolution that became unstoppable. With the passage of time, the SIB would become more and more independent of the BEM.

The issue of using single local women in church work presented a problem to the SIB, as within their local culture 'there could be serious moral temptations' if women went out on their own or even when they did so two by two. The SIB discussed three proposals. Firstly, local women should be appointed to teach in the Bible School. This was obviously an impractical suggestion in view of the number of single women, as there were more people than positions available. Secondly, they should team up to work with the BEM single women missionaries. Thirdly, a reliable woman in the local church should be appointed to chaperone the single local women pastors and be responsible for their welfare.[194] The latter two suggestions were implemented with some measure of success.

Since the most capable people occupied posts in the central SIB leadership, there was a tendency for the districts to look to their leaders at Lawas for guidance and advice. Realising that this practice would only create dependency in the long term, the SIB leadership at the SIB Conference urged the district conferences and leaders to play a greater role instead of looking to Lawas to

---

[190] Interview with Tagal Paran, 22 September 2004. Also, interview with John Urud, 15 September 2004.
[191] Interview with John Urud, 15 September 2004. John Urud is the son-in-law of Racha Umong.
[192] *Combined BEM/SIB Executive Meeting*, 27 October 1966, 7-8.
[193] Interview with Jok Wan, 16 September 2004.
[194] *BEM NL*, February 1962, 2.

deal with the placing of pastors, coordinating evangelism, stimulating fellowship and coping with problems. This encouragement of district and local initiatives was reminiscent of the BEM's style of encouraging indigenous leadership and initiatives. Further, the SIB Conference dealt with the difficult issue of deacons who had outlasted their usefulness in service. As there was no machinery to deal with the problem then, the proposal that all deacons faced an automatic election biannually was adopted 'after much discussion'.[195] Thus, the SIB leadership proved itself able and willing to make difficult decisions and exercised prudent leadership in dealing with and solving important problems facing them as a church; experiences that augured well for them in the 1980s.

The established pattern of work between the BEM and SIB was that, in every area of ministry, an indigenous person or couple would invariably understudy and work alongside the missionary with the aim of taking over that particular ministry. The process of handing over the ministries from the BEM missionaries took its natural course, when the missionary went on furlough or when the BEM officially ceased its work in Sarawak. By 1980, the SIB had taken over the specialized ministries which included the Bible schools, evangelist training programmes, Studio Bahagia (radio ministry) and literature ministry and also had Coordinators for the Sunday School, Youth Fellowship, Women's Fellowship, Film Ministry and Evangelism.[196]

Since 1963, the SIB had increasingly taken on the responsibility of negotiating directly with the government regarding matters pertaining to the SIB. In 1963, the SIB dealt directly with the Sabah government for entry into a new area. Also, the SIB applied successfully for a piece of land for the Chinese Christians to build a church at Lawas.[197] Moreover, now that Racha Umong, President of the SIB, sat on the Lawas District Council and on the Council Negeri,[198] SIB was given some recognition by the government as an indigenous church.

The issue of self-support has been an issue that has often kept churches from being truly 'Three-Self'. In the SIB churches, the culture of self-support was instilled almost from the beginning as the churches collected, kept and disbursed their own funds, since all church expenses were the responsibility of the church itself. Further, they were responsible for their own buildings.[199] The reason for this emphasis on self-support was three-fold. Firstly, during the

---

[195] *BEM NL*, February 1971, 1.

[196] *SIB Handbook and Rules*, 21-22.

[197] *BEM NL*, December 1963, 2.

[198] *BEM NL*, August 1963, 4; October 1963, 1.

[199] 'It should be made clear to villages asking for pastors that they must be prepared to support a resident pastor completely from the beginning of his time in the village'. See *BEM Field Conference Minutes*, 15-26 July 1960, 7. *BEM NL*, December 1958, 2. Shortly after WWII, when Southwell returned to Sarawak, the church at Gaya had built its own new church building in time for Christmas 1947. See Southwell, *Uncharted Waters*, 184.

Japanese Occupation, the churches were self-supporting and self-governing out of necessity. As noted in an earlier chapter, a few churches had invited indigenous pastors and teachers from across the Kalimantan border and some support was given to them. Secondly, an early case of supporting the 'first two pastors to the Kayan tribe' out of BEM funds had 'the sad and far reaching result that for many years that church did not learn to give'.[200] As a result of this salutary experience, the BEM adopted a firm rule that no mission funds were to be used for any local church; as a result, self-support became a matter of necessity.[201] From 1961, the BEM adhered with renewed vigour to its original policy of being 'opposed to the principle of supporting native workers out of Mission funds'.[202]

The principle of tithing, which became a widely accepted practice in the SIB, was first introduced in the 1948 BEM Easter Conference among the Lun Bawang. The churches unanimously accepted the principle, and treasurers were appointed over different districts to collect the tithes. Also, they agreed that half of the tithe collected was for the support of students at LBS.[203] This support for the LBS students was handled by a committee of students from LBS under the presidency of the missionary-in-charge of the Lun Bawang Church.[204] Since becoming Christians, the Lun Bawang had experienced successively good harvests so that they not only tithed in kind but also sold the excess rice or exchanged it for buffaloes or cattle and gave them in support of the students at Lawas.[205] By 1949, when the first indigenous pastors, who had been trained at LBS, were sent into the interior churches,[206] the Lun Bawang churches had been educated to support their pastors, by building a house for the pastor and his wife, and supporting them with gifts in kind. In a rural situation, it was customary for all, including the headman and, hence, the pastor also to have his small plot of land to cultivate crops or breed livestock for his own consumption.

On the one hand, both the students at LBS and the pastor at the local church were expected to have an attitude of dependence upon God alone for their

---

[200] Lees, *Jungle Fire*, 88. 'It is now our firm policy not to put mission money in the support of Bornean personnel'.

[201] 'We aim to build a church which is independent of western missions. It must therefore be independent of western money from the start'. Lees, *Jungle Fire*, 88. *BEM NL*, January 1961, 2 & June *1967*, 1. 'No Mission funds are used to support the church'.

[202] *BEM Principles and Practices* (1939), 5, art. 13.

[203] *BEM NL*, June 1948, 3. The principle of tithing was first introduced by the BEM missionaries. See also Pollock, *Earth's Remotest*, 262.

[204] *BEM Fifteenth Annual Report*, December 1948, 5. *BEM NL*, December 1948, 2.

[205] *BEM NL*, August 1949, 1; December 1949, 4.

[206] *BEM NL*, December 1949, 4. Libat and Riong were sent to the Lun Bawang churches in Ba Kelalan in the interior.

financial support (a policy inherited from the BEM).[207] On the other hand, the church was taught about their responsibility of supporting their students at LBS and their pastor in their local church. In one instance in 1957, the question was raised as to why the sending church of a student was not supporting him so that he had to be supported by other churches.[208] The question implied that the local church should bear the responsibility of supporting the student. It was, however, recognized that many of the churches were too poor even to support a student or pastor. In 1960, seventy-six churches out of 186 churches (41%) were either unwilling or unable to support a pastor.[209] During the 1950s, though some churches were unable to support a pastor, some of the older churches not only supported their own pastors, but also supported the stipend of the Chairman of SIB and the Bornean staff at LBS and shared in the support of their missionaries to areas 'where there is not yet a church to do this'.[210] The situation seemed to worsen during the 1960s. The fact that a deacon at the Inter-Tribal Conference in 1960 spoke of the need of adequate support for the pastors meant that support had been insufficient. The suggested level of support for the first graduates from LBS sent as pastors to the churches in 1949 had not been revised, so that it was just sufficient for a married couple, but not for a pastor with a large family. This became a reason for the large number of 'dropouts' from the fulltime ministry among pastors with large families, especially those with school-going children.[211] By the end of the 1960s, it was reported that there was poor support for the pastors, with only a few who were well supported, since only half of the financial requirements of the SIB were being met. Responding to this situation, the BEM assisted the SIB in teaching the people about the need to support their pastors, with the result that 'a large number of the pastors continued in the work'.[212]

During the 1960s, a cash economy was increasingly impacting Sarawak, with its effects being felt first along the coastal towns, sub-coastal towns and then into the interior. The impact was unevenly felt among the SIB pastors. As most of the churches were in the interior, the impact of a cash economy was not drastically felt until their children had to move to the towns for education. For

---

207 Pollock, *Earth's Remotest*, 262. *BEM.NL*, June 1955, 2. 'Students live by faith'. 'The Mission does not give any financial support to these students and *all look to the Lord alone* for sustenance'.

208 *BEM NL*, June 1957, 3.

209 *BEM NL*, January 1961, 1.

210 *BEM NL*, January 1961, 2.

211 *BEM NL*, August 1970, 3. From 1960 to1970, 85 pastors had withdrawn from the work, which included 'those who had dropped out through sickness, age, *large families that cannot be supported on a pastor's allowance*, spiritual problems, etc'. See *BEM NL*, December 1969, 2. The monthly school fee of one child was equivalent to one month's allowance for one of the parents. Often the provision came through relatives. The pastors that had financial lack were pastors of large churches.

212 *BEM NL*, October 1969, 1.

the married pastors without children or with small children, they could continue to live off the land even when their monthly stipend was low.[213] But this would not be possible when they had school-going children. The SIB tried to deal with this issue of support for the pastor in 1968 by doubling the monthly allowances for the pastor, which included their monthly stipend and children's allowances on per child basis.[214] Another significant factor that helped SIB and its pastors overcome the difficulty of having to find cash to support their children for higher education was the award of government scholarships from the 1970s onwards to their children by virtue of their status as bumiputras;[215] thus giving the SIB church and the pastors more time to adjust towards their participation into the national economy. By 1980, the SIB had made reasonable progress towards the support of its pastors by communicating and spelling out more clearly for the local churches their responsibility to their pastor.[216] However, the SIB leadership recognized that the basic problem could not be solved by human management alone but believed that 'the Holy Spirit must do his own work of engendering liberality in individual hearts'.[217]

Until the mid-1950s, the BEM supported pioneer indigenous missionaries to the other unevangelized tribes.[218] In 1956, the SIB leadership indicated that SIB was ready to assume financial responsibility to support indigenous missionaries.[219] The SIB devised a system for financing evangelistic trips into new areas (for example, that of Balang Selutan and Tama Galang visiting the Kayan and Iban in the Bintulu River) by having the money collected on Christmas Day by the local churches to be sent to the central fund at the SIB headquarters in Lawas.[220] Though there had been a query about this practice, the SIB leadership was able to convince the local churches of its necessity, especially when the local churches would have liked to use the money to support their own pastors.[221] The competent handling of this issue highlighted

---

[213] *BEM NL*, February 1968, 2. It was reported that 101 pastors had been supported except for four; a generally good sign for the SIB.

[214] *BEM NL*, February 1968, 4.

[215] *Bumiputra* literally means 'son of the soil'. After the racial riots in Peninsular Malaysia in 1969, the New Economic Policy (NEP) was introduced so that the Malays and the indigenous peoples collectively known as *bumiputras* were given special privileges, of which the awarding of scholarships was one of them.

[216] The responsibility of the local church to its pastor included providing for his accommodation, utilities, monthly allowance, special allowances for his children's education, his travel and medical needs. See *SIB Handbook and Rules*, 20.

[217] *BEM NL*, February 1971, 1.

[218] This matter is to be distinguished from the BEM policy of not supporting local pastors who were resident within their own ethnic group. The BEM was keen to hand over this responsibility to the SIB as soon as possible. See *BEM Field Executive Minutes*, 7-14 October, 1955.

[219] *BEM Field Executive Minutes*, 5-15 March 1956, 3.

[220] *BEM NL*, December 1962, 1. Pollock, *Earth's Remotest*, 262. Lees, *Jungle Fire*, 88.

[221] *BEM NL*, December 1962, 1.

the ability of the SIB to balance their self-governing function with those of self-propagation and self-support.

The annual hosting of irau or conventions and also the Inter-Tribal Conferences, which were big events ranging from two thousand to four thousand people in attendance, were mainly supported by resources from the local churches, so that these events continued even after the BEM had withdrawn from Sarawak after 1979.[222]

In short, the SIB took on the challenge to be truly 'Three-Self' and showed itself to be reasonably competent in its self-propagation and self-governance. Though it managed its self-support satisfactorily within an agrarian economy and without any financial support from the BEM, the one area of greatest difficulty was sufficient support for pastors with large families; a continuing problem which the SIB has tried to rectify. Also, the assistance that the BEM gave toward the SIB was an important one, that of encouraging and teaching the SIB churches to properly support the needs of their pastors,[223] a task that was easier for the BEM than the SIB to do. Further, this difficulty was somewhat alleviated through government scholarships for the children of pastors going for higher education in the towns or to Peninsular Malaysia.

The Relationship between the BEM and SIB after 1959

The formal establishment of the SIB in 1959 marked a new phase of relationship between the BEM and the SIB. This relationship was spelt out in the Constitution of the SIB as follows:

> The SIB recognizes the BEM as the parent body. Although the two bodies are truly independent one from the other, they are one in their love for Christ and in their fellowship and cooperation in the all important task of proclaiming the Gospel in Borneo. All matters affecting both the SIB and BEM will be decided by the SIB and BEM meeting in conference.[224]

---

[222] In *BEM NL*, December 1962, 3, it was reported by a missionary that 'God is giving gifts to the SIB in a remarkable way. As I watched them organize the annual three day convention for the Murut Christians, any doubts I may have had been dispelled. Rice to feed 2,000-4,000 guests for three or four days, 10-20 heads of cattle, accommodation, everything is carried through smoothly and efficiently…in all aspects of the running of the convention is convincing evidence that the Lord is giving the gifts necessary for self-government'.

[223] *BEM NL*, February 1971, 1. With regard to giving, the SIB identified two major problems; that of poor communication and poorly understood objectives of the SIB that had considerably hamstrung the SIB's giving and in turn, affected its ability to function more effectively. The *BEM Field Executive Minutes*, 5-14 March 1968, 8, recorded that 'it was resolved that missionaries take every opportunity to stress the importance of giving by the churches towards the support of SIB's own workers'.

[224] *BEM NL*, February 1962, 1.

Underlying this statement was an understanding of the relationship in terms of a parent-child relationship. But when Racha Umong, President of the SIB, spoke at a BEM Rally held in Melbourne on 11 November 1962 in Nash Memorial Hall, MBI, the metaphor of the relationship changed to that of a younger brother and older brother.[225]

Even in the use of this 'younger brother-older brother' metaphor, there seemed to be a sense of dependence on the older brother (BEM), so that the BEM consciously clarified their relationship as follows: 'The SIB is not subject to the BEM but they want us to work with them and make a contribution they are as yet unable to make'.[226] However, BEM was conscious of the danger of 'SIB, the little brother leaning on the big brother… for too long', and also of the possibility that 'little brother might resent big brother and say "You should have enabled me to stand on my own feet earlier."'[227] By 1966, the relationship was clarified even further by Racha Umong: the two options of either BEM controlling SIB, or SIB controlling BEM, were rejected in favour of the option of 'cooperating alongside each other' as 'equal partners'.[228]

During the period from 1960 to 1963, the BEM had some uncertainties about the future; by virtue of the fifteen-year policy, the reality of withdrawal in 1965 was a difficult prospect and its re-interpretation provided the BEM with some way of continuing its work with the SIB. The SIB was, however, reluctant to see any premature withdrawal of the missionaries with whom they had a happy relationship, so that they were thinking of ways in which the relationship could continue, forging a new way forward. By 1963, it was clear that SIB needed BEM's help in translating the Scriptures and in areas of work which the SIB had been unable to initiate or as yet do for themselves.[229] Also, even through the later 1960s, there were repeated calls for the BEM to continue working with the SIB, as there were continually new challenges. These calls were first conveyed to Belcher[230] and later to Harold McCracken when he

---

[225] *BEM NL*, December 1962, 3. 'The SIB and BEM' are 'brothers – one is the younger, the other the older;' together the 'BEM and SIB are fellow labourers with God'.

[226] *BEM NL*, January 1961, 2.

[227] *BEM Field Executive Minutes*, March/April 1963, 3. This viewpoint was a suggestion from Harold McCracken to which the Field Executive fully agreed. Underlying this viewpoint was the fear that the BEM would be charged for being too slow or unwilling to hand over responsibilities to the SIB.

[228] *BEM NL*, October 1966, 3.

[229] *BEM NL*, October 1962, 3. The SIB made a request to the BEM, 'We don't want you to leave us yet. We want you to help us to provide us with more vernacular Scriptures and to do those things for us which we cannot do for ourselves yet'. Even though this report may be taken with some caution, it remained true that such a request was made.

[230] Letter of Belcher to Harold McCracken and John Smith, 26 May 1966 (OMF). Racha Umong made the request to the BEM. 'We don't want you to have a heavy hand on us or to withdraw or leave us alone, but to work in fellowship with us'. Their request was 'evidence of their desire for our fellowship'.

visited Lawas in 1968.[231] In a 1968 meeting between the SIB Executive, the BEM Executive and representatives from the Home Council, Balang Selutan commented that though the KINGMI church agreed that it could stand on its own feet, 'in view of recent happenings, it would seem that pastors are not able to fully assume responsibility and the fact is that the church is now stagnant... If we are forced to say yes and to stand completely on our own, we will wobble in certain areas where outside help is still needed... we want BEM to stand alongside us in partnership'. Another SIB leader, Tama Galang, said that 'if BEM wants to withdraw, we would think of looking to someone else who could help us'.[232] This appeal of the SIB leadership struck an empathetic chord in McCracken's heart, as was seen in his address to the BEM Rally on September 1968 in Melbourne. There he said that 'from the perspective of the SIB, in laying more and more responsibility to SIB so as to make SIB self-reliant and yet at the same time to withdraw its support, it appeared to SIB that BEM has lost interest in or is fed up with the SIB'.[233] From another perspective, the requests from the SIB could be a way of using the BEM to fulfil its agenda, even to the extent of putting the BEM in a dilemma.[234] In short, BEM was constrained by the need to continue to work with SIB and also to move into new specialized areas of ministries as requested by the SIB.

The new way forward had many different contributory factors. Firstly, there was the ongoing work of translating the Scriptures which had lagged behind schedule. Secondly, the SIB pastors and missionaries were facing difficult problems after continuously working for years without any provision for furlough or rest. There were difficult past moral problems,[235] personal problems of physical and psychological exhaustion or 'burnout' in the work, pressures

---

[231] Unpublished Address of Harold McCracken to the BEM Rally in Melbourne 1968. 'SIB leaders pointed to the tragedy of the KINGMI church in Indonesia where the missionaries left them a bit too early to stand on their own feet. It resulted in the KINGMI pastors being unable to fully resume responsibility so that the church is now stagnant'.

[232] Paper documenting 'Comments made by Members of SIB Executive at Meeting with BEM Executive and Representatives of Home Council' (n.d). Though this paper is undated, the meeting would have taken place in 1968 during the time of the BEM Field Conference, as Balang Selutan resigned as SIB President the following year and also in 1969, McCracken did not visit Sarawak. See Unpublished Address of McCracken at BEM Rally 1968, where much of what he said echoed the comments of the SIB leaders documented in the above paper.

[233] Unpublished Address of Harold McCracken to the 29 September BEM Rally in Melbourne 1968 (OMF).

[234] The BEM later acceded to the SIB request to get help to put up church buildings in the towns. See Combined BEM/SIB Executive Minutes, 27 October 1966, 9-10, where Balan Seling made the case for raising monetary aid from the BEM supporters overseas for SIB projects, making comparison that the SIB got no monetary aid from the BEM, while the Iban Methodist church got whatever it wanted free.

[235] *BEM NL*, October 1965, 1. Problems were varied; there was a case of someone having attempted to shoot a pastor and he was experiencing much psychological trauma.

exerted on pastors by their own family to return to village life, and also financial pressures they faced when their children were entering school-going years in view of their insufficient monthly stipend.[236] The issue of giving pastoral care to these indigenous pastors became an urgent one, a role which the BEM missionaries were asked to assume.[237] Thirdly, the rural-urban drift of young people in the 1960s was causing some grave concern among the SIB leadership as some of the SIB young people were becoming secularized by western education and had succumbed to the 'influence of worldliness'. In some cases, they became hostile to the Christian faith, trying to influence others from going to church.[238] The urgency of work among the SIB young people in the coastal towns had become a priority.[239] The concern of the BEM was that 'it would be tragic if other Christian groups were to skim off the cream of SIB young educated people in the towns, thus greatly reducing the potential for leadership in the SIB in years to come'.[240] Also, youth conferences in the interior and the towns became a new feature of work.[241] Further, these migrant people constituted the emerging group of working class and professional class SIB people who were unlikely to return to their villages or longhouses, so that the need arose to start churches among them in the towns. Another focus was also to increase evangelism to the other larger surrounding tribes.[242] Fourthly, the rise of literacy among school students resulted in the expansion of the existing literature ministry and the development of more specialized ministries for the BEM, such as radio ministry, Bible study on cassette tapes and Bible correspondence courses and Vacation Bible Schools (VBS).[243] Fifthly, with rising educational standards in the country, there were higher expectations of the SIB pastors and missionaries. This necessitated the introduction of the Advanced Bible School, which had its roots in the Pastors' Refresher course in Bahasa Malaysia,[244] the upgrading of the standards in all Bible schools and

---

[236] *BEM NL*, December 1969, 2.

[237] *BEM NL*, October 1965, 1.

[238] This problem was beginning to rear its head in the late 1950s especially among the Kelabit. See *BEM NL*, December 1958, 2. By 1965, it had become a serious concern among the SIB leadership.

[239] *BEM NL*, October 1966, 4. The SIB was very slow in responding to this problem of rural-urban migration, and hence, SIB relied heavily on the missionaries. Interviews with Winston Edip, 15 September 2004; with Pengiran Gugkang, 16 September 2004; with Balang Anid, 17 September 2004; and with Gerawat Maran, 23 September 2004.

[240] *BEM Field Director's Report to the BEM Australian Conference*, 24-27 April 1975, 3.

[241] *BEM NL*, October 1971, 4.

[242] There was the realization that the Orang Ulu only constituted 5% of the total population of Sarawak and the largest indigenous tribe is the Iban.

[243] *BEM NL*, October 1967, 1; February 1971, 4 and August 1971, 1.

[244] *BEM NL*, April 1970, 3. Bahasa Malaysia or Malay language is the National Language.

developing a Bible school that met Western standards using English as the medium of instruction.[245]

The cumulative effect of this complex web of events and factors propelled the BEM to initiate new areas of work in the coastal towns, partnering with and often playing an influential role in evangelical para-church groups such as the Scripture Union, Nurses' Christian Fellowship (NCF)[246] and Teachers' Christian Fellowship (TCF),[247] and sponsoring the entry of OMF missionaries to pioneer churches among the Chinese in Miri and Kuching which soon broadened their congregations to include different races and classes of people. While handing over the established work to the SIB, the BEM continued its work at Lawas by helping to conduct the Advanced Bible School and provide pastoral care for the SIB pastors at Lawas.[248] More importantly, it re-focused its work towards new and specialized ministries in the coastal towns.

In 1972, with the help of Colin Reasbeck and Bob Burton, the BEM formulated its new policy, the 'Twin Primary Tasks', which involved, firstly, evangelistic outreach and church planting and, secondly, Bible teaching and leadership development. The new statement of policy argued that BEM had so far confined its work among the Orang Ulu which constituted only five per cent of the population of Sarawak, and that the evangelization of the larger groups of unevangelized people who were open to the gospel was the joint task of both BEM and SIB.[249] This policy was partly a response to the ten-year ruling on missionary residence which came into force in 1967.[250] The other aspect of its twin task was leadership development, and the BEM initiated the establishment of the Miri Bible College (MBC) in 1972, with Ken Coleman as its first principal, to provide theological education that met the standards in western countries and catered for the needs of the more educated SIB people in the

[245] *BEM NL*, August 1971, 1 and November 1976, 4.

[246] *BEM Field Conference Report* March 1970, 34-35. The NCF was initiated by Margaret Wyber, an OMF missionary based in Kuching. See *BEM NL*, October 1968, 2.

[247] *BEM NL*, October 1966, 2. The first TCF conference was initiated by Dr Bill Hawes so that an executive committee was formed with three BEM missionaries as Advisory Board members.

[248] *BEM/OMF Conference Report*, March 1975, 8, on 'Advanced Training for Pastors'. 'SIB Executive leaders, lay leaders and pastors have put high priority on this type of training.... SIB leaders have expressed that this is still one area of ministry in which they look to BEM'.

[249] *BEM Field Conference Minutes*, March 1972, 6-7. *BEM NL*, August 1972, 1-3. Colin Reasbeck was responsible for presenting the paper on 'Task: Evangelistic Outreach and Church Planting' and Rev. R.N. Burton presented 'Task: Bible Teaching and Leadership Training'.

[250] *BEM Field Executive Minutes*, 2-8 November 1966, 1 & 23-31 May 1967, 1. *BEM NL*, December 1966, 3. The ten-year ruling was effective from 1 January 1967. See also Chapter 8.

towns.[251] These twin tasks further sharpened the rationale of the BEM's work which began initiating new areas of work and specialized ministries even with the few more years left for them as a result of the government ruling on missionary residence in the country.[252]

Ken and Maureen Coleman

Some areas of development in the work of the BEM after 1965 coincided with some key recommendations made in Eric Fife and Arthur Glasser's book, Missions in Crisis: Rethinking Mission Strategy, which was becoming influential among evangelical mission circles. Fife and Glasser called the Church to take the offensive (a) to face the challenge of the cities, their importance in the future, and their strategic position in the evangelization to the surrounding areas; (b) to reach the students, which was a growing, needy and strategic group of people; and (c) to use literature and radio as means of evangelization and Christian nurture.[253] The move to work in coastal towns entailed fulfilling the first two recommendations. In addition, work among the students, youth conferences[254] and VBS in the interior[255] and in towns was

[251] *BEM NL*, August 1972, 2. Later, MBC became known as the Malaysia Evangelical College (MEC). At the same time, the first national Principal, Tagal Paran, was appointed to Lawas Bible School.

[252] See Chapter 8.

[253] Eric S. Fife and Arthur F. Glasser, *Missions in Crisis: Rethinking Missionary Strategy* (London: Inter-Varsity Fellowship, 1962), 178-239. The BEM's student ministry was also directed at the students who had gone overseas to study and had become Christians there and had return to Sarawak as leaders of the churches. See *BEM NL*, December 1964, 2. Reference to Fife and Glasser's book was made in *BEM NL*, August 1968, 4.

[254] *BEM NL*, October 1971, 4; October 1972, 3.

being initiated and organized by BEM missionaries. The literature ministry of the BEM (which had the aims of distributing literature to SIB Christians, stimulating the church to be discerning readers and perceptive distributors, establishing key centres for literature distribution and having training programmes for booksellers and appropriate conferences and also encouraging people to be writers of Christian literature)[256] was given an extra boost in the 1960s when the demand for Christian literature increased greatly at the BEM bookroom at Lawas.[257] The development of Bible correspondence courses increased greatly in the late 1960s due to their popularity among students.[258] In short, the BEM was able to refocus its priorities from 1968, beginning with the change of the Field Director and crystallizing in 1972 with the 'twin tasks', enabling it to chart out new areas of work and specialized ministries which allowed the BEM and SIB sufficient room to work, grow and cooperate together.

Executive Members of the Sidang Injil Borneo
Left to right: Tama Galang (Treasurer), Racha Umong (Chairman), Balang Selutan (Vice-Chairman), Kelasi Ating (Secretary)

---

[255] *BEM NL*, October 1967, 1. Vacation Bible Schools were held in Bario from August 21-26. *BEM NL*, April 1969, 2. VBS were also held at Lawas.

[256] *BEM Field Conference Report* March 1970, 21-23. *BEM NL*, December 1969, 3. The Lawas Book Depot was started in 1960 with portions of translations in the various native languages, Bibles in Indonesian Malay, Christian literature and also materials in Malay and English to promote literacy in both languages. See *BEM NL*, September 1960, 2. By 1972, the Lawas Book Room had a national manager, Arun Selutan. See *BEM NL* August 1972, 4.

[257] Sales figures of $5,000 (1961), $8,000 (1964), $15,000 (1968).

[258] *BEM NL*, October 1966, 4 and October 1967, 1. In 1966, there were 2,500 correspondents with the Bible correspondence courses. In 1964, there was one part-time worker on this work, in 1966, four full-time workers.

Conclusion

Any successful implementation of the 'Three-Self' policy requires both the mission society to be willing to maintain a sustained pursuit of the policy without attempts to subvert or reverse it, and also the indigenous church to rise up to the challenge of becoming truly 'Three-Self'. It is observed that there have been two common types of unsuccessful attempts: firstly, the policy has been tardily implemented by mission societies; and secondly, indigenous churches were unable to become truly 'Three-Self' even when they had achieved autonomy, as they were still dependent on the mission societies for financial aid, which in turn, has led to an indirect control by the mission societies.

In contrast, the BEM formulated a unique fifteen-year policy that gave its work a clear focus and goal that led to the establishment of the SIB in 1959, that is, after only nine years. It further fulfilled its objective of completing and distributing the Lun Bawang New Testament in 1962. A characteristic of the BEM was its constant monitoring of the implementation of its policies. For the first decade, the monitoring of this fifteen-year policy exercised a 'count-down' mentality among the missionaries on its progress at every biannual BEM Field Conference. But in 1960, the subtle change in the interpretation of the fifteen-year policy justified a prolongation of their stay in Sarawak as each new tribal work opened up, so that a justification for withdrawal in 1975 could be made. This prolongation of BEM work beyond 1965 worked out well for both the BEM and the SIB, as the SIB was still unable to assume full responsibilities from the BEM and the BEM had lagged behind in their schedule in translation work. Also, the BEM was able to help the SIB face more confidently the challenge of the rural-urban drift from the mid-1960s onwards, a new phenomenon with which the SIB was unfamiliar. Despite this prolongation, the BEM was mindful of the need to train and hand over responsibilities to the SIB. As for the BEM missionaries, a vital ingredient pertained to their mental attitude and confidence in native abilities. Despite their mildly paternalistic attitude, the BEM missionaries were particularly encouraging of native ability to the extent that they seemed to be pushing the SIB to assume more responsibilities than the SIB wished (as in the case of 1968), so that the pace of the handover of responsibilities was moderated by the SIB itself. So, this extended the time for the full transfer of responsibilities and, in turn, allowed the SIB to grow steadily in its confidence in order to assume full responsibilities when BEM ceased as a mission in 1975. Significantly, in the implementation of the 'Three-Self' policy, the BEM did not at any time work to consciously undermine or reverse it, so that there was no struggle between the BEM and SIB in the handing over process. The slowness in assuming full responsibilities by the SIB and the lack of Mission-church conflict had an important contributory factor, which was the lack of secondary education among the key SIB leadership in the decade of the 1960s.

The policies and practices of the BEM developed a culture of Christian mission work from which the SIB formulated its own pattern of mission and which also nurtured both the grass-roots church work and the SIB leadership. The Lawas Bible School played a central role in the training and supply of pastors for the emerging indigenous church. Its philosophy of developing Christian spirituality and character, analytical thinking skills, and practical ministerial training was adjusted to the rising educational standards of the country. Missionary policy was generally encouraging of indigenous initiatives, and participatory involvement in joint ministries of both BEM missionaries and national pastors at every level of BEM activities which extended to deacons' schools, short-term Bible schools and annual conventions. At the local church level, the more established congregations were cared for by indigenous pastors with minimal missionary supervision. By 1956, this supervisory role had been taken over by the Inter-Tribal Conference. On a wider scale, the BEM encouraged the formation of the SIB as a separate ecclesial entity from the BEM, with the BEM having 'no voice' within its structure, minimizing drastically the danger of BEM dominating or supplanting the SIB. The gradual but sustained transfer of responsibilities from the BEM to the SIB was such that by 1959, the SIB could function as a 'Three-Self' church with self-propagation as its greatest strength and self-support as its weakest. Even with self-support, the SIB had been able to take some remedial steps to overcome its weakness. In conformity with its ethos, the BEM provided no mission funds for the SIB. The assistance from BEM took the ultimately more valuable form of educating church members to their responsibilities toward their pastors, which was of great help; they could do this because of their moral authority among the people with whom they had worked. The progress of SIB indigenous leadership in accepting the challenge to be 'Three Selfs' was slower, but nevertheless steady, first assuming full responsibilities for work among the local churches, then the schools in the interior, the short term deacons' and Bible schools, the regional conventions and district conferences, and later the Lawas Bible School. It was also able to exercise prudent discernment in the problems facing the SIB, making wise but necessary decisions, even though some of these may have been especially difficult when they pertained to long-standing cultural practices, for instance, the issue of bride wealth in marriage.

The evidence surveyed in this chapter suggests that the relationship of the BEM and the SIB was an unusually harmonious one, without any need to struggle for independence by SIB from BEM. Rather the BEM had to be patient with the SIB until it was able to assume responsibilities from them. In 1968 the BEM/SIB relationship began to enter into a new phase with a more definite shift in the work of the BEM and the change of BEM Field Director. The BEM was beginning to re-focus its mission as a result of the new opportunities that had opened up owing to the socio-cultural, educational and economic trends that had been impacting Sarawak. This process of re-focusing created an internal rift within the BEM leadership so that only with the change of Field

Director could the new proposals be implemented. The process of re-focusing mission priorities to respond to important political events such as the formation of Malaysia and, in particular, the Brunei uprising, began with the proposals from Dr Bill Lees in 1963, and was reinforced by Harold McCracken in 1966, by younger missionaries in 1967, and also, by Dr Bill Hawes, the new Field Director, in 1969. These proposals finally crystallized with the formulation of the 'twin tasks' in 1972, a proposal that was able to chart new areas of ministries for the BEM. In handing over some of the established work of the interior churches to the SIB, the BEM was then able to direct its work to the coastal towns and later to move its headquarters to Miri in 1974, starting churches in the towns especially in the seventies, developing new areas of ministries and specialized ministries relevant to the new situation in which BEM found itself. True to its philosophy of being 'mobile', the BEM planted and established a 'Three-Self' church, the SIB, and then handed over responsibilities and moved on to initiate and develop new areas of work. It now remains for us to examine in the next two chapters the impact of revivals on the SIB in its attempt to maintain vibrant church life, and also how the BEM and SIB faced the process of social, economic and political change and new challenges under an independent Malaysian government.

Chapter 7

REVIVAL MOVEMENTS AND THE CONSOLIDATION OF THE CHURCH IN A CHANGING SOCIAL CONTEXT

With the rapid growth of the SIB churches through mass conversions in the post-war era, there was a variety of responses to Christianity ranging from firm commitment to a shallow adherence to Christianity, as it was shown in Chapter 4. Whatever commitment to Christianity a community of believers might have, there is the likelihood of a decline in spiritual fervour with the passage of time. This is especially so with evangelical Christianity with its emphasis on an individual's direct relationship with God, a process which is not easy to sustain or nurture. It is in these situations of spiritual declension that revival movements often surfaced, serving to restore the sense of spiritual vitality and also to transform both the lives of individuals and that of the SIB churches.

In the historiography of church growth and Christian revival movements, the tendency has been to explain these happenings in terms of both exogenous and endogenous factors.[1] In addition, as it has been noted in Chapter 3, a 'revival' exhibits a number of characteristics; namely, (a) its participants anticipate a reviving and renewing act of God; (b) it involves some sort of dramatic conversion or intense spiritual experience in individuals; and (c) it is a community experience, involving the whole life of the Christian community.[2] In short, a 'revival' highlights the revitalization of the Church. Furthermore, as Stuart Piggin has noted, 'revival' is also 'preceded by an extraordinary unity and prayerfulness among Christians', 'the conversion of large numbers of unbelievers' and 'the diminution of sinful practices in the community'.[3]

In this chapter, there will be an examination of the revival among the Lun Bawang in 1952 and then the revivals which began in 1971, occurring in localized areas before becoming a pan-SIB movement. The revival first occurred among the students at LBS (1971), then among those at the various

---

[1] See Robert Currie, Alan Gilbert and Lee Horsley, *Church and Churchgoers: Patterns of Church Growth in the British Isles since 1700* (Oxford: Clarendon Press, 1977), 5-9. Blumhofer and Balmer, *Modern Christian Revivals* (Urbana/Chicago: University of Illinois Press, 1993).

[2] See Chapter 3.

[3] Piggin, '"Towards a Theoretical Understanding of Revival", 13-33.

conventions (1972), and later at the deacons' school in Bario, and then among the school children and church at Bario among the Kelabit (1973). From Bario, the revival movement spread rapidly throughout Sarawak. An analysis on the circumstances surrounding each revival itself, the revival proper and the impact on the life of the indigenous church will be made.

The Revival among the Lun Bawang (1952)

The Context of the Revival

To appreciate the localized revival among the Lun Bawang in 1952, it is needful to examine the various contributory factors. There were two almost paradoxical external developments. First, the post-war years of the early 1950s, as it has been shown in the last chapter, were uncertain and anxious times, which fueled fears of a communist takeover of Southeast Asia and a possible persecution of the Christian Church.[4] Then, the Korean War of 1950 caused a rubber boom in rubber growing countries, including Sarawak that enriched the Lun Bawang who had been cultivating rubber. This rubber boom brought them into greater contact with the coastal towns as a result of trade. Missionaries feared that this mix of sudden wealth and increasing western influence would lead the Lun Bawang of the lower Trusan to 'become worldly minded and less keen to serve the Lord with the whole heart'. Hence, within the BEM this grave concern became an item of prayer for them.[5] By 1951, as a result of the rubber boom, some of the Lun Bawang took their children out of the school conducted by the indigenous pastor, Lawai, to help in tapping rubber, which was viewed by the BEM missionaries as 'a sure sign that these people are allowing worldly things to come in'.[6] Though the new found wealth could contribute toward financial self-sufficiency of the Lun Bawang church, the concern of the missionaries here was that the Lun Bawang were being distracted from spiritual matters of the Christian faith.

There were other internal factors that contributed toward an expectation of and prayer for a revival. Within Lun Bawang society, there was, firstly, a widespread epidemic of pneumonia, tuberculosis and other diseases that led to some deaths and a discernible decline in population. In early 1950, constant reports for some months of many cases of pneumonia amongst the Lun Bawang, and an epidemic between the areas of Mengalong and Pa Matong reminded the missionaries of a similar but more widespread epidemic that swept through Lun Bawang country when the Lun Bawang first embraced

---

[4] *SG*, March 1975, 43.

[5] 'A degree of westernization is also approaching Borneo with new ideas and many attractions and allurement which can easily corrupt the believer side-tracking him from the spiritual life and stifling any desire for service'. *BEM NL*, October 1949, 1, 4.

[6] *BEM NL*, February 1951, 4.

Christianity in the 1930s.[7] This would certainly have brought anxious moments for the missionaries. Further, the BEM literature reported that concern was expressed about the indigenous leaders who had contracted the disease, and they included Iki, wife of Udan Rangat,[8] Riong Awa of Long Semadoh and also Balang and Rigo from Tang Lepadan.[9] It is not surprising that in response to such situations indigenous Christians were moved either to pray to God or alternatively to pray to the spirits of their former religion for healing. There was the ever-present temptation for the Lun Bawang to return to their old ways of appeasing the spirits to gain healing, which was viewed in missionary parlance as making 'compromises with paganism'.[10] It should also be noted that the missionaries' prayer requests sounded very urgent, asking that the Mission may be able to give the necessary medical treatment and advice so as to save the Lun Bawang from dying out,[11] and that the 'epidemic may be used of God to bring about a revival to the Lun Bawang'.[12]

Secondly, problems of different kinds were brewing slowly within the Lun Bawang churches and these matters were raised as prayer requests to the BEM supporters. A letter from Southwell to McCracken in March 1948 revealed that, the relationship between the Lun Bawang and the Kelabit was greatly strained as a result of the murder of four Lun Bawang at Long Luping by a visiting Kelabit who was given hospitality. This matter required the intervention of the Resident, government officers and Southwell, who had been asked to investigate the matter. Despite Southwell's preaching on Christian love and forgiveness, there were some Lun Bawang Christians who called for revenge and for returning to their traditional custom of a trial by ordeal, a pagan ceremony as a way of proving the innocence of the accused. Further, Southwell was alarmed that the Lun Bawang wanted to claim tohad or blood compensation, which involved another of their traditional ceremonies.[13] Among

[7] *BEM NL*, April 1950, 4.
[8] *BEM NL*, February 1951, 4.
[9] *BEM NL*, June 1952, 4.
[10] *BEM NL*, December 1952, 1.
[11] The prayer request of the missionaries that 'the Mission may be able to give the necessary medical treatment and advice to save these people as it is tragic indeed if this tribe which knows Christ were to die out' suggest a real anxiety and fear among the missionaries. For instance, the village of Batu Lapan, which was once a large village, had only about 20 people when the Belchers made a visit there. See *BEM NL*, February 1951, 4.
[12] *BEM NL*, April 1950, 4.
[13] 'All this is very sad and wrong, especially some of the ones concerned in these claims are elders…some are even opposing the government's attempt to effect a just settlement'. Letter of C.H. Southwell to H. McCracken, 8 March 1948 (OMF). See also Morrison, *Fair Land Sarawak*, 44. Morrison was involved in trying to settle the issue of compensation due from the Kelabit to the Lun Bawang for the murder. 'The Lun Bawang…demanded blood money and the Kelabit agreed to pay several heads of cattle

the Lun Bawang, especially the relatives of the deceased, there was much bitterness and anger. A grave concern arose among the BEM missionaries, who interpreted the situation thus, noting that the 'first rapturous experience' of their conversion in the 1930s 'so manifested with the visitation of God's Spirit amongst the Muruts is passing … into easy complacency'.[14] The Lun Bawang were said to have become 'embittered and revengeful and as a result lost their spiritual glow'.[15]

Other missionary reports about the Lun Bawang at this time included 'backsliding and compromises with paganism'.[16] There were those who had 'fallen into sin at Ba Kelalan', so that Libat and Riong Awa were assigned there to bring them back to repentance.[17] There were also reported instances of 'carnality and dissension' within the church especially in the Pa Matang district.[18] Further, there was some opposition to the leadership in the churches at Tang Lepadan and Long Tengoa in the Trusan region, so that prayer was requested for the deacons that they 'may be delivered from the fear of man and become bold for Christ'. At Long Litong, there was some hindrance to the building of the church and also to Tai Kelasi's joining Bible school.[19]

There was also a report of a problem brewing among the leadership within the local churches, relating the lack of confidence among some deacons in leading their churches, as they were illiterate and untaught. Further, it was noted that their preaching was limited to telling the same Bible stories repeatedly, so that the BEM initiated the short-term deacons' school among the Lun Bawang at Lawas in October 1951, aiming to equip them for their task. Even then, some found the classes difficult and continued to show their lack of self-confidence by commenting: 'I'm not so clever; therefore it is useless to try.'[20] Such a comment could also be interpreted as a face-saving defensive mechanism when some leaders were unable to understand and apply what was taught. The outcome for these deacons meant that, without the benefit of being better equipped, leading their churches became a drudgery and a chore rather than a joy and challenge. If all these reports of what were happening in the various churches were true, it is not surprising that by 1952, these problems had

---

and some valuable jars in compensation'. A partial handover was done in Indonesian territory where an Indonesian official and Morrison were witnesses.

[14] *BEM NL*, April 1948, 3.

[15] *BEM NL*, December 1948, 1.

[16] *BEM NL*, December 1952, 1.

[17] *BEM NL*, December 1949, 4. Though the matter was not elaborated, the matter was serious enough to warrant the sending of two senior Lun Bawang pastors, Riong and Libat, to deal with the problem.

[18] *BEM NL*, June 1950, 4. The prayer request was that the Spirit of God may turn the churches from their carnality and dissension to a new walk in the Spirit.

[19] *BEM NL*, August 1950, 3. The deacons at Tang Lepadan and Long Tengoa were Belan Ho and Pengai respectively.

[20] *BEM NL*, February 1952, 2.

contributed to a waning of spiritual fervour among the churches and, understandably, a corresponding call to prayer for revival.

Among the BEM missionaries, it could be detected that by the 1950s, there were signs of weariness among the missionaries and a difference of opinion about work assignments between Belcher and Southwell. The fifteen-year policy adopted in 1950 added much pressure on the BEM to ensure that progress was made year on year. From 1950, repeated prayer requests were sought for Alan Belcher as Field Chairman of the BEM, 'that he may be truly led of God in all the decisions that he as Chairman will have to make'[21] and for 'grace to cope with the opportunities and problems of the work'.[22] Just prior to the 1950 Field Conference, McCracken wrote to Belcher stressing the need for unity as 'one of the most important parts of the work and we must pray greatly that in the forthcoming Field Conference that will be greatly manifested'.[23] All these prayer requests could be indicative that all was not well within the Mission. In August 1951, the prayer requests broadened to include the other BEM missionaries, Madge Belcher and Dorothy Summerson at LBS and Bruce Morton at the headquarters, that they might have renewed strength for ministry.[24] The main difficulty at that time was the relationship between Southwell and Belcher which became very strained after the BEM Field Conference of 1948 when Belcher was elected as the Chairman of BEM. This event came as a great shock to Southwell.[25] Its repercussions affected the other missionaries as well so that there were not only differences in matters of policies, but also of attitudes to one another. In his unpublished account of the situation prior to the 1952 BEM Field Conference, Southwell revealed that 'some difficult matters … needed solution… But more important than issues, such as policies, strategy and methods, was the matter of attitudes both towards

---

[21] *BEM NL*, October 1950, 4. Alan Belcher had been elected as Field Chairman in the Field Conference in 1948.

[22] *BEM NL*, June 1951, 3.

[23] Letter of H. McCracken to A. Belcher, 5 July 1950 (OMF).

[24] *BEM NL*, August 1951, 4.

[25] Southwell, *Uncharted Waters*, 265-66. 'To my complete surprise, it was suggested that Alan Belcher should stand for election as chairman with full administrative responsibility, and it was clear that Alan himself had wanted this position. I could hardly believe this was happening.... My initial reaction was to fight this decision. But I knew that was not the right answer. Such conflict could destroy the Mission…I felt then, and still believe, that a change in leadership of the Mission was, at best, premature. I was devastated…but I had to accept it'. On the other hand, Southwell had not realized the extent of the missionaries' frustrations because of his frequent trips away from the headquarters, which led to the general feeling that Southwell was an absentee leader. Also, there was the dissatisfaction about Southwell's inappropriate use of funds designated for a particular missionary as general fund. See Peter Elliott, *Asang: The Story of Trevor White and the Dusuns of Sabah* (Cleveland: Delia Wilson, 1997), 44. In the interview with Dorothy Summerson, 31 October 2004, she commented that when Southwell and Belcher were both at the home base the atmosphere was rather tense.

God and before men, especially our fellow missionaries'.[26] This uneasy tension was increasingly felt among the missionaries, particularly when Belcher as the Field Chairman assigned the Southwells to work at Marudi doing translation of the Bible into the Kayan language; a move which Southwell felt was unsuitable. At that time, Marudi was receiving only transient Kayan visitors. Also, as there were no available resident language informants, his task was made more difficult.[27]

To overcome these problems within the Lun Bawang churches and among the BEM missionaries, the BEM missionaries believed that only a revival could cause a breakthrough and make a real difference. From their revivalistic tradition, they believed that revival might come through prayer meetings and Bible teaching given at the organized Bible conferences. In the light of the Long Luping murder incident, Southwell hoped that at the Easter Conference of 1948, the indigenous leaders would be 'blessed by spiritual blessing and revival'.[28] Concern for the Lun Bawang churches was expressed as an item of prayer in the BEM newsletters: 'that the Holy Spirit will continue the blessing of the various Christmas meetings, and specially that the Muruts at the Trusan convention of 1950 will be instruments of revival as they return home',[29] and 'that the Lord will bless with revival the Murut churches during the Easter convention of 1951 at Brayong'.[30] A similar request was also made for the 1952 Easter convention.[31] It is obvious from the evidence cited that the tone of these prayer requests for the Lun Bawang revealed a sense of urgency and expectation of a revival.

The prayer requests for the spiritual needs of the missionaries also sounded serious and urgent. As Belcher wrote, 'Our greatest need is for revival among us missionaries ... when our eyes are open to God's will and plan for us and for the Mission'.[32] Also, they requested prayer 'for an outpouring of God's Spirit on the Field Conference reviving and uniting the missionary force into a closely

[26] Southwell, *Unpublished Memoirs*, 269. The Field Conference was held in August 1952.

[27] Southwell, *Uncharted Waters*, 312. The Southwells complied with the assignment, though they felt that they should still be stationed at Long Tebangan. When the Hammers, another missionary couple, went on furlough, there was no one available for Long Tebangan, so that the Southwells were asked to return to Long Tebangan in early 1953, having been in Marudi only for a few months.

[28] *BEM NL*, April 1948, 3. As a result of the Long Luping incident, 'the danger is that the Murut churches will settle down in complacency, if not stirred again by the Spirit of God. *This is why the conference of native elders which was fixed for Easter is so important*'. (Italics mine).

[29] *BEM NL*, February 1950, 4.

[30] *BEM NL*, April 1951, 4.

[31] *BEM NL*, April 1952, 4. The request was 'for an outpouring of God's Spirit upon the Easter Convention resulting in the Murut church being revived and purified to fulfill God's purpose for the whole Church in Borneo'.

[32] *BEM NL*, August 1952, 4.

compacted Spirit-filled unit to build Christ's Church in Borneo in God's appointed time'.[33] These prayer requests shed further light on the relationship between Belcher and Southwell and hinted at the difference between them in discerning God's will for the BEM as well as a lack of unity that had become rather serious.[34] Further, they revealed a heightened sense of the need for unity among the missionaries and the expectation of a revival amongst their midst and so encouraged BEM supporters to be in urgent prayer for the work.

Seeds of Renewal among the BEM missionaries

The beginnings of a renewal, as reported in the BEM newsletter, first surfaced at the July 1952 BEM Field Conference, which led the missionaries to the conviction that 'the outpouring of the Holy Spirit' was vital to empower the indigenous church to thrive and withstand persecution. The Conference had three special speakers. The first, Dr Delwyn Rees, a CIM medical missionary from northwest China, spoke on the Person and Work of the Holy Spirit, stressing the need for the fullness of the Spirit in the life of the missionary.[35] The second, Stafford Young, dealt with the sin of unbelief in fulfilling the task in thirteen years, stressing the lack of faith on the part of the missionaries as the limiting factor. The third, Rev. John Chen of the Overseas Chinese Missionary Society, spoke of the revival in the lives of the Christians in North China.[36] Just as Christians in China were experiencing mass revitalization, the BEM missionaries had similar hopes for revitalization within their midst and also among the Lun Bawang churches. There were two emphases of the Field Conference. The first was on the 'Fullness of the Spirit', and the second on the building of an indigenous church. The missionaries believed that the test of a truly indigenous church that had been established by divine enablement was its ability to 'withstand persecution … Such an outpouring is needed in Borneo if the indigenous church … was to stand against the persecution that inevitably would fall upon it'.[37] The fear of the march of Communism throughout

---

[33] *BEM NL*, June 1952, 4.

[34] Like the Roman Catholics and the Anglicans, Southwell was very keen on running schools. Interview with Ray Cunningham, 8-9 November 2004.

[35] Dr Delwyn Rees had just been released from two years' detention by the Communists. See *BEM NL*, October 1952, 2. Southwell, *Uncharted Waters*, 308, 310. It was Harold McCracken, the BEM Home Council President, who recommended Dr Rees to Alan Belcher to be the speaker at the 1952 Field Conference. Before the Conference, Belcher admitted to being quite apprehensive about Dr Rees' understanding of the 'Fullness of the Spirit'. See *BEM NL*, February 1976, 3.

[36] 'Hearing reports of the native church in North China, the working of the Holy Spirit in the lives of consecrated Chinese Christians has challenged us anew'. See *BEM NL*, October 1952, 2.

[37] *BEM NL*, October 1952, 2. They felt that 'the two subjects were very closely linked, because it is the Lord who builds this church by the Holy Spirit and without the fullness of the Spirit no truly indigenous church will be built'.

Southeast Asia, as it has been noted earlier, anticipated the possibility of persecution of the Christian church under a communist regime.[38]

The BEM missionaries themselves expressed the desire for 'a real outpouring of the Holy Spirit to revive us', believing that the empowerment of the Spirit, which is the birthright of every Christian, was essential for them to complete their task of establishing an indigenous church in thirteen years. Despite their planning and exertion of energies, they realized that 'unless each one is fully controlled by the real power from on high it will all be in vain and the work will not stand ... During the time that remains, a tremendous task lies ahead – one for which we, in ourselves, are quite unequal, but by the power of the Holy Spirit indwelling and filling each of us, God has shown that it is possible', and 'the limiting factor is in us and not God'.[39]

It seems that with this attitude of openness and dependence solely upon God by the missionaries, they were reported to have experienced spiritual renewal and a new sense of excitement during the conference: 'We are on the fringe of a new thing here in Borneo. Oh, for the rivers of Living Water for us missionaries and our native workers! ... Never have we witnessed such unity and corporate, Spirit-led thinking. I cannot imagine anything better.'[40] Here the tone set for the conference facilitated the business sessions, stimulated discussion and enabled them to reach many important decisions.[41] The unity and harmony of mind during these sessions to reach important decisions was attributed to the Holy Spirit.[42]

A result of this renewal among the missionaries was a strengthened resolve and confidence in the power of the Spirit of God to establish an indigenous church that would stand and endure persecution. Their renewed confidence may be detected in the manner in which they expressed their task as 'essentially finishable', emphasising 'not (only) to evangelize every town or village', but also the need to commit 'the work to faithful men who would (be able to) teach others also (2 Tim 2:2)' and to teach them 'the whole counsel of God'. A substantiating case in point was the Kelabit who, on their own initiative, were passing on the message to the Penan. Further, 'the missionary task to establish a church could only be conceived as finished' when 'the Scriptures had been translated into their own language'. Lessons were cited 'from church history

---

[38] See Chapter 6.

[39] *BEM NL*, October 1952, 2. 'For some months a growing conviction had come to the missionaries that there must be a revival among the native church. As they so prayed for this revival God showed that there must be revival amongst the missionaries as well. Increasingly in the last few weeks, the missionaries felt that God was going to do this'.

[40] *BEM NL*, October 1952, 2.

[41] There were three sessions each day for the six days of Conference.

[42] *BEM NL*, October 1952, 2. As one missionary said, 'There was no argument; just a collective building up of the thoughts and ideas. At the end of each session, the chairman summed up the contributions and these were obviously the clear decisions of the Conference'.

regarding the Nestorian and North African churches' that these churches did not continue to exist as they did not have the Scriptures in the vernacular.[43]

Despite this heightened sense of 'divine' presence in the Field Conference, it needs to be pointed out that there was no outburst of public repentance or confession of sin to one another and no outward signs of reconciliation among the missionaries, which often accompanied revivals. However, there was quiet confession of sins, as the missionaries believed that the fullness of the Spirit could only be received when 'all that was crooked and sinful was forsaken', which involved the removing of any stumbling blocks or hindrances, 'walking in the light' and 'striving for peace with all men'.[44] This call to confession and to purity of life is best interpreted as a veiled reference to the strained relationship between Belcher and Southwell. According to Dorothy Summerson, an atmosphere of uneasy tension prevailed when both Belcher and Southwell were present in the Field Conferences.[45] But as it has been pointed out earlier, the uneasy tension continued as Southwell was assigned to Marudi much against his own wishes. According to Southwell's account, he complied, going there only for a few months before being reassigned to Long Tebangan. The difference of opinion between Belcher and Southwell regarding work in the Baram finally led to Southwell's resignation from the BEM in 1954.[46]

In short, the renewal, not amounting to a revival, among the missionaries was localized and short-lived.

Revival among the Lun Bawang churches

The revival among the Lun Bawang triggered a spiritual revitalization among the Lun Bawang churches with confession of sins, setting right what they were convinced was wrong, obtaining forgiveness of sins and receiving the assurance of peace. According to Tubu Padan, the 1952 revival was confined to the Lawas Bible School and Lawas.[47] Both Tubu Padan and the Mission account agree that the revival first began at Lawas among the Bible School students, and it was sparked off by the event of the drowning of Singha Achang's three-year-old son, Pengiran, on 25 August 1952. This incident was catalytic to a series of all-night prayer meetings, where many made public confession of their sins.[48] The Mission account further reported that the students, who had been

[43] *BEM NL*, October 1952, 4.
[44] *BEM NL*, October 1952, 1.
[45] Interview with Dorothy Summerson, 31 October 2004.
[46] Southwell, *Uncharted Waters*, 319.
[47] Interview with Tubu Padan, 24 September 2004. Jok Wan, a former SIB President, and Sara Mulang, a former SIB Secretary, have hardly any recollection of this revival. Jok Wan joined LBS as a student in 1955. Interviews with Jok Wan, 16 September 2004 and with Sara Mulang, 22 September 2004.
[48] Singha Achang was the head prefect in the Lawas Bible School. Tubu Padan observed that the incident triggered an all night prayer among the students. Interview with Tubu Padan, 24 September 2004. See also *BEM NL*, October 1952, 1.

away from LBS during Pengiran's drowning, came under the conviction of sin when told of the recent event. The BEM newsletter of October 1952 carried this report:

This movement has spread and developed, and never before has there been such a conviction of sin amongst the school people before … Some have been awakened at night by the burden of their sin, and in the last week many of them have also been terribly burdened because of their debts … there is a widespread desire to confess and put right the things which are wrong … Some have even asked to be able to go out of school in order to pay their debts, as they believe there is no point in them staying in school until they have dealt with this matter which God has so clearly spoken to them.[49]

A later report noted that following this series of events, the people were said to be revived and have a greater desire in spiritual matters,[50] though these events could be interpreted differently as some form of mass hysteria with cathartic effects.

Special revivalistic meetings were arranged for a teachers' conference at Lawas on 8 September for the purpose that teachers in the local churches might also experience divine aid and enablement. From the Mission account, there seem to have been two discernible results. Firstly, Rigo, the wife of one of the teachers, regained her sense of joy and confidence in teaching, when previously she had a hard time teaching in the school, becoming so unhappy that she had been unable to eat. During the second day of the conference, all the teachers publicly confessed their sins, and 'it was as if a burden had rolled off. A spirit of prayer came over them'. Next, 'there came a deep longing to be filled with all the fullness of God … and such a hunger that we had never witnessed', according to Madge Belcher. The result was joy and confidence, according to Rigo, 'that the Lord Jesus will keep me and teach me in my heart so that I can teach in the school'.[51] Secondly, there was another surprising result. Kuda, a Kelabit, who had attended the teachers' conference, was so concerned for his people that he arranged for Racha Umong to visit and conduct teaching sessions among his Kelabit community.[52] It can be argued that this invitation for Racha to visit the Kelabit community paved the way to repair the Lun Bawang and Kelabit relationship, which had become estranged following the Long Luping incident in 1948.

It is significant that during the revival there was an accompanying sense of liberty in worship after the public confession of sins. For instance, the BEM newsletter reported that in the church at Lawas at one Sunday service, many in the congregation, including the headmen and community leaders, came under

---

[49] *BEM NL*, October 1952, 1.

[50] The people who experienced the revival were reported to have a 'deep hunger and longing for God's fullest blessings'. *BEM NL*, December 1952, 1.

[51] *BEM NL*, December 1952, 1.

[52] *BEM NL*, December 1952, 4.

great conviction of sin. One after another publicly confessed their sin, including one who 'confessed to compromise with Islam'. Also, those who came to the short-term deacons' school held on 13 October at Lawas had similar experiences, with some thirty-five men publicly confessing their sin. In these cases, the result that followed was a sense of liberty and spontaneity in worship with heart-warming prayers that even surprised the BEM missionaries present.[53]

When the revival spread into the interior churches as far as Long Beluyu, it can be argued that revival had the effect of emboldening people in the preaching of the gospel, at times leading them to cast aside cultural norms in doing so. For instance, in Racha Umong's letter to Mrs Belcher from Long Beluyu, which was made public in the BEM newsletter, Racha Umong wrote of his unusual experience that, in response to his preaching, the penghulu or village headman immediately confessed his sin and was likewise followed by many others. Further, it was revealed that Racha had expressed his fear about preaching to the penghulu: 'I was a little frightened because he is a chief, but as I prayed, the Lord helped me, and I was not frightened, because the Lord was in my heart.' In his letter, Racha asked for prayers as he preached to the other villages. 'Please pray for me when I visit the churches in this area, that I may exhort men with humility and with a heart filled with blessing and power of the Holy Spirit so that many more will be entreated by me.'[54] In short, revival provided the means of emboldening people to preach to authority figures, such as the penghulu or village headman, which in ordinary times was not culturally acceptable.

This revival also played a significant role in infusing moral confidence in and spiritual empowerment of the indigenous leaders to take up the challenge of inaugurating a 'Three-Self' church, as they felt they had experienced spiritual empowerment for their ministry. It is not unreasonable to perceive significance in the fact that the revival took place after the first annual Conference of Native Christians in 1948 and the adoption of the fifteen-year policy by the BEM in 1950, when the process of starting a 'Three-Self' church was in its early stages, but just before the first Pastors' Conference in 1952, which subsequently led to the formation of the first Inter-Tribal Conference in 1954 with its first Committee of indigenous leaders and the acceptance of responsibility by the Inter-Tribal Conference for all matters relating to Bornean churches in 1956.

It can then be concluded that the revival among the Lun Bawang, which lasted from July until the end of 1954, not only spiritually reinvigorated the Lawas Bible School students, native leaders and deacons of the Lun Bawang churches, but also had begun a reconciling and a strengthening effect on the relationship between the interior Lun Bawang and Kelabit. Further, both the

---

[53] *BEM NL*, December 1952, 1.
[54] *BEM NL*, October 1952, 1.

BEM missionaries and indigenous leaders experienced a new moral confidence and spiritual empowerment that affirmed their ability to fulfill their God-given vision of completing their task of establishing a strong indigenous church even in the face of uncertain times, which might include persecution for their faith.

The Pan-SIB Revival (1971-1976)

The decade from the mid-sixties to the mid-seventies witnessed significant developments in Sarawak. The formation of Malaysia on 16 September 1963 drew Sarawak into contact with the more dominant Peninsular Malaysian culture, which is predominantly Malay-Muslim. The fears of the Christian churches during the formation of Malaysia focused on the restrictions on freedom granted to other religions, particularly Christianity.[55] These fears were reinforced when Christian missionaries in Malaysia were given a limit of ten years residence in the country beginning from 1 January 1967.[56] They were further exacerbated when neighbouring Sabah under its Chief Minister, Tun Datu Mustapha Harun, decided to use the emergency powers vested in him as the Chairman of the State Operation Committee[57] to summarily expel Christian missionaries from March 1970 onwards.[58] His repressive actions climaxed in December 1972, when force was used to arrest and deport the Roman Catholic priests in the interior of Sabah. As the situation in Sabah showed, even the missionaries with permanent resident status could still have their status revoked and be expelled at any time, so that an atmosphere of uncertainty and unease among the Christian missions and churches prevailed.[59]

---

[55] *BEM NL*, June 1963, 1; April 1964, 1. It was reported that 'religious freedom of the past will be threatened by the Federation'. Further, Balang Selutan and Balan Seling had noted that, 'there is more religious freedom in Sarawak and British North Borneo (now Sabah) than in Malaya'.

[56] Chew, *Journey of the Catholic Church*, 156-59, 203-204. The new policy came into effective on 1 January 1967 through a directive dated 1 September 1966 from the Controller-General of Immigration. It meant that all foreign missionaries would have to leave the country by 1977.

[57] This situation was brought about by the promulgation of a state of national emergency after the race riots of May 1969 in Peninsular Malaysia and special powers were vested in the Chairman of National Operations Council and the Chairmen of the various State Operation Committees.

[58] By the end of the year, Sabah had expelled forty-one missionaries and refused entry for twelve new missionaries. As for the BEM, there were three cases of expulsions, (that is, one cancellation for a permanent resident status and two for work passes) and four new entries were refused. For the BEM, the cancellation of work passes for Wes and Doreen Battle into Sabah and refusal of entry permit for John and Jan Shattock into Sarawak. These were regarded as 'serious setbacks' for the Mission. See *BEM NL* August 1971, 1.

[59] See Chew, *Journey of the Catholic Church*, 157-58.

Certain trends which first began as a trickle in the early and mid-sixties, slowly developed in the later sixties to become a stream by the early 1970s. Social and economic changes resulting from urbanisation, the rural-urban drift for both higher education and employment and the development of a national market economy in Sarawak had profound effects on both the Orang Ulu societies and the Orang Ulu migrants to the coastal towns. The Orang Ulu communities experienced a steady loss of their older teenagers and young adults so that the resultant Orang Ulu societies consisted mainly of older people and the young children except for centres like Bario and Marudi, which had secondary schools. Further, the young people and young adults who had moved into the towns for higher education or employment, had to cope with a changed situation such as (a) a different and more cosmopolitan culture from their own,[60] (b) the danger of being lured away by this more sophisticated culture, and (c) the problem of social dislocation and disorientation from their familiar social network of relationships.

As the Orang Ulu represented only five per cent of the total population of Sarawak,[61] they keenly felt their minority status in the rapidly growing coastal towns. They also experienced a 'felt' sense of inferiority in relation to the other better educated Malaysians, in particular the urban Chinese, who did not seem to believe in Christianity; this only served to raise for them the issue of the relevance of Christianity for urban people. This problem was exacerbated not only by the influence of higher education but also by those urbanised Orang Ulu who had become hostile to their Christian faith.[62] This was a phenomenon which the Orang Ulu youths had initially been unable to cope with adequately, resulting in a number of backsliders.[63] Furthermore, the missionaries expressed concern about the shallowness of the faith of the Orang Ulu youths.[64]

It is important to note that by 1970, the rapidly growing literacy rate among the Orang Ulu community posed a challenge to the older indigenous pastors

[60] It is observed that whereas previously the church had been the centre of life and activity among the rural *Orang Ulu*, in their current situation the church was marginal to urban society.

[61] In 1947, the Orang Ulu population was 29,867 (5.5%) out of total population of 544,385. In 1975, the Orang Ulu population was 57,713 (5.2%) out of total population of 1,116,111. See Noakes, 'Sarawak and Brunei', 635. *BEM NL*, 50th Anniversary Issue 1978, 3.

[62] As noted earlier, these urbanised Orang Ulu have tried to discourage others from going to church. See Chapter 6.

[63] *BEM NL*, October 1969, 1. These youths were reported to have difficulties in adjusting to life in the towns and were influenced by 'temptations from non-Christian friends, drinking, evil film shows' among other things.

[64] The *Orang Ulu* youths, who were second-generation Christians, were said to follow their Christian faith as part of their culture and had an 'almost total ignorance of a personal experience of conversion' and little understanding of the Christian faith. See *BEM NL*, October 1968, 1; October 1969, 1. Sunday schools and special youth meetings were specially geared for them to alleviate the problem.

and also to the training provided by the Bible School.[65] Further, this trend of a higher level of literacy among young people, young adults and congregation compared to that of their pastors and leaders presented other problems to the SIB. For instance, the parents and pastors had problems answering their questions about the Christian faith; hence it necessitated the organizing of youth conferences, particularly among the Kayan, where some of their questions were dealt with by the BEM missionaries.[66] With better education, it was natural for the more literate youths and young adults to have a sense of greater confidence in their own knowledge and abilities in relation to their older leaders and pastors (who had much less formal education than themselves) and also to look up to leaders who were deemed capable enough to gain their respect. This leadership ability of the young people was affirmed by Mr John Ironside-Wood, an English secondary schoolteacher in Limbang, who expressed his deep impression about the leadership abilities of these young Christians in the schools.[67]

There were grave concerns by the SIB leadership regarding the 'low spirituality' among the Orang Ulu churches, their 'over-concern about politics in some churches' and pursuit of 'worldly' possessions with a corresponding neglect of reading the Scriptures.[68] Concerns were also expressed that some people were falling back to their old indigenous practices of making a feast and having special prayers for the sick, in view of the presence of much sickness among them.[69] There was even an instance of a former traditional healer professing to be a Christian and quietly practising white magic purported to be for good causes,[70] a practice forbidden by the SIB leadership. Further, the BEM literature noted that a leading SIB pastor had taken a second wife and had left the ministry some years earlier.[71]

As the revival of 1973 spread nation-wide from Bario in the Kelabit Highlands, it is necessary to examine the situation among the Kelabit community. Two major developments affected the Kelabit community after the formation of Malaysia in 1963.[72] Firstly, during the period of the Indonesian

---

[65] *BEM NL*, October 1971, 1. Many of them have been 'embarrassed because they find that they cannot answer the kind of questions that are being asked of them; no longer can they satisfy growing numbers of their congregation whose capacity to appreciate expository preaching and sound Bible study is increasing'.

[66] *BEM NL*, October 1971, 4.

[67] *BEM NL*, October 1969, 1. 'They have all the friendliness of unsophisticated people: qualities which had been deepened by their Christian faith. They were models of independence—the boys provided their own speakers and their own pattern of worship was based on the practice of their home churches'.

[68] *BEM NL*, October 1969, 1. According to Tagal Paran, an SIB Chairman, these were 'some of SIB's deepest needs' at the time.

[69] *BEM NL*, August 1969, 3.

[70] *BEM NL*, April 1973, 4.

[71] *BEM NL*, June 1972, 3.

[72] The formation of Malaysia occurred on 16 September 1963.

Confrontation (1963-1966), when Indonesia opposed the formation of Malaysia, there were Indonesian military incursions into the Third and Fourth Divisions of Sarawak along the Kalimantan border in late 1963 and 1964. Consequently, the scattered Kelabit villages in the Kelabit Highlands near the border were re-grouped together in Bario, forming one large community.[73] This resettlement, which presented opportunities as well as problems for the Kelabit community, had social and economic implications. There were changes in agricultural activities for those resettled from hill farming to wet paddy cultivation. The school children there had to move from small, scattered schools into a large, centralized school with more teachers, and the SIB churches became more accessible due to the proximity of the villages to one another, which facilitated intensive visitation. The proximity of these villages to one another confronted them with two issues: (a) for the older generation of Kelabit, the resettlement, which involved a return to Bario, brought to the surface memories of 'old family feuds and bitter quarrels', which 'had forced them to move to their present location', away from Bario; and (b) the varying moral standards among the villages, even among Christian ones. The BEM newsletter reported thus: 'some were lax about brewing and drinking rice beer. Some tolerated promiscuous relationships between the sexes, while others upheld the Christian virtues of chastity and continence', which undoubtedly generated some unease and tension in the relationship among the villages. Moreover, the presence of a large number of military servicemen at Bario with 'many new ideas' and 'new morality' was in the view of the BEM and SIB, 'a stumbling block to many'.[74] Of greater concern was the division of a Christian Kelabit village into two separate longhouses, five hundred yards apart, and the pastor who resided in the longhouse, where church worship took place, was being pressured to refrain from visiting the other longhouse. It was reported that a compromise proposal of building the church half-way between the two longhouses did not materialize and a lack of fellowship between the two longhouses continued. Similar petty divisions and quarrels also weakened the communal relationship among the longhouses and villages.[75] The negative impact of these influences was perceived to be a greater sense of worldliness, a lowered standard of morality and unresolved tensions in relationships that were understood to be choking the spiritual life of the church.

The economic benefits of resettlement became obvious to the Kelabit community. The large boarding school and the presence of the army provided them with a ready market for their abundant agricultural produce, subsidized by

---

[73] See Robert Lian Saging and Lucy Bulan, 'Kelabit Ethnography: A Brief Report', *SMJ* 60.61 (December 1989), 91. *BEM NL*, April, 2, and December 1964, 3. Amster, 'Community, Ethnicity and Modes of Association among the Kelabit of Sarawak', 24 noted that this resettlement had the effect of creating Bario as 'the unofficial capital of the Kelabit people'. Bala, *Changing Borders and Identities*, 42.

[74] *BEM NL*, December 1964, 3.

[75] *BEM NL*, August 1971, 4.

government aid that gave them a taste of affluence. This was exhibited in their ability to purchase new luxury goods flown in by the weekly air service and in the building of superior houses or impressive 'two storey' longhouses. The BEM missionaries viewed this situation with some concern, commenting that 'the seeds of materialism are beginning to germinate'.[76] It was noted that despite their growing affluence, there has not been any 'big increase in church giving generally', though the local women's guild had donated a substantial amount to the SIB for its evangelism and Scripture translation work.[77]

Through the establishment of a primary school in 1963 and a secondary school in Bario in 1967, the Kelabit were soon acknowledged as the most educated tribe among the Orang Ulu,[78] and the concern was that there was no suitably qualified SIB pastors to work among the Kelabit students, as most of the pastors from the LBS had only attained a formal primary education except for the few who were already busy at LBS. Further, the headmaster at that school, who held allegedly 'liberal' views on theology, was of the view that the BEM and SIB were not of much use in helping the students.[79]

In short, the Kelabit, by 1971, were fragmented by village quarrels, had become 'increasingly materialistic' as a result of their growing affluence and were losing their older teenagers and young adults to the towns so that only the young children and the elderly were left in the Highlands.

Within the SIB leadership, there were two important developments at this time. Firstly, a major difficulty facing the pastors was that of insufficient support to look after their large families; a problem which has been examined in the previous chapter, noting that there was a greater dropout rate among the older pastors from ministry.[80] Secondly, there was some hesitancy on the part of the SIB to assume full responsibility as a 'Three-Self' church from the BEM, as was evident at the 1968 meeting between the BEM Field Executive and SIB leadership. The appointment of an indigenous pastor as the principal of LBS was delayed until 1972, instead of December 1968, as intended by the BEM. This development was due to a lack of self-confidence among the older members of the SIB leadership after their seeming inability to deal with some of the problems raised by the social, economic and educational trends that had been impacting the Orang Ulu society, in particular that of the youths from the later 1960s. Hence, there came the request by the SIB to the BEM to help them work among the youths in the towns.[81] It was observed that the challenge for

---

[76] *BEM NL*, December 1964, 3

[77] *BEM NL*, August 1971, 4. The collection through sales of work amounted to $1,081 (Malayan).

[78] W.M. Toynbee, 'Educational Progress in the Kelabit Highlands', *SG*, 31 July 1965, 218-19.

[79] *BEM NL*, December 1964, 3.

[80] *BEM NL*, June 1968, 2; December 1969, 2; August 1970, 3.

[81] See Chapter 6.

SIB was that 'the SIB, a rural Church', had 'to learn the relevance of Christianity to the new world of towns'.[82]

In view of the above problems and challenges facing the BEM and SIB, the BEM and SIB leadership issued a call to pray for a genuine renewal and revival,[83] especially in view of the prevalent perception that there had been a slowdown in church growth from 1963 to 1969. This slowdown was attributed to two reasons: firstly, a waning in spiritual fervour and secondly, the saturation of the areas with the gospel. According to the BEM, the statistics of 211 churches in 1963, 226 churches in 1965, 244 churches in 1967 and 266 churches in 1969 represented a slowdown in the rate of church growth.[84] For the BEM and SIB, this slowdown was a cause for alarm. So, on the eve of the revival, the political, social and economic trends which had begun to affect the BEM missionaries and impact the Orang Ulu communities were giving the SIB grave concern about its future, and the conditions for a revival seemed to be in place.

The revival that took place among the SIB churches was initially a series of localized occurrences before becoming a pan-SIB movement after the Bario revival. The following pages will discuss: first, its beginning at LBS; second, its spread through the various Easter conventions where Dr Petrus Octavianus was the speaker;[85] third, its impact on the deacons' school at Bario; and fourth, the appearance among the school children at Bario of a spontaneous outbreak of revival, which quickly spread through the interior and down to sub-coastal and coastal towns including Miri and Kuching.

The Revival at Lawas Bible School

The beginnings of the revival are traceable to November 1971 when several students at the Lawas Bible School, according to the BEM newsletter, sought permission to be absent from classes on the grounds that the teaching from the Bible was 'penetrating them like a knife'.[86] But George Ngo clarified that it was through listening to David Pawson's Bible teaching through tapes that the students, especially the head student and the graduating students, experienced a desire to pray for revival and be empowered by the Holy Spirit to be effective ministers of God.[87] The BEM literature further reported that this head prefect

---

[82] *BEM NL*, October 1969, 4. 'This new life is a glittering attraction to the people of Borneo. It offers a regular salary, respectable government employment and numerous 'mod cons' of which the cinema, the watch, camera and the radio are much sought after. 'Pop culture' and the latest dress fashion are keenly watched and imitated'.

[83] *BEM NL*, August 1970, 3.

[84] *BEM Field Conference Reports*, March 1970, 32. *BEM NL*, August 1970, 3.

[85] *BEM NL*, February 1973, 1; August 1973, 3.

[86] *BEM NL*, April 1972, 3.

[87] The tapes were supplied by a BEM missionary, Dorothy Evans, to the students. Rev. David Pawson was then the Pastor of Guildford Baptist Church, and a pioneer of charismatic renewal in Britain. Interview with George Ngo Epoi, 7 October 2004.

had an earlier reconciliation with a fellow student and later met to pray late into the night. They were joined slowly by other students, the number growing to eight people. The turning point came when the whole of one Saturday night was spent in prayer and fellowship, punctuated by confessing to one another those things that had hindered mutual fellowship at a deeper level. By early morning, the mood of prayer had given way to praise and joy. The following week it had spread to the women students. A similar pattern of conviction of sin, confession and repentance followed. That weekend witnessed a gathering of a large number of students continuing all night in prayer and fellowship. As it was reported by one missionary, 'Probably the keynote throughout has been the intense love that had been generated one for another ... There is a reality there in a wonderful way. The Lord has made some of them spiritually mature overnight'.[88]

It is significant that the revival among the LBS students led to a new surge in evangelism, resulting in the next few weeks of preaching teams moving out to share the joyful news to the local villages. The missionaries noted that these meetings were 'charged with power and a presence of the Lord'. Further, many people were attracted to the church at Lawas. With the onset of the long vacation, the students banded themselves into fifteen teams as they returned to their home villages for the purpose of preaching the gospel, 'with a deep assurance that the Spirit is bearing witness with them'. 'Lives have been transformed and possessed with a power and radiance that have filled them with a child-like wonder. Timidity had given way to boldness in proclaiming the gospel.'[89] Though this comment may sound patronizing, it was expressing the fact that there were visible changes in the lives of the students as they proclaimed the gospel.

It was recorded in the BEM newsletter that the student teams returned with positive reports. Firstly, they claimed to have experienced the enabling of the Spirit in their preaching and reported to have beneficial results on both preachers and hearers. There was also a heightened sense of the need for 'an awakening and revival amongst the churches'.[90] Secondly, at least one married student in one of the teams experienced the 'wonderful' divine provision for his material needs. His wife and two children who were sick had to go to hospital and surprisingly, he received a timely gift of ten dollars for the badly needed food for them. Then, for his return trip to LBS, two people on separate occasions provided him with a hundred and twenty dollars, all in answer to fervent prayer. Thirdly, there were reports of 'blessings' among the different tribes when the student teams returned. Among the Kelabit, the team that returned home to their longhouse had the permission of the pastor and deacons to preach at the Sunday worship and also visited every room in the longhouse,

[88] *BEM NL*, April 1972, 3.
[89] *BEM NL*, April 1972, 3.
[90] *BEM NL*, June 1972, 2.

speaking the Word and praying with each family. Tears followed, with confession of sin and then a sense of joy and praise to God. Some waited until midnight for the student team to visit them in their rooms and later wanted them to make a return visit.[91] Another team felt the burden to preach to their own Iban people and went to the Iban at Batu Niah, with the result that the church at Batu Niah was eager for more teaching. Accompanied by the Iban of Batu Niah, they visited surrounding Iban longhouses. A different team that visited the Bisaya church at Ranggu was invited by the leading man of the village, who had earlier been quite apathetic to Christianity, but then showed an openness of heart to the gospel.[92] In short, it is to be noted that there was a sense of excitement and empowerment to preach and evangelize among the LBS students.

The BEM newsletter also reported that the young people were being 'awakened' by the movement. For example, one LBS student, who had returned to his home village, re-gathered the scattered group of young people in his village, who had earlier met for Bible study in 1971 prior to his joining LBS. Further, a Kayan student, Usun, was concerned for her sister who was adamant about marrying a Roman Catholic who was suspected of practising powerful witchcraft. Persuasion from the headman, pastor and deacons failed to make her change her mind. But when Usun spoke to her sister, her sister broke down into tears, saying, 'My sin is great', and as she attended the Long Bemang convention with Usun, she wept and realized that she had gone astray.[93] At the Long Bemang convention in the Baram, a large proportion of the 2,000 people who attended were youths. Many of them received Christ and most of them were second-generation Christians.

There was a growing concern among the LBS students for those with a shallow faith whether as second-generation Christians or as nominal adherents, for those who had backslidden in their faith, and also for the 'youths, both boys and girls in their primary and secondary schools, who had been led astray in boarding schools, away from their parents'. This concern of the missionaries led to a call to pray for revival so that the students at LBS continued to meet for hours of prayer two or three nights a week.[94] Since the students joining LBS by 1972, were mostly young people and not actual leaders as in the past,[95] it is evident that the revival had the effect of emboldening the students with a sense of spiritual ability and empowerment to meet the challenges of the ministry ahead of them and so prepare the next generation of future SIB leaders.

---

[91] *BEM NL*, April 1972, 3. 'We have never prayed before apart from meal times'. Mina Tigan reported on the blessings among the Kelabit in the Bario as a result of her sharing. See *BEM NL*, August 1972, 2.
[92] *BEM NL*, June 1972, 3.
[93] *BEM NL*, June 1972, 3.
[94] *BEM NL*, June, 1972, 3; August 1972, 2.
[95] *BEM NL*, August 1972, 2.

Ministry of Dr Petrus Octavianus of Batu Malang, Indonesia

The ministry of Dr Petrus Octavianus from Batu Malang, Java, among the Orang Ulu was another milestone in the progress of the revival. His ministry as the guest speaker for the SIB Biannual Conference in December 1972[96] led to further invitations to speak at the SIB Easter conventions for three successive years. With each successive year, the numbers grew until it was reported in 1974 that crowds 'exceeded previous convention numbers'. Accompanying the conventions, there were also major rallies each year first at Miri in 1973[97] and then at Lawas in 1974.[98]

At the 1972 SIB Biennual Conference, Octavanius was reported to have exercised a ministry that combined spiritual power with solid teaching over a wide area of evangelical truth and Christian doctrine, especially about sin in the Christian life, spiritual warfare and exposing witchcraft and occult practice. After each meeting, there was confession and counselling, with queues of people waiting until midnight and appearing early at six in the morning. Sins confessed included witchcraft, stealing, covetousness, adultery, keeping fetishes, and receiving 'Satan's medicines' among others. Of significance was a public admission of moral failure by a former president of SIB. Further, many married couples experienced reconciliation. These experiences were reported to be followed by a sense of joy and liberty, which led to praises to God.[99]

There were missionary reports of similar happenings in 1973, as Octavanius spoke at four of the eight 'Keswick-type' conventions,[100] and also at an SIB rally in Miri;[101] The conventions drew large numbers of people with 3,000 at Long Kerembangan and 4,600 at Long Atip. The results were quite visible. For

---

[96] Dr Petrus Octavianus was Chairman of the Indonesian Missionary Fellowship (an outgrowth of WEC) and also associated with the Bible Institute at Batu Malang, East Java, Indonesia (*BEM NL*, February 1973, 1). Detmar Scheunemann was director of the Bible Institute at Batu Malang from 1957 to 1987 and a regional director of WEC International for East and Southeast Asia. According to Kurt Koch in *The Revival in Indonesia* (Grand Rapids: Kregel Publications, 1971), 8, Octavianus was one of the most important spiritual leaders of the revival … (He) was a principal of a high school in Malang, East Java, a president of a teachers' institute and later a lecturer at a university. Octavianus was referred to as 'Pak Elias' in Koch's, *Revival in Indonesia*, 167-79, which gives an account of his life and ministry as a revivalist in Indonesia and Timor. See Kurt Koch, *Wine of God: Revival in Indonesia, Formosa, Solomon Islands and South India* (Laval, Canada: Christian Evangelism Publications, 1974), 65, which explicitly states that Pak Elias is Petrus Octavianus.

[97] *BEM NL* June 1973, 2-3.

[98] *BEM NL* August 1974, 1.

[99] *BEM NL*, February 1973, 1.

[100] The conventions were held at Long Atip among the Kayan, Long Kerebangan among the Lun Bawang, Bario among the Kelabit and Mendalang among the Lun Bawang. See *BEM NL*, April 1973, 4. It was reported that some 13,000 people attended the four conventions in April. See *BEM NL*, October 1973, 2.

[101] *BEM NL*, June 1973, 3.

example, it was noted that among the Lun Bawang churches, a well-respected leader confessed his sin; the pastor confessed to the barrenness of his ministry; a 'hardened witch-doctor' denounced and rejected his profession; husbands and wives were reconciled and crowds of people both young and old rededicated their lives to God. Among the Kayan churches, 'many nominal Christians and backsliders had been brought back. Sin has been confessed, many people were baptized and churches that were half empty are now full'. Further, what was regarded as 'fetishes or Satan's medicines' were discarded.[102]

The impact of the revival became clear during the SIB conventions in Sarawak in 1974.[103] Two conventions were particularly significant: the one at Long Temarub along the lower Trusan River had some 5000 people. The other at Long Liam had some 2000 visitors which included Kayan, Kenyah, Kelabit, Lun Bawang and Penan. At the end of the conventions, it was reported that many had pledged to support the work of spreading the gospel. It is significant that the conventions were reported to be 'a family affair', signifying the strengthening of the bond that had occurred between different tribes and churches, as highlighted in an earlier chapter.[104] These conventions then constituted a significant factor toward the cultural integration and creation of a corporate Orang Ulu identity. The revival had the effect of strengthening this cultural integration and identity among the Orang Ulu, especially in the face of the emerging national culture most pronouncedly felt in the towns. It is important to note that the challenge issued at the end of each convention reminded participants that 'revival is not plain sailing', and the church was urged to recognize and deal with the excesses that accompanied revivals and to continue to stand and thrive in spite of times of external testing.[105] What the revival also imparted was spiritual empowerment and confidence to face their fears of an uncertain future and overcome the difficulties under a more restrictive Malaysian government, evidence of which had earlier been felt in neighbouring Sabah.

Deacons' School at Bario

This beginning of the revival at the deacons' school at Bario in early 1973 was a prelude to the greater wave that was to come a few months later. From the account in the BEM newsletter, it began when a church leader publicly apologized for impatience, a sharp tongue and constant criticism of others on the final day of the school. There followed the conversion of the former penghulu or village chief and of a fourteen-year-old girl, filling them with joy and praise for God. In addition, a woman experienced the lifting of her burden

102 *BEM NL*, June 1973, 2.
103 *BEM NL*, June 1974, 2. Dr Octavianus was again invited for the Conventions in April 1975 but was subsequently banned from entering Sarawak thereafter.
104 Chapter 6.
105 *BEM NL*, August 1974, 1, 3.

of guilt for a past deed, which was their custom of burying her baby twins alive; a guilt which she had carried for years before her confession of her sin. There were fears about the temptations that the young people, once free from parental control, would face in the towns as they went there for further education, and their parents and the SIB leaders expressed the need for these young people to experience spiritual empowerment and revival,[106] so that they would be able to overcome the 'worldly' temptations of city life and be faithful Christians.

Revival at Bario and beyond

The first three occurrences of the revival, which has just been examined, reached a climax with the revival in Bario which then spread throughout Sarawak. The Mission account reported that the revival which started in mid-October 1973 had almost completely affected the Bario Highlands within a month. Various preaching teams, comprising school teachers, young people, church deacons, district and village chiefs, were formed and began to disperse in different directions, one going to Ba Kelalan, another to Long Lellang, another to Long Peluan and Lio Matu and down the Baram, another to Long Bemang, Long Atip and Long Bedian and others reaching Marudi, Miri, Kuching, Lawas, and Limbang.[107] By August 1974, the 'reviving work of the Holy Spirit had touched churches from the extreme north to Kuching at the other end of the country'.[108]

In Bulan's book 'The Bario Revival', the spontaneous revival in Bario was said to first involve students from the School Christian Fellowship in the Secondary School and later spread to the headmaster, his wife, two school teachers and students of the school.[109] At the Primary School, the headmaster, teachers and students were similarly affected. The dramatic movement was described thus: 'For two days the primary school pupils were so under the influence of the Holy Spirit that the teachers could not hold classes ... The children were all crying or singing or prophesying ... what these young children said when they prophesied' was found to be 'Scriptural'. The revival spilled over to the others during church services which were said to be 'so different from what had been experienced before'.[110] Unusual happenings were reported:

> People begin to cry out in loud wailing (sometimes 20 or 30 people at the same time) calling out to God for forgiveness of sins and some people calling out the

[106] *BEM NL*, February 1973, 2.

[107] Bulan and Bulan-Dorai, *The Bario Revival*, pp 109-22. *BEM NL*, February 1974, 4; April 1974, 3; November 1976, 2.

[108] *BEM NL*, August 1974, 1.

[109] Bulan and Bulan-Dorai, *The Bario Revival*, 7-14. Solomon was one of the school teachers at Bario involved in the revival. *BEM NL*, December 1973, 3.

[110] *BEM NL*, April 1974, 1.

> names of those with whom they have been quarreling in a desperate desire to get reconciled. Many pending court cases have been cancelled because the parties involved have been reconciled in a very dramatic manner with tears and embraces of godly love. After the sin problems have been dealt with by the Lord and forgiveness granted, then the service goes on with loud singing of praises while tears of joy are still flowing. With some hard ones the Holy Spirit has been severe. They would fall flat on the floor unconscious for 20 minutes or two or three hours, then others would pray over them and they usually begin to shake all over then sat up and began to call out to God for forgiveness.[111]

In his anthropological study of the Kelabit of Sarawak, Matthew Amster noted a few perspectives from the people present at the time of the revival. Some saw the revival as a genuine work of the Holy Spirit. Those who were sceptical described it sociologically as a type of mass hysteria. Ironically, some of the young people who were among the first to be involved in the revival later became cynical about their experience. Equally ironic is that others who were initially sceptical at the time of the revival subsequently changed their opinion. Amster concluded that this Bario revival in 1973 has 'become inscribed in the historical consciousness of the Kelabit community' and has become such a pivotal point in their history that Christianity became a defining feature of their identity.[112] Similarly, Poline Bala, a Kelabit anthropologist, in her reflections on growing up in a Kelabit village in Sarawak, maintained that the revival in 1973 converted the whole tribe to Christianity and they have ever since fully embraced Christianity.[113]

Initially, it was pointed out that the local SIB leadership at Bario was opposed to these unusual happenings and prohibited the students from preaching or evangelizing in all the village churches, as they were concerned about their falling into 'trances', which were common during their pre-Christian days. They attributed their 'disorderly worship' as not from God.[114] However, Balang Anid, who was then the SIB district superintendent at Bario, admitted that he was at first unsure of the genuineness of the revival, but only became convinced through the timely intervention from Balan Seling, a well respected leader among them.[115] It was later reported that it led to the lifting of

---

[111] *BEM NL*, April 1974, 1. Bulan and Bulan-Dorai, *The Bario Revival*, 92-97.

[112] Amster, 'Community, Ethnicity and Modes of Association among the Kelabit of Sarawak', 284-85, 288. See also Matthew H. Amster, '"New Sacred Lands": The Making of A Christian Prayer Mountain in Highland Borneo', in Ronald A. Lukens-Bull (ed.), *Sacred Places and Modern Landscapes: Sacred Geography and Social Religious Transformations in South and Southeast Asia* (Tempe: Program for Southeast Asian Studies, Arizona State University, 2003), 137-40.

[113] Bala, *Changing Borders and Identities*, 50.

[114] Interview with Balan Seling, 29 July 2005. Bulan and Bulan-Dorai, *The Bario Revival*, 83-87.

[115] Interview with Balang Anid, 17 September 2004.

the ban on the activities of the students.[116] According to Bulan, the local leadership was further convinced that this revival was truly a divine visitation during a combined prayer and worship meeting held on 21 October at the Penghulu's house (Ulung Palang) for all the churches in Bario.[117]

During the revival, there were excesses which have been well documented in Bulan's book. These excesses included lengthy and loud prayers as a sign of spirituality, a pre-occupation with dreams and visions, exclusive claims of guidance from God, a castigation of many traditional practices as demonic, and excessive emotionalism in prayer.[118] Important leaders within the SIB leadership acknowledged that it was Balan Seling, who helped discern the genuine move of the Spirit from the excesses. His presence and wise advice during the revival enabled the SIB to accept this revival as from God and to discard its more excessive practices.[119]

It can be argued that a number of effects resulted from this revival.[120] Firstly, it was a movement that gave a prominent role to young people, especially the Kelabit and Kayan youths. In a church in the Kelabit Highlands, where there was no pastor for a month or so, the young people who had been 'touched by the Spirit' assumed temporarily a leadership role in the church and took the place of the deacons,[121] who were at a loss about how to deal with the revival. Winston Edip perceptively pointed out that the SIB leadership was first taken by surprise at the movement. They were later not only divided in their views about the movement, but found that the movement could not be stopped.[122] The translation of young people into leadership roles, even though temporarily, proved to be of some significance. It is arguable that the 'touch of the Spirit'

---

[116] Bulan and Bulan-Dorai, *The Bario Revival*, 90-92.

[117] Bulan and Bulan-Dorai, *The Bario Revival*, 92-97.

[118] Bulan and Bulan-Dorai, *The Bario Revival*, 185-96. According to Winston Edip, one negative effect was the near absolute reliance of dreams and visions as a means of divine guidance to the neglect of relying on and reading the Bible. Interview with Winston Edip, 15 September 2004.

[119] Jok Wan, a former SIB President, acknowledged the significant role of Balan Seling as advisor and counsellor who visited the different areas where revival occurred. See Interview with Jok Wan, 16 September 2004. Balang Anid, as the SIB *ketua daerah* (or district superintendent) of Bario during the revival, noted that Balan Seling was crucial in discerning and giving guidance during the Bario revival. Interviews with Winston Edip, 15 September 2004; with Balang Anid, 17 September 2004; and with George Ngo Epoi, 7 October 2004.

[120] One explanation of the revival suggests that 'the revival was a response by the rural people to their situation of the out-migration of the Kelabit' that led the majority of Kelabit to reside in urban areas. 'From this perspective, the revival can be seen as a form of renewal experience for rural dwellers'. Also, the revival can be seen as 'a way for the rural community to advance itself in relation to the people who migrated to town areas'. See Amster, '"New Sacred Lands"', 137-38.

[121] *BEM NL*, April 1974, 2. Amster also notes that the revival movement was 'at least initially a youth movement'. See Amster, '"New Sacred Lands"', 140.

[122] Interview with Winston Edip, 15 September 2004.

not only gave them confidence to lead a church but also 'poured out new gifts upon these people to enable them to serve Him more acceptably'.[123] In the longer term, both George Ngo Epoi and Winston Edip agree that the revival prepared a set of younger leaders to assume the leadership vacuum created by the departure of the missionaries.[124]

Secondly, it is noted that the operation of these gifts confronted situations of spiritual compromise. The BEM newsletter recorded an instance in which a young man with the gift of discernment was 'convinced that right in the pastor's house was a jimat or a charm with satanic power', an accusation which the pastor denied. A search was made but nothing was found, and the young man was denounced, but other young people supported the young man's accusation. Another more thorough search was made by an older member of the household, who discovered the charm. Then, the young man was reported to have said that the Spirit of God had told him that there was another charm, which was also found. After which he pointed out the place of a third charm in the unlikely place beneath a banana palm, which was later found. This episode resulted in confession of sins by the pastor.[125] The report of this incident about the pastor was too dramatic for the BEM missionaries to believe as they were not only outsiders to the event who were also unaccustomed to, or sceptical about, such incidents. It seems that its inclusion in the BEM newsletter was due to the fact that this kind of incident has parallels in their literal reading of the Acts of the Apostles, so that the BEM missionaries' initial scepticism gave way to belief. Also, when Cunningham was invited to give some 'biblical teachings' on these strange practices, it was said that he had some reservations but he experienced the revival himself that convinced him of the presence of God in it.[126]

If the above dramatic account provided by the BEM newsletter was true, incidents of these sorts would have caused a sense of awe and fear among the church members and even leaders and so boosted the confidence, status and prestige of these young people who had experienced unusual guidance by the power of the Spirit of God. It is maintained that as a result of the revival, the youths 'often form a virile part of the local congregation and they are beginning to take an increasing part in the life and leadership of the local churches -- some becoming deacons, Sunday school teachers and youth leaders'.[127] This fact is also attested by Gerawat Maran, who further observed that there was an influx

[123] *BEM NL*, February 1974, 2.

[124] Interview with Winston Edip, 15 September 2004; and with George Ngo Epoi, 7 October 2004.

[125] *BEM NL*, April 1974, 2. Amster notes that 'at the time of the revival, there were many cases of youths confronting their elders and pressing them to cast off their 'pagan' habits'. See Amster '"New Sacred Lands"', 140.

[126] Bulan and Bulan-Dorai, *The Bario Revival*, 194-95. See Cunningham, *Longhouse Open Doors*, 128.

[127] *BEM NL*, August 1975, 2.

of young people into Bible schools from 1975 for a few subsequent years.[128] Furthermore, according to Balan Engan, another effect was that a large majority of the youths who went to Bible School from the Baram were from the lower class of the local society. As a result, the revival facilitated their move into leadership positions as pastors in the SIB.[129] During this time, younger indigenous pastors and leaders such as Balan Seling (a Kenyah) and Jok Wan, (a Kayan) who had been able to provide spiritual discernment, guidance and leadership were highly regarded.[130] Importantly, this revival led to a revitalizing of spirituality and standard of morality in the churches.

Thirdly, this revival led to a new surge in evangelism throughout the SIB churches, first initiated by the preaching teams in the Bario Highlands, which radiated to the other parts of Sarawak and finally reaching Kuching.[131] As these preaching teams moved out in different directions from the Bario Highlands, a general pattern of events emerged. Church services became unusually long with many people confessing their sins publicly, dramatic conversions among 'die-hard sinners', backsliders restored, old addictive habits discarded, and marital relationships restored. Further, many pending court cases were settled amicably, people apologized to one another for wrongs done and sought forgiveness, which effected reconciliation and in some cases, sick people were healed immediately.[132] It was reported that the Kenyah and Kayan churches in the Baram were also 'touched significantly by the Spirit's work through the teams'.[133] According to Balan Engan, the revival first began among the Sunday school children in Long Jee, Baram, in October 1973. It later resulted in the whole village becoming Christian.[134]

---

[128] Interviews with Gerawat Maran, 23 September 2004 and with Balan Engan, 18 September 2004. According to Balan Engan, at least fifty-three young people from the Baram area entered Bible schools whether at LBS or at Long Lama.

[129] Interview with Balan Engan, 18 September 2004.

[130] Balan Seling had become a Council Negeri member and Jok Wan was Treasurer of the SIB. Jok Wan was later to become the SIB Chairman. Balan Seling was in Bario just after the revival started and discerned that it was a movement of God. While not curbing the revival or condoning any excesses, he wrote a couple of letters outlining issues raised by the revival. His letters were: a) on 'Dreams, Visions and Voices' (dated 28 December 1973); b) on guidelines for the SIB Executive Council on how to oversee the revival, (dated 20 January 1974); c) on 'Growing in Christ' (dated 17 January 1974); d) on 'Guarding against slander of the name of Jesus on our account' (dated 23 January 1974); and e) on 'Beware of the Devices of the Devil', providing helpful guidelines in curbing the excesses of the revival (dated 12 February 1974). *BEM NL*, June 1974, 2; 50th Anniversary Issue, 1978, 4.

[131] Interviews with Winston Edip, 15 September 2004; with Balang Anid, 17 September 2004; with Gerawat Maran, 20 September 2004; with Balan Engan, 18 September 2004; and with George Ngoi Epoi, 7 October 2004.

[132] *BEM NL*, April 1974, 3.

[133] In a report by Dr Bill Hawes to the BEM/OMF Conference in 1976. *BEM NL*, November 1976, 2.

[134] Interview with Balan Engan, 18 September 2004.

Fourthly, reports claimed that unusual signs were leading people to conversion and strengthening of the faith of many SIB Christians. These reports were recorded in the BEM newsletter. In Miri, on the night of 19 November 1973, a light in the sky in the form of a cross was purported to be sighted by a non-Christian solider on sentry duty. He related the episode to his six other friends, one among them a Lun Bawang Christian who witnessed to him, which subsequently led to his conversion.[135] In the Upper Baram region, an unusual series of signs in the sky was reported to be seen on 16 January 1974. While eleven people were out harvesting together, they saw what looked like a chest, then a hand with nail-marks, which were blood red, and then a crown of thorns and finally the face of Jesus Christ. It was further reported that the next day, they purportedly saw the empty tomb of Jesus with many shining people walking about happily. It is not uncommon to regard these reports as the creative imaginations or hallucinatory experiences of the people. But the sightings of these signs were recorded to have resulted in 'large numbers of people praying hard and all flocking to church in the morning and evening';[136] that, perhaps, convinced the missionaries, though not necessarily others who were more skeptical, of the working of a divine hand. However, it is not surprising to find an ambiguity in response to such phenomena. On the one hand, people may have flocked to the church out of curiosity, and on the other, the faith of many SIB Christians were being strengthened.

The revival that spread to coastal towns had effects that were less dramatic but nonetheless real. In the coastal towns such as Kuching and Miri, the churches not only had a mix of all the various Orang Ulu communities but also of other ethnic groups, the Iban, Bidayuh and Chinese not normally found elsewhere in the rural SIB churches.[137] The revival at Kuching was reported to have begun at one Saturday prayer meeting when a testimony from a Kelabit boy who had been reading Roy Hession's 'The Calvary Road' triggered a movement involving public confessions of sins with weeping and tears, confession to those who have been wronged followed by apologies and reconciliation and the sudden outburst of a frightening case of a demonized girl who was subsequently delivered.[138] There followed a surge of evangelistic activities to the surrounding Iban villages through teams of both missionaries and young adults, as it was reported, 'week by week the van goes out loaded with witness teams from the SIB English-speaking church'.[139] During this phase of the revival, there was a strong emphasis on evangelistic outreach to the Iban

[135] *BEM NL*, April 1974, 3.
[136] *BEM NL*, April 1974, 4.
[137] Interview with Gerawat Maran, 20 September 2004.
[138] *BEM NL*, February 1974, 1. Roy Hession's book, *The Calvary Road* (London: Christian Literature Crusade, 1950) was readily available in the local BEM bookroom and it is unlikely that the Kelabit boy knew much about the East African revival, except that what he read made sense of what was happening in the Kelabit Highlands.
[139] *BEM NL*, November 1974, 3.

in Kuching, Sibu and Bintulu.[140] Not only was there outreach to another new group of people, the Bidayuh,[141] but there were also 'open homes' as a means of evangelism.[142]

In Miri, the movement first spread to the relatives of the Kelabit who were serving as Police Field Force personnel and resulted in many conversions, and the spiritual awakening and growth of both the Malay-speaking and English-speaking sections of the church.[143] From Miri, the church carried out regular church planting and teaching trips to the scattered groups working along the Miri-Niah road with reports of much interest and result.[144]

This new phenomenon of the rise of SIB churches with members belonging to both the working and professional classes and people of all ethnic groups represented in Sarawak except for the Malays, necessitated cultural adjustments to each other within the SIB churches. It is likely that the revival had the effect of facilitating the process of social integration among the various people groups within the SIB churches as a social institution and of forging a distinctive SIB identity in relation to the other Christian denominations and the wider society.

The cumulative effect on the SIB churches suggests a general deepening of spiritual enthusiasm, commitment and vitality within the churches, an evangelistic fervour to witness, enhancement of the role of young people within the churches which prepared them for leadership positions, reconciliation within the churches and the strengthening of relational bonds across the Orang Ulu communities leading to the creation of a distinctive SIB identity in the urban centres.

Conclusion

Common features of the 1952 and 1973-1976 revivals included numerous conversions, the renewal of spiritual vitality and enthusiasm within the SIB churches, and noticeable social effects on community life. Also, both revivals were preceded by expectant prayer in response to political and social changes that were causing widespread anxiety. During the 1950s, the turbulent political events in Southeast Asia heightened fears of a communist takeover of the region. Further, the spiritual fervour among the indigenous churches had been waning as a result of the sudden wealth that the Lun Bawang acquired through the rubber boom of the 1950s, the alarming spread of infectious diseases such as tuberculosis and pneumonia, the strained relationship between the Lun Bawang and the Kelabit because of the Long Luping incident, and the lack of confidence by deacons within the churches. All of these factors together with

140 Interview with Gerawat Maran, 20 September 2004.

141 *BEM NL*, April 1974, 3-4.

142 *BEM NL*, December 1972, 3.

143 *BEM NL*, February 1975, 1.

144 *BEM NL*, August 1975, 3.

the weariness of the BEM missionaries contributed to urgent and united prayers being made toward God for and an expectation of a revival which was seen as being able to set matters right for both the BEM and the indigenous churches. During the late 1960s and early 1970s, the prayer concern for revival among other things focused on the moral and spiritual condition of the young people who were migrating to the urban centres for education and employment.

The revivals were significant in a number of ways. Firstly, they played a significant role in infusing moral confidence in, and spiritual empowerment of the indigenous leaders, both the deacons and pastors, not only to lead their churches but also to rise to the challenge of planting and developing a 'Three-Self' church during the 1950s; that is, they helped prepare the indigenous leadership to assume their responsibilities as a 'Three-Self' church and work toward the formation of the SIB. In addition, they were a means of bringing about reconciliation between the Lun Bawang and Kelabit churches so as to make possible the 'Three Selfs' vision. For the BEM missionaries, the revival had the effect of assuring them that their fifteen-year policy was a God-given vision and a 'finishable task', thereby renewing their resolve toward the task at hand.

The revival of the 1970s brought the role of the youths and young adults to the fore and was catalytic in the new surge of their evangelistic activities across Sarawak, where they grouped themselves into preaching teams. The thrust of this evangelism was often towards new areas and new groups of people, particularly the Iban and Bidayuh along the sub-coastal areas and coastal towns, and the effects were still being felt into the late 1970s. Further, the revival was instrumental in affirming and forging an Orang Ulu identity in the rural areas, and also in enhancing the process of their social integration with Christians of other ethnic groups in urban towns so as to create a distinctive SIB identity in relation to the wider Christian community and society. This social integration is also seen in the building of a new social network with other evangelical para-church groups such as the Inter School Christian Fellowship (ISCF), NCF and TCF, as they worked alongside evangelical Christians of other ethnic groups, and were thus introduced to a wider social integration with the emerging national culture. The revival not only provided inner courage toward social integration but also social empowerment of the Orang Ulu to work as equals among the other more sophisticated and more educated people in the towns; that is, it boosted their sense of self-confidence in relation to the other ethnic communities in urban Sarawak. This boost was a necessary ingredient for the SIB to be really 'Three-Self' as Sarawak moved towards greater modernization with the passage of time.

The revival of the 1970s was not initially accepted by the SIB leadership as a genuine move of the Spirit of God. The SIB leadership only became convinced because of Balan Seling, a prominent SIB leader, who was instrumental in discerning the genuineness of the movement and in giving guidance to the movement from falling into excesses and deviant practices. The result was an indigenous movement spread rapidly throughout Sarawak, becoming widely accepted especially within the SIB churches. The BEM missionaries, though they found themselves on the margins of this movement, sought to provide guidance when necessary.

Positively, the revival prepared the SIB for the eventual departure of the BEM missionaries and for the assumption of full responsibilities as a 'Three-Self' church. It also acted as a catalyst to a process of change which saw the older leaders replaced by younger men who were more in tune with the rapidly changing situation of Sarawak, and better able to provide the necessary leadership and guidance during the period of the revival. Further, the revival was beginning to facilitate the process of an upward mobility of the lower class among Orang Ulu society into leadership positions of the SIB as pastors. In tandem with the fact that the revival had its most significant effects among the Kelabit and Kayan, the senior leadership within SIB passed from Lun Bawang to Kayan and Kelabit personnel, when in 1975, Jok Wan, a Kayan, was elected SIB Chairman and Balan Lugan as SIB Secretary.[145] In commenting on this new set of key SIB leaders, the BEM newsletters reported that, 'the SIB is moving into a new era'.[146] This more progressive set of leaders was rightly placed to help SIB to begin its process of changing from a rural church to an urban church and to face the challenges confronting Sarawak as a state under Malaysian government rule. The next chapter will examine the challenges which the BEM and SIB faced under the Malaysian government and their response to them.

---

[145] *BEM NL*, February 1975, 3. Jok Wan was described as 'a young Kayan man of excellent spirit', and Balan Lugan as 'young but experienced and comes with exuberance to the task'.

[146] Jok Wan was SIB Chairman from 1975 to 1987 with only a short break. Gerawat Maran, a Kelabit, became the next SIB Chairman after Jok Wan. See *BEM NL*, February 1975, 3; March 1983, 1-2; 1st Quarter 1985, 2.

Chapter 8

The Response of the BEM and SIB to Political, Social and Economic Challenges 1959-1979

The work of the BEM spanned the period from 1928 to 1979 during which time the SIB as a 'Three-Self' church was formally established in 1959 as a separate entity from the parent mission body, the BEM. In Chapter 5, it was shown how the SIB was constituted and began to function as a 'Three-Self' church. In Chapter 6, it was argued that the revival of 1952 was a means of infusing spiritual confidence, courage and empowerment to the indigenous leadership to rise to the challenge to take practical steps toward inaugurating a 'Three-Self' church. Further, the revival of 1972-1976 was a means of emboldening a younger set of leaders to assume leadership positions within the SIB but also of empowering them to meet the challenges under the Malaysian government. In addition, it acted as a catalyst toward creating and strengthening a pan-Orang Ulu identity among the Orang Ulu and in facilitating the process of greater social integration with Christians of other ethnic groups. Thus, it began the process of forming a distinctive SIB identity in the churches in the urban townships. The reality of life in the coastal towns brought the SIB closer to the challenges presented by the socio-economic and political developments that were impacting Sarawak.

The socio-economic changes and political challenges in Sarawak under independent Malaysia had both positive and negative effects on the BEM and the SIB. To be a truly 'Three-Self' church, it was vital for SIB to capitalise on the positive benefits and to overcome, circumvent and minimize the negative effects of these changes. This chapter will examine the attempts of the BEM and SIB in making the transition from the rural to the urban context and their response to socio-economic and political challenges along their way.

Socio-Economic Challenges and the BEM/SIB

Social Migration and SIB churches

The most significant impact on the Orang Ulu communities as a result of the various socio-economic trends was the widespread social migration of the Orang Ulu; a process which began to gain momentum from the 1950s. But social migration and urbanisation were inseparably linked to educational and economic changes that had been taking place in Sarawak from the 1960s, leading to the growth of major coastal, sub-coastal and interior towns with large influxes of people.[1] These groups of people, which were once geographically segregated, were brought together in the larger towns, making them more cosmopolitan, with all the ethnic groups in Sarawak now represented in the towns. By 1980, a serious concern was raised about the growing towns slowly emptying out the people from the interior.[2]

This global phenomenon of urbanisation prompted evangelical missiologists to write about its challenge from the 1960s. Eric Fife and Arthur Glasser's book Missions in Crisis: Rethinking Mission Strategy was an early example.[3] Within evangelical Bible colleges and missionary bodies, this book became standard reading on urban missions, as missiological thinking on this phenomenon was still in its infancy. Even by 1980, there was a dearth of literature in evangelical missiological circles discussing how an indigenous church could make the transition from its rural to urban context, though the subject of urban church planting was being discussed.[4] Evangelical mission activity during this period was directed at individual personal salvation with little regard for any ecclesiological polity. Further, even the OMF, working in the new East Asian fields from the 1950s, was ambivalent on this issue.[5] Being an interior mission,

---

[1] The various groups of people include: a) the young people going for secondary or higher education or government employment as teachers, nurses, dispensers, dentists and doctors or the school dropouts working in the low paying jobs; b) the older people and school dropouts joining the Police Field Force, the Land Schemes in the sub-coastal areas near the towns or the timber camps, first in the sub-coastal areas and later from the mid-1970s towards the interior; c) the returnees from institutions of higher learning or universities abroad from the 1970s onwards; and d) the group of Peninsular Malaysian civil servants who were to occupy senior positions in Sarawak; among whom were a few Christians.

[2] *BEM NL*, May 1980, 1. The Baram had experienced the greatest percentage decline in population of the Orang Ulu due to the process of social migration. The per centages of the total Orang Ulu population located in the Baram were 57.9% in 1939, 57.4% in 1947, 50.3% in 1960, 49.6% in 1970 and 47.5% in 1980. But the Iban population had increased from 21.3% in 1939 to 32% in 1980 of their total population. See Joseph Ko, 'Changing Patterns of Sub-National Ethnic Distribution', 1-11.

[3] See Chapter 6.

[4] From 1965 to 1975, there were only three relevant articles in the *Evangelical Missions Quarterly* on this subject; namely, Raymond J. Davis, 'What missions must do to survive in the 70s', *EMQ* 6.4 (Summer 1970), 221-26; Roger S. Greenway, 'A Church-Planting Method That Works in Urban Areas', *EMQ* 6.3 (Spring 1970), 152-58 and John K. Branner's interview with McGavran, 'McGavran speaks on Roland Allen', *EMQ* 8.3 (Spring 1972), 165-74. However, Roger Greenway has written a couple of books on Urban Mission, namely, *Guidelines for Urban Church Planting* (Grand Rapids: Baker Book House, 1976), and *Apostle to the City: Biblical Strategies for Urban Missions*.

[5] See David A. Huntley, 'The Withdrawal of the China Inland Mission from China and their Redeployment to New Fields in East Asia' (PhD dissertation, Trinity Theological

OMF did not place urban mission as their priority, and prior to 1968, the BEM under the leadership of Belcher held a similar attitude.[6]

However, prior to 1968, there were some voices within the BEM calling for work to be started in the sub-coastal and coastal towns in tandem with the migration of the Orang Ulu. First, as discussed in Chapter 5, there was Dr Bill Lees' proposal in the 'Year of Decision', and then, another similar proposal by Harold McCracken, the BEM President, in 1966. Other voices came from younger missionaries such as Marion Baker and Viola Taeni calling for the move to the towns and ministry among students.[7] Further, by this time, Southwell, who had moved to Marudi, saw the need for establishing a Christian fellowship among secondary school students and started a suburban church. He later advocated at the 1968 BEM Field Conference the need to start a secondary school and urban churches to cater for the needs of the SIB members migrating to the coastal towns.[8]

Following the change of Field Director in 1968, the BEM through its younger missionaries took more seriously the mission strategy propounded by Fife and Glasser, which was first evident in Colin Reasbeck's article on 'Change', discussing the changes which were occurring in the spheres of education and urbanisation in Sarawak.[9] Then, at the BEM Australasian Conference in 1969, Dr Bill Hawes, the new BEM Field Director, envisioned among other things: (a) the establishment of urban SIB churches with missionaries in strategic towns; (b) the establishment of Christian Unions in schools and teacher training colleges; (c) the priority given to the use of mass media in propagating the gospel, as there was an offer from Far Eastern Broadcasting Corporation (FEBC) to build a studio at Lawas to produce tapes

---

Seminary, 2003), 108-16. Prior to CIM's withdrawal from China, the converts through the CIM remained largely independent or had formed groups unconnected with the churches. The CIM or OMF did not have any clear official policy on church structures in their work in the new fields in East Asia from 1952. Their missionaries worked as part of a denomination, or linked with a denomination, or worked independently of any existing denomination. In this latter option, the 'OMF church-plants in Malaya' had 'no viable OMF-type church structure' when missionaries withdrew. But in Thailand, as the church-plants were numerous, they later formed an association of congregations – a new denomination in its own right. In short, having a church structure was an afterthought in the mission policy of OMF.

[6] See Chapter 6.

[7] See Chapter 6.

[8] Though Southwell had officially left the BEM in 1954, his heart was still with the work. From 1965 to 1968, Southwell was in Marudi and in 1968, Southwell was invited to be acting Principal of St. Aidan's School in Miri. See Southwell, *Uncharted Waters*, 314-45. Interviews with Cunninghams, 8-9 November 2004; and also with Winston Edip, 15 September 2004 and with George Ngo Epoi, 7 October 2004.

[9] *BEM NL*, August 1968, 4. 'There is no need to elaborate this description by Fife and Glasser except to say that it can be applied in detail to the situation developing in this land'.

for radio broadcasts from Manila, and, in addition, the setting up of book centres or bookrooms in the various towns; and (d) the challenge for SIB to be integrated with the Church in Southeast Asia and be mission-minded.[10]

Social migration thus presented opportunities for the expansion of the work of the BEM and SIB. Firstly, the migration toward the urban centres led to the establishment of SIB town churches in the coastal areas. Secondly, there was a reverse migration of individuals back into the administrative centres in the sub-coastal and interior areas, establishing SIB churches there. Thirdly, the SIB work spread outward from the towns to their surrounding areas focusing particularly on the Iban, though the Bidayuh and Melanau were not excluded. It is these developments that will now be explored.

The opportunities opened up by the migration of Orang Ulu resulted in SIB working in conjunction with BEM to establish urban work from the later 1960s onwards in the three major coastal towns of Kuching in 1969, Miri in 1973,[11] and Sibu in 1974.[12] As highlighted in Chapter 5, the BEM/SIB networked with other mission and para-church organisations such as the OMF, TCF, NCF and SU to fulfil their aims of both reaching the students and planting urban churches. For instance, the OMF started work in Miri in 1963 under the sponsorship of the BEM and later continued to provide the necessary missionaries to work in urban centres, especially in Kuching and Sibu,[13] as there was a shortage of BEM missionaries who could take charge of urban churches. Moreover, in response to these trends of urbanisation and migration, the BEM formulated their policy on the 'twin tasks' of evangelism and church planting, and Bible teaching and leadership training in 1972,[14] which bore much resemblance to the recommendations of Fife and Glasser.[15] It resulted in the

---

[10] These aims were also those recommended by Fife and Glasser. Other concerns include missionaries acting as pastors to the SIB pastors and 'the threat of false teaching from Baha'i and other sects'. *BEM NL*, June 1969, 1-2. See Chapter 6 above.

[11] Percy King of the OMF helped in starting the Chinese work in Miri, which gave rise to the Miri Gospel Chapel. But this work did not become affiliated with the SIB, so that no SIB church was established until 1973. See *BEM NL*, June 1963, 1; August 1963, 3; August 1969, 1.

[12] Work in Sibu was started by Graeme Buntrock in 1974. The original composition of the church consisted of teachers, nurses, civil servants, with some policemen in the Field Force and construction workers at the shipyard. Its outreaches included Sarikei, Mukah and Kapit. See *BEM NL*, May 1975, 3; August 1977, 2; May 1980, 1-4.

[13] The Kuching church had a succession of three English pastors, Percy King, Douglas Sadler and Tony Horsfall. The Sibu church had Graeme Buntrock and Brian Newton. See *BEM NL*, May 1980, 3.

[14] *BEM NL*, August 1972, 1.

[15] Fife and Glasser, *Missions in Crisis*, 85-86, argued for a missionary strategy that focused on planting a national church 'in the cities among the educated classes, the two per cent that will produce the future leaders of the nation', on training a vigorous and able leadership for the national churches and on developing a missionary-minded national church. The formulation of this strategy arose from the lessons learnt from the failure of missionary work in China.

BEM missionaries being involved in evangelistic outreach and church planting among the Iban from the First to Fourth Divisions in Sarawak, and also in leadership development in the Advanced Bible School in Lawas,[16] and Miri Bible College (MBC) in Miri, and so the BEM missionaries were stretched to the limit.

The formal establishment of the Kuching Evangelical Church (KEC) in 1972 was of strategic importance. The multi-racial mix of KEC, with its growing number of young professionals worshipping in a modern church building, represented the beginning of the modern phase of the SIB. Many of these professionals became committed Christians overseas in their student days. Though they came from different church denominations, they now made KEC their home church and provided KEC with a ready-made leadership team. For instance, Nicholas Patrick, an Iban engineer, and Thomas Chung, a medical doctor, were then prominent lay leaders.[17] In turn, KEC became catalytic in encouraging the formation of other town churches when some of these professionals moved to other towns. When three of the leaders from KEC were transferred to Miri in 1973 because of employment, they became responsible for the formal establishment of the English speaking church in Miri.[18] Moreover, KEC pioneered a new evangelistic thrust, organizing local church teams under local leadership in evangelistic outreach and church planting efforts to the Iban, particularly in the First and Second Divisions of Sarawak.[19] In contrast, the older established pattern had been a church planting team consisting of a BEM missionary and an SIB pastor to pioneer a new area. The new pattern of outreach from urban churches under local lay leadership comprised a team of a few indigenous lay people, (only occasionally including a BEM missionary), so that indigenous initiative became primary.

From the three major towns of Kuching, Sibu and Miri, the movement of SIB members to other town centres such as Bintulu,[20] Sarikei[21] and Kapit[22] led

---

[16] The Advanced Bible School or Sekolah Teologia Atas was started in 1974 at the request of SIB to upgrade pastors and Bible School teachers. See *BEM NL*, February 1980, 1.

[17] *BEM NL*, May 1980, 3.

[18] See Reasbeck, 'The Growth of the Gospel among the Iban People in Sarawak', 58. Colin Reasbeck was a BEM missionary from 1964 to 1978 and focused his ministry among the Iban.

[19] *BEM NL*, May 1977, 1, 4; May 1980, 3.

[20] Bintulu was a fast growing town with massive development with facilities for a deep water port and had projects for an LNG processing plant, an aluminum plant, a hydro-scheme and a campus of an Agricultural University. See *BEM NL*, May 1980, 3-4.

[21] The Sarikei church first began as a Bible study group in 1975, which formed the nucleus of the church that was formally established in 1977. By June 1977, it had its first pastor in Winston Edip, a Bidayuh. See *BEM NL*, November 1978, 1.

[22] The region in the upper Rajang was later delineated as the Seventh Division, in which Kapit was the administrative centre. The Sibu SIB church had helped in ministering to the emerging group in Kapit. See *BEM NL*, August 1978, 4.

to the establishment of SIB churches there. The distinctive pattern of this work was the leadership role played by young professionals. In Kapit, the administrative centre for the upper Rajang, Third Division, Dr Bob Baru, a dentist, played a vital role in organizing the small group of individuals who were then meeting informally into a SIB church in 1977. In Lundu, a town in the First Division, two women teachers converted during their teacher training days in Kuching formed the core of the group there.[23] These groups of English-educated leaders played a vital leadership role in the emerging town churches throughout Sarawak.[24]

The pastors of the town churches at Kuching, Miri and Sibu were mainly OMF or BEM missionaries,[25] who had been exposed to the world of the ulu and the world of the town. From within the SIB leadership, there was initially no pastor who was suitably qualified to take charge of the English-speaking congregations of the urban churches or deal with the problems presented by the alternative culture and lifestyle of the towns, the social displacement and rootlessness of the young migrants and the need to understand the relevance of Christianity to city life. The pastoral care and guidance of the BEM/OMF pastors and lay leaders and the communal bond within the social life of the town churches served as a bulwark against the alternative culture and lifestyle of the towns, and also provided a sense of belonging and identity. But the problem of the relevance of Christianity to city life was helpfully alleviated by the presence of Christian graduate teachers and professionals from overseas who had come under the various voluntary organizations, such as the Voluntary Service Overseas (V.S.O.), Colombo Plan, Canadian University Volunteers and the Peace Corps, to work in the secondary schools in Sarawak, most of which were largely boarding schools.[26] In view of the dire shortage of qualified secondary school teachers in Sarawak resulting from the rapid expansion of schools in the 1960s and 1970s, they were warmly welcomed by the Sarawak government. It was reported that 'a number of committed Christians have come to Sarawak … in these capacities'. In addition, there were the 'fine Chinese brethren from Singapore and Malaya'.[27] The presence, friendship and counsel

---

[23] *BEM NL*, November 1978, 2.

[24] *BEM NL*, November 1978, 4; and May 1980, 3-4.

[25] The three missionary couples, Horsfalls, Nightingales and Newtons, 'each involved in a town pastorate' were appointed at the 'request of the leaders of the SIB who feel that they do not have an adequate number of qualified men to fill these positions'. See *BEM NL*, August 1977, 2. In reviewing the history of the BEM town ministry, Reasbeck stated that, 'The need of the SIB in the towns first brought BEM missionaries out of the *ulu* and at the request of the SIB for help for those people moving to the towns from interior churches'. See Colin Reasbeck, 'Town Ministry', in *BEM/OMF Conference Reports*, March 1975, 22. As for indigenous pastors (including women pastors) in the coastal towns, the SIB did not have any until 1980.

[26] *BEM NL*, February 1967, 2.

[27] *BEM NL*, October 1965, 4.

of these highly qualified teachers and government civil servants from overseas exercised a positive influence on the SIB members, assuring them that it was not incompatible to be a Christian and be highly educated, affirming the belief that Christianity is relevant to urban society. Further, the growing number of university graduates and professionals among the nationals bolstered their sense of confidence as Christians among their own communities. These pioneering batches of university graduates and professionals were held in high regard by their own communities, so that they exercised an unconscious impact on them, especially when they went out in outreach teams from the town churches to the longhouses or villages in the surrounding areas.[28]

From the mid-1970s, SIB evangelism focused more sharply on the other larger indigenous tribes, the Iban, Bidayuh and Melanau, in the sub-coastal and coastal regions. The urban drift in search of education and employment, the migration of people into the land resettlement and agricultural schemes, and improved communication systems, especially with the opening of new roads, brought the Orang Ulu into contact with other indigenous groups; for example, the Iban in the Marudi-Miri-Bintulu triangle,[29] in the areas covering Bintagor, Sarikei, Julau River and Entabai-Kanowit River and in the areas surrounding Kuching.[30] The result was a combination of initiatives by individual SIB members dovetailing with outreach teams from local SIB urban churches, teams of students from Miri Bible College, and the planned strategy of the BEM/SIB. For instance, from Miri, regular church planting trips and visits were made to groups in the palm oil estates along the Miri-Bintulu road, to the Iban longhouses in Batu Niah[31] and the Kayan villages along the Tubau River.[32] Specifically, teams from both the Miri Evangelical Church (MEC) and Miri Bible College (MBC) responded to an invitation to help the group at the Commonwealth Development Land Scheme at Mile 26, Miri-Bintulu Road by constructing a church building (known as Commonwealth Development Church) and providing them with a weekend pastor in David Kellawing Jok, then a student at MBC in 1977.[33] Also, new evangelistic efforts by both BEM missionaries and SIB pastors and individuals were directed at the Iban in the

---

28 Personal communication with Dr Jerip Susel, a Bidayuh medical doctor and a former SIB elder, at KEC.

29 Palm oil had continued to be an important part of the economy even until the 1990s. See 'Highlights of Mid Term Review of the Second Malaysia Plan, Sarawak', *SG*, 31 January 1974, 2-8. Work among the Iban was concentrated along the Bakong River in the Baram, the Niah River, and the agricultural schemes along the Miri-Bintulu road in the Fourth Division. See *BEM NL*, April 1965, 1; February 1975, 4; November 1978, 2; February 1979, 4.

30 *BEM NL*, May 1977, 1. The Iban outreach team consisted of eight Iban from Kuching Evangelical Church (KEC) doing longhouse visitation during the weekends twice a month.

31 *BEM NL*, February 1975, 4.

32 *BEM NL*, May 1976, 4; May 1977, 3.

33 *BEM NL*, November 1978, 2.

region encompassing Binatang (later known as Bintagor), Sarikei, the Julau River, the Entabai and Kanowit Rivers and Kapit in the Third Division,[34] and also at the Iban in Simanggang, the centre of the Second Division. Work among the Iban in Simanggang also had help from Iban Christians from the Kuching church.[35] For the work among the Melanau in Mukah, though the initiative to establish the church in 1977 came from a local teacher, help also came from students of MBC and the Sibu SIB church.[36] By 1979, the initiatives toward the planting and growth of the SIB churches among the Iban and other tribes were firmly in the hands of both the SIB pastors and young professionals from urban churches.

Education, Urban Lay Leadership and Pastoral Leadership in the SIB

The presence of a growing number of educated people in urban churches made it difficult for the SIB leadership to find suitably qualified pastors to work among them. From the mid-1960s, there was a slow but growing dichotomy between those who entered Bible school and those who entered tertiary colleges or universities. By the early 1970s, the best students from the SIB community were continuing their studies at university level, while those who were unable to do so entered Bible school to be SIB pastors. While the SIB pastors had no difficulty working among the Malay-speaking congregations in the urban churches or in rural churches, they faced a crisis of confidence among the more educated English-speaking congregation in the urban churches. Hence, the urban churches, though initially pastored by either BEM or OMF missionaries, became increasingly led by capable lay leaders.

This problem was partly exacerbated by the negative perception of Bible school training held by the English-educated section of the SIB who tended to believe that entry into the fulltime ministry was for those with low academic qualifications. The emerging pattern in the urban churches in the 1970s was the image of a capable professional who was able to spend time in active SIB evangelistic outreach or ministry within a local church without going through Bible college training. This became the preferable option as it allowed them to have an avenue for meaningful Christian service as well as enjoy the benefits of material wealth as professionals. The proposal from the churches in Bario in the Kelabit Highlands to set up a Bible school in that area was well intentioned, with the aim of providing school dropouts with skills that would help them to do productive work in the interior, thereby checking their migration to the

[34] *BEM NL*, May 1976, 2-3. Graeme Buntrock and his indigenous team visited the Iban longhouses in the region between the Julau, Entabai and Kanowit Rivers. George Pandong, an MBC student, from the Sarikei church had done extensive visitation among the longhouses between the Sibu-Binatang main road. See *BEM NL*, February 1979, 1-2.
[35] *BEM NL*, October 1972, 2. Simanggang had visits from two separate teams: the first by Colin Reasbeck with Iban from the Batu Niah church and the second team comprising Unak, Icha, Menin and George Jackson.
[36] *BEM NL*, May 1977, 2; November 1978, 3.

coastal towns.[37] But for these dropouts, a return to farm work had become an unattractive option, as they were perceived as failures. However, this kind of proposal also served to enhance the prejudices of those in the urban churches toward Bible school training, even though the setting up of this Bible school did not finally materialize.

There was a twofold attempt to produce SIB pastors who would be able to meet the needs of the urban churches and the rising level of literacy in Sarawak. Firstly, the priority among the BEM and SIB leadership was to select the most promising indigenous pastors for further training in Bible colleges overseas so that they could return to serve in the Bible schools, take charge of the town churches, or serve in the central SIB leadership.[38] However, the small number of such SIB pastors meant that most urban churches continued to be lay-led.

Secondly, there was a need to upgrade MBC to meet western standards of training. The aim of MBC was to provide training to meet the various needs within the SIB. These needs included pastors for the town churches in the English or Malay medium, trained evangelists and missionaries, youth leaders, Bible teachers and leaders who could also skillfully manage inter-church relations, and skilled leaders in handling correspondence courses and in handling personnel, operating an efficient office which included financial responsibilities.[39] Due to stringent immigration rules and personal factors among the missionaries, the BEM missionary-teachers were unable to serve at MBC for longer than a term of four years. The relatively quick turnover of BEM lecturers hastened the urgency to train a local group of leaders who could take over MBC. Despite the indigenisation process whereby SIB had a fully Malaysian staff by 1981,[40] MBC continued to produce SIB pastors who were more at ease working in the rural churches than in urban churches. The

[37] It was proposed that the Bible school with some agricultural training would orientate them back to rural life, so that they would not become 'wanderers in the towns' in search of the illusive 'good life'. See *BEM NL*, December 1968, p.1. A solution to the problem of school-dropout with two or three years of secondary education in Sarawak was 'to encourage a greater interest in the land and if possible to inculcate some practical knowledge of agriculture', as Sarawak was a rural economy based on three main crops, rubber, sago and pepper, and the dropouts could not be absorbed into government or European business occupations. See *SG*, April 1958, 56.

[38] *BEM Field Executive Minutes*, June 1975, 5. Among those who were sent to Bible colleges overseas, it was acknowledged that 'they are the best available for training but not the best in whole SIB'. See above in this chapter.

[39] *BEM Field Council Minutes*, 18-19 April 1975, 2. MBC was also intended to provide sufficient Bible training for those who could then continue further specialized training elsewhere.

[40] *BEM NL*, First Quarter 1985, 3. Elisa Paul was groomed for the Principalship, but he declined it in 1978 and later became a staffworker in 1980 with the Fellowship of Evangelical Students, working among East Malaysian students in tertiary colleges in Peninsular Malaysia. See *BEM Field Council Minutes*, 25-29 September 1978, 4. George Ngo Epoi was earmarked for further studies. *BEM NL*, February 1980, 4.

challenge that remained, involved long-term planning for progressive faculty development and upgrading of the level of training at MBC so as to attract better educated people into theological training and to produce pastors for both the rural and urban churches.[41]

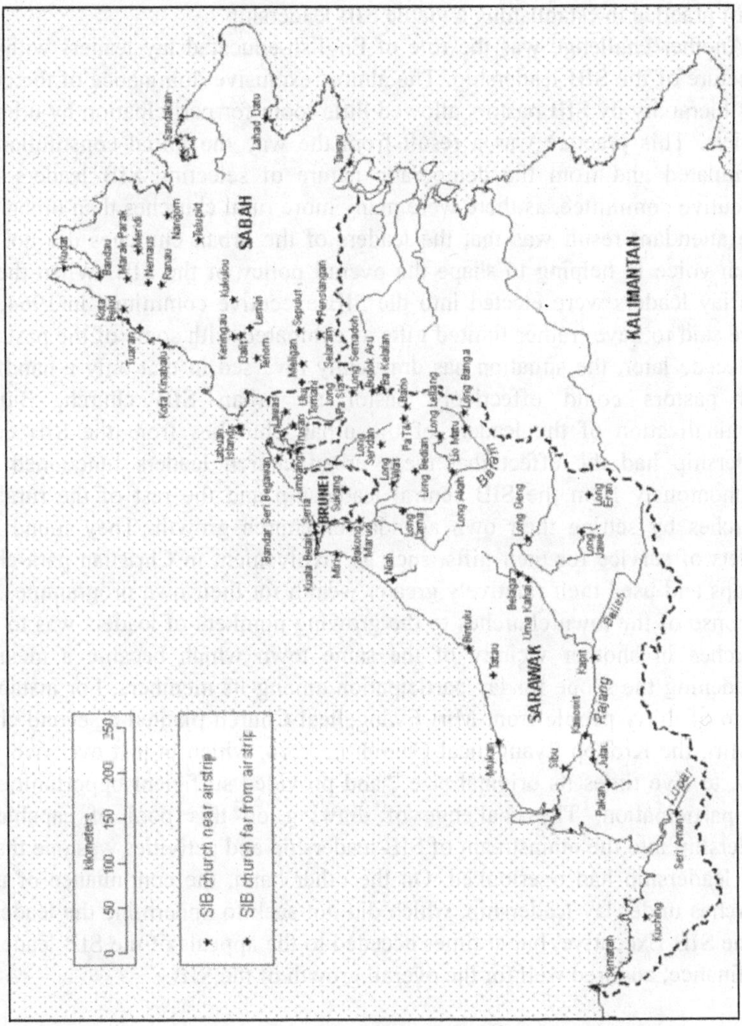

Map 7: Distribution of SIB churches in Sarawak and Sabah (1980)

[41] This issue is beyond the scope of this study.

In response to the needs of the town churches, the BEM Executive Council resolved in 1977 that 'any missionary holding the position of pastor in a town church should at the earliest opportunity delegate responsibility' to a local pastor or local leadership.[42] This decision was consistent with the pattern of BEM practice in establishing a viable SIB leadership.

Another challenge was the role of English-educated lay leaders within the structure of the SIB leadership. The almost exclusive dominance of the central SIB hierarchy by SIB pastors allowed little room for participation by urban lay leaders. This practice was a result from the way the initial constitution was formulated and from the democratic nature of selecting SIB leaders to its executive committee, as there were many more rural churches than urban ones. The attendant result was that the leaders of the urban churches did not have much voice in helping to shape the overall policy of the SIB. When the first two lay leaders were elected into the SIB executive committee in 1964, they were said to have 'rather limited gifts as compared with some of the pastors'.[43] A decade later, the situation has drastically reversed in that only a handful of SIB pastors could effectively pastor an urban SIB church. But the marginalization of the leaders of the urban churches from the SIB central leadership had the effect that these urban church leaders functioned quite autonomously from the SIB central leadership and the rest of the rural SIB churches by setting their own agenda for church growth. They found other outlets of service for their gifts, such as involvement in Christian para-church groups and used their relatively greater wealth for their own programmes. One response of the town churches to the growing numbers of leaders was to plant churches in another vicinity of the same town which became a means of broadening the scope for lay participation among its members. For instance, a group of thirty people from Miri Evangelical Church planted a second church in Miri, the Krokop Evangelical Church in 1984, which in just over two years grew to five times its original size,[44] and provided sufficient opportunities for lay participation. The challenge of drawing on this pool of capable lay leadership into the mainstream of SIB leadership and activities was one that the SIB leadership had overlooked. On the other hand, the continuance of urban churches under lay leadership, which did not seek to undermine the leadership of the SIB Executive, but at times acceded to the appeals of the SIB leadership for finance, augured well for the overall growth of the SIB.

---

[42] *BEM Council Minutes*, 19-23 September 1977, 5. Though the BEM merged with OMF in 1975, the BEM Executive Council continued to function until 1979.
[43] *BEM NL*, February 1964, 2. The sermons of these lay leaders were said to be often less profitable.
[44] *BEM NL*, Third Quarter, 1986, 2.

Between Two Worlds: The Economic Challenge

Although most SIB churches were still rural by 1980, there was a small but growing number of urban churches, so that the SIB had begun to operate across two economic worlds: one, agrarian and the other, an urban cash economy.[45] In the ulu or rural situation where subsistence farming and growing of cash crops continued,[46] the rural SIB churches were generally self-sufficient with the ability to build their own churches and support their pastors from the produce of their land, though their salaries were rather low. Their situation worsened when the 'inexorable exodus' of youths to the towns from the mid-1960s left the rural areas bereft of young people and their farms untended.[47]

A different situation prevailed in the urban SIB churches. Their numerical growth was matched by their material wealth, which was sufficient to finance their operational costs, but they still experienced difficulty in raising sufficient funds to erect church buildings that had to conform to more exacting building standards. According to Balan Seling, the vice-president of SIB, in 1966, 'it is comparatively easy for SIB to manage its own affairs in the Ulu but much more difficult in the towns, for instance, for two years, SIB have collected money to build a church at Marudi'. The need for a church building was urgent, but only a third of what was needed had been collected. According to Balan, 'SIB had been backward in mentioning their financial needs to the BEM' so as not 'to upset the indigenous principles of the BEM'. But he suggested that 'foreign aid' would not necessarily weaken the SIB.[48] Further, the BEM policy of providing no financial support for the SIB represented the other extreme to the policy of the Methodist Church, which built churches solely from mission funds for the Iban. He then requested whether BEM could on behalf of SIB mention the needs of the SIB churches to the supporters of the BEM in the home countries, suggesting that 'some Christians in Australia and England might like to specifically pray for and give to the SIB as distinct from BEM'.[49] Beyond the mention of the lack of prayer on the part of the BEM for the financial needs of the SIB and the need for both BEM and SIB to trust in the Lord, there was no commitment from the BEM in response to the request from the SIB. However, a practical initiative was taken to assist the town churches by the BEM. In December 1970, a New Zealand team of twenty builders and

---

[45] There were only 16 town churches in comparison with 237 rural churches in 1985. See *BEM NL*, First Quarter, 1985, 3.

[46] In other words, the cash economy was in the rural areas also.

[47] Joachim Ulok Laeng, 'The Inexorable Exodus', *SG*, 31 March 1974, 49-50. The young people returned to a warm welcome during festive occasions, on short trips of vacation or to attend to personal family matters, and they brought with them new ideas from the towns and gifts in the form of material resources or cash for their family members.

[48] *Combined BEM/SIB Executive Minutes*, 27 October 1966, 9-10.

[49] *Combined BEM/SIB Executive Minutes*, 27 October 1966, 15.

technicians was invited by the BEM to help build the SIB church at Marudi.[50] In the case of the churches in Kuching and Miri, the BEM raised the funds for both these projects mainly from BEM supporters overseas, purchasing a bungalow as a church in Kuching which was also used to house a missionary couple in 1974.[51] As these were considered BEM projects, there was justification for the use of mission funds; hence not contradicting the BEM policy of providing funds directly for SIB work.

This situation was to change somewhat after the merger of BEM with OMF in 1975. The OMF had a definite financial policy of assisting national churches to erect church buildings, and it was acceptable to OMF to have a centrally-operated revolving church fund from which individual churches could borrow. Further, Rev. Denis Lane, Overseas Director of the OMF, felt that particular help should be given for SIB church buildings in towns.[52] When the SIB set up their Central Church Building Revolving Fund with help from OMF, this Fund was to provide for not more than two-thirds of the cost of the church building and the remaining third was to be raised by the local church.[53] This scheme encouraged a spate of modern church buildings in the towns from the mid-1980s, which helped to project a modern urban image of the SIB. For example, Kuching Evangelical Church (KEC) in 1985 had an average attendance of three hundred and fifty each Sunday, of whom only forty per cent came from an SIB background and most of whom were English-educated professional people.[54] The numerical growth of the urban SIB churches had economic implications for the whole SIB, since not only the leadership gifts but also the material resources of these town churches could be made available to assist SIB in their programmes of outreach, church planting and leadership development. But this largely remained an untapped resource. It was the resources of the town

---

[50] *BEM NL*, April 1971, 1-2.

[51] *BEM Field Executive Minutes*, 6-17 October 1972, 3. See also *BEM NL*, February 1974, 1.

[52] The following reasons were cited: a) the SIB consists largely of rural people who have slender resources of cash; b) the SIB can and does provide all the church buildings in the rural areas, but the churches in the towns need to conform to a certain standard; c) town churches are needed to retain an educated leadership and to present an appropriate image before the community; d) the growth of the SIB has a very particular significance for future development of the country; e) the number of such buildings are limited; and f) in the case where a church building has been erected with foreign money as in one of the larger churches in Sarawak, this has encouraged and not hindered national leadership. See *Minutes of meeting of BEM Council with OMF Overseas Director and Homeside Representatives*, 23 September 1976.

[53] *BEM Council Minutes*, 27 February and 1 March 1979.

[54] *BEM NL*, Fourth Quarter 1985, 3. When KEC first started in 1969, it had a Sunday attendance of 30 people. By 1974, it had doubled to 60 and most of the congregation had just left school and were in training as nurses, teachers and technicians. By 1985, these professionals include doctors, engineers, accountants, teachers, nurses, office workers and students. See *BEM NL*, February 1970, 3; February 1974, 1.

churches that helped SIB to be more self-supporting and also helped it to straddle an agrarian economy and the emerging national economy. By 1979, the SIB was just beginning this process of transition to becoming a church in the modern world.

Political Challenges and the SIB/BEM in Sarawak

The formation of Malaysia in 1963 brought a number of new political developments into Sarawak with implications for the BEM and SIB. These included the electoral process and party politics, Malaysianization and the ten-year immigration ruling, the Malay language as the medium of instruction, the special rights of the Orang Ulu as bumiputras, and the status of Islam and Islamization.

The Electoral Process and the Orang Ulu

The development of a modern Sarawak and the formation of Malaysia in 1963 exposed the Orang Ulu to involvement in politics.[55] The attitude of the BEM leadership to political involvement by SIB members was cautiously negative in 1963. But the BEM newsletter in June 1963 reported that the leadership nevertheless realized that the situation which the SIB faced 'was totally different' from that which the missionaries 'had been familiar with in their home countries'. Alan Belcher conceded that it 'could be right temporarily' for the SIB leaders to be involved in politics provided that 'SIB was convinced that the Lord was leading them',[56] but left the final decision to the SIB leadership. In this situation, according to Tagal Paran, the SIB decided against the advice of the BEM,[57] so that what was reported in the June 1963 BEM newsletter was a way of rationalizing the actions of the SIB to their Christian constituencies in their home countries.

The Orang Ulu were drawn into politics, firstly, out of necessity, and secondly, as a response to the perceived threat regarding the loss of religious freedom in Sarawak.[58] A third factor was the necessity to have representatives to look after their communal welfare. In 1963, the Lun Bawang were the dominant Orang Ulu sub-group in the SIB and provided them with key leaders, who were either community leaders or the most educated people among them.

---

[55] See Porritt, *British Colonial Rule*, 101-103. The June 1963 elections, the first of its kind in Sarawak, provided Sarawak with a ministerial government before Malaysia was formed on 16 September 1963.

[56] *BEM NL*, June 1963, 1. Belcher believed that 'the principal leader of the Church should not be involved in politics, but under present circumstances it could be right temporarily'.

[57] Interview with Tagal Paran, 22 September 2004.

[58] The SIB leader, Balan Seling observed that 'there is more religious freedom in Sarawak and British North Borneo (Sabah) than in Malaya' and that 'religious freedom of the past will be threatened by the Federation'. See *BEM NL*, June 1963, 1.

So the SIB church leadership unanimously chose Racha Umong, the SIB President, to contest the 1963 elections for the State Legislature as an independent candidate.

Coming from a relatively 'sheltered' political environment and being unschooled in the machinations of democratic party politics, the intention of the SIB leaders to be involved in politics was noble but the perception of their potential influence was, at times, a bit naïve. The reply of the SIB to the initial objections of the BEM about SIB leaders' involvement in politics seemed idealistic. It argued that (a) the SIB representative would not be a member of any political party, which would overcome the problem of adequately serving those of his flock who favoured a different party; (b) the SIB representative would only take up this extra sphere of service temporarily; and (c) politics was not time-consuming nor was there any monetary remuneration.[59] In reality, each of these answers was proven wrong as the harsh reality of politics dictated that alignment with a political party was a necessity, and once in politics, it was difficult to extricate oneself from it, an admission made by Racha Umong during the Combined BEM/SIB Executive Meeting in October 1966.[60] It also was not only time-consuming but had accompanying perks that befitted a State assemblyman or Parliamentarian, including monetary remuneration, many times more than what an SIB pastor could earn. After the 1963 local elections, Racha Umong, though initially an independent candidate, joined the indigenous party, Party Pesaka Anak Sarawak (PESAKA) led by Temenggong Jugah, the leader of the Iban in the Third Division and whose leadership was mainly made up of indigenous (mostly Iban) communal leaders.[61] But by the next election in 1970, SIB members were generally divided between those belonging to PESAKA and those belonging to the Sarawak National Party (SNAP). The situation arose that two SIB leaders, Racha Umong (PESAKA) and Pudun Rangat (SNAP), stood against each other for the Lawas state seat among three

---

59 *BEM NL*, June 1963, 1.

60 Racha Umong admitted that 'as an independent candidate of Council Negeri, no one takes notice. The BEM have said it is better for me not to be in a party, but to be outside a party is to be pushed this way and that way. Once you are in you have committed yourself. Previously, Balan and I wanted to form one party, then we had to choose one of two parties. The party Balan has joined has separated from the government...If Balan and I are in separate parties, although the two of us may have good fellowship together, the members of our parties will later push us to oppose one another. This may lead to division in the church'. See *Combined BEM/SIB Executive Minutes*, 27 October 1966, 15.

61 PESAKA was known as a party of the *penghulus* or 'aristocrats', and Racha Umong himself was a former *penghulu*. So, it is understandable for him to join PESAKA instead of Sarawak National Party (SNAP), the ruling indigenous party, whose leaders were from the ranks of the commoners but whose membership was appreciably better educated than those in PESAKA. See Michael Leigh, *The Rising Moon: Political Change in Sarawak* (Sydney: Sydney University Press, 1974), 36-37.

other contestants, with the result that neither was elected.[62] This situation served to underline the division within the SIB leadership and church. For a decade from 1966 to 1975, there was a period of strong anti-Federal feelings in Sarawak in view of what was perceived as Federal intrusion into the politics of Sarawak. This led to a division among SIB members between those on the side of the ruling government, including those appointed by PESAKA or government as town councillors or as penghulu, and those on the side of the opposition party SNAP, which constituted a larger number.[63] Sensing this cleavage within the SIB, the SIB leadership resolved that it was better for SIB pastors not to be directly involved in politics,[64] disallowing any SIB pastor from active participation in politics.[65] So, at the December 1967 SIB Conference Racha Umong declined election for the post of SIB president, citing among other reasons that he had been long enough in that position and also explained the problems of simultaneously being the SIB president and a member of Council Negeri.[66] Similarly, in 1967, Balan Seling resigned as vice-president when he decided to enter politics and he later became the state assemblyman for Baram.[67] The BEM newsletter later reported that these two changes in the SIB leadership resulted from the leaders' involvement in politics, a reference to Racha Umong and Balan Seling.

---

[62] SNAP, another indigenous (also mostly Iban) party, was originally the ruling party but disagreement with the Federal government led to its exclusion from the Government coalition. In the 1970 election, Racha Umong lost, but he was appointed to chair the Lawas district council. However, two SIB candidates stood under SNAP, and one under the Sarawak United People's Party (SUPP). Two won their State seats: Balan Seling (SNAP) for the Baram, Nyipa (SUPP) for Belaga and one candidate, Luhat Wan (SNAP) won the Federal seat of Baram. See Leigh, *The Rising Moon*, 211-12 and *BEM NL*, October 1970, 3.

[63] Pastor Bagul Luping of Lower Trusan and Giso Agong of Long Tuma, Lawas, were made *penghulu*. See *BEM NL*, October 1973, 4. Of the five SIB people who contested the 1970 election, three were with SNAP, one with SUPP and one with PESAKA. During this period (1966-75), SNAP was in the Sarawak opposition. After the 1974 election, the success of SNAP led to its acceptance into the ruling *Barision Nasional* (BN) or National Front Government. See Peter Searle, *Politics in Sarawak, 1970-1976: The Iban Perspective* (Singapore: Oxford University Press, 1983), 184-95.

[64] Balan Seling himself said that it was not good for SIB pastors to be in politics; rather, if a pastor 'is called to politics, then let him go into it completely…but it is difficult to do both'. Balan Seling has urged Racha Umong to choose between politics or church and 'if Racha chooses politics', it was recognized that 'there will be political parties in the SIB'. See *Combined BEM/SIB Executive Minutes*, 27 October 1966, 15.

[65] 'The SIB is not a political organization. As such, it does not engage in political activities. Its members…as loyal and responsible citizens of Malaysia are encouraged to participate fully in the life and development of the nation in righteousness and integrity…. SIB full-time workers may not engage in party politics unless they first resign from their church responsibilities'. See *Sidang Injil Borneo Handbook and Rules*, 65.

[66] *BEM NL*, February 1968, 1-2.

[67] *BEM NL*, April 1967, 1.

> This period (of the 1960s) has been marked by several big upheavals in the historical experience of the country: ... the attaining of independence within the context of the new nation of Malaysia, the emergence of political parties. All these have tended to threaten the equilibrium of the people and bring with dramatic suddenness new challenges and temptations into their traditional life patterns. The two changes in SIB leadership in this decade were not unrelated to the above factors.[68]

Even in this news report, a sense of disappointment by the BEM leadership in the 1960s about the loss of two outstanding SIB leaders to politics may still be detected, which was indicative of a negative attitude towards political involvement by SIB leaders at that time.

By 1969, there was an 'over concern with politics' among SIB church members, according to Tagal Paran, the then SIB vice-president.[69] This was a euphemistic reference to the campaigning during the 1970 election, which caused some division among SIB members over political alignments.[70] It soon became accepted that there would be different political views among SIB members. In taking care not to allow these differences to distract them from their mission as a Church, the SIB leadership heeded the earlier advice of the BEM leadership that in principle, 'the leader of the Church should not be involved in politics'.[71] Racha Umong and Balan Seling, who became involved in politics, held their offices as president and vice-president of SIB respectively until 1967.[72] In keeping a separation between holding church office and political office at the same time, the SIB became more focused, concentrating on its church planting and evangelistic activities, which, in turn, were fueled by the flame of revival from late 1973 to 1976.[73]

Though the two SIB leaders in politics represented different political parties, they were surprisingly able to put aside political differences when it came to promoting the cause of the SIB church. Further, their relationship with the SIB remained warm and cordial, being present when invited to important occasions of both the BEM and SIB. As for Balan Seling, even when he was a Sarawak state assemblyman, he continued to preach in SIB churches and also acted as

---

[68] *BEM NL*, August 1970, 3. In 1974, there was another change in leadership when Racha Umong was re-elected as a Federal Member of Parliament in August 1974. See *BEM NL*, November 1974, 1.

[69] *BEM NL*, October 1969, 1.

[70] Earlier Alan Belcher had written to Harold McCracken saying, 'There is a great need to pray as party politics is presenting great problems to the Church'. Letter of A. Belcher to H. McCracken, 20 November, 1964 (OMF).

[71] See *BEM NL*, June 1963, 1. Though SIB allowed Racha Umong to be involved temporarily in both church leadership and politics in 1963, it became unwise to continue the practice when Balan Seling, the Vice-Chairman, stood as a candidate in the opposition party, SNAP, for the 1970 election.

[72] *BEM NL*, February 1966, 3; February 1968, 2.

[73] See Chapter 7.

interpreter for Dr Petrus Octavianus during the 1973 convention at Long Atip among the Kayan.[74] Further, he provided the necessary spiritual discernment, advice and guidance as a corrective to some of the excesses during the time of the Bario revival in 1973, through his personal presence in Bario and his letters of advice to SIB pastors, leaders and members from 1974 to 1976.[75] As for Racha Umong, when he lost in the 1970 State elections, he returned to an active role as SIB president again for one year only before becoming pastor of the Lawas Church and adviser to the SIB,[76] and he continued to travel extensively on preaching and teaching trips among the churches for a short time. The conduct of both these politicians was exemplary as they generally refrained from using church activities as a political forum and to divide the church any further, recognising that their party members might want them to oppose each other.[77] Interestingly, both these leaders showed themselves to be examples of Christian statesmanship, unity and service for the work of the SIB. In view of their example and stature in the SIB communities, their combined influence helped the work of the SIB to continue without much hindrance till the departure of the BEM from Sarawak.[78]

The attitude of the BEM leadership towards the involvement of SIB members in politics became more favourable from the mid-1960s as new missionaries joined the BEM at that time.[79] In the 1968 BEM newsletter, Colin Reasbeck, a BEM missionary from Britain, wrote about the changes that were taking place in Sarawak and argued that 'there was nothing unhealthy' about church leaders leaving the ranks of church leadership for politics as there was a need for Christians to be 'in leading positions in Sarawak and Sabah in twenty or thirty years' time'. His article implied the need for both BEM and SIB to

---

[74] Bulan and Bulan-Dorai, *The Bario Revival*, 101. *BEM NL*, June 1973, 3.

[75] Interview with Balan Seling, 29 July 2005. Bulan gives details of Balan Seling's ministry during the Bario revival especially that of Balan's caution against the excesses of the 'new practices', such as dancing in the Spirit, hugging and embracing each other in 'brotherly love' (especially between the sexes), loud, long and domineering prayers, uncontrolled gestures and movements during worship, indiscreet exposure of sin and indiscreet confession of sins, especially of adultery. See Bulan and Bulan-Dorai, *The Bario Revival*, 101-105, 185-96.

[76] *BEM NL*, February 1971, 2; August 1973, 3. Racha Umong was SIB President for 1971.

[77] See *Combined BEM/SIB Executive Minutes*, 27 October 1966.

[78] It is arguable but speculative that the departure of Balan Seling and Racha Umong from the SIB leadership did hinder the rate of transfer of responsibilities from the BEM to the SIB. But they continued to exercise some influence through their appointment as SIB Advisors. Balan Seling continues to be one till today.

[79] The new missionaries from Great Britain included Dr W.E. (Bill) Hawes, Iain and Beatrice Clayre, Margaret Bradley (later Margaret Reasbeck), Sheila McLeod and Viola Taeni, and later Colin Reasbeck. The new missionaries from Australia included Rev. Bob Burton, Ken Coleman, George Jackson and Keith and Marion Baker. See *BEM NL*, June 1964, 1; June 1967, 1.

have a proper Christian perspective on politics so that Christianity in Sarawak could take the initiative in making an impact on the political history of the country. Otherwise, in Reasbeck's interpretation, Christianity would face a similar situation to post-war Britain where it initially provided leaders such as Ernest Bevin, Britain's Foreign Secretary, but with Bevin's conversion to socialism, socialism took over the lead and became a major influence in the country.[80] This paper represented the thinking of a more progressive wing in the BEM that at least legitimized participation in politics by SIB members. The concern was that committed SIB Christians should make their contribution to the country through politics, assuming that those who entered politics would maintain close links with the Church and promote its cause, which Balan Seling did after he became a state assemblyman in 1970 and later State Minister for Local Housing. However, the unaddressed issue was the formulation of a Christian perspective on politics, and this was no simple task. But within both BEM and SIB circles, there was no expertise to provide sufficient guidance or any support system for those involved in politics. Their lack of expertise in the political arena and the suddenness with which they were thrust into the electoral process meant that the SIB needed time to formulate a Christian perspective on politics, a task which proved so difficult that their response to politics was ad hoc and pragmatic.

Malaysianization and the Ten-Year Immigration Ruling

The issue of Malaysianization of the civil service in Sarawak was a contentious issue between the Federal and State governments. Not having enough local people to assume the jobs in the civil service, which were then performed by British expatriates, the first Sarawak Chief Minister, Kalong Ningkan, tried to retain them for as long as possible until suitably qualified Bornean candidates could replace them. The general belief among the indigenous people was that expatriates were more likely to protect their interests than West Malaysians. But the Federal government wanted to speed up the process of Malaysianization, which in effect meant replacing expatriates with Peninsular Malaysians. So, when the next new State government took office in 1966, the removal of all the top expatriate officers in the administration was effected within a year.[81]

In line with Malaysianization, an immigration ruling was issued, putting a ten-year limit on the residence of all Christian missionaries in Malaysia with effect from 1 January 1967. This move was interpreted by some Christians as the federal government's 'measure to restrict Christian mission work among the

[80] *BEM NL*, June 1968, 4. The issue here is not whether Colin Reasbeck's analysis of British politics is accurate, but that his view had an impact on the BEM.

[81] The second Chief Minister was Tawi Sli (1966-1970). See Leigh, *The Rising Moon*, 99-102, 107, 113.

interior natives'[82] and increased Christian fears that restrictive federal measures on their freedom of worship would follow. The government had sent a message to the Christian mission bodies that their days in the country would end in the foreseeable future.

The urgency of the situation led to the formulation of the 'twin tasks' in 1972 and also spurred the BEM and SIB leadership to select the most promising indigenous pastors for further training in Bible colleges overseas so that they could return to serve in key positions in the Bible schools, the town churches or the central SIB leadership.[83] Among them were Elisa Paul who went to All Nations Christian College (ANCC) in England; Kalip Besar and Winston Edip to the Bible College of South Australia; Gerawat Maran to the Bible College of Victoria, (formerly known as MBI), Australia, and George Ngo Epoi to Asia Theological Seminary in the Philippines.[84] They returned to be leaders in the SIB Executive Council.[85] One served as pastor to a town church and another on the staff of MBC.[86] This move, in effect, helped to groom the next generation of key SIB leadership.

In contemplating its future in Sarawak as a result of the ten-year ruling, the BEM Field Executive first considered the possibility of integration with OMF just prior to the revival. This matter of a merger with the OMF was later raised at the BEM Field Conference in 1972, but its discussion was overshadowed by the discussion on redefining the tasks of the BEM in Sarawak, which resulted in the formulation of the policy of the 'Twin Tasks', and necessitated a re-examination of the resources of the Mission.[87] It soon became clear that the whole future of the BEM was to be viewed in the light of the fact that all its missionaries would have to leave Sarawak by 1977, raising the grim possibility of the closure of BEM as a Mission. By the end of January 1973, Dr Bill Hawes, the BEM Field Chairman, then on leave at ANCC considered the possibility of a closer working relationship with the OMF and met with Dr Michael Griffiths, General Director of the OMF, who was then visiting ANCC. This preliminary meeting led to further discussion first with Rev. Denis Lane, Overseas Director of the OMF in Singapore, and later with Mr Ben Draper in Lawas, when he was visiting OMF personnel in Sarawak in March 1973.

---

82 Gordon P. Means, *Malaysian Politics* (London: Hodder & Stoughton, 1976 [1970]), 372.

83 *BEM Council Minutes*, 6-10 June 1975. Those sent were 'the best available for training but not the best in the whole SIB'.

84 *BEM NL*, 50th Anniversary Issue 1978, 4. See also *BEM Council Minutes*, 27 February and 2 March 1979, 1.

85 Gerawat Maran and Kalip Besar later served as SIB Presidents. Elisa Paul was in the SIB Executive and also as lecturer in MBC for a short time.

86 Winston Edip was first pastor at the Sarikei SIB church and later became lecturer at MBC. George Ngo Epoi became the first indigenous Principal of MBC in 1985. MBC is now known as Malaysia Evangelical College (MEC).

87 *BEM NL*, August 1972, 1-3.

Subsequently, the BEM Field Executive presented a paper on the matter and a revised version was circulated among the BEM missionaries. The BEM Australian Council was also notified for its feedback before the BEM Field Conference, which gave its endorsement for the merger of BEM with OMF on 28 March 1974.[88] This merger was effected in 1975 so that the OMF was able to continue the work of the BEM for a few more years after its termination when Dr Bill Hawes, the BEM Field Director left Sarawak in 1979.[89] In short, the ten-year ruling provided the impetus for the merger of BEM with OMF in 1975. Its rationale was to allow OMF to deploy some of its experienced missionaries to work in Sarawak so as to provide continuity of personnel and potential leadership resources for as long as was possible. For instance, when Dr Bill Hawes left Sarawak in May 1979, Brian Michell, an OMF missionary to Indonesia, provided the leadership continuity in the transition from BEM to OMF. The merger also enabled BEM missionaries who were leaving Malaysia to continue service in Southeast Asia in other OMF fields,[90] and it was hoped that new missionaries from the OMF could replace the expected loss of the BEM missionaries. But the government's insistence on Malayanisation offered little hope of any prolonged stay of new missionaries,[91] and this finally led to the closure of BEM's work in Sarawak in 1979.

The strict implementation of the ten-year ruling by the Malaysian government signalled the reality that the SIB would have to continue without the presence of BEM missionaries.[92] As the BEM's commitment to establish

---

[88] *BEM Field Executive Minutes*, 2-5 April 1974. Appended as Appendix A is 'The Joint Statement of BEM and OMF in Integration Move'. *BEM NL*, June 1974, 1.

[89] The work of the BEM in Sabah and Sarawak became part of the overall work of the OMF, and after 1975, the BEM Field Chairman became known as the Area Director of East Malaysia, OMF.

[90] *BEM NL*, May 1978, 1. Thelma Johnson was redirected to the Philippines.

[91] Missionary work had come under very close government scrutiny; the BEM observed that 'some types of activity are evidently not favoured for expatriate missionaries, for instance translation of the Scriptures and youth work'. See *Area Director's Field Report to the Australian Conference*, April 1975 and East Malaysia Area Director's Report 1976 (Progress since 1973). Even Peninsular Malaysian Christians were subject to the ten-year immigration ruling. In the *BEM Council Minutes*, 12-22 July 1976, 1, it is noted that 'there has been a stricter application of the existing rulings. Localisation is being insisted on wherever possible'. Questions about the 'ordination' of its missionaries had also been raised.

[92] The BEM Council was informed that the Malaysian Immigration did not allow any replacements for missionaries who have completed their ten-year stay in Sarawak. But replacements were possible for those missionaries who have not completed their ten-year period, provided those replacing them continued in the same work for the remainder of that ten-year period. See *BEM Council Minutes*, 5 December 1977, 2. Two missionary couples, the Nightingales and the Jacksons, and three single women missionaries, Susan Hallmark, Sheila McLeod and Marion Gill, had their visas terminated. The application for a missionary couple and two single women missionaries as replacements were not approved. See *BEM NL*, August 1976, 1.

and prepare SIB 'to stand on its own feet' began as early as 1939, which led to the establishment of SIB with a formal ecclesial structure in 1959, there had been sufficient time to prepare itself to become a truly 'Three-Self' Church. A drawback was the loss of friendship, support and advice from the BEM missionaries, though missionaries such as the Lees, the Reasbecks and Alf Tharratt continued to visit them for as long as their health permitted or their situation allowed. However, the SIB was compensated by the presence of the few OMF missionaries in the town churches for a short period of time, and later, links were made with evangelical churches in Peninsular Malaysia and the NECF that helped SIB become an integral part of the pan-Malaysian evangelical community in the mid-1980s.

The Malay Language as the Medium of Instruction

The use of English as the medium of education for all government schools in Sarawak began in 1961 and the subsequent changeover to the Malay language in 1976 had a dichotomizing effect on rural Sarawak society with a spill-over effect on the SIB. The SIB churches welcomed the implementation of the national language policy as they had already been using Malay together with vernacular languages in their church activities. Within Orang Ulu society, the older people and school dropouts among the indigenous people were more fluent in the vernacular and Malay, in addition to the rural school children who began schooling after 1975. However, a sizeable number of urban SIB members were English-speaking as a result of the influence of English education since 1961 and had also become bilingual or trilingual. This dichotomizing effect divided Sarawak society into the English-speaking elite and the Malay- and vernacular-speaking working class in the urban centres.

When BEM/SIB started work in the major towns such as Miri and Kuching to which the Orang Ulu had been migrating, the Orang Ulu congregated into two separate linguistic groups, (that is, English-speaking and Malay-speaking) usually at different geographical locations, as in the case at Kuching. At Miri, however, the two groups met in the same building, but held separate services at different times catering to their different linguistic needs. This was a pragmatic response of the BEM and the SIB to a difficult situation, realizing that many SIB Malay-speaking members had difficulties with English, though 'in fact quite a number freely interchange between the two services'.[93] Interestingly, the English-speaking congregation began to attract other ethnic groups, including the Chinese, who were not fluent in Malay, so that it was difficult just to have one single congregation to cater for the needs of everyone. In time as both congregations grew, it became an entrenched practice to have linguistically separate congregations, each having a separate leadership in the urban centres. The natural development of the homogeneous grouping of people, whether because of geographical or linguistic factors, within each congregation was an

[93] *BEM NL*, August 1977, 3.

aid toward evangelism. The homogenous unit principle of church growth as advocated by Donald McGavran of Fuller Theological Seminary was then influential in evangelical circles and made such a practice acceptable.[94]

Among SIB churches, the use of the Alkitab (Indonesian Bible) was the norm.[95] But the free use and distribution of the Alkitab was viewed with grave concern by the Federal government, which led to the prohibition of not only the Alkitab in 1981 but also of the use of certain words in the Malay language by the Christian community.[96] This issue has remained a thorny issue, and its discussion goes beyond the scope of this study.[97]

Special Rights of Orang Ulu as Bumiputras

The system of 'special privileges' for the Malays in Peninsular Malaysia was also extended to the Malays and indigenous people in Sabah and Sarawak; they are collectively known as bumiputras.[98] With the implementation of the New Economic Policy (NEP) in 1970, the bumiputras, especially the Malays, became the main beneficiaries, though the other indigenous people of East Malaysia were not neglected.[99] The decades of the 1970s and 1980s saw the opening of many job opportunities for the bumiputras, including the Orang Ulu, in both the public and private sectors especially in the urban areas. The award of Federal and State scholarships to the bumiputras for studies in institutions of higher learning in Peninsular Malaysia from 1970 onwards was a major source of their upward social mobility, creating within two decades a significant group of middle-class workers and professionals and also firmly entrenching them into the national economy. Economic prosperity increased the material resources of these people, which they were willing to use for evangelistic

---

[94] Donald McGavran had advocated the homogenous unit principle for church growth, which was widely adopted in evangelical missions from the 1960s until the early 1980s.

[95] The Malay language and the Indonesian language are very similar. The *Alkitab* has been the Bible used by the *Orang Ulu*.

[96] Chew, *The Journey of the Catholic Church*, 279-81. There were originally 36 forbidden words.

[97] Representations made by the Malaysian churches as a whole in the 1980s led to a partial lifting of the ban but limiting the distribution of the *Alkitab* to specific distribution outlets and the reduction of the forbidden words to four. Despite this unsatisfactory situation, the SIB has continued to use the Alkitab for its church activities and evangelism, arguing that it is unconstitutional to ban the Holy Book of another person's religion and that as a matter of principle, no government has the right to forbid anyone from using any word in any language. The Federal government has, thus far, turned a blind eye, as long as the *Alkitab* was not perceived as being used in evangelism among the Malays.

[98] *Bumiputra* literally means 'son of the soil' or the indigenous people.

[99] The NEP with a two prong aim of eradicating poverty irrespective of race and the restructuring of society to eliminate identification of economic function with race, had specific targets for *bumiputra* ownership (30% of corporate share capital) and employment in the private sector.

outreach, especially to unevangelized tribes. For instance, a group of Lun Bawang churches collected a sizeable amount of money which was handed over to the SIB for outreach to the Melanau in Mukah.[100] Also, during the Bario revival of 1973, the members of the preaching teams from Bario had just received arrears in their salaries so that they were able to use this resource to finance various preaching teams that reached across the length of Sarawak.[101] It is significant that as a predominantly bumiputra church, most SIB members can lay claim to bumiputra privileges and it remains to be seen how the SIB will make further use of these privileges enjoyed by its members for their work.[102]

However, the Sarawak Foundation, which was established in 1971, also sponsored Form One students to study in Peninsular Malaysian schools. Students from a number of Orang Ulu families, (mostly Christian ones) were placed under the charge of Malay-Muslim foster parents or in boarding schools reserved for Malay students during the time of their study in Peninsular Malaysia with attempts to Islamize them.[103] Initially, SIB was unaware of this intention and made no response, but it later tried to discourage Orang Ulu parents from accepting the scholarships for secondary education but only to send their children over to Peninsular Malaysia for tertiary education;[104] a move which was not wholly successful.

Islam and Islamization

Though Sabah and Sarawak agreed to accept Islam as the official religion of Malaysia, there were provisions that placed some limits on the influence of Islam in these states. Of note were the stipulations that federal financial aid to Muslim institutions in these states was prohibited unless approved by the Yang Di-Pertua Negara (Governor); and federal funds, which in other states were grants in the support of Islam, were to be donated instead to general social

---

[100] *BEM NL*, December 1970, 2.

[101] *BEM NL*, April 1974, 3.

[102] Though there were Chinese members in the SIB town churches, there was no Chinese pastor in Kuching before 1980 nor were there any other Chinese-speaking SIB churches outside Lawas. Until 1980, the only Chinese-speaking church in Lawas continued to exist alongside but outside the SIB ecclesial structure. Hence, the SIB was predominantly a *bumiputra* church.

[103] The concern was expressed that many of the youths who had completed their primary or secondary schools were being 'led astray in boarding schools'. *BEM NL*, June 1972, 3. Interview with Gerawat Maran, the former SIB President of Sarawak, (1988-2001) on 23 September 2004. The children under Malay foster parents were given the songkok and prayer mats.

[104] Interview with Gerawat Maran, 23 September 2004. With regards to the children who were already in boarding schools, links were made with particular Peninsular Malaysian churches in the mid-1980s onwards to request help to care for the children concerned. Part of a long-term solution came with the aspiration of Sarawak to have its own university; a move which SIB Assemblymen had no difficulty supporting so that in time, UNIMAS, the university in Sarawak became a reality.

welfare purposes.[105] Also, any state law intended to restrict non-Muslims proselytizing Muslims required a two-thirds majority in the State Legislative Assembly.[106] The Islamic resurgence in Peninsular Malaysia, which fuelled the process of Islamization in Peninsular Malaysia from the mid-1970s onwards and gained momentum in the decade of the 1980s,[107] did not affect Sarawak to the same extent. As the Muslim population in Sarawak was in a minority, the process of Islamization in Sarawak has been slower, but nonetheless created concern among the Christian denominations in Sarawak in the 1970s.[108] The process of Islamization, which included instilling Islamic values into the federal governmental administration, and the establishment of Shariah courts alongside the civil court system and Islamic banking in the 1980s, had some spillover effect into Sarawak.[109] A side effect of the Islamization process in Malaysia was to impel the SIB to become part of the National Evangelical Christian Fellowship (NECF), so as to be part of a united Christian voice in making representation to the government.

In 1972, there was a government-sponsored attempt to convert the new settlement of Kayan in Long Busang, Belaga, (where twelve Kayan longhouses had moved from Indonesia to Long Busang), by promising them the necessary amenities and privileges, which resulted in some two hundred conversions to Islam. In response, the SIB sent two pastors to Long Busang, Belaga, and over a number of years contributed to re-converting most of them back to

---

105 Means, *Malaysian Politics*, 372.

106 *Malaysia, Agreement Concluded between the United Kingdom of Great Britain and Northern Ireland, the Federation of Malaya, North Borneo and Singapore* (London: HMSO, 1963), Articles 64-65.

107 Chandra Muzaffar, *Islamic Resurgence in Malaysia* (Petaling Jaya: Penerbit Fajar Bakti Sdn Bhd, 1987). The Islamic resurgents wanted the formation of an Islamic state in which there was a new social order with an Islamic system of education, economy, jurisprudence and political order. For the major policy initiatives that aimed to Islamize Malaysia during the decade of the 1980s, see Husin Mutalib, *Islam and Ethnicity in Malay Politics* (Singapore: Oxford University Press, 1990).

108 The Muslim population consisted of 30% in 1947, 31% in 1960 and 26.3% in 1980 of the total population in Sarawak; the Christian population was 8% in 1947, 16% in 1960 and 28.5% in 1980. See L.W. Jones, *The Population of Borneo* (London: Athlone Press, 1966), 144. Gordon P. Means, *Malaysian Politics: Second Generation* (Singapore: Oxford University Press, 1991), 165. Govt. of Malaysia, Department of Statistics, *1980 Population and Housing Census of Malaysia, Population Report, Sarawak Part 1* (Kuala Lumpur: Department of Statistics, 1983), 66 and 228.

109 Hussin Mutalib argues that the Islam practiced in Malaysia was more in its ritualistic and symbolistic aspects prior to 1980. From 1981 onward, under the Mahathir administration, Islamization accelerated and affected governmental administration, the legal and economic institutions and the foreign policies of the government. Hussin Mutalib, *Islam in Malaysia: From Revivalism to Islamic State* (Singapore: Singapore University Press, 1993), chapters 3 and 4.

Christianity.[110] Until 1980, Islamization did not pose a serious threat or really hinder the work of the SIB or BEM, as the Muslims were still mainly confined to the coastal towns.[111]

The SIB: On Becoming a Modern Malaysian Church

In Chapter 5, it was shown that the SIB had begun to function as a 'Three-Self' indigenous church by the early 1970s. The SIB has grown to be one of the largest Protestant denominations in Malaysia today, and this fact witnesses to its ability to stand on its own two feet, and highlights the trajectory which the SIB has undergone towards becoming a modern Malaysian church.

In becoming a modern church in Malaysia, this journey by the SIB was made jointly with the BEM. In the late 1950s, with its outlook characterized by its famous dictum, 'We are a jungle outfit and we wouldn't be at home in the towns', the BEM tended to insulate itself from the realities of the effects of urbanisation and modernization in Sarawak.[112] But the change in the BEM Field Director in 1968 signalled the beginning of a move toward work in the coastal towns. In Chapter 6, we demonstrated that with its move to the coastal towns, the BEM re-focused its ministry and reformulated its policy, advocating the 'Twin Primary Tasks' in 1972.[113] The 'twin tasks' as formulated by the BEM were based on two underlying beliefs. Firstly, the task of the Mission was not only to assist the indigenous church but also to have a direct role in evangelism and church planting. Secondly, the evangelization of untouched parts of East Malaysia was 'also the immediate responsibility of the BEM' as there 'remained large tribal populations (and Chinese and others) virtually untouched by the gospel'. It was recognised that the Mission was 'tragically lacking in missionaries who could be engaged in the twin primary tasks', and this fueled greater cooperative efforts between SIB and BEM.[114]

The BEM's philosophy of the 'twin tasks' seemed a reversal of its earlier fifteen-year policy, for not only did it legitimize placing BEM or OMF missionaries as pastors of SIB churches, as in the three coastal towns of

[110] Interview with Gerawat Maran, 23 September 2004. 'The Kayan families at Long Busang were originally Christians under the C&MA mission in Kalimantan. By 1992, most of those who had converted to Islam were reconverted to Christianity'. *BEM NL*, June 1970, 2, reported that there were some 800 newcomers from the Indonesian border into the Belaga and initial visits to these people were made by two SIB pastors.

[111] Interview with George Ngo Epoi, 7 October 2004.

[112] Reasbeck has argued for the need to be aware and to respond to the changes in 'the spheres of materialism and politics' and also 'education and urbanization'in Sarawak. See *BEM NL*, June 1968, 1 and August 1968, 4. Interview with Colin Reasbeck, 29 May 2004. At about the same time, both Reasbeck and Hawes advocated the move to work in the coastal towns.

[113] See Chapter 6.

[114] *BEM Field Executive Minutes*, 21-27 January 1972, 2.

Kuching, Miri and Sibu (a practice hitherto unknown in the BEM), but it also allowed BEM's continued involvement in direct evangelism and church planting. This reversal of policy, which appeared to legitimize the indefinite stay of the missionaries, arose from the sense of urgency imparted by the knowledge that the Mission's stay in Sarawak was soon coming to an end, and that this posed a pressing need to reach the larger tribal groups, especially the Iban and the Chinese. This was to be their last big effort before leaving the country. However, rather than making the SIB more dependent upon the BEM, as might be supposed, this modification of the fifteen-year policy had the effect of further stimulating the outreach and church planting activities of the SIB to spread as rapidly and as extensively as possible.

The move to establish churches in the towns had significant implications for both the BEM and SIB. First, there was the need for both BEM and SIB to come to terms with the process of urbanisation and modernity. Within the BEM, the older generation of missionaries did not seem at first to understand that the trend of the urban drift was an irreversible one. There was initially a naive expectation that the young people would return to their villages after their education in the towns or overseas, so that there was resistance to establishing churches in the coastal towns in the 1960s;[115] hence the delay in taking the decision to establish churches in coastal towns, which was eventually made in November 1970.[116]

Further, the move to the coastal towns raised the issue of the location of Lawas as the BEM headquarters. The spread of the work towards Kuching made Lawas administratively more isolated, less central and strategic. The older generation of BEM missionaries, who had grown used to linking the work of the BEM mainly with the Lun Bawang and Kelabit, wanted Lawas to continue as the headquarters. But the younger missionaries viewed Miri as more central in relation to the whole of Sarawak.[117] Similarly, the reluctance of the SIB leadership to move from Lawas to Miri represented an unwillingness to move out of Lun Bawang country, where Lawas is the centre, to Kayan country, where Miri is the centre.[118] As the SIB leadership was still strongly influenced by Lun Bawang and Kelabit leaders, this resistance to the move to Miri was understandable. When the BEM eventually moved its headquarters to

---

[115] Interviews with Colin Reasbeck, 29 May 2004; and with George Ngo Epoi, 7 October 2004.

[116] *BEM Field Executive Minutes*, 20 October-3 November 1970, 5. Ultimately, the town churches would be cared for by SIB pastors, who would need a higher standard of education both general and theological. BEM sought to provide for one aspect of this through the English Bible School.

[117] Interview with Colin Reasbeck, 29 May 2004. The issue of the aircraft and the flying programme was a major consideration to any move from Lawas as headquarters. See Colin Reasbeck's 'Paper for the consideration of BEM Executive in June 1973 on the location of the Mission headquarters'.

[118] Interview with Dr Bill Hawes, 17 May 2004.

Miri in December 1974 with the seeming approval of the SIB, it was later revealed to the BEM that SIB was unhappy with the move.[119] This also served to underline the difference in opinion within the SIB itself. The SIB president, a Kayan, had given his approval, but the objection came from the SIB vice-president, a Kelabit.[120] The move to Miri by the BEM in a sense paved the way for SIB to be more strategically placed in modern Sarawak, and SIB followed suit in 1988.[121] Of greater significance was the ability of SIB to raise sufficient funds for the new headquarters at Miri; eighty per cent of which came from within the SIB churches,[122] which was an indication of the growing material wealth of the town churches.

Conscious of the need to hand over responsibility, the BEM adopted a five-year prayer goal in 1975 in which it sought prayer for a significant increase in more highly qualified SIB fulltime workers, who were able to pastor town churches, teach at the higher levels in the Bible schools, supervise the state-wide literature outreach programme, head up the youth training programmes, conduct effective evangelistic/teaching Bible studies and move out in missionary work overseas.[123] Though the implementation was slower than expected, most of the goals were fulfilled except for the provision of sufficient pastors for the town churches, especially in the English-speaking section. The appointment of the first indigenous principal of the Advanced Bible School took place in 1977; but in the case of MBC, the implementation of a similar goal was delayed when Elisa Paul was seconded to student work in West Malaysia in 1980, so that only in 1985 did George Ngo become the first indigenous principal.[124] The SIB Literature Board was formed in 1977 with the appointment of a local coordinator.[125] The Youth work was handed over to a group of key youth leaders working under the SIB Youth Work Committee in 1980.[126] As for its vision beyond Sarawak, the idea of starting an SIB church in Kuala Lumpur, the capital of Malaysia, was first mooted in 1975 but did not materialize until the early 1990s. Further, exploratory trips had been made to

---

[119] See *Area Director's Field Report to the Australian Conference*, April 1975, 5-6. See also discussion in Chapter 6.

[120] Interview with Dr Bill Hawes, 17 May 2004.

[121] Souvenir Programme SIB Sarawak: Opening of new SIB Miri Headquarters 1988.

[122] The cost of the Miri headquarters amounted to $489,422.66 for the first two phases and the money received was $531,369.32, so that the balance was set aside for the third phase of development. Of this money, $393,925.19 (80%) came from the SIB churches and members.

[123] *Area Director's Field Report to the Australian Conference*, April 1975, 6.

[124] Elisa Paul was seconded to the Fellowship of Evangelical Students (FES) Malaysia in 1980 to work among the SIB students in the tertiary colleges in Peninsular Malaysia. Mr Lee Hong Kwang, a West Malaysian Chinese Christian, was appointed as the Principal of MBC in 1980 and he was succeeded by George Ngo in 1985.

[125] *BEM NL*, February 1978, 3.

[126] Souvenir Programme SIB Sarawak: Opening of new SIB Miri Headquarters 1988, 92.

the Sengoi, an indigenous people group in West Malaysia in 1975,[127] the tribal people in Mindoro, Philippines, and also to southern Thailand.[128] The vision of looking for fields beyond Sarawak is an indication of their commitment to missions abroad. By 1979, the SIB had taken over all major responsibilities from the BEM, so that SIB had taken tentative but definite steps toward becoming a 'Three-Self' church.

After 1979, the contribution of expatriate missionaries was minimal except for the moral encouragement given to the SIB and periodic visits by former BEM missionaries, though the OMF provided continuity to the work of the BEM for another few years on a skeletal staff.[129] OMF, being a larger mission body, was more helpful in providing some assistance in the form of scholarships to deserving SIB pastors or leaders as their contribution toward the leadership development of the SIB. In short, any external assistance from both the BEM and OMF in the subsequent years was negligible in comparison to the overall work of the SIB.

Conclusion

In the face of rapid social changes occurring in Sarawak, the BEM was rather slow to respond to the process of migration and urbanisation, as the older generation of BEM missionaries, epitomized by Belcher, did not realize that the process was irreversible; they were further hampered by their philosophy of BEM as an interior mission. In contrast, the team of younger BEM missionaries led by the new Field Director, Bill Hawes, forged ahead in the new direction and moved to establish urban churches to cater to the needs of the SIB members. The BEM mission strategy drew its inspiration largely from the recommendations advocated by Fife and Glasser and focused on the planting of urban churches, on student work and on the use of mass media and the promotion of Christian literature. Similarly, the 'twin tasks' formulated in 1972, which focused on (a) evangelism and church planting and (b) Bible teaching and leadership development, also drew upon the insights of Fife and Glasser, on lessons learnt from the failures of mission in China, namely, the failure to plant national churches and train a vigorous and able leadership for them.

In meeting the social challenge, the move to the coastal towns saw BEM focusing on planting urban churches, starting student work in the secondary schools and the teacher training colleges, partnering with the OMF to provide missionaries to pastor churches in the towns, initiating Christian Union groups in schools, Teachers' Christian Fellowships, and Nurses Christian Fellowships,

[127] *BEM NL*, August 1975, 3; November 1975, 3.

[128] *BEM NL*, November 1975, 3.

[129] The OMF Area Director, Mr Brian Michell, relocated first to Singapore, then to Kuala Lumpur after only four years in Miri.

and promoting Christian literature among SIB members. Further the beginning of urban churches especially in Kuching, Miri and Sibu had the catalytic effect of sparking the formation of churches in other sub-coastal and coastal towns like Bintulu, Sarikei, Kapit, and Lundu, and outreach to the other larger tribes, the Iban, Bidayuh and Melanau in the surrounding areas. In addition, migration to the land resettlement and agricultural schemes and the opening of new roads helped BEM and SIB to focus work on the Iban in the Marudi-Miri-Bintulu triangle with a combination of initiatives from not only individual SIB members, but also outreach teams from the local SIB urban church, teams of students from MBC and the planned strategy of the BEM/SIB. By 1979, though the OMF and BEM missionaries continued to pastor the urban churches, the initiative for outreach to the other tribes lay firmly in the hands of both SIB pastors and young lay leaders from the urban churches.

Another effect of this social migration and the education policy was the rise of linguistically separate congregations, where the English-speaking congregations were more cosmopolitan, attracting Christians from other tribes and ethnic groups and making them a microcosm of Sarawakian society. But these English-speaking congregations were more lay-led, especially by young professionals, who had gone for tertiary education in Peninsular Malaysia or overseas. By this time, the rise in literacy among the Orang Ulu had caused a reverse situation; at one time the SIB pastors had been the most educated people in the community, but the situation had reversed in the urban churches, so that their English-speaking congregations had difficulties finding suitable pastors from within the SIB. The BEM responded by selecting the most promising of the SIB pastors available for further training overseas so that they could return to fill this gap in the urban churches as well as groom the next generation of SIB leaders. Further, the BEM tried hard to upgrade the Bible college training through starting the Advanced Bible School for re-training SIB pastors and an English-speaking Bible college that met western standards of theological training. Both these efforts were moderately successful and met the pressing needs for another decade after the departure of the BEM from Sarawak. However, though the educated lay leaders were not sufficiently incorporated into the SIB central hierarchy, they nevertheless channelled their resources and energies by not only supporting the work of the SIB but also in initiating outreach work to the other indigenous tribes, starting new urban churches, and getting involved in evangelical para-church work such as Scripture Union (SU), TCF and NCF. The challenge for the SIB beyond 1980 was whether the human and material resources which the urban churches had to offer could be harnessed for the overall good and growth of the SIB, or whether the urban churches would continue to function independently with their own agenda.

By 1980, the SIB churches were still largely rural, though urban churches had sprouted in the various towns, and the SIB was taking tentative but definite steps toward adjusting to the urban context and integrating into the national cash economy. But the continued growth of urban churches beyond 1980s could bring about a widening gap between the rural and urban churches, or it could also mean a situation where the SIB could become more self-sufficient or self-supporting by benefiting from the resources of the urban churches. This challenge, however, requires further research which goes beyond the scope of this study.

As for the political challenges, especially those posed by Malaysianization and the ten-year immigration ruling, the response of the BEM, on the one hand, was the formulation of its 'twin tasks' and its handing-over of responsibilities to the SIB. The 'twin tasks' policy was a last concerted effort by the BEM and SIB at teaching and training the SIB leadership and also at reaching out to the larger unreached tribes, especially the Iban. On the other hand, as to its existence as a mission body, the BEM saw in the Malaysian government policies the signals for the impending exit of the work of the Mission, resulting in its closure in 1979 with the departure of the last Field Director. Anticipating its closure, the BEM merged with the OMF in 1975 so that BEM missionaries could be deployed to other fields in which OMF worked; but more importantly, the BEM hoped that the OMF could provide the continuity in missionary personnel, leadership and resources to the SIB. By this time, though the aid provided was useful, it had become secondary to the overall SIB work. Thus the political challenges had little effect on the SIB, which had been sufficiently prepared since 1959 toward being a 'Three-Self' church and taking its place as an independent indigenous church in Malaysia.

Chapter 9

Conclusion

The legacy of the BEM has been the planting, emergence and development of an indigenous church, the SIB. The central objective of its mission policies was the 'speediest evangelization of Borneo' and the establishment of a 'Three-Self' church.

The concept of the establishment of a 'Three-Self' church had been in vogue in Protestant mission circles from the time of Henry Venn and Rufus Anderson, its most ardent proponents. But its implementation, as has been pointed out in Chapter 6, did not often succeed in the manner it was first envisaged, and was often prolonged, undermined, subverted or even reversed by succeeding missionaries; nor was there the planned euthanasia of the mission.[1] The establishment of genuine 'Three-Self' churches was generally delayed until after decolonization and the enforced removal or reduction of the power of western missionaries. But the story of the BEM is one with a difference.

Why is the BEM story different? Firstly, the BEM was exceptional among mission bodies in not simply having a policy of planting a wholly autonomous indigenous church but also in carrying out its intention of handing over responsibilities to the SIB in a sustained manner and within a limited time frame. Evidence for the specific commitment of the BEM to a 'Three-Self' policy can only be traced back to 1939 (see Appendix 5), though it is quite possible, as noted in Chapter 4, that it may have been part of the original intention from the inception of the BEM. However, the implementation of the 'Three-Self' policy was not trouble free, as significant modifications to the policy were adopted, such as the re-interpretation of the fifteen-year policy in 1960, the shift from interior mission work to urban mission, and the adoption of the policy of the 'twin tasks' in 1972. Nevertheless, the BEM retained a clear exit strategy, which was a key factor to its success in implementing its 'Three-Self' goals. Secondly, the BEM was a small mission body which lacked financial, administrative and personnel resources. Hence, it was prudent to delegate the duties of the missionary at a station as quickly as possible to the indigenous pastor, as it was shown in Chapter 5. Being small in size, the BEM had an institutionally 'light' structure which allowed it to make and implement

[1] See Chapter 5.

decisions quickly as well as to act rapidly to adapt itself to whatever difficult situations might arise.

A third factor relates to the particular theological stance of the BEM. As it was noted earlier in Chapter 3, the BEM was an inter-denominational evangelical mission body that consciously modelled itself on the mission philosophy and practices of the CIM. Hence, the BEM placed a primary emphasis on missionaries 'being mobile' and on the practice of a widespread dissemination of the gospel. There was also an equally strong emphasis on the training of indigenous pastors and teachers to assume leadership positions in the local church from its inception and the translating of the Scriptures into the vernacular. However, in planting an indigenous church, the BEM adopted the teachings of Roland Allen alongside their literal reading of the Scriptures, (particularly, the Gospels and the Acts of the Apostles), as shown in Chapter 6. It may seem a curious development that a conservative evangelical mission body should adopt the teachings of a High Anglican churchman, especially his distinctive Catholic pneumatology (the confidence that the Holy Spirit will always guide the Church into the path of the truth), and his adherence to the Pauline pattern of church planting and nurture, (that of the missionary planting a church, training the local leadership there over a short period of time, then leaving them to manage their own church; after which, the missionary moved on to pioneer a new area of work). However, Roland Allen's emphasis on adherence to the apostolic pattern of mission was perceived by the BEM as being fundamentally scriptural, in accordance with the teaching of the Acts of the Apostles. Thus, the BEM was willing to adopt it despite the Anglo-Catholic background of its proponent, and Roland Allen's writings became the textbook of the BEM, enforcing the lesson that the missionary was meant to work himself out of a job. The ability of the BEM to implement the teachings of Roland Allen is also due to its light institutional mission structure. In the aftermath of the fall of China to Communism, as discussed in Chapter 6, many mission bodies re-discovered and re-examined the thinking of Roland Allen. However, those which had heavy institutional structures generally found it more difficult to adopt or even adapt Allen's teachings.

Fourthly, the challenges posed by regional political developments in China and Malaysia played an important role in the formulation and implementation of the policies of the BEM. The distinctive fifteen-year policy of the BEM was formulated during a political atmosphere of uncertainty and anxiety in Southeast Asia in the aftermath of the fall of China to Communism in 1949, and the perceived threat of Communism to the region. The urgency of the situation, as discussed in Chapter 6, provoked important questions for the BEM which led to the adoption of this fifteen-year policy. Without the grave threat of Communism over the region, it is unlikely that the fifteen-year policy would have been formulated.

Next, the spectre of the communist threat in Sarawak, and particularly the Brunei uprising in December 1962, and also the social-economic trends that were impacting Sarawak provoked a process of re-evaluation of BEM's policies and its time-table of handing over responsibilities to SIB so as to 'complete its task'.[2] Further, the governmental ruling of Malaysianization (1963) and the ten-year limit to missionary residence (1967) helped to hasten the time-table of handing over responsibilities to the SIB, as the signs were already on the wall of an impending closure of the BEM as a mission in the foreseeable future.[3] These developments led to a shift in the implementation of BEM's policies with the formulation of the 'twin tasks' in 1972 which was meant to be a last combined effort of the BEM and SIB to reach the larger tribes of Sarawak of the First to Third Divisions of Sarawak. The 'twin tasks' policy, rather than reinforcing dependence on the Mission, in fact encouraged the SIB to make its own response to the challenge. In the light of these factors and constraints, the BEM re-evaluated its original policy and implemented it with a renewed sense of urgency. The Borneo story is thus different from that of the experience of many missions in China, where the devolution of authority and autonomy to the indigenous church was hastily conceived and implemented under irresistible political pressure, without the long-term planning and periodic re-focusing demonstrated by the BEM during the twenty-nine years before it finally withdrew from Sarawak.

In what ways, then, was the implementation of the BEM policies distinctive? The objective of the BEM was given a bold and specific focus when it accepted the fifteen-year policy in 1950 with the understanding that by 1965, the BEM would complete its work, withdraw or support the SIB Church, when needed, in other specialized ministries; a policy that was possibly unique in the history of missions in the Asian context. But its implementation, as shown in Chapter 6, was not trouble free. This policy was re-interpreted in 1960 in the light of a few factors. Firstly, the progressive serial expansion that was taking place among the Kayan, Kenyah, and Penan during the 1950s and the Iban in 1960 meant that the fifteen-year policy was impractical when it came to be applied to the Penan and the Iban, especially in the areas of training the indigenous leaders and translating the Scriptures into the vernacular. Secondly, though the translation of Scriptures for the Lun Bawang was on schedule, the translation for the other tribes had lagged behind by 1960, which was due to another factor, i.e. the lack of missionary translators. Further, when the fifteen-year policy was first formulated, only the Lun Bawang churches were rather well established; whereas the work among the Kayan and Kenyah was in its infancy, and that among the Penan and the Iban had not yet begun. Also, the field was expanding so rapidly that the human resources of the BEM were stretched to their limit, especially with the need for the time-consuming work of travelling and teaching and also the painstaking work of translation. The fifteen-year policy was then re-interpreted as applying to each given tribe from the date

[2] See Chapter 6.
[3] See Chapter 8.

when work first started with them, so that work among the Iban which began in 1960 could continue until 1975. Consequently, this clarification justified a prolonged stay of the BEM in Sarawak should new tribal churches be established. In effect, fifteen years became twenty-nine, when the BEM finally ceased its work in Sarawak in 1979. Nevertheless, the series of political events mentioned above provided the BEM with a sense of urgency and a time-bound impetus to 'finish the task'. In the process, the year 1965 passed without any mention by the BEM of its original significance; after which, the fifteen-year policy lapsed from its mission vocabulary.

There were significant gains resulting from the fifteen-year policy. First, there was the formal establishment of the SIB which gained a centralized ecclesiastical structure with its own decision-making and implementation mechanisms independent of the BEM in 1959, and a finalized constitution in 1961, whereby it could and did function as an independent indigenous church, not answerable to the parent mission body, the BEM. This was a major contributing factor towards the promotion of indigenous initiatives. A significant feature of the BEM-SIB relationship was the progressive handing over of responsibilities from 1956 onwards as the SIB was able to accept them, so that by 1980, all the important ministries of the BEM had in effect been handed over to SIB personnel. Second, in training the 'native church to stand on its own two feet', the BEM gave priority to the training and grooming of indigenous leaders and the strengthening of the spiritual life of the members. This training took numerous forms. In the first two decades, the Lawas Bible School trained selected students with the best potential (who were regarded as the 'cream of the churches') for leadership positions in the SIB, which was an important factor in the vibrant growth and development of the SIB. Most of these students were senior men and recognized leaders of the community from which they came. Other forms of training included the deacons' schools, the short-term regional Bible schools and the annual Keswick-type conventions which enhanced the spiritual, educational and social life not only of the leaders but also of its grass-root members.

Further, there was a conscious effort at promoting indigenous initiatives. From its inception, self-propagation was the greatest strength of the SIB. As shown in Chapter 6, the SIB was sufficiently prepared and proved its capacity for self-governance. Prior to the formal establishment of the SIB in 1959, the Inter-Tribal Conference took over the administration of the Bornean churches in 1954, and the task of assigning the LBS-trained indigenous pastors to their field of work in 1956. The Conference thus had to deal with a variety of church issues, including thorny ones, as they arose. As for self-support, the BEM philosophy forbade the provision of any funds for the SIB, and encouraged it to be self-sufficient from its inception, which was the case, especially during the Japanese Occupation. From its inception, the SIB churches functioned quite self-sufficiently in their rural agricultural setting, having adopted the principle of tithing among their members. However, from the 1960s, the crunch came when the process of change towards a cash economy began to impact Sarawak. Despite the initial difficulties faced by SIB pastors with school-going children, a combination of factors alleviated the problem. These included the remedial steps which SIB and BEM took cooperatively, and also the provision of government scholarships for children of indigenous SIB pastors for higher education from the 1970s.

In the implementation of BEM policy, it is significant that at no time did the SIB have to wrest control from the BEM. Instead it was the SIB which delayed the process of the transfer of responsibilities in the late 1960s, but assumed the responsibilities when it felt able to do so at its own pace, finally doing so by 1980. In response, the BEM did not force the issue or consciously subvert the process. By then, as the SIB had already been in existence for nearly a decade, the BEM had encouraged a process which it could not now stop. The issue then was the rate at which SIB was willing and able to assume full responsibilities from the parent mission body.

Surprisingly, there appears to have been no major tensions between the BEM and the SIB in the course of devolution of authority and autonomy. Several possible reasons may be suggested for this. First, not only were the BEM missionaries as white people highly regarded and respected during the colonial period, but the BEM missionaries were initially regarded by the Orang Ulu as their 'parents' and 'teachers' in the Christian faith. Second, indigenous testimony indicates that the Orang Ulu felt grateful and indebted to the missionaries for the spiritual and temporal benefits which they brought.[4] Culturally, it would have been highly improper and disrespectful of them to disagree openly with the missionaries, though there were culturally polite ways of doing so. These factors, however, applied equally to many mission situations where tension between church and mission became much more evident. A more important factor is that literacy was first introduced by the missionaries in the post-war period and secondary education by the government only from 1962 onwards. Any indigenous expression of vocal dissent was therefore unlikely until the Orang Ulu leaders had at least a secondary education, giving them the confidence to challenge missionary opinion.[5] It was shown that signs of real dissent only began to appear from 1963 onwards. In the situation where the BEM disapproved of the SIB leaders to be involved in politics, the BEM nonetheless came around to accept the decision of the SIB leadership.[6] Hence, the general lack of secondary education among the SIB leadership up to the 1960s was an important contributory factor to the lack of Mission-church conflict and also to the delay in the transfer of full responsibilities to the SIB.

---

[4] Interview with George Ngo Epoi, 7 October 2004.

[5] See Chapter 6. By 1975, secondary education became available to all school children in Sarawak.

[6] See Chapter 8.

Orang Ulu culture dictated that, even if indigenous leaders disagreed with the missionaries, they should allow the missionaries to do whatever they suggested out of deference to their authority. But this did not mean that the Orang Ulu leaders did not express their own views or disagreement to the missionaries. The issue of the move of the headquarters to Miri in 1974 illustrates this point well. The Orang Ulu appeared to have expressed their preferences in their customary polite manner but their quietly stated objections might have been misunderstood as lacking full conviction. Hence, as shown in Chapter 6, at the time when the new Field Director had assumed office in 1968, and when the BEM wanted to set a time-schedule for handing over responsibilities to the SIB, the Orang Ulu leaders informed the BEM missionaries that they should pay attention to some Orang Ulu customary practices; a veiled way of implying that BEM missionaries were not understanding the polite objections of the Orang Ulu to their suggestions.

Further, what the BEM missionaries had suggested and begun to do, namely to establish a 'Three-Self' church, was welcomed by the Orang Ulu. In the light of the care shown by the missionaries for their general well being (spiritually, medically and educationally) the general perception among the Orang Ulu appears to have been that the missionaries had their interests at heart, and would not do things that would bring harm to them. This is particularly true of the Lun Bawang, who were in a state of serious depopulation when the BEM took an interest in them. Hence they were rather trusting, though not undiscerning, of the paternal advice and leadership given by the BEM. Finally and quite significantly, no hard evidence has been uncovered of gross missionary interference in the decision-making process of the SIB, which could have created major tension between the BEM and SIB. Rather the relationship between the Field Director and SIB President appears to have been so close that their decisions were often taken on a mutual basis.

It has been shown in Chapter 6 that the constant monitoring of the implementation of its policies in the light of the changing socio-cultural and political circumstances proved to be BEM's greatest strength, and evaluation of its performance was done at least every two years during the Field Conferences. The result was a definite and sustained progress during the period of its fifteen-year policy, and also sensitivity to the context which might demand any policy change. It was noted that this constant assessment of its policy from 1950 to 1960 promoted a 'count-down' mentality at each successive Field Conference so that it was reported that there were 'thirteen years', then 'eleven years' more to complete the task; hence, inculcating a sense of commitment and seriousness among the BEM missionaries.

In being sensitive to the changing socio-political context, the BEM acted prudently enough in response to anticipated eventualities, formulating important policies with far-reaching significance for the SIB, as it was discussed in Chapter 6 and also in Chapter 8, and thus prepared the BEM for its own euthanasia (or its absorption into OMF) as a mission in 1975. In so doing, the BEM may be said to have fulfilled Henry Venn's vision of establishing a 'Three-Self' indigenous church and the euthanasia of a mission within a period of fifty years of its existence; a process that has relatively few parallels in mission history.

Perhaps the most important consideration facilitating the realization of the objectives of the BEM relates to the mass movement of the Orang Ulu into Christianity, first among the Lun Bawang in the pre-war period, and then among the Kayan, Kenyah and Penan in the immediate post-war period, as discussed in Chapter 5. In the case of the mass movement of the Lun Bawang into Christianity, the BEM missionaries harnessed the gains of this indigenous movement by organizing the converts into local churches that bore a close resemblance to their native patterns of leadership. As for the mass movement in the Baram, the situation was more complex. In a sense, Southwell was responding to a trend which had already begun with the conversion of Temenggong Lawai Jau, the paramount chief of the Kayan in the Baram, to Roman Catholicism. It was also true that not every longhouse in the Baram which Southwell visited converted to Christianity, but he was instrumental in facilitating the conversion of a number of the Kayan longhouses in the Apoh and Tutoh River area. In short, the BEM responded appropriately to a process of indigenous conversion and was also catalytic in encouraging the development of the mass movements. It was these mass movements that contributed greatly to translating the objective of the BEM from intention into reality. This was despite the fact that the missionaries believed that a small proportion of the community had succumbed to the pressure of conforming to the new religion without any genuine personal experience of conversion.

The receptivity of the Orang Ulu to the Christian message and the nature of their conversion were diverse in character. As discussed in Chapter 4, the Lun Bawang's change of religious allegiance helped them regain a new sense of identity and worth, delivering them from a situation of hopelessness and despair. This process of conversion re-orientated and restored meaning to their lives in the aftermath of a shattered world-view after the cessation of head-hunting, and through a spiritual encounter experienced Christianity as a superior religion. However, the conversion movement among the Orang Ulu in the post-war period, as discussed in Chapter 5, was slightly different. The impact of outside western influence during WWII on their religion and culture made them re-evaluate their religion and cultural practices. In turn, this re-evaluation made them open to western culture, education and Christianity. Further, their interaction with the Christian message led to a re-orientation of their world-view and helped them to make the transition from their old religious worldview to an indigenized Christian worldview. The missionary message, which increasingly emphasized the claims of the superiority of the power of Christ over the spirits and freedom from their various and burdensome religious practices, proved experientially validated in their conversion process. Conversion to Christianity, on the one hand, meant identification with a world religion that had become associated with a more advanced culture, technology and civilization. On the other, it meant a change of allegiance to a superior supernatural power or resources based on the evangelical belief in the authority of Christ over the spirits. As for the Kayan, Kenyah and Penan, later conversions laid greater emphasis on allegiance to a superior supernatural power or resources.

The BEM policies would not have succeeded if the SIB leadership had not been able to rise to the challenge of becoming a 'Three-Self' church. In addition to what has been said earlier about the encouragement of indigenous initiatives by the BEM and the corresponding response of the SIB, the experience of the revival movements, first in the 1950s and then in the 1970s, left an indelible mark on the SIB. Though the BEM missionaries were in no sense in control of these movements, they nevertheless attempted to influence and guide them where possible. It was argued in Chapter 7 that the revival in the 1950s played a significant role in infusing moral confidence in the indigenous leaders, both pastors and deacons, to lead their churches and to rise to the challenge of becoming a 'Three-Self' church, working steadily toward the formation of the SIB. For the BEM missionaries, the revival was an assurance that their 'fifteen-year' policy was rightly conceived and that their task was 'finishable', thereby strengthening their resolve to the work at hand. The revival in the 1970s, which was pan-Orang Ulu in scale, brought a new dimension to the life of the SIB. It empowered the youths and young adults, bringing them to the forefront of ministry and using them to spark a new surge of evangelistic activities throughout Sarawak and preparing them, especially those who entered Bible school, for future leadership roles. But this revival movement was not without its problems of excesses and its initial resistance by the SIB leadership, who were only convinced of the genuineness of this revival by the wise counsel of a prominent indigenous leader. Positively, the revival was instrumental in forging and affirming a pan-Orang Ulu identity in the rural areas and also a distinctive SIB identity in the urban towns. In the process of wider social integration in the urban areas, SIB members acquired the inner courage to integrate socially with others, and gained the self-confidence and social empowerment to work with the other more sophisticated and educated ethnic communities in the towns. Further, the revival acted as a catalyst to begin a process of change in the SIB leadership from an older set of leaders to a younger generation who were more in tune with the rapidly changing scene of Sarawak and were better able to provide the appropriate leadership for the changing times. In short, at a time when the BEM missionaries were preparing to leave the country, the occurrence of the revival greatly consolidated the work of the SIB, gave renewed confidence to the SIB leadership, and prepared a new generation of younger leaders for future leadership positions.

The changing social, cultural and political trends occurring in Sarawak from 1959 also aided the development of the SIB toward a 'Three-Self' church in a way which the SIB leaders regarded as almost providential. The process of urbanisation created a complex situation of social movements, first a movement toward the coastal towns, and then a movement toward the suburban and rural towns and their surrounding areas in Sarawak. All these movements aided the spread of the SIB into hitherto unevangelized areas, extending their ministry to the other larger ethnic groups such as Iban, Bidayuh and the Chinese. In this process, the establishment of the coastal town churches, especially the Kuching church, was instrumental in spearheading the planting of other SIB town churches. In tandem with the rise in educational opportunities for higher learning through government scholarships offered under the Malaysian government to them as bumiputras, some of these SIB young people then returned as young professionals, becoming part of a social movement from the major towns to the smaller towns and their surrounding areas, where they assumed leadership in various spheres of Christian work, as shown in Chapter 8. Significantly, the outreach work of these professional lay people often dovetailed with the work of the students from the Miri Bible College. It also complemented the work of other local churches and the planned strategy of the SIB/BEM, which was constantly looking for new opportunities of expansion. In seizing the available opportunities and working cooperatively, the SIB as a whole took confident charge of outreach activities to the other tribes, making good progress of growth in a modern world, despite the problems they continue to face as the church makes the transition from its rural context to an urban context.

The dilemma posed by the higher educational levels of the lay people meant that these urban churches had difficulties finding suitably qualified SIB pastors, and consequently these urban churches increasingly became led by these highly-educated young lay professionals. To alleviate this problem, the BEM in conjunction with the SIB selected the best available young people for higher theological training overseas in the later 1970s, so that they could return to fill positions in the urban churches and key leadership positions in the SIB. This was a prudent move that provided the SIB with sufficient leadership personnel for the next decade. Further in line with the policy of the 'twin tasks', the BEM began the process of upgrading their Bible school training, especially with the establishment of the English-language Bible School (MBC), in order to meet western standards of training and provide the SIB churches with pastors who could minister relevantly to a context of rising educational expectations.

The political factors of Malaysianization and the ten-year immigration ruling hastened the process whereby the SIB assumed all the key responsibilities from the BEM. The SIB was less affected by the process of Islamization in Sarawak than might have been expected. Instead the Orang Ulu's status as bumiputra and the privileges which were accorded to them had the positive effect of creating middle-class professional elites among the SIB members, who felt comfortable relating to both the rural and the urban context in Sarawak and Malaysia. By 1980, though the SIB churches were still largely rural, this group of professionals and the urban churches had begun to fill the gap to help SIB take tentative but definite steps toward becoming a modern 'Three-Self' indigenous church in Malaysia.

In short, the policies of the BEM to plant and develop a 'Three-Self' indigenous church were often reformulated and refined in response to the changing political contexts in Southeast Asia, Malaysia and Sarawak, facilitated by the mass movements of the Orang Ulu into Christianity, and reinforced by the ability of the indigenous leaders to rise to the challenge by gradually assuming various positions of leadership. As a result, the SIB has taken its place as a growing 'Three-Self' church within the context of modern Malaysia.

Appendix 1
Oral Research: Interview Guide

I. BEM Mission Policies

1.1. What were the significant policies of the BEM that encouraged the formation and nurture of the SIB? (e.g., church building, worship and management, church leadership – appointments, assignments and discipline, use and availability of money for projects)

How were the policies implemented over the years? (fifteen-year policy, place of Bible Schools, policies regarding areas of work; range of ministries of BEM – their rationale; vision and forward planning, faith principle and role of women)

How did BEM respond to the changes in the country (e.g., rising educational standards? political events? urbanisation?) How were policies reviewed (1958, 1964, 1972)? What modifications (if any) were made and why? (e.g., in 1958 a suggestion was made in Field Conference that the fifteen-year policy be understood without any time limit and change to 'with all possible speed' in regard to its fulfillment. It was turned down. Who raised it? Why was it turned down?) What were their subsequent effects on BEM and SIB? What were the reactions/opinions of missionaries to changes in policies? How did the missionaries respond to meeting these challenges (e.g., the move to the coastal towns)?

With an egalitarian form of decision making process, what difficulties did the BEM face in its decision making process (e.g., 1964, 1966 and 1968 Field Conferences)? What issues were debated? How were they overcome or not overcome? What effects did they have on BEM and SIB?

1.2. Before the formation of the SIB, describe the selection or appointment of deacons among the various tribes (e.g., Lun Bawang, Kelabit, Kayan, Kenyah). The numbers selected, the criteria, the role of the church and missionaries in the process? What about after the SIB was established?

How were pastors appointed before the SIB was formally established?

When pastors were sent to the various places, how were the decisions made and by whom?

What role did the BEM missionaries played in this process? What about after SIB was established?

If difficulties arose between the pastors and headmen or deacons, how were the problems resolved?

Were pastors disciplined? For what reasons? Who took action? Were they rehabilitated? If so, how? What effect did it have on church and SIB?

1.3. How did SIB respond to the handing over of responsibilities to the indigenous church? Procedure and Pace of handing over? Properties?

II. SIB Church

2.1. How did SIB make their decisions and formulate their policies (for example, the SIB Constitution)? Under what situations do they seek the advice of the BEM missionaries (from the Belchers and other senior missionaries)?

What role (if any) did the BEM missionaries play in their decision-making?

Was BEM advice always heeded? What were the advice that were not taken by SIB and why?

2.2. How did the SIB view and respond to the 'Three Selfs' policy, 15 years policy of BEM and change in BEM Field Chairman in 1968?

How did SIB seek to be self-supporting? How did BEM help or point to ways for SIB of finding financial resources?

How did the BEM and SIB relate to each other after 1959 (give an image)? What major difficulties (if any) did they face and how were they resolved?

2.3. What roles did the pastors' conferences, annual conventions, and deacons' schools play in the life of SIB? What was the impact of each of these events? What roles did the missionaries play in these events? Who made the final decisions and how were they made?

2.4. What role did the Bible School play in the life of SIB? How did SIB develop or not develop it after 1959? Who and why did many people choose to go full-time? What opportunities were seen to be provided by BEM/SIB to meet the aspirations of indigenous people?

2.5. Did the tribes have difficulties integrating with each other? Why? What steps did SIB take to overcome them?

2.6. How did the revivals (e.g., in 1952 and in 1973) happen? What effects did they have on the life of the Church? How did the missionaries view and respond to them? How were the excesses dealt with by the BEM and SIB leadership?

III. Conversion and Indigenous Culture

3.1. What within their culture made them receptive to Christianity? Why?

3.2. What cultural practices continued even after their conversion? What practices were discontinued? Why?

3.3. What new practices were introduced as a result of their conversion? What were modified from their culture? why?

IV. Governmental Help or Hindrance

4.1. What political events affected and shaped BEM policies? (e.g., Japanese Occupation, Fall of China to communism, Korean War, Zoning policy of the government, the Confrontation, Brunei Rebellion, Ten-Year Ruling for missionaries)

4.2. How did government policies affect and shape the work of BEM?

When did the SIB take over the task of dealing directly with the government instead of the BEM (e.g., for permission to work into new areas, etc.)? Under what circumstances and with what results?

How did government policies affect and shape the work of SIB? (e.g. the Confrontation, Brunei uprising 1962, zoning policy of the government, ten years ruling on missionaries, educational policies, Islamization policies, Bumiputra status of Orang Ulu). How did SIB meet those challenges?

4.3. How did the (a) BEM and (b) the SIB respond to the urban drift of the Orang Ulu to the towns from the 1960s?

Appendix 2
Interviews with BEM missionaries

	Missionaries	Description	Date interviewed
1	Dr Bill Hawes	British missionary from 1963 to 1979. Third BEM Field Director, 1968-1979. A medical doctor by training.	17 May 2004
2	Colin Reasbeck	British missionary with BEM 1966-1978.	29 May 2004
3	Dr Bill Lees	British missionary from 1951 to 1966. A medical doctor by training.	14 June 2004
4	Dr Beatrice Clayre	British missionary from 1964 to 1968.	16 May 2004
5	Alan Belcher	Australian missionary from 1940 to 1988. Second BEM Field Director, 1948-1968.	29-30 October 2004
6	Dorothy Summerson	Australian missionary from 1950 to 1965.	31 October 2004
7	Lois Freeman	Australian missionary from 1961 to 1974.	31 October 2004
8	Ken Cooper	Australian missionary from 1948 to 1966.	4 November 2004
9	Rev. Ken Coleman	Australian Anglican missionary from 1964 to 1975.	8 November 2004
10	Ray and Evelyn Cunningham	Australian missionaries from 1949 to 1990.	8-9 November 2004
11	Keith Napper	Australian missionary from 1953 to 1972.	8 November 2004

Questionnaire/Correspondence from BEM missionaries

1	Rev. Robert N. Burton	Australian missionary from 1964 to 1979. A Baptist minister.	30 November 2004
2	Alf Tharatt	Australian missionary from 1960 to 1966.	22 November 2004

Interview with missionary from other denominations

1	Rev. Peter Varney	Anglican priest in Sarawak from 1967 to 1968.	7 March 2006

Interviews with SIB pastors and elders

	Pastors/Elders	Description	Date interviewed
1	Winston Edip	Student at LBS (1971) and MBC (1972-1973). Pastor at Sarikei Church (1978) and Kuching (1983). Lecturer at MEC (till now)	15 September 2004
2	John Urud	MEC Principal (1998 till 2009)	15 September 2004
3	Jok Wan	SIB President (1977-1987)	16 September 2004
4	Pengiran Gugkang	Teacher at Buduk Aru Bible School (1970-1975; 1979-1982) and at LBS (1983-1984). Student at Batu Bible School, Malang, Indonesia (1985-1987). Teacher at Sekolah Theologia Atas, Lawas (1988-1997).	16 September 2004
5	Balang Anid	Pastor in Baram (1960-1962), in Long Peluan (1962-1966), in Bario (1966-1979) and in Miri (1981-2004).	17 September 2004

6	Balan Engan	Student, Long Lama Bible School (1983-1984), MBC (1985-1987) and New Zealand Bible College (1993-1995). Pastor among the Penan, Baram (1988-1992). Pastor, Krokop Evangelical Church, Miri (2001-2004).	18 September 2004
7	Gerawat Maran	President of SIB (1988-2002). Treasurer of SIB (1983-1987). Student at LBS (1969-1971). Teacher at LBS (1972-1973). The second national Principal of LBS (1974-1975). Principal at Long Lama Bible School (1975-1976). Student at BCV (1977-1980). Teacher at Sekolah Theologia Atas, Lawas (1981-1982).	20 September 2004
8	Lawai Asi	Pastor at Long Tukon, Trusan (1940-1952)	21 September 2004
9	Satu Lakui	Secretary of SIB (1966-1969). Pastor among the Lun Bawang in the churches in the Lawas district (1957-1999).	21 September 2004
10	Sigar Bee	Secretary of SIB (1970-1971). Teacher at Buduk Aru Bible School (1967-1969). Pastor (1973-1990).	21September 2004
11	Udan Rangat	Secretary of the Inter-Tribal Council (1956-1958). Student at MBI (1959-1961). Teacher at LBS (1953-1964).	21 September 2004
12	Sara Mulang	Secretary of SIB (1977-1978). Teacher at LBS (1957-1960). Student at Tahlee Bible School (1961-1962).	22 September 2004
13	Tagal Paran	President of SIB (1970-1972). The first national Principal of LBS in 1972.	22 September 2004

14	Tubu Padan	President of SIB (1976-77). Translator of Old Testament into Lun Bawang (1963-1965). Student at New Zealand Bible Institute (1965-1967). Teacher at LBS (1967-1976). Pastor in Lawas (1978-1981).	24 September 2004
15	George Ngo Epoi	Coordinator for the SIB Basic Bible Schools (1979-1980). The first national Principal of MBC (1984-1989).	7 October 2004
16	Datuk Balan Seling	Vice President of SIB (1965-1966). Student at MBI (1960-1962). Teacher at LBS (1963-1964).	29 July 2005

Appendix 3
An Outline of Events Leading Up to the Formation of a Borneo Fellowship

During the middle term of 1927, two students at the Melbourne Bible Institute were moved to pray for the evangelization of Borneo. Enquiries were made and an accurate large-scale map was drawn to help visualize the Island, and further, a request was made through the local Secretary of the Worldwide Evangelization Crusade for any information they possessed relative to Borneo.

Meanwhile others had been moved to pray, and when in February 1928 a reply was received from the Worldwide Evangelization Crusade, interest and prayer was greatly stimulated by the information obtained. By May 16th 1928 it was felt that some forward step should be taken.

Great confirmation to this decision was given on May 17th when Mr C.H. Southwell received from Mr E. Stafford Young an offer of up to £ 50 for preliminary expenses that may be necessary and for sending someone to the field.

On May 18th, after consultation together, Rev. C.H. Nash suggested a Borneo Fellowship as a germinal idea and during the ensuing vacation it was resolved that all interested should make future developments a matter of special prayer.

On June 11th the Lord's hand was clearly seen when Mr F. T. Davidson, while visiting Yallourn, was providentially brought into touch with M. A. Henderson who had spent seven years in Borneo as a trader. A conference was arranged and on June 23rd Messrs. F.T. Davidson, C.W. Tolley and C.H. Southwell met Mr Henderson at Yallourn. This meeting was made possible through the kindness of Mr H. Jeffrey. Mr Henderson returned to Melbourne with the party and spent the weekend discussing the possibilities of work in Borneo.

On June 20th a circular was suggested and drawn up setting out the present position and future prospects. From time to time informal meetings were held by those immediately interested and various suggestions were discussed.

June 28th. Discussion took place on the character of the proposed missionary work in Borneo. Rev. C.H. Nash suggested that the Borneo Fellowship should consist of members who are such on the understanding that each desires to further the work as God lays it on the heart; - there would be a consciousness of personal responsibility. These Fellowship members might be in two broad divisions differing only in function not in degree of membership. A ratio of one field member for every ten home members was mentioned as desirable proportion in order that the home base may be sufficiently strong.

A doctrinal standard would be drawn up. Membership would be safeguarded on suitable lines. As a basis of Government it was suggested that administration should be in the hands of a Field Director and a Home Director. Around each Director there would be Advisory Councils and decisions would be made by the Director without formal motions, the desire being to attain unanimity, the final decision however would lie with the Field Director who would be General Director.

June 29th. A further discussion did not result in any new decisions. Some time was spent discussing various suggestions as to a Home Director, but we have no clear light on that question. The printing and distribution of Circular was considered to be the next step.

The discussion showed that at first the Home Base should be supreme and a Field Secretary should be appointed with Mr Henderson as Leader.

July 14th. After prayer, the feeling was unanimous that we must quietly follow the Lord's leading step by step rather than develop any complete organization at present. Mr Tolley reported an interview with Mr W.L. Wright who was keenly interested in the work and requested a lantern lecture early in August. He kindly volunteered to pay for the making of some lantern slides.

Mr Davidson called on Mrs John Griffiths by request. Mrs Griffiths was greatly interested and desired to be kept informed of the work. A visit to Miss Beath was also reported relative to the operation of the Dohnavur Fellowship. After further discussion it was decided that some definite association should take shape and that a Minute Book be opened, the first formal statement being:-

On July 4th, 1928, at a informal gathering of a few persons interested in the Evangelization of Borneo held in the Principal's room of the Melbourne Bible Institute, 38 Williams Road, Windsor, Victoria, the following persons being present: Rev. C.H. Nash MA, Messrs R.S. Tregaskis, C.W. Tolley, C.H. Southwell, and F.T. Davidson. It was resolved to take steps for the formation of a Borneo Fellowhip. Rev. C.H. Nash was asked to act as Chairman of the group, Mr C.H. Southwell to act as Honorary Secretary, and Mr R.S. Tregaskis as Honorary Treasurer. A statement for circulation was adopted setting before the Christian Public the present position.

A Borneo Fellowship July 4, 1928

A Statement issued concerning proposed Missionary Work in Borneo.

GEOGRAPHY, CLIMATE AND TOPOGRAPHY.

Borneo is the second largest island in the world, and is the most central of the Malayan Group. It is exactly astride the Equator, and is roughly 800 miles long and 700 miles broad – ten times the size of Tasmania, or one-ninth the area of Australia.

Climatic conditions and rainfall are typically tropical, but it is not considered unhealthy. It is a land of abundant rivers, which are well distributed, and form the main highways for communication. The northern half is more mountainous, the main mountain ridge averaging four to five thousand feet, with occasional peaks of 8,000 and 10,000 feet. The highest mountain is 13,000 feet, but is not a portion of the main mountain system.

POPULATION AND HISTORY

Borneo's aboriginal inhabitants are inclusively known as Dyaks, but these vary greatly in type and distribution; the greater number being in the northern section. There is a large immigrant population of Malays, who are principally itinerant traders, and as traveling facilities increase, these are pushing further into the interior, carrying Islam's Crescent with them. There is also a large immigrant population of Chinese, which, however, live chiefly in communities, and are not religiously aggressive. The total population is estimated to exceed 3,000,000.

Borneo was first made known to Europe by the early Portuguese navigators, but after the decline of Portuguese sea power, the Dutch took control over the major portion of the island. The northern section, roughly one-ninth of the total area, is controlled by the British North Borneo Company under Royal Charter. Lying to the south-west is first the small native state of Brunei, and then a large independent state of Sarawak, under the sovereignty of the Englishman, Rajah Brooke.

MISSIONARY WORK

The societies working in Borneo are:

The Basel Mission. This is a German Mission which has about 24 workers engaged around Banjermassin, in the extreme south and neighbouring rivers. They have had a hard battle, but are doing good work, though they have not touched the pagan heart of the island – nor apparently do they contemplate it.

Anglican Missions. The Society for the Propagation of the Gospel is working in the northern coastal region, in the diocese of the Bishop of Labuan and Sarawak, but their work is mainly among the Malay and Chinese. They have nine European workers in the field.

Roman Catholics. These have been granted a large territory for their exclusive occupation in the east of Borneo. They also have isolated stations in British territories.

Other Missions. The Methodist Episcopal Mission had one or two stations in West Borneo, which they are now abandoning to concentrate on Sumatra. Seventh Day Adventists also have a small work.

The World-wide Evangelization Crusade contemplated an advance into Central Borneo, and made enquiries from the Dutch authorities through the Basel Mission. The information then obtained has been kindly placed at our disposal.

THE PRESENT POSITION

For some time past the needs of Borneo's unevangelized millions have been laid on the hearts of some of the students at the Melbourne Bible Institute, and a little band has met to pray for the Evangelization of the untouched pagan tribes of Central Borneo. Enquiries were made from all sources available, and gradually, as information has been gathered, the call to the work has become more definite.

By a series of providential leadings, three men have come to the point of offering their lives for such service, and the time now appears ripe for the issue of a first statement to be put forth among the Lord's people in Australia in the confident belief that it is His good pleasure that preparations should be made for advance.

The first requirement is PRAYER. Without this, and the further revelation of the Divine will in consequence, untimely and unwise attempts may be initiated. It is hoped that the project may eventually be related to some existing missionary organization of an inter-denominational character, to obviate the addition of yet another to the many existing societies. Meanwhile, this statement is issued as an invitation to prayer.

The call to prayer is urgent because:

The Mohammedan Malay trader is rapidly advancing among the pagan tribes.

The field is near to Australia, and is the special responsibility of the Church in Australia.

Definite offers of immediate service are available.

It is felt that the time is ripe for a wider fellowship in prayer that God may make clear His will as to the next move; and that the way may speedily open up for a strong forward movement into Borneo. We therefore invite communications from those upon whose hearts this burden is laid, with a view to their incorporation in this Fellowship for Borneo.

By filling in the accompanying form and forwarding it to the Hon. Secretary, Borneo Fellowship, Melbourne Bible Institute, 38 Williams Road, Prahran, S.1., Victoria, any reader of this statement may get into touch with the Borneo Fellowship.

Issued with the consent and authority of Rev. C. H. Nash, Principal, and the Executive Committee of the Melbourne Bible Institute.

Since the above statement was written God has wonderfully brought us into contact with a Christian man who has spent seven years trading in all parts of Borneo. He knows the language and customs of the people, and, though no longer young, he is willing to consider the leadership of a band of young men for an initial period of two to three years. By this time those going with him should have sufficient grasp of the language and native conditions. We would ask for special prayer in this regard.

To Hon. Secretary, Borneo Fellowship, 38 Williams Rd, Prahran, S.1., Vic.
Please send me further particulars of the Borneo Fellowship.

Name ………………………………………………………
Address………………………………………………….
Date………………………………………………………

Note: Any expressions of opinion relative to this work will be gladly received by the Secretary.

Source: BEM Home Council Minutes Book 1928, BCV, Melbourne.

Appendix 4
Provisional Constitution of the Borneo Evangelical Mission (1928)

1. The Borneo Evangelical Mission is a company of believers in the Lord Jesus Christ associated on a common basis of faith and practice for the purpose of giving the Gospel to the native races in Borneo with a view to the formation of a Christian Church from among them.

2. Doctrinal Basis

(1). The Divine Inspiration and supreme authority of all the Scriptures of the Old and New Testaments.

(2). The Triune Godhead, Father, Son and Holy Spirit.

(3). The twofold nature of our Lord Jesus Christ, God and Man. His Virgin birth, vicarious death and bodily resurrection, His eternal Deity; His present Majesty; His future coming in Glory.

(4). The fall of man and his consequent moral depravity and need of regeneration. Justification by faith through the substitutionary death of Christ. Sanctification by the Holy Spirit. Resurrection of the body, both of the just and unjust. Eternal life of true believers and eternal punishment of disbelievers.

Every member of the Council, responsible officer and authorized representative of the Mission, whether honorary or salaried, is required to signify his sincere agreement with the doctrinal basis by signing and forwarding to the Secretary a copy of this Constitution and to undertake to continue in office only so long as his belief shall remain unchanged.

3. Support

The Mission looks to God alone for all the needs of its members, no appeals for financial aid or collections being made by or authorized for this Mission. No more is expended than is received by the Mission, going into debt being considered inconsistent with the principles of entire dependence on God.

4. Organisation and Government

The centre of the organization is the Borneo Evangelical Mission Council consisting of the following Foundation Members viz:-

Messrs C.H. Perrin; E. Stafford Young; H.J. Jeffery; Miss Beath; Rev. C.H. Nash; Messrs R.S. Tregaskis; A. Henderson; C.W. Tolley; F.T. Davidson; C.H. Southwell.

The Council is maintained in continuity by addition to their numbers chosen as occasion may require with the unanimous consent of all the existing members. No less than five members shall be resident in Australia. This council directs and supervises all affairs of the Mission except so far as provision is made under its authority for local administration, receives and accounts for all moneys and gifts, and is generally responsible for the well being and progress of the Mission.

It also elects its own Officers as they may be required from time to time.

The local administration on the Field is in the hands of an Executive committee consisting of those members of the Council located on the Field, and consent of all its members must be given for all operations on the Field. The Council appoints a Field Secretary (who, under direction of the Executive committee will report fully the progress of affairs on the Field), and any other Officers found necessary.

This constitution with the exception of clauses 2 and 3 may be completely reviewed at the end of two years.

At any subsequent time judged desirable and found practicable in the opinion of a Council meeting consisting of a three fourths majority of all existing members, the responsibility for Government and administration may be placed in the hands of a General Director, assisted by an Advisory Council.

5. The Borneo Evangelical Mission Fellowship is a body of helpers who, constrained by the love of Christ, and the need of Borneo, desire to take an active interest in the Evangelization of its people.

All members must approve of the doctrinal standard of the Mission.

Members are admitted to the Fellowship by approval of the Council, and all members undertake:-

(1). To support the work by regular prayer.

(2). To assist the Mission by forming, and maintaining prayer circles, or otherwise promoting the objects of the Mission.

The Council may appoint a Fellowship Secretary, who may from time to time convene gatherings of the Fellowship for conference and prayer, and exercise a general supervision.

(Presented to BEM Home Council on 1 September 1928 and ratified on 11 September 1928).

Source: BEM Home Council Minutes Book 1928, BCV, Melbourne.

Appendix 5
Statement of the Character, Principles and Practice of Borneo Evangelical Mission.

The Mission was founded in 1928 to evangelize the tribes of the interior of Borneo. It is evangelical in aim and character; its members are chosen without any regard to denominational connection, and its work is carried on by the gifts which come in answer to prayer. The following extracts are drawn from the Constitution, and the Principles and Practice of the Mission.

OBJECT. The speediest possible Evangelization of the native tribes of Borneo, with the building up of a self-supporting and self-propagating indigenous Church.

DOCTRINE.

1. The Divine Inspiration and supreme authority of all the Scriptures of Old and New Testaments.
2. The Triune Godhead, Father, Son and Holy Spirit.
3. The twofold nature of our Lord Jesus Christ, God and Man, His Virgin Birth, vicarious death and bodily resurrection; His eternal Deity; His present Majesty; His future coming in Glory.
4. The fall of man and his consequent moral depravity and need of regeneration. Justification by faith through the substitutionary death of Christ. Sanctification by the Holy Spirit. Resurrection of the body, both of the just and unjust. Eternal life of true believers and eternal punishment of disbelievers.

Each member of the Governing Field Conference, the Home Council, responsible officer and authorized representative of the Mission, whether honorary or salaried, is required to signify his sincere agreement with the Doctrinal Basis by signing and forwarding to the Secretary of such Conference or Council a copy of the Constitution, and to undertake to continue in office only so long as his belief shall remain unchanged. Any member, responsible officer, or representative shall be required to subscribe to the Doctrinal Basis when called upon to do so by any member of the Conference or Council.

ORGANISATION AND GOVERNMENT. The government and administration of the Mission vests in a Governing Field Conference. In addition there is a Home Council who is responsible for the administration of the affairs of the Mission at home.

Membership of the Governing Field Conference is open to all missionaries of the Borneo Evangelical Mission who have signed the Principles and Practice of the Mission and who have served a term of two years, or such other time as the said Conference shall determine in the case of any individual missionary, but not less than one year. Until the expiration of such period of two years or other such period as shall be determined such missionary shall be deemed to be a probationary member and will not have the right to attend such Conference. Notwithstanding anything to the contrary a probationary missionary may be invited by the Executive Committee to attend the Field Conference.

The Governing Field Conference meets at least once in every two years, provided always that such Conference may be called at any time on the requisition of at least two thirds of its members.

The Governing Field Conference once in every two years elects from its members a Chairman and an Executive Committee to conduct its business, or alternatively, delegates the election of its Chairman to such Committee. Subject to the over-ruling power of the Executive Committee and/or the Governing Field Conference, the Chairman is responsible for the administration of the affairs of the Mission on the Field. The Chairman and/or such Executive Committee are in either case responsible to the Field Conference. The Executive Committee may be called at any time by the Chairman or the a majority of its members

The Governing Field Conference or Executive Committee may appoint a Field Secretary and Treasurer and such Executive and administrative officers as it may require from time to time. In the event of furlough or other temporary absence from the Field of the Chairman in the Executive Committee appoints a Deputy to act for him for a period not exceeding one year.

SUPPORT. The Mission looks to God alone for all the needs of its members, no appeals for financial aid or collections being made by or authorised for the Mission. No more is expended than is received by the Mission, going into debt being considered inconsistent with the principle of entire dependence on God.

The Mission then, depending as it does entirely on the faithfulness of God through voluntary gifts of His people, as He may dispose them to contribute, offers no guarantee of any fixed amount of support to its workers. It seeks faithfully to distribute the funds available and to meet the need of each worker as those funds allow.

Every member of the Mission is expected to realize that his dependence for the supply of all his need, both temporal and spiritual, is on God, Who called him and for whom he labours, and not on the human organisation. As the great founder of the CIM has said – 'the funds might fail, or the Mission might cease to exist, but if they put their trust in Him He will never fail or disappoint them'.

EXPENDITURE. At present (1939) the arrangement of finances at home is as follows:- The Home Treasurer is responsible for the handling of all monies received in Australia and is responsible to deduct necessary home expenses before forwarding drafts to the Field. He also divides to missionaries on furlough their share of allowance out of the Field Draft. The Home Treasurer is also responsible for preparing the Mission account for audit, and publication in the annual report.

The Field Chairman will be responsible for the disbursement of all monies received from the Home bases, or received directly on the Field, and also for seeing that accounts are regularly and strictly kept by each section of the Field.

CANDIDATES. Candidates are expected to satisfy themselves as to the Principles and Practice of the Mission, and not to offer themselves unless they cordially approve of them and heartily desire to carry them out. As the CIM puts it, 'They must count the cost, and be prepared to live lives of toil, of privation, of loneliness, of danger, - to be looked down upon by their own countrymen, and to be despised by the natives; to live in the interior, far from the comforts and advantages of society and protection such as they have enjoyed at home. They will need to trust God, as able to meet their need in sickness as well as in health, since it will usually be impossible to have recourse to the aid of qualified physicians. But, if faithful servants, they will find in CHRIST and in His Word a fullness, a meetness, a preciousness, a joy and strength, that will far outweigh all that they have sacrificed for Him'.

SOUND IN FAITH. Candidates are expected to satisfy the Home Council to which they apply as to their soundness in the faith on all fundamental truths by handing in together with their schedule of application, a written statement of their convictions as to the Divine inspiration and authority of the Scriptures, the Trinity, the fall of man and his consequent moral depravity and need of regeneration, the atonement, justification by faith, the resurrection of the body, the eternal life of the saved, and the eternal punishment of the lost. They must be catholic in their views, and able to have fellowship with all believers holding these fundamental truths, even if widely differing in their judgment as to points of Church government. If conscious that their views differ in any important point from those usually held by Evangelical Christians, they are expected candidly to state this. Should the views of any one on any of the above mentioned points change subsequently, he must, if in the Field, inform the Chairman of Conference, or his deputy, of the change; and, if at home, the Home Council for the country from which he went out; and whether in the Field or at Home he must be prepared to resign his connection with the Mission.

PROBATIONERS AND MEMBERS. Candidates are those who have filled in the official application forms and are seeking acceptance by the Home Council for service in the Foreign Field. Those who are accepted become Probationers. Probationers will be under the direction of the Home governing body until they reach the Field, when they will be under the Field Conference, its Chairman and Executive Committee. Should Probationers have approved themselves after two years on the Field and remain in a satisfactory state of health, they will be accepted as full missionary Member. But should they prove unstable, or unable to cope with the difficulties of the language or the work generally, to bear the climate, to harmonize with their brethren, to adapt themselves to the natives, or otherwise show themselves unsuitable, Conference will either prolong their probation or will make the best arrangements in their power to facilitate their retiring.

Even though members on the Field should supply a proportion of their own support this does not free them from the need of full-hearted obedience to the executive of the Mission.

SPHERES OF LABOUR. On the Field a Probationer must be loyal and obedient in all things, willing to go anywhere and do anything, and this with joy. However, missionaries will never be appointed to permanent spheres of labour without their cordial concurrence. When appointed to a permanent post they should remain at their post unless circumstances of great urgency compel them to leave. Should they not feel happy in their work they must inform the Chairman, and even though the cause be irremediable, they must still be prepared to remain for 6 months or over till suitable arrangements can be made to carry on the work without them.

Patient perseverance is needed; it should be borne in mind that difficulties and discouragement are to be expected in the beginning of every work; and that the absence of immediately apparent results is no ground for abandoning a work begun for God. In every case, except the unexpected occurrence of alarming illness requiring immediate removal, at least 6 months' notice must be given by Probationers and Missionaries before leaving their work. Should illness necessitate leaving the district, the sanction of the Chairman should be obtained; and if it is needful to leave the country, a medical certificate should also be procured.

The Missionary in charge of a Station will be responsible for the work and workers in his sphere. Probationers, where practicable, will be placed under the superintendence of senior missionaries in charge of stations, with whom they may reside, and whom they will assist in the work as far as they can. Should the convictions of any Probationer differ on some points from those of the Missionary in charge, he is not to attempt to unsettle the minds of the converts and native helpers. If the difference of convictions be such as to prevent happy fellowship, the Chairman or his deputy will, when requested, endeavour to arrange for his residence at some other station as soon as circumstances permit.

For the good of the work it is most necessary that Probationers and Members should be perfectly frank with the Chairman, informing him not only of the successes but also of the difficulties, hindrances and disappointments of their work.

All should be constantly mindful of their professed objective in leaving home – the speediest Evangelization of all native tribes. They should therefore shield the Mission from every unnecessary expense, remembering that under God the extension of the work depends on the funds available for pressing forward to the regions beyond. It is equally necessary to be very careful about the economy of time, for no one knows how soon the time for work will end, by loss of health, death or any other cause. A waste of time or money must necessarily delay the Evangelization of the World.

FURLOUGH. Furlough is considered advisable as an aid to the maintenance of an all round efficiency in service on the Field, and is viewed primarily in this light. The climate in Borneo is enervating, and in the absence of an annual rest in a hill station four years is considered to be the normal period of service. Both the Mission and the Missionary should plan their service with this period in view, provided that in exceptional cases an application may be made to the Chairman of the Governing Field Conference for a variation of this time. Furlough will consist of nine months, not including the time taken for traveling to and from the homeland, providing that the Home Council may enlarge or abridge this period in the case of exceptional circumstances. Missionaries at home on furlough shall be under the control of the Home Council, who shall be responsible for allotting time for deputation work and provided always that no deputation work be done within three months of the arrival in the home country.

BETROTHAL AND MARRIAGE. The weighty bearings of these questions on Missionary work render special caution necessary on the part of all concerned. Married candidates will only be considered, accepted, and sent out after careful consideration of the suitability of both husband and wife. Unmarried candidates who are engaged must candidly state this, and will only be accepted when the case of both parties have been considered; and candidates who have any attachment which might lead to an engagement should be frankly state the fact. Probationers and Missionaries are earnestly recommended to be most thoughtful and prayerful before committing themselves to an engagement and are asked to consult with the Home Council or Field Chairman in their engagement.

In general the Mission will consider it advisable for any Probationer to remain a period of from one to two years on the Field before marriage. Both Probationers and Missionaries are expected to ask the permission of the Field Executive before marriage. In any case, should the Executive not grant its permission or feel that a marriage taking place without their permission is unsuitable, they have full right to ask the retirement of those concerned and in the case of non-compliance to exercise their powers of dismissal.

RETIREMENT AND DISMISSAL. Should a Probationer or Member desire at any time to sever his connection with the Mission he must, if in the Field, give six months' notice through the Chairman who will take whatever steps may be necessary in the case. If he be at home, he must give at least one month's notice to the Home Council for the country from which he went out, who will likewise take such action in the case as may be needful.

In all cases where the Mission is satisfied that retirement is really necessary from failure of health or other adequate cause, it will not expect any refund. In other cases, any one leaving the Mission before the end of the second year of residence in Borneo will be expected, as soon as able, to refund in full any sum expended by the Mission towards his or her outfit or passage money; if during the third year, three-quarters of that amount; if during the fourth year, half; if during the fifth, one-quarter; after that time no refund will be looked for. In the case of any Probationer or Member leaving the Mission within three years of arrival in Borneo for marriage, or salaried employment, or for purposes of trade, the amount expended on the support of such Probationer or Member from the time of his arrival in Borneo should be added to the outfit and passage money above mentioned, and be repayable in like proportion. Anyone leaving the Mission must hand over all Mission monies or properties in his charge into the hands of the person appointed to receive them.

Should any occasion of sufficient gravity ever raise, the Mission has the power of summarily terminating the connection of any worker with the Mission, in which case they would, of course, act with all possible consideration.

MISSION PREMISES. For the effective carrying on of localized Missionary work, Mission premises are of course required, and these should be rented when economically preferable. It may in some cases be needful to secure sites and to erect premises. The money required for such purpose is ordinarily supplied in whole or in part from the general or special funds of the Mission, as circumstances require and the funds permit. The Field Conference of the Mission cannot be responsible for any expenditure not authorized by them, or for any outlay of personal funds on Mission property. But Missionaries may, if they wish it, use their own monies or contributions from their friends for securing, improving, or building premises, on the understanding that all such premises, however secured or improved, are to be held as Mission property; the Mission, and not the individual Missionary, being considered the tenant, or owner, as the case may be; and the funds so used being regarded as donations to the Mission. Where new premises are to be erected, or extensive alterations involving change in external appearance, are to be made in those already existing, whether with private or Mission funds, the plan and character of the proposed building or alterations are first to be submitted, through the Chairman for approval before such work is commenced.

NATIVE HELPERS. The Mission has adopted the principle of a self-supporting Church and is opposed to the principle of supporting native workers out of the Mission funds, but in special cases native workers may be placed on the Mission list when recommended by the Missionary-in-charge and sanctioned by the Governing Field Conference or its Executive Committee, when they will thenceforth be supported by sharing in Mission funds. The employment of a native helper, even by a Missionary at his own expenses, must be first approved by the Missionary-in-charge and the Field Chairman. All native helpers should be considerately dealt with, and should not lightly dismissed or summarily treated. If any offence requiring it has been committed by one of them, definite Church action must be taken; or, should such action not be required, the helper may be suspended from office by the Missionary-in-charge until the difficulty can be referred to the Field Chairman, who may personally, or by deputy, investigate the matter if sufficiently grave; but if the difficulty arises rather from want of happy co-operation, opportunity must be allowed to remove such helper to another district, where he may work better.

CHURCH GOVERNMENT. The Mission recognizes a local Church as a body of baptized Christians, and regards it as a God-formed agency through with the Holy Spirit works for the building up of believers and the Evangelization of surrounding regions. The Mission believes that the teaching of the New Testament indicates there should be local individual Churches with powers of self-government, and that when these increase in number, they should be organized into a larger body, a Conference, which should exercise authority over the local churches. So long as the principles of self-support and self-propagation be kept in mind together with co-operation with other activities of the Mission, the Missionary-in-charge may, in consultation with the Christians, decide details of organization and government in his district or tribe. A Church having been organized, the form of Church government already instituted must not be changed by a succeeding Missionary, unless with the approval of the Field Conference.

The raising up of self-supporting and self-extending Churches must ever be kept in view. Converts must be stimulated and encouraged in the study of the Word of God; suitable opportunities should be afforded them for the manifestation of spiritual gifts; and they should be encouraged to help by material giving, according to their ability, in the work of God. Native helpers especially should be afforded all possible help and encouragement; as they become able they should be allowed to bear responsibility, and the element of foreign teaching, pastoral care, and supervision, be gradually withdrawn.

This section is intended as a guide only, and the Mission looks for its confirmation or modification in the light of future experience.

RELATIONS TO GOVERNMENTS. Everyone shall be subject to Government laws and regulations, and urge this duty upon Native Christians.

The Chairman, or any he may deputize, alone is authorized to make an appeal to the Government or deal with the Government in general.

'To those who are considering offering to our fellowship, we say earnestly, Do not offer unless you are prepared to spend and be spent out to the uttermost, which means nothing heroic, but just a loving and lowly life, in which self and its natural desires do not count at all.'
(The Dohnavur Fellowship)

Signatories: Frank T. and Enid Davidson
E. Strafford Young
Roland A. Bewsher
Hudson and Winsome Southwell

Jesselton, B.N.B.
September, 1939.

Source: OMF Archive, Kuala Lumpur

Appendix 6
Constitution of the Sidang Injil Borneo (Evangelical Church of Borneo)

Introduction

The Sidang Injil Borneo was formally constituted in 1959. As part of the Church Universal it recognizes and acknowledges the Lord Jesus Christ as the only King and Head of the Church, and the word of God, that is the scriptures of the Old and New Testament, as its sole standard and authority.

Rule 1. Name, Postal Address and Place of Meeting

(1) The Society shall be known as the Sidang Injil Borneo.

(2) Its place of meeting shall be at Tanah Baru, Lawas, Sarawak, or at such other place or places as may from time to time be decided on by the executive committee.

(3) Its postal address for correspondence shall be Sidang Injil Borneo P.O. Box 47, Lawas, Sarawak.

(4) The place of meeting of the Sidang Injil Borneo shall not be changed without the prior approval of the Registrar of Societies.

Rule 2. Objects of the Sidang Injil Borneo

The objects of the Sidang Injil Borneo are those which is has received from its divine Lord as expressed in holy scripture, namely –

(1) To witness to the Lord Jesus Christ (Acts 1:8)

(2) To establish and care for the church (John 21:17)

(3) To preach the gospel where it has not been heard (Matt. 28:18-20)

Rule 3. Relationship of Sidang Injil Borneo to Borneo Evangelical Mission

(1). The Sidang Injil Borneo recognizes the Borneo Evangelical Mission as the founding body. Although these two bodies are truly independent the one from the other, they are one in their love for Christ, and in their fellowship in the gospel and the two will always work in fellowship and co-operation in the all important task of proclaiming the gospel in Borneo.

(2) All matters affecting both the Sidang Injil Borneo and the Borneo Evangelical Mission shall be decided by the Sidang Injil Borneo and the Borneo Evangelical Mission meeting in conference.

Rule 4. Doctrinal Basis

The Sidang Injil Borneo believes that God used the Borneo Evangelical Mission as His instrument in its birth and development. In seeking, therefore, to express and formulate the doctrines of holy scripture upon which the Sidang Injil Borneo is founded it has taken as its basis of belief the doctrinal basis of the Borneo Evangelical Mission, namely:-

(1) The divine inspiration and supreme authority of all the scriptures of the Old and New Testament.

(2) The triune Godhead, Father, Son and Holy Spirit.

(3) The twofold nature of our Lord Jesus Christ, God and man, his virgin birth, vicarious death and bodily resurrection, his eternal deity, his present majesty, his future coming in glory.

(4) The fall of man and his consequent moral depravity and need of regeneration, justification by faith through the substitutionary death of Christ, sanctification by the Holy Spirit, resurrection of the body, both of the just and the unjust, eternal life of true believers and eternal punishment of unbelievers.

Rule 5. Membership of the Sidang Injil Borneo

The Sidang Injil Borneo comprises all local churches in Sarawak, Sabah and Brunei, which at the daté of this constitution are united to form the Sidang Injil Borneo together with all such other local churches in other lands which maybe admitted by the general conference to membership of the Sidang Injil Borneo.

Rule 6. Local Churches

A local church is a congregation of believers meeting together to worship God according to the teaching of the gospel of our Lord Jesus Christ and in accordance with the aims and beliefs of the Sidang Injil Borneo. Such members of a local church who accept the doctrinal basis of this constitution and whose life shows signs of repentance and faith shall be entitled to elect such representative or representatives to the district branch conference as the general conference shall from time to time decide. No local church shall make rules which are contrary to this constitution.

Rule 7. District Branches

The general conference of the Sidang Injil Borneo shall divide the local churches into district branches.

A conference of the representatives of the local churches of each such district branch shall be held at least once in every two years, at least one month prior to a general conference.

Notice and agenda for each district branch conference shall be forwarded to all member churches of the district branch at least fourteen days before that date fixed for the meeting.

Such conference shall elect from their members such representative or representatives as the general conference shall from time to time decide. Each district branch conference shall appoint a Chairman and such other officer or officers as it shall think fit. A district branch conference shall, subject to the over-ruling power of the executive committee, have power to legislate in relation to all matters relating to the common interest of the local churches within its boundaries and in relation to the common interest as may be remitted to it by a local district church. It shall also have the right to act as a court of appeal from a decision of a local church.

A district branch conducts no financial transactions.

Rule 8. General Conferences

(1) Representatives

(a) The representatives of each district branch together with the members of the executive committee shall constitute the general conference of the Sidang Injil Borneo. More that 50% of those who are eligible to attend the general conference shall constitute a quorum.

(b) Each member of the general conference shall be entitled to one vote on every occasion that voting occurs in a meeting of the general conference.

(2) Meeting

(a) The general conference of the Sidang Injil Borneo shall meet at least once in two years at such time and place as shall be decided by the executive committee.

(b) Noticc and agenda for each meeting of the general conference shall be forwarded to the members of the Executive Committee and the chairman of all district branches with sufficient copies for distribution to all elected representatives of their respective district at least fourteen days before the meeting.

(3) Rights and Authority of the General Conference

All the powers of the Sidang Injil Borneo shall vest in and be exercisable by the general conference. Such power shall include the power to make rules and regulations in relation to doctrine, worship, discipline and government, and all matters affecting the well being of the Sidang Injil Borneo and the extension of the kingdom of Christ in the world, and in particular the power to:

(a) decide all disputes concerning doctrine

(b) discipline a church or district branch which through teaching or behavior brings shame or harm to the Lord's name and church

(c) examine and advise in all affairs and activities of the local churches

(d) create new district branches or divide or unite existing district branches.

The business of the meeting of the general conference shall include:

(a) receiving the executive committee's report on the working of the Sidang Injil Borneo

(b) receiving the Treasurer's report and the audited accounts of the Sidang Injil Borneo

(c) appointing an auditor or auditors for the period until the next general conference

(d) election of the executive committee for the period until the next general conference

(e) deciding the year and month of the ensuing meeting of the general conference

(f) dealing with such other matters as may be put before it.

4) Extraordinary meeting of the General Conference

An extraordinary meeting of the general conference of the Sidang Injil Borneo shall be convened:

(a) whenever the executive committee deems it desirable

(b) at the joint request of not less than one third of district branches or one third of member churches.

An extraordinary meeting requisitioned by district branches or member churches shall be convened for a date within sixty days of the receipt of such requisition.

Rule 9. Executive Committee

(1) Election

Each general conference shall elect by ballot from members of the local churches comprising Sidang Injil Borneo a President, Vice-President, Secretary and Treasurer who shall hold office until the next general conference and who, with the Principal of the central Bible School, a representative of the founding body, and such other persons as the general Conference shall from time to time decide, constitute the executive committee of the Sidang Injil Borneo.

(2) Vacancies

In the event of an executive seat becoming vacant for any reason whatsoever, the executive committee shall appoint another member of a local church of Sidang Injil Borneo to such vacant office to hold that office until the next meeting of the general conference provided always that if the office of the President becomes vacant the Vice-President shall hold office as Acting President until the next ensuing meetings of the general conference.

(3) Function

The executive committee shall hold office between meetings of the general conference and shall:

(a) implement all instructions and laws of the general conference

(b) act on behalf of the general conference between meetings of the general conference.

(4) Meetings

The executive committee shall meet at least twice a year at such time and place as the President or half of the members of the executive shall decide, and half of the members of the members of the executive committee shall constitute a quorum. Fourteen days' notice of each meeting shall be given to all members of the executive committee.

Rule 10. Duties of Office Bearers

(1) The President and Vice-President

The President shall:

(a) preside over all meetings of the general conference and meetings of the executive committee

(b) perform such functions as the general conference and executive committee shall decide.

In the absence of the President the Vice-President shall preside over the meetings of the general conference and meetings of the executive committee.

(2) Secretary

The Secretary shall:

(a) keep minutes of all meetings of the general conference and the executive committee

(b) conduct the business of the Sidang Injil Borneo in accordance with its rules, and shall carry out the instructions of the general conference and of the executive committee

(c) be responsible for conducting all correspondence and keeping all books, documents and papers except the accounts and financial records.

(3) Treasurer

The Treasurer shall:

(a) be responsible for the finances of the Sidang Injil Borneo

(b) give and receive receipts for all monies received and disbursed

(c) keep accounts of all its financial transactions and be responsible for the correctness of the said accounts.

Rule 11. Trustees

(1) The general conference of the Sidang Injil Borneo shall appoint at least three trustees who are members of local churches of the Sidang Injil Borneo to hold office as trustees during the pleasure of the Sidang Injil Borneo.

(2) All immovable property of the Sidang Injil Borneo in Sabah shall vest in three of such trustees on the behalf of the Sidang Injil Borneo.

(3) All immovable property of the Sidang Injil Borneo shall vest in three of such trustees for and on behalf of the Sidang Injil Borneo.

(4) The trustees shall be responsible to the executive committee and under the authority of the executive committee who shall have power, at their absolute discretion to dismiss any trustee and appoint another in his place who shall be a member of a local church of the Sidang Injil Borneo, such trustee to office until a new trustee shall have been appointed by a meeting of the general conference of the Sidang Injil Borneo.

Rule 12. Financial Provisions

(1) The income of the Sidang Injil Borneo shall be derived from gifts and freewill offerings, and may be expended for any purpose necessary for the carrying out of its object.

(2) The Treasurer may hold a petty cash advance not exceeding $2,000 at any one time. All money in excess of this sum shall within seven days of receipt be deposited in a bank approved by the executive committee. The bank account shall be in the name of the Sidang Injil Borneo.

(3) All cheques or withdrawal notices on the Sidang Injil Borneo's account shall be signed jointly by two of the following – President, Vice-President, Secretary or Treasurer.

(4) No expenditure exceeding $500 at any one time shall be incurred without the prior sanction of the executive committee, and no expenditure exceeding $20,000 at any one time shall be incurred without the prior sanction of the general conference.

Rule 13. Audit of Accounts

(1) The accounts of the Sidang Injil Borneo shall be audited each year by an auditor or auditors appointed by the general conference and who shall hold such office until the next meeting of the general conference. No member of the executive committee may be such auditor.

(2) The Auditor/auditors shall be required to audit the accounts of the Sidang Injil Borneo for the year, and to prepare a report or certificate for the meeting of the general conference. He/they may also be required by the President to audit the accounts of the Sidang Injil Borneo for any period within their tenure of office at any date, and to make a report to the executive committee.

Rule 14. Relationship of the Sidang Injil Borneo to Government

The Sidang Injil Borneo gives its loyalty to the constituted Government of the country in accordance with the statement of scripture such as that contained in Romans 13-1-3a as follows:

'Let every person be subject to the governing authorities. For there is no authority except from God, and those that exist have been instituted by God. Therefore he who resists the authorities resists what God had appointed, and those who resist will incur judgment. God rulers are not a terror to the good works, but the evil.'

Rule 15. Alteration to Constitution

This constitution may be altered provided the motion has been passed by a two-thirds majority of the general conference.

Such alterations or amendments shall take effect from the date of their approval by the Registrar of Societies.

Lawas: December 1961; Amended December 1965; July 1969; December 1970.

Source: OMF Archive, Kuala Lumpur

Appendix 7
Important Personalities in the BEM

Charles Hudson Southwell

Hudson Southwell was born on 28 June 1900 of devout Christian parents who had lofty ambitions for him to be a missionary. He obtained a scholarship to study for a degree in Science at the University of Melbourne, majoring in Chemistry in 1921. After fulfilling his contract with the Department of Technical Education in 1926, he studied at the Melbourne Bible Institute (MBI) under the Rev. C.H. Nash from 1927 to 1928. Together with Frank Davidson and Carey Tolley, they became the three pioneer missionaries of the newly formed Borneo Evangelical Mission (BEM) to Sarawak in 1928. Hudson Southwell was married to Winsome Howell at St Matthew's Church, Melbourne on 29 April 1932. He was first the Field Secretary of the BEM from 1928 and later the Field Director/Chairman of the BEM from 1939 until 1948. He died in Perth in 2000.

Sources: Uncharted Waters, 51-7. BEM Field Conference Minutes, 25-31 August 1939.

Frank T. Davidson

Frank Davidson, the second son of the managing director of Morgan and Marshall the publishers, was born in England and belonged to the Anglican Church. His family emigrated to Australia when Frank was sixteen. He had an English public school education and 'considered himself an Englishman'. He studied at MBI during the same time as Southwell and Tolley. He married Enid Gray, a graduate of the University of Sydney, in February 1935, and they went out to Sarawak later the same year. They first worked among the Kelabit in the Medihit but later relocated to work among the Lun Bawang at Trusan in 1939. Davidson died in internment at Kuching on 27 April 1945.

Sources: Drunk before Dawn, 24, 51, 79-80, and BEM Field Conference Minutes, 26 January 1935 and 3-4 March 1935.

Carey Tolley

Carey Tolley, an Australian from the Brethren church, was one of the three pioneer missionaries of the BEM in 1928 after his studies at MBI. In 1935, he was married to Florence Roberts Thomson, who joined him to work in the

Lubai area, Limbang valley, until he resigned from the Mission in January 1939. He died in Currimbin, Queensland, on 2 January 1969.

Sources: Drunk before Dawn, 24; BEM Seventh Annual Report 1936, 1; BEM NL February, 1969, 4.

Alan Belcher

Alan Belcher, an Australian, joined the BEM as a missionary in 1940, working in Sabah. He was interned at Kuching together with Southwell, Davidson, and Tolley from 1941 to 1945. After his internment, he returned to Australia and later married Madge Hill on 16 November 1946. They returned to work in Sarawak in January 1948, and Belcher succeeded Southwell as the second Field Director/Chairman from August 1948 to 1968. He now lives in retirement in Benalla, Victoria, Australia.

Sources: Drunk before Dawn, 71-72, 92-93; BEM NL September 1946, 4 and February 1948, 4.

Dr Bill Lees

Bill Lees, an Englishman, was a medical doctor by training. He was a member of Westminster Chapel, London, when he joined the BEM in 1951. Both he and Shirley, his wife, were mainly involved in translation work among the Tagal in Sabah. Bill Lees was Secretary-Treasurer of the Mission in 1958 and was Deputy Chairman during Alan Belcher's furlough in 1963. He returned to England on furlough in 1966 and thereafter continued to be active in deputation ministry for the BEM in the U.K. He now lives in retirement in Reading, England.

Sources: BEM NL June 1952, 3; December 1958, 1 and December 1966, 2.

Dr Bill Hawes

Bill Hawes was trained as a medical doctor at the University College of London and subsequently worked for two years at the Mildmay Mission Hospital. He later became an assistant minister at the Landsdowne Evangelical Church, Norwood, South London before joining the BEM in 1963. He became the third BEM Field Director/Chairman in August 1968 at the age of thirty-two. He was married to Dr Valerie Myatt, another English doctor, on 29 May 1971. When BEM merged with OMF in 1975, he continued as Director until 1979 when he returned to the U.K. He now lives in Plaistow, South London.

Sources: Drunk before Dawn, 166. BEM NL August 1968, 1 and August 1971, 3.

Colin Reasbeck

Colin Reasbeck went out originally as a missionary teacher with the Missionary Society of the Methodist Church, England, to Sarawak. He taught at the Methodist Secondary School in Sibu from September 1961. During his four years in Sarawak, he came into contact with BEM work among the Iban in the Third Division. When he returned to England, he spent two years at All Nations Missionary College as preparation to return to Sarawak as a BEM missionary. He joined the BEM in June 1967 and worked among the Iban in the Third Division until 1978. He now lives in Doncaster.

Sources: BEM NL June 1964, 1; August 1967, 4 and June 1971, 1-2.

John Harold MacCracken

John Harold MacCracken studied law in the University of Melbourne (1924-28). In university, he was a foundation member of the Melbourne University Evangelical Union, and had encouraged his contemporaries to serve as foreign missionaries. He was President of the Crusader Union of Victoria from 1929 to 1950 and had come to know Alan Belcher when he was a boy at Trinity Grammar School, Melbourne. He was invited by Rev. Nash to join the BEM Home Council first as a member in 1933 and later became the BEM President from 1935, serving in this capacity for thirty-five years until 1971. He had worked alongside three BEM Field Directors, Southwell (1939-1948), Belcher (1948-68) and Hawes (1968-71). He died in Melbourne in 1999.

Sources: BEM NL, October 1971, 2; BEM Eighth Annual Report 1937, 3; John Harold MacCracken, Summing Up, 120-23, 139, 180-89.

Bibliography

Primary Sources

UNPUBLISHED SOURCES

Bible College of Victoria Library, Melbourne

Minutes of the BEM Home Council, 1928-1934, 1937-1941, December 1945-May1946

Minutes of the BEM Field Conference October 1934-December 1941, 1948-1974

Minutes of the BEM Field Executive 1950-1979

An Outline of Events Leading to the Formation of a Borneo Fellowship, and the Early Minutes of the Borneo Evangelical Mission, July 1927 to February 1929.

Charles Hudson Southwell Unpublished Memoirs

Overseas Missionary Fellowship (OMF), Kuala Lumpur

BEM Home Council Minutes and Correspondence 1934-1941

Letter of BEM Home Council to M. Perrin, 16 March 1932.

Letter of Harold McCracken to Rev. C.H. Nash, 10 May 1935.

Letter of Winnie C. Mills to H. McCracken, 12 October 1939.

BEM Field Conference Minutes 1934-1941

Letter of Norman Grubb to Stafford Young, 4 January 1938.

Letter of Stafford Young to Norman Grubb, 11 May 1938.

Memorandum Letter for F.T. Davidson regarding Council and Home matters, 28 July 1938.

BEM Field Correspondence: Field Chairman and Field Conference/Executive 1939-1941

Letter of Stafford Young to Field Conference members, 28 March 1939.

Letter of R.A. Bewsher to Field Conference, 12 December 1940.

Letter of F.T. Davidson to Field Executive, 3 August 1940.

Letter of Enid Davidson to Field Executive, 6 August 1940.

Letter of C.H. Southwell to F.T. Davidson and Field Executive, 17 September 1940.

Letter of F.T.Davidson to R.A. Bewsher, 1 October 1940.

Letter of R.A. Bewsher to F.T. Davidson, 28 October 1940.

Letter of C.H. Southwell to Field Conference, 4 November 1940.

Letter of F.T. Davidson to Field Conference, 4 December 1940.

Letter of R.A. Bewsher to Field Conference, 12 December 1940.

Letter of C.H. Southwell to Field Conference, 24 April 1941.

Letter of C.H. Southwell to Field Executive, 8 May 1941.
Letter of Stafford Young to Field Conference, 23 June 1941.
Letter of R.A. Bewsher to C.H. Southwell, 16 August 1941.
Letter of Stafford Young to Field Conference, 1 October 1941.
BEM Correspondence: Field Chairman and President 1947-1969
Letter of C.H. Southwell to H. McCracken, 8 March 1948.
Letter of C.H. Southwell to H. McCracken, 12 April 1948.
Letter of H. McCracken to A. Belcher, 5 July 1950.
Letter of H. McCracken to A. Belcher, 21 July 1950.
Letter of H. McCracken to Bill Lees, 26 March, 1963.
Letter of H. McCracken to Bill Lees, 28 May 1963.
Letter of Alan Belcher to H. McCracken and John Smith, 26 May 1966.
Letter of H. McCracken to Dr Bill Hawes, 18 September 1969.
BEM Newsletter/Prayer Notes 1940-1941
BEM Field Executive Minutes 1950-1968
BEM Field Reports 1967-1968
Balan Seling's letters of advice concerning the revival
Balan Seling, 'A Brief Guide concerning the work of the Holy Spirit at this time.' 23 October 1973.
_____, Letters to the SIB churches in Bario, 3 and 10 November 1973.
_____, 'Dreams, Visions and Voices', Sarawak, 28 December 1973.
_____, Letter to the SIB Executive Council, 20 January 1974.
_____, 'Growing in Christ', 17 January 1974.
_____, 'Guard against slander of the Name of Jesus on our account', 23 January 1974.
_____, 'Buah-buah Rohu'l Kudus', 8 May 1974.
_____, 'Awas tiga senjata tajam Iblis', 16 February 1976.
_____, 'Buah-buah Rohu'l Kudus (sambongan)', 23 February 1976.
Statement of the Character, Principles and Practice of the BEM, September 1939.
Collection of Ray Cunningham, Sydney
Letters of Resident, Fourth Division, to C.H. Southwell , 4 February 1948 (Ref. No. 14 in O/4/IV).
Letter of Resident, Fourth Division, to Alan Belcher, 3 April 1952 (Ref. No. 14 in 0/7/50).
Letter of Resident, Fourth Division, to Alan Belcher, 20 June 1952 (Ref. No. 24 in 0/7/50)

PUBLISHED SOURCES

Bible College of Victoria Library, Melbourne
Borneo Evangelical Mission Annual Reports 1928-1951.
Borneo Evangelical Mission Newsletters, July 1936-January 1942; 1946-1986
Borneo Prayer Notes, May 1936-February 1940, August 1941.
Borneo Prayer Fellowship Notes, 1963, 1979-1990.

BEM Prayer letters (cyclostyled) October 1932-March 1936.
BEM Praying Borneo, 1964-1986.
BEM, 'Jungle Keswick - Brayong 1951', (Melbourne, n.d.).
Sidang Injil Borneo Headquarters, Miri
SIB Handbook and Rules 1980 (1st edn), 1989 (2nd edn).
SIB Souvenir Magazine, Sarawak, 1988.

NEWSPAPERS
New Life (Melbourne)
The Life of Faith (Melbourne)

Secondary Sources

Aichner, P., 'Adat Bungan'. *Sarawak Museum Journal* 7:8 (December 1956), 476-477.

Allen, Roland, Missionary Methods: St Paul's or Ours? London: R. Scott, 1912.

——. Missionary Principles and Practice. London: R. Scott, 1913.

——. *Pentecost & the World.* London: Oxford University Press, 1917.

——. *The Spontaneous Expansion of the Church.* London: World Dominion Press, 1927.

Amster, Matthew H., 'Community, Ethnicity, and Modes of Association among the Kelabits of Sarawak, East Malaysia'. PhD thesis. Brandeis University, 1998.

——. 'New Sacred Lands: The Making of a Christian Prayer Mountain in Highland Borneo'. In *Sacred Places and Modern Landscapes: Sacred Geography and Social Religious Transformations in South and Southeast Asia*, 131-160. Ed. Ronald A Lukens-Bull. Tempe: Program for Southeast Asian Studies, Arizona State University, 2003.

Andaya, Barbara W. and Y. Leonard Andaya. *A History of Malaysia.* London: Macmillan, 1982.

Anderson, Gerald, Ed. *Biographical Dictionary of Christian Missions.* New York: Simon & Schuster Macmillan, 1998.

——. *Mission Legacies.* Maryknoll: Orbis Books, 1994.

Archer, John Belville. *Glimpses of Sarawak between 1916 and 1946.* Hull: Department of SEA Studies, University of Hull, 1997.

Aulen, Gustaf. *Christus Victor.* New York: MacMillan, 1960; Reprint. London: Society for Promoting Christian Knowledge, 1975.

Bala, Poline. Changing Borders and Identities in the Kelabit Highlands: Anthropological Reflections on Growing Up in a Kelabit Village near the International Border. Kota Samarahan: University Malaysia Sarawak, 2002.

Banks, Edward. 'Murut Morons'. *Sarawak Gazette* (31 July 1939), 107.

Baring-Gould, S. and C.A. Bampfylde. *A History of Sarawak under its Two White Rajahs.* London: Henry Sotheran, 1909.

Barrett, David B., Ed. *World Christian Encyclopaedia.* Oxford/New York: Oxford University Press, 1982.

Barrett, David B., George T. Kurian, and Todd M. Johnson, Eds. *World Christian Encyclopaedia.* Oxford/New York: Oxford University Press, 2001.

Baur, John. *2000 Years of Christianity in Africa.* Nairobi: Paulines Publications Africa, 1994

Beaver, R. Pierce, Ed. To Advance the Gospel: Selections from the Writings of Rufus *Anderson.* Grand Rapids: Eerdmans, 1967.

Bebbington, David. Evangelicalism in Modern Britain: A History from the 1730s to the 1980s. London: Routledge, 1993.

—. Holiness in Nineteenth-Century England. Carlisle: Paternoster, 2000.

Bediako, Kwame. *Christianity in Africa: The Renewal of a Non-Western Religion.* Edinburgh/Maryknoll: Edinburgh University Press/Orbis Books, 1995.

Bennett, J.C. 'Charles Simeon and the Evangelical Anglican Mission Movement: A Study of Voluntaryism and Church Mission Tensions'. PhD thesis. University of Edinburgh, 1992.

Bewsher, R.A. 'Correspondence: Ulu Lordsfeed'. *Sarawak Gazette* (31 March 1957), 69.

—. 'The Bisaya Group'. *Sarawak Gazette* (31 December 1958), 239-241.

Bible College of Victoria (BCV) Faculty Handbook 2002.

Blumhofer, Edith L. and Randall Balmer. *Modern Christian Revivals.* Urbana and Chicago: University of Illinois Press, 1993.

Borneo Evangelical Mission. *Towards the Goal.* Melbourne: The Austral Printing and Publishing Co., 1954.

—. *From Every Tribe*. Lawas: Borneo Evangelical Mission, n.d.

—. *Commit Thou to Faithful Men.* Melbourne: Spectator Publishing Co, c. 1957.

—. *Headhunter's Daughter.* Lawas: Borneo Evangelical Mission, n.d.

Bowie, Fiona, Deborah Kirkwood and Shirley Ardener, Eds. *Women and Missions: Past and Present*. Oxford: Berg Publishers, 1993.

Branner, John K. 'McGavran speaks on Roland Allen'. *Evangelical Missions Quarterly* 8:3 (Spring 1972), 165-174.

Bray, Jenny. *Longhouse of Faith.* Melbourne: Borneo Evangelical Mission, 1971.

—. *Longhouse of Fear.* Melbourne: Borneo Evangelical Mission, n.d.

—.*Jewel From the Darkness.* Melbourne: Borneo Evangelical Mission, 1971.

Breward, Ian. *A History of the Australian Churches.* Sydney: Allen & Unwin, 1993.

—.*A History of the Churches in Australasia.* Oxford: Oxford University Press, 2001.

Brooke, Charles. *Ten Years in Sarawak.* 2 volumes. London: Tinsley Brothers, 1866; Reprint. Singapore: Oxford University Press, 1990.

——. Queries, Past, Present and Future. London: Planet, 1907.

Brooke, Sylvia. *Queen of the Headhunters.* London: Sidgewick and Jackson, 1970; Reprint. Kuala Lumpur: Oxford University Press, 1990.

Broomhall, A.J. *Hudson Taylor and China's Open Century.* 6 volumes. Sevenoaks: Hodder and Stoughton, 1981-89.

Bulan, Lucy and David Labang. 'The Kelabit Harvest'. *Sarawak Museum Journal* 27, 48 (1979), 43-52.

Bulan, Solomon and Lillian Bulan-Dorai. *The Bario Revival.* Kuala Lumpur: Home Matters Network, 2004.

Bunyon, C.J. *Memoirs of Francis Thomas McDougall and of Harriette His Wife.* London: Longmans, 1889.

Bullock, F.W.B. *The History of Ridley Hall,* Vol. I. Cambridge: University Press, 1941.

Carpenter, Joel and W.R. Shenk, Eds. Earthen Vessels: American Evangelicals and Foreign Missions, 1880-1980. Grand Rapids: Eerdmans, 1990.

Cartwright, F.T. *Tuan Hoover of Borneo.* New York: Abingdon Press, 1938.

Chambers, David. *Tempest-Tossed: The Life and Teaching of the Rev. C.H. Nash, MA.* Melbourne: Church Press Publications, 1959.

Chan Lean Choi, Lily. 'Christian Missions and the Ibans of Sarawak during the Brooke Rule 1840's to 1940's'. BA thesis. Australian National University, 1975.

Chew, Daniel. *Chinese Pioneers on the Sarawak Frontier, 1841-1941.* Singapore: Oxford University Press, 1990.

——. 'Social and Cultural Trends in Sarawak'. *Sarawak Museum Journal* 47:68 (December 1994), 85-100.

Chew, Maureen K.C. *The Journey of the Catholic Church in Malaysia, 1511-1996.* Kuala Lumpur: Catholic Research Centre, 2000.

Christensen, Torben and W.R. Hutchison, Eds. *Missionary Ideologies in the Imperialist Era: 1880-1920.* Aarhus, Denmark: Aros Publishers, 1990.

Christie, Clive J. Southeast Asia in the Twentieth Century: A Reader. London: I.B. Tauris, 1998.

Clack, W.S., Ed. We Will Go: The History of 70 years of Training Men and Women for World Missionary Ministry, 1920-1990. Melbourne: Bible College of Victoria, 1990.

Clark, Sidney J.W. *The Indigenous Church.* London: World Dominion Press, 1928.

Comaroff, Jean and John Comaroff. *Of Revelation and Revolution: Christianity, Colonialism and Consciousness in South Africa.* Vol. 1. Chicago/London: University of Chicago Press, 1991.

——. Of Revelation and Revolution: The Dialectics of Modernity on a South African Frontier. Vol. 2. Chicago/London: University of Chicago Press, 1997.

Conley, William, W. The Kalimantan Kenyah: A Study of Tribal Conversion in Terms of Dynamic Cultural Themes. Nutley: Presbyterian and Reformed Publishing Co., 1976.

——. 'Kenyah Cultural Themes and Their Interrelations'. *Sarawak Museum Journal* 12:43 (1974), 303-310.

——. 'Kenyah Receptivity and Response to Christianity'. *Sarawak Museum Journal* 12:43 (1974), 311-324.

Cowan, C.D. Nineteenth Century Malaya: The Origins of British Political Control. London: Oxford University Press, 1961.

Crain, J.B. 'Murut Depopulation and the Sipitang Lun Dayeh'. *Journal of the Malaysian Branch of the Royal Asiatic Society* 45:2 (1972), 109-121.

Cramb, R.A. and R.H.W. Reece, Eds. *Development in Sarawak.* Clayton: Centre of Southeast Asian Studies, Monash University, 1988.

Cunningham, Ray. Longhouses Open Doors: God's Glory in Borneo. Ormond: Hudson Press, 2002.

Currie R., A. Gilbert and Lee Horsley. Churches and Church Goers: Patterns of Church Growth in the British Isles since 1700. Oxford: Clarendon Press, 1977.

Davidson, Enid. The Lun Bawang and the Gospel. n.d. Unpublished paper.

Davis, G.C. 'A Hundred Days Drunk'. *Frontier* 6:1 (Spring 1963):50-54.

Davis, Raymond J. 'What missions must do to survive in the 70s', *Evangelical Mission Quarterly* 6:4 (Summer 1970):221-226.

Deegan, James L. 'Some Lun Bawang Spirit Chants'. *Sarawak Museum Journal* 18:36-37 (July-December 1970), 266.

——. 'Change Among the Lun Bawang, a Borneo People'. PhD thesis. University of Washington, 1973.

——. 'Community Fragmentation among the Lun Bawang'. *Sarawak Museum Journal*, 22:43 (January-December 1974):229-247.

de Windt, Henry. *My Restless Life.* London: Grant Richards, 1909.

Dickey, Brian, Ed. *The Australian Dictionary of Evangelical Biography.* Sydney: Evangelical History Association, 1994.

Dickey, Brian. 'Evangelical Anglicans Compared'. In *Amazing Grace: Evangelicalism in Australia, Britain, Canada and the United States.* Eds. George A. Rawlyk, and Mark Noll. Grand Rapids: Baker Books, 1993, 215-240.

Doering, Otto C. 'Government under Charles Brooke'. *Journal of the Malayan Branch of the Royal Asiatic Society* 39:2 (1966), 95-107.

Edwards, Leonard and Peter W. Stevens. *Short Histories of the Lawas and Kanowit Districts.* Kuching: Borneo Literature Bureau, 1971.

Etherington, Norman. 'Recent Trends in the Historiography of Christianity in Southern Africa', *Journal of Southern African Studies* 22:2 (June 1996), 201-219

Elliott, Peter. Asang: The Story of Trevor White and the Dusuns of Sabah. Cleveland: Australia: Delia Wilson, 1997.

Evans, Ivor H.N. *Among Primitive Peoples in Borneo.* London: Seeley Service, 1922.

Fiedler, Klaus. *The Story of Faith Missions.* Oxford: Regnum Books/Lynx Communications, 1994.

Fife, Eric S. and Arthur F. Glasser. *Missions in Crisis: Rethinking Missionary Strategy.* London: Inter Varsity Fellowship, 1962.

Fisher, Humphrey. 'Conversion Reconsidered: Some Historical Aspects of Religious Conversion in Black Africa'. *Africa* 43 (1973), 27-40.

——. 'The Juggernaut's Apologia: Conversion to Islam in Black Africa'. *Africa* 55 (1985), 153-173.

Fitly Framed: Diocese of Borneo, 1855-1955. Kuching: Centenary Committee of the Diocese of Borneo, 1955.

Freeman, Derek. Iban Agriculture: A report of the shifting cultivation of hill rice by the Iban of Sarawak. London: HMSO, 1955.

——. *Report on the Iban of Sarawak.* Kuching: Government Printing Office, 1955.

——. *The Iban of Borneo*, London School of Economics Monographs on Social Anthropology No. 41, 1955. Reprint. Kulala Lumpur: S.A. Majeed & Co, 1992.

Glover, Willis B. Evangelical Nonconformists and Higher Criticism in the Nineteenth Century. London: Independent Press, 1954.

Government of Malaysia, Department of Statistics. *1980 Population and Housing Census of Malaysia, Population Report, Sarawak Part 1.* Kuala Lumpur: Department of Statistics, 1983.

Greenway, Roger S. 'A Church-Planting Method That Works in Urban Areas'. *Evangelical Missions Quarterly* 6:3 (Spring 1970), 152-158

——. *Guidelines for Urban Church Planting.* Grand Rapids: Baker Book House, 1976.

——. Apostles to the City: Biblical Strategies for Urban Missions. Grand Rapids: Baker Book House, 1978.

——. 'Don't Be an Urban Missionary Unless ...' *Evangelical Missions Quarterly* 19:2 (April 1983), 86-94.

Grijpstra, B. G. *Common Efforts in the Development of Rural Sarawak, Malaysia, 1976.* Wageningen: Centre for Agricultural Publishing and Documentation, 1976.

Hanciles, Jehu. Euthanasia of a Mission: African Church Autonomy in a Colonial Context. New York: Praeger Publishers, 2002.

Harford, C.F., Ed. *The Keswick Convention.* London: Marshall, 1907.

Harford, John B. and McDonald, Federick C. *Handley Carr Glyn Moule, Bishop of Durham: A Biography.* London: Hodder and Stoughton, 1922.

Harrisson, Tom. *Classifying the People.* Kuching: Govt. Printing Press, 1950.

——. 'Robert Burns - the first Ethnologist and Explorer of Interior Sarawak', *Sarawak Museum Journal* 5:3 (November 1951), 463-477.

——. 'Outside Influence on the Kelabits'. *Sarawak Museum Journal* 6:4 (December 1954), 104-125.

——. 'Ulu Problem. A Wing and a Prayer'. *Sarawak Gazette* (31 May 1956), 114-116.

——. 'Ulu Problem II. Zealots and Dreams'. *Sarawak Gazette* (30 June 1956), 145-147.

——, Ed. *The Peoples of Sarawak.* Kuching: Borneo Literature Bureau, 1959.

——. *World Within: A Borneo Story.* London: Cresset Press, 1959; Reprnt. Singapore: Oxford University Press, 1990.

Hefner, Robert W., Ed. Conversion to Christianity: Historical and Anthropological Perspectives on a Great Transformation. Berkeley: University of California Press, 1993.

Hepburn, B.A. St. J., (comp). The Handbook of Sarawak: Comprising Historical, Statistical and General Information Obtained from Official and Other Reliable Records. Singapore: Malaya Publishing House for the Government of Sarawak, 1949.

Hession, Roy. *The Calvary Road.* London: Christian Literature Crusade, 1950.

Hewitt, Gordon. The Problem of Success: A History of the Church Mission Society, 1910-1942. Vol.II. London: SCM, 1977.

Hodges, Melvin. *The Indigenous Church.* Springfield, MO: Gospel Publishing House, 1953.

——. On the Mission Field: The Indigenous Church. Chicago: Moody Press, 1953.

Hoke, Donald, Ed. *The Church in Asia*. Chicago: Moody Press, 1975.

Hong, Evelyne. 'Kenyah Society in Transition: A Baram Case Study'. MSocSc thesis. University Sains Malaysia, 1977.

Hood, George. *Neither Bang nor Whimper: The End of a Missionary Era in China.* Singapore: The Presbyterian Church of Singapore, 1991.

Horton, R. 'African Conversion'. *Africa* 41:2 (1971), 86-108.

——. 'On the Rationality of Conversion, Parts I & II'. *Africa* 45:3 (1975), 219-235 & 373-399.

Hunt, Everett N. 'The Legacy of John Livingston Nevius'. *International Bulletin of Missionary Research* 15:3 (July 1991), 120-124.

Hunt, Robert, K.H. Lee and John Roxborogh, Eds. *Christianity in Malaysia: A Denominational History.* Kuala Lumpur: Pelanduk, 1992.

Huntley, David A. 'The Withdrawal of the China Inland Mission from China and their Redeployment to New Fields in East Asia'. PhD dissertation. Trinity Theological Seminary, 2003.

Hutchins, Ruth Presswood. *No Sacrifice Too Great: The Story of Ernest and Ruth Presswood.* Camp Hill: Christian Publications, 1993.

Hutchinson, Mark, Edmund Campion and Stuart Piggin, Eds. *Reviving Australia. Essays on the History and Experience of Revivalism in Australian Christianity.* Sydney: Centre for the Study of Australian Christianity, 1994.

Hutchinson, Mark and G. Treloar, Eds. *This Gospel Shall be Preached: Essays on Australian Contribution to World Mission.* Sydney: Centre for the Study of Australian Christianity, 1997.

Ingleson, John E. *Expanding the Empire: James Brooke and the Sarawak Lobby 1839-1868.* Perth: Centre for SSEA Studies, University of Western Australia, 1979.

Irwin, Graham. Nineteenth Century Borneo: A Study in Diplomatic Rivalry. Kuala Lumpur: University of Malaya, 1955.

Jackson, J.C. *Sarawak: A Geographical Survey of a Developing State.* London: University of London Press, 1968.

James, Lawrence. The Rise and Fall of the British Empire. London: Abacus, 1998.

Janowski, Monica. 'Gender, Power and Christianity among the Kelabit of Sarawak'. Unpublished paper presented at the Association of South-east Asian Studies United Kingdom (ASEASUK) annual meeting, 25-27 April 1996.

Jensen, E. *The Iban and Their Religion.* London: Oxford University Press, 1974.

Jerusalem Meeting of the International Missionary Council, 1928. 8 vols. London/Oxford: Humphrey Milford/Oxford University Press, 1928.

Jones, L.W. *The Population of Borneo.* London: Athlone Press, 1966.

Joseph, Terence. 'The Longhouse Church in Sarawak'. ThM thesis. Southern Methodist University, 1964.

Keppel, Henry. *The Expedition to Borneo of HMS Dido for the Suppression of Piracy with Extracts from the Journals of James Brooke Esq.* 2 vols in 1. London: Chapman and Hall, 1846; Singapore: Oxford University Press, 1991.

Kim, Sebastian C.H. In Search of Identity: Debates on Religious Conversion in India. New Delhi: Oxford University Press, 2003.

King, Victor T., Ed. *Essays on Borneo Societies.* Oxford: Oxford University Press, 1978.

——. *The Peoples of Borneo.* Oxford: Blackwell, 1993.

——. *The World Within: The Ethnic Groups of Borneo: Essays on Borneo Societies.* Oxford: Oxford University Press, 1978; Reprint. Kuala Lumpur: S.A. Majeed and Co, 1994.

Kirkwood, Deborah. 'Protestant Missionary Women: Wives and Spinsters'. In *Women and Missions: Past and Present.* Ed. Fiona Bowie, D. Kirkwood and S. Ardener. Oxford: Berg Publishers, 1993, 23-42.

Ko, Joseph Tee Hock. 'Changing Patterns of Sub-National Ethnic Distribution in Sarawak, 1939-1980'. *Sarawak Museum Journal* 36:57 (December 1986), 1-11.

Koch, Kurt. *The Revival in Indonesia.* Grand Rapids: Kregel Publications, 1971.

——. Wine of God: Revival in Indonesia, Formosa, Solomon Islands and South India. Laval, Canada: Christian Evangelism Publications, 1974.

Koepping, Elizabeth. 'Hunting with the Head: Borneo Villagers Negotiating Exclusivist Religion'. *Studies in World Christianity,* Vol 12.1 (2006), 59-78.

Kraemer, Hendrik. From Missionfield to Independent Church: Report on a decisive decade in the growth of indigenous churches in Indonesia. 1st British ed. London: SCM Press, 1958.

Kraft, Marguerite. 'Reaching Out For Spiritual Power: A Study in the Dynamics of Felt Needs and Spiritual Power'. PhD dissertation. Fuller Theological Seminary, 1990.

Laeng, Joachim Ulok. 'The Inexorable Exodus'. *Sarawak Gazette* (31 March 1974), 49-50.

——. 'The lonely plight of the Old Ulu Folks'. *Sarawak Gazette* (31 August 1975), 181-182.

——. 'Educational Problems in the Ulu'. *Sarawak Gazette* (30 November 1975), 269-270.

Lamb, Christopher and Bryant M. Darrol. *Religious Conversions: Contemporary Practices and Controversies.* London/New York: Cassell, 1999.

Langub, Jayl. 'Adaptation to a settled life by the Punan of the Belaga Sub-District'. *Sarawak Museum Journal* 22:43 (1974), 295-301.

——. 'Ethnic Self Labelling of the Muruts or Lun Bawang of Sarawak'. *Sarawak Gazette* (December 1987), 30-35.

——. 'Some Aspects of the Life of the Penan'. *Sarawak Museum Journal* 60:61 (December 1989), 169-184.

Lee, Boon Thong and Tengku Shamsul Bahrin. 'The Bario Exodus: A Conception of Sarawak Urbanisation'. *Borneo Review* 4: 2, 113-28.

Lees, Shirley. *Jungle Fire.* London: Borneo Evangelical Mission, 1964.

——. *Drunk before Dawn.* Sevenoaks: Overseas Missionary Fellowship, 1978.

Lees, William C. *The Mission of the Church.* Lawas: Borneo Evangelical Mission, n.d.

——. *Second Thoughts in Missions.* Dorset: The Overcomer Literature Trust, 1964.

Lees, William C. and Shirley Lees. *Is it Sacrifice? Experiencing Mission and Revival in Borneo*. Leicester: Inter Varsity Press, 1987.

Lee, Yong Leng. 'The Population of Sarawak'. *Geographical Journal, London* 131:3 (Sept, 1965), 344-356.

——. *Population and Settlement in Sarawak.* Singapore: Donald Moore for Asia Pacific Press, 1970.

Leigh, Michael B. *The Chinese Community of Sarawak: A Study of Communal Relations.* Singapore: Malaysia Publishing House Ltd for the Department of History, University of Singapore, 1964.

——. The Rising Moon: Political Change in Sarawak. Sydney: Sydney University Press, 1974.

——. 'Local Government: Its Origins and Early Development'. *Sarawak Museum Journal* 23:44 (1975), 9-27.

——. 'Reflections on Poltical Change, Sarawak in Malaysia, 1963-1983'. *Sarawak Museum Journal* 32:63 (August 1983), 159-166.

Lewis, Rodger. Karya Kristus di Indonesia: Sejarah Gereja Kemah Injil Indonesia sejak 1930. Bandung: Yayasan Kalam Hidup, 1995.

Liong, Yuk Chong. 'A Historical Inquiry into the Quest for a Post-Independence Identity: The Chinese Methodist Church in Sarawak, Malaysia, 1963-1988'. PhD thesis. University of Birmingham, 2000.

Loane, Marcus. *The Story of the China Inland Mission in Australia and New Zealand 1890-1964.* Sydney: China Inland Mission/Overseas Missionary Fellowship, 1965.

——. 'The Keswick Convention and the Missionary Movement'. *Southern Cross Booklet* No. 3 (Sydney: Diocese of Sydney, n.d), i-vii.

Lockard, Craig Alan. 'Charles Brooke and the Foundation of the Modern Chinese Community in Sarawak, 1863-1917'. *Sarawak Museum Journal* 19:38-39, (July-December 1971), 77-108.

——. From Kampong to City: A Social History of Kuching, Malaysia, 1820-1970. Athens: Ohio, 1987.

Long, Bob. Z Special Unit's Special War: Operation Semut1 soldiering with the headhunters of Borneo. Baywater: W.A.B. Long, 1999.

Long, Charles Henry and Anne Rowthorn. 'The Legacy of Roland Allen'. *International Bulletin of Mission Research* 13:2 (April 1989), 65-68.

McCracken, Harold. *Summing Up: John Harold McCracken (1906-1999).* Aranda, ACT: Heather and Paul Shelley, 2003.

McDonald, Malcolm. *Borneo People.* London: Jonathan Cape, 1956; Singapore: Oxford University Press, 1985.

McGee, Gary. 'The Legacy of Melvin Hodges'. *International Bulletin for Missionary Research* 22:1 (January 1998), 20-24.

Malaysia, Agreement Concluded between the United Kingdom of Great Britain and Northern Ireland, the Federation of Malaya, North Borneo and Singapore. London: HMSO, 1963.

Marsden, George, Ed. *Evangelicalism and Modern America.* Grand Rapids: Eerdmans, 1984.

Means, Gordon Paul. *Malaysian Politics.* 2nd ed. London: Hodder and Stoughton, 1976.

——. *Malaysian Politics: The Second Generation.* Singapore: Oxford University Press, 1991.

Metcalf, P.A. 'The Baram District: A Survey of Kenyah, Kayan and Penan Peoples'. *Sarawak Museum Journal* 22:43 (January-December 1974), 29-42.

——. 'The Passing of the Folk Religion in Central North Borneo'. *Sarawak Museum Journal* 25:46 (July-December 1977), 101-105.

Michell, Brian John. 'The Role of Missionary Partnership in Indigneous Church Development: A Malaysian Case Study'. DMiss thesis. Asia Graduate School of Theology, Philippines, 2004.

Morrison, Alastair. 'Ulu Lordsfeed'. *Sarawak Gazette* (31 January 1957), 4-7.

——. *Fair Land Sarawak: Some Reflections of an Expatriate Official.* Studies on Southeast Asia Program (SEAP). Ithaca, New York: Cornell University, 1993.

Mundy, R. Narrative of Events in Borneo and Celebes, Down to the Occupation of Labuan: From the Journals of James Brooke Esq., Rajah of Sarawak and Governor of Labuan, Together with a Narrative of the Operations of HMS Iris. Vol. I. London: John Murray, 1848.

Munting, Jonathan Jelanding. 'History of the Iban Church in Sarawak'. Research Paper. Trinity Theological College Singapore, 1979.

Mutalib, Husin. *Islam and Ethnicity in Malay Politics.* Singapore: Oxford University Press, 1990.

——. *Islam in Malaysia: From Revivalism to Islamic State.* Singapore: Singapore University Press, 1993.

Muzaffar, Chandra. *Islamic Resurgence in Malaysia*. Petaling Jaya: Penerbit Fajar Bakti Sdn Bhd, 1987.

Needham, Rodney. 'Penan and Punan'. *Journal of the Malayan Branch of the Royal Asiatic Society* 27 (1954), 73-83.

Nelson, Jack, 'The Indigenous Policy: Ideals and Realities'. *Mission Studies* XI-1, 21 (1994), 27-42.

Nevius, John Livingston. *The Planting and Development of Missionary Churches.* Studies in the World Church and Missions 4. Ed. Harvie Conn. Nutley, NJ: Presbyterian & Reformed Publishing, 1958 [1885].

Newberry, Warren B. 'Contextualising Indigenous Church Principles'. *Asian Journal of Pentecostal Studies* 8:1 (2005), 95-115.

Newton, Brian. 'A New Dawn Over Sarawak'. MA thesis. Fuller Theological Seminary, 1988.

Nightingale, Ken, *Headhunter's Daughter.* Melbourne: Borneo Evangelical Mission, n.d.

——. *Tribe in Transit.* Melbourne: Borneo Evangelical Mission, n.d.

——. *One Way Through the Jungle*. London: Overseas Missionary Fellowship/Borneo Evangelical Mission, 1975.

Noakes, J.L. *A Report on the 1947 Population Census.* Kuching: Government Printer, 1950.

——. 'Sarawak and Brunei: A Report on 1947 Population Census'. *Sarawak Museum Journal* 5:3 (November 1951), 628-644.

Noll, Mark A., David Bebbington and G.A. Rawlyk, Eds. Evangelicalism: Comparative Studies of Popular Protestantism in North America, the British Isles and Beyond. Oxford: Oxford University Press, 1994.

Okorocha, Cyril C. The Meaning of Religious Conversion in Africa: The Case of the Igbo of Nigeria. Aldershot: Groves Publishing Co. Ltd, 1987.

Ongkili, James. The Borneo Response to Malaysia, 1961-1963. Singapore: 1961.

——. *Modernization in East Malaysia,* 1960-1970. Kuala Lumpur: Oxford University Press, 1972.

Ooi, Keat Gin. Of Free Trade and Native Interests: The Brooke Rule and the Economic Development of Sarawak, 1841-1941. Kuala Lumpur: Oxford University Press, 1997.

Orr, J. Edwin. *Evangelical Awakenings in the South Seas.* Minneapolis: Bethany Fellowship Inc, 1976.

Pannikar, K.M. Asia and Western Dominance: A Survey of the Vasco Da Gama Epoch of Asian History 1498-1945. new edition. London: 1953.

Paproth, Darrell Neil. 'C.H. Nash and his Influence'. PhD thesis. Deakin University, 1993.

——. 'Revivalism in Melbourne from Federation to World War I: The Torrey-Chapman Campaigns'. In *Reviving Australia: Essays on the History and Experience of Revivalism in Australian Christianity.* Ed. Mark Hutchinson, Edmund Campion, and Stuart Piggin. Sydney: Centre for the Study of Australian Christianity, 1994, 143-69.

——. 'The Melbourne Bible Institute: Its Genesis, Ethos and Purpose'. In *The Furtherance of Religious Beliefs: Essays on the History of Theological Education in Australia.* Ed. G. Treloar. Sydney: Centre for the Study of Australian Christianity, 1997, 124-55.

——. *Failure Is Not Final: A Life of C.H. Nash.* Sydney: Centre for the Study of Australian Christianity, 1997.

Parker, David. *The Bible College Movement in Australia.* Paper presented at the 9th Conference of the South Pacific Association of Bible Colleges (SPABC), 22-27 August 1980, 1-9.

——. 'The Evangelical Heritage of Australian Protestantism: Towards An Historical Perspective'. *History Teacher*, May 1981, 16-31.

——. 'Fundamentalism and Conservative Protestántism in Australia, 1920-1980'. PhD thesis. University of Queensland, 1982.

——. 'The Bible Union: A Case Study in Australian Fundamentalism', *Journal of Religious History* 14:1 (June 1986), 74-79.

——. 'Theological and Bible College Education in Australia: An Evangelical Perspective'. *Journal of Christian Education,* Papers 86-87 (July & December 1986), 5-18 & 29-40.

Paton, David. M. Christian Missions and the Judgement of God. London: SCM, 1953.

Payne, Robert. *White Rajahs of Sarawak.* London: Robert Hale, 1960.

Peel, J.D.Y. *Religious Encounter and the Making of the Yoruba.* Bloomington & Indianapolis: Indiana University Press, 2000.

Phoon, W.O. 'Malaysia-Singapore'. In *The Church in Asia.* Ed. Donald Hoke. Chicago: Moody Press, 1975, 411-33.

Pickett, J. Waskom. *Christian Mass Movements in India.* New York: Abingdon, 1933.

Pierson, D.L. *Arthur T. Pierson: A Biography by his Son.* London: Nisbet & Co., 1912.

Piggin, Stuart. *Making Evangelical Missionaries, 1789-1858.* Appleford, Oxford: Sutton Courtenay Press, 1984.

—. 'Pietism, Pluralism, and Provincialism: The Divergent Paths of Melbourne and Sydney Evangelicalism, 1848-1988'. *Southern Cross,* February 1991.

—. 'The American and British Contributions to Evangelicalism in Australia'. In *Evangelicalism: Comparative Studies of Popular Protestantism in North America, the British Isles, and Beyond, 1700-1990.* Eds. Mark Noll, David Bebbington, and George A Rawlyk. New York: Oxford University Press, 1994, 290-309.

—. 'Towards a Theoretical Understanding of Revival: Recent Developments in the Historiography of Revival'. In *Reviving Australia: Essays on the History and Experience of Revival and Revivalism in Australian Christianity.* Eds. M. Hutchinson, E. Campion and S. Piggin. Sydney: Centre for the Study of Australian Christianity, 1994, 13-33.

—. Evangelical Christianity in Australia: Spirit, Word and World. Melbourne: Oxford University Press, 1996.

—. Firestorm of the Lord: The History of and Prospects for Revival in the Church and the World. Carlisle: Paternoster Press, 2000.

Pirouet, Louise M. Black Evangelists: The Spread of Christianity in Uganda, 1891-1914. London: Rex Collings, 1978.

—. 'East African Christians and World War I'. *Journal of African History* 19:1 (1978), 117-130.

Pollard, Elizabeth. *Kuching Past and Present.* Kuching: Borneo Literature Bureau, 1972.

Pollard, F.H. 'The Muruts of Sarawak'. *Sarawak Museum Journal* 4:13 (July 1933), 139-155.

—. 'Some Comparative Notes on Muruts and Kelabits'. *Sarawak Museum Journal* 4:14 (December 1935), 223-227.

Pollock, D. 'Conversion and Community in Amazonia'. In *Conversion to Christianity.* Ed. R. Hefner. Berkeley: University of California Press, 1993, 165-197.

Pollock, John C. *Earth's Remotest End.* London: Hodder and Stoughton, 1960.

Porritt, Vernon L. *British Colonial Rule in Sarawak,* 1946-1963. Kuala Lumpur: Oxford University Press, 1997.

—. *Bapak Guru Orang Bisaya: A Pioneer in Social Experimentation in Sarawak, Ro Bewsher,* 1910-1998. Hull: Department of South East Asian Studies, University of Hull, 1999.

Porter, Andrew. 'Cambridge Keswick, and Late Nineteenth Century Attitudes to Africa'. *Journal of Imperial and Commonwealth History* 5 (1976-1977), 5-34.

——. Religion versus Empire? British Protestant Missionaries and Overseas Expansion, 1700-1914. Manchester: Manchester University Press, 2004.

Prattis, Ian. 'The Kayan-Kenyah 'Bungan Cult' in Sarawak'. *Sarawak Museum Journal* 11:21-22 (July-December 1963), 64-87.

Price, Charles and Randall, Ian. *Transforming Keswick.* Carlisle: Paternoster, 2000.

Pringle, Robert M. *Rajah and Rebels.* London: Macmillan, 1970.

——. 'The Brookes of Sarawak: Reformers inspite of Themselves'. *Sarawak Museum Journal* 19:38-39 (July-December 1971), 53-76.

Rambo, Lewis R. *Understanding Religious Conversion.* New Haven/London: Yale University Press, 1993.

Randall, Ian. Evangelical Experiences: A Study in the Spirituality of Evangelicalism, 1918-1939. Carlisle: Paternoster, 1999.

Ranger, Terence. 'Christianity and Indigenous Peoples: A Personal Overview'. *Journal of Religious History* 27:3 (October 2003), 255-71.

Rawlins, Joan. *Sarawak 1839 to 1968.* 2nd edn. Basingstoke/London: Macmillan, 1969.

Rawlyk, George A. and Mark Noll, Eds. Amazing Grace: Evangelicalism in Australia, Britain, Canada and the United States. Grand Rapids: Baker Books, 1993.

Reasbeck, Colin Arthur. 'The Growth of the Gospel among the Iban People of Sarawak'. MA dissertation. University of Sheffield, 2003.

Reinhardt, J.M. 'Administrative Policy and Practice in Sarawak: Continuity and Change Under the Brookes'. *Journal of Asian Studies* 29:4 (August 1970), 851-862.

Ride, Lindsay T. 'The Problem of Depopulation with Special Reference to British North Borneo'. *The Caduceus* 13 (1934), 169-184.

Rivers, W.H.R. *Essays on the Depopulation of Melanesia.* Cambridge: Cambridge University Press, 1922.

Rooney, John. Khabar Gembira: A History of the Catholic Church in East Malaysia and Brunei, 1880–1976. London: Burns and Oates, 1981.

Roosma, Gary Dean. 'Guiding Toward Independence: The Borneo Evangelical Mission and the Planting of the Borneo Evangelical Church'. ThM thesis. Regent College, Vancouver, 2006.

Rousseau, Jerome. *Central Borneo: Ethnic Identity and Social Life in a Stratified Society.* Oxford: Clarendon Press, 1990.

——. 'The Kayan'. In *World Within: The Ethnic Groups of Borneo.* Ed. Victor King. Kuala Lumpur: S.A. Majeed & Co, 1994, 120-159.

——. Kayan Beliefs: Ritual Life and Religious Change in Central Borneo. Leiden: KITLV Press, 1998.

Roxborogh, John. 'Christian and Missionary Alliance'. In *Dictionary of Asian Christianity*. Eds. Scott Sunquist, D.C. Wu, and J.H.C. Chew. Grand Rapids: Eerdmans, 2001, 160.

Runciman, Steven. *The White Rajahs: A History of Sarawak.* Cambridge: Cambridge University Press, 1960.

Russell, Sue A. *Conversion, Identity and Power: The Impact of Christianity on Power Relationships and Social Exchanges.* Lanham/New York/Oxford: American Society of Missiology/University Press of America, 1999.

Rutter, Owen. *The Pagans of North Borneo.* London: Hutchinson & Co., 1929

——. Rajah Brooke and Baroness Burdett Coutts. London: Hutchinson & Co., 1935.

Sagan, Jacob Dungau. 'The Kenyah of Sarawak'. *Sarawak Museum Journal* 60:61 (December 1989), 119-141.

Saging, Robert Lian. 'An Ethno-history of the Kelabit Tribe of Sarawak: A Brief Look at the Kelabit Tribe before World War II and After'. BA thesis. University of Malaya, 1976/77.

Saging, Robert Lian and Lucy Bulan. 'Kelabit Ethnography'. *Sarawak Museum Journal* 60:61 (December 1989), 89-118.

St. John, Spenser. *The Life of Sir James Brooke of Sarawak.* Edinburgh: Blackwood, 1879; Kuala Lumpur: Oxford University Press, 1994.

——. Rajah Brooke: the Englishman as Ruler of an Eastern State. London: Unwin, 1899.

Saint, Max. Twenty Years in Sarawak, 1848-1868: A Flourish for the Bishop and Brooke's Friend Grant. Braunton: Merlin Books, 1985; Kuala Lumpur: S.A. Majeed and Co., 1992.

Samporoh, Richard. 'The Establishment, Growth, Strengths and Weaknesses of the SIB Church'. BTh thesis. Malaysia Bible Seminary, 1992.

Sandeen, E.R. *The Roots of Fundamentalism.* Chicago: University of Chicago Press, 1970.

Sarawak Education Department. 'Outline of the History of Education in Sarawak'. *Journal of the Malaysian Historical Society, Sarawak Branch* 5 (June 1980), 11-19.

Saunders, Graham 'James Brooke and Asian Government'. *Brunei Museum Journal* 3:1 (1973), 105-117.

——. 'Bishops and Brookes: The Anglican Mission and the Brooke Raj in Sarawak, 1848 – 1941'. PhD thesis. University of Hull, 1989.

——. Bishops and Brookes: The Anglican Mission and the Brooke Raj in Sarawak, 1848 – 1941. Singapore: Oxford University Press, 1992.

Searle, Peter. *Politics in Sarawak, 1970-1976: The Iban Perspective.* Singapore: Oxford University Press, 1983.

Seling, Ding and Jayl Langub. 'The *Orang Ulu*: An Overview'. *Sarawak Museum Journal* 60:61 (December 1989), 19-36.

Sellato, Bernard. Nomads of the Borneo Rainforest: The Economics, Politics and Ideology of Settling Down. Honolulu: University of Hawaii Press, 1994.

Seymour, J. M. 'Education in Sarawak under Brooke Rule, 1841-1941'. *Sarawak Gazette* (30 June 1970), 113-119; (31 July 1970), 139-143; (31 August 1970), 156-159.

——. 'Objectives of Primary Education in Sarawak'. *Sarawak Museum Journal* 19:38-39 (July-December 1971), 167-183.

Shearer, Diana and Mina Tigan. 'Australians and Indigenous Church of Borneo: An Overview of Australian Contributions to Sarawak and Sabah through the Borneo Evangelical Mission and Overseas Missionary Fellowship'. In *This Gospel Shall be Preached: Essays on Australian Contribution to World Mission*. Eds. Mark Hutchinson and G. Treloar. Sydney: Centre for the Study of Australian Christianity, 1997, 147-163.

Shenk, Wilbert R. 'The Origins and Evolution of the Three-Selfs in Relation to China'. *International Bulletin for Missionary Research* 14:1 (January 1990), 28-34.

Simpson, A.B. *The Challenge of Missions*. New York: Christian Publishing Co., 1926.

Sloan, W.B. 'The Influence of the Keswick Convention on Missionary Work'. *International Review of Mission* 3:12 (October 1914), 708-720.

Smith, John. 'Borneo Evangelical Mission'. In *The Encyclopaedia of Modern Missions*. Ed. Goddard, Burton L.; Kerr, William N.; Lane, William L.; and Scholer, David M. London/New Jersey: Thomas Nelson and Sons, 1967, 92.

Sng, Bobby E.K. *In His Good Time: The Story of the Church in Singapore 1819-1978*. Singapore: Graduates Christian Fellowship, 1980.

Sormin, H.C. 'A History of the Seventh Day Adventist Church in Sarawak from 1915-1956'. MA thesis. Philippines Union College, 1971.

Southwell, C. Hudson. 'The Muruts'. *Sarawak Gazette* (30 April 1948), 85-86.

——. 'The Upriver People: Kayan and Kenyah'. *Sarawak Gazette* (30 September 1958), 160-164.

——. 'The Kayans and Kenyahs'. In *The Peoples of Sarawak*. Ed. T. Harrisson. Kuching: Sarawak Museum, 1959, 39-56.

——. 'The Baram Cultures'. *Sarawak Gazette* (31 May 1970), 95-96.

——. *Kayan-English Dictionary*. Marudi, Baram: 1980.

——. *Uncharted Waters*. Calgary: Astana Publishing, 1999.

——. *Unpublished Memoirs*. Manning, West Australia: ca. 1988.

Stanley, Brian. The Bible and the Flag: Protestant Missions and British Imperialism in the Nineteenth and Twentieth Centuries. Leicester: Apollos/IVP, 1990.

——, Ed. *Christian Missions and the Enlightenment*. Grand Rapids/Surrey: Eerdmans/Curzon, 2001.

——. 'Christianity and Civilization in English Evangelical Mission Thought'. In *Christian Missions and the Enlightenment.* Ed. Brian Stanley. Grand Rapids: Eerdmans, 2001, 169-197.

——. 'Conversion to Christianity: The Colonization of the Mind?' *International Review of Mission* 92;366 (July 2003), 315-331.

Stevens, Peter W., 'A History of Kanowit District'. *Sarawak Gazette* (31 Jan 1970), 2-9; (28 Feb 1970), 33-41; (31 Mar 1970), 51-57; (30 April 1970), 75-84.

Sunquist, Scott, David C.S. Wu and John H.C. Chew, Eds. *A Dictionary of Asian Christianity*. Grand Rapids: Eerdmans, 2001.

Sutlive, Vison H. Jr. *The Iban of Sarawak: Chronicle of a Vanishing World.* Prospect Heights: Waveland Press, 1988; Reprint. Kuala Lumpur: S.A. Majeed & Co, 1992.

Taber, Charles R. The World is Too Much with Us: 'Culture' in Modern Protestant Missions. Macon: Mercer University Press, 1991.

Tambaram Meeting of the International Missionary Council, 1938. 7 vols. London/Oxford: Humphrey Milford/ Oxford University Press, 1939.

Tarling, Nicholas. *The Burthen, the Risk and the Glory: A Biography of Sir James Brooke.* Kuala Lumpur: Oxford University Press, 1982.

Tarling, Nicholas, Ed. *The Cambridge History of Southeast Asia*: *From World War II to the Present.* Vol. 2, Part 2. Cambridge: Cambridge University Press, 1999.

Taylor, Brian. *The Anglican Church in Borneo,* 1848-1962. Bognor Regis: New Horizon, 1983.

Taylor, Dr & Mrs Howard. *Hudson Taylor and the China Inland Mission: The Growth of a Work of God.* London: China Inland Mission, 1918.

Templer, John C., Ed. The Private Letters of Sir James Brooke, K.C.B., Rajah of Sarawak, Narrating the Events of His Life from 1838 to the Present Time. 3 vols. London: Richard Bentley, 1853.

Tham, David. 'British Attitudes towards the Greater Malaysia Proposal'. In *Borneo 2000: Proceedings of the Sixth Biennial Borneo Research Conference.* Ed. Michael Leigh. Kuching: Universiti Malaysia Sarawak, 2000, 313-337.

The Sarawak Education Department. 'Outline of the History in Sarawak'. *Journal of Malaysian Historical Society, Sarawak Branch,* June 1980, 11-23.

Thompson, H.P. Into All Lands: The History of the Society for the Propagation of the Gospel in Foreign Parts 1701-1950. London: Society for Promoting Christian Knowledge, 1951.

Thompson, Roger C. *Religion in Australia: A History.* Melbourne: Oxford University Press, 1994

Thomson, A.T. 'The Missionary Situation in Australia'. *International Review of Mission* 15, 60 (October 1926), 675-91.

Tien Ju-Kang. *The Chinese of Sarawak: A study of social structure.* London: Department of Anthropology, The London School of Economics and Political Science, Monographs on Social Anthropology, No. 12, 1853.

Torrey, R.A. *Let My People Go: The Life of Robert A. Jaffray.* Camp Hill: Christian Publications, 1990.

Treloar, G., Ed. The Furtherance of Religious Beliefs: Essays on the History of Theological Education in Australia. Sydney: Centre for the Study of Australian Christianity, 1997.

Toynbee, W.M. 'Educational Progress in the Kelabit Highlands', *Sarawak Gazette* (31 July 1965), 218-219.

Tucker, Ruth. From Jerusalem to Irian Jaya: A Biographical History of Christian Missions. Grand Rapids: Zondervan, 1983.

Tuma, A.D. Tom. Building a Ugandan Church: African Participation in Church Growth and Expansion in Busoga 1891-1940. Nairobi: Kenya Literature Bureau, 1980.

Turnbull, C.M. 'Regionalism and Nationalism'. In *The Cambridge History of Southeast Asia: The Nineteenth and Twentieth Centuries*, Vol 2. Ed. Nicholas Tarling. Cambridge: Cambridge University Press, 1992, 596-603.

Urquhart, I.A.N. 'Some Kenyah-Penan Relationships'. *Sarawak Museum Journal* 8:10 (1957):113-116.

Urud, John Edison. *Datuk Racha Umong: Memories of the Great Rhinoceros Hunter Live On.* Kota Kinabalu, Sabah: H and A Media Publishing, 2004.

Uyo, Lah Jau. 'Kayan People of Sarawak'. *Sarawak Museum Journal* 40:61 (December 1989), 57-88.

Van der Weer, Peter, Ed. Conversion to Modernities: The Globalisation of Christianity. New York/London: Routledge, 1996.

Varney, Peter D. 'The Anglican Church in Sarawak from 1848 to 1852'. *Sarawak Museum Journal* 16:32-33 (1968), 377-406.

——. 'Some Early Iban Leaders in the Anglican Church in Sarawak'. *Sarawak Museum Journal* 17, 34-35 (1969), 273-289.

Wagner, Ulla. *Colonialism and Iban Warfare.* Stockholm: OBE-Tryck Sthim, 1972.

Walker, J.H. *Power and Prowess: The Origins of Brooke Kingship in Sarawak.* Honolulu: University of Hawaii Press/Allen and Unwin, 2002.

Walls, Andrew. 'British Missions'. In *Missionary Ideologies in the Imperialist Era,1880-1920.* Eds. Torben Christensen and W.R. Hutchison. Aarhus: Aros Publishers, 1982, 159-165.

——. The Missionary Movement in Christian History. Maryknoll: Orbis Books, 1996.

——. *The Cross-Cultural Process in Christian History.* Maryknoll/Edinburgh: Orbis Books/T and T Clark, 2002.

Ward, A.B. *Rajah's Servant.* Data Paper 61. Ithaca, New York: South East Asia Program, Department of Asian Studies, Cornell University, 1966.

Ward, A.B. and D.C. White, (comps). *Outlines of Sarawak History under the Brooke Rajahs, 1839-1946*. Kuching: Sarawak Government Printing Office, 1957.

Warren, M.A.C. The Missionary Movement from Britain in Modern History. London: SCM, 1965.

—. Social History and Christian Mission. London: SCM, 1967.

Warren, Max, Ed. *To Apply the Gospel: Selections from the Writings of Henry Venn*. Grand Rapids: Eerdmans, 1971.

Webster, John. 'British Missions in India'. In *Missionary Ideologies in the Imperialist Era. 1880-1920*. Eds. Torben Christensen and W.R. Hutchison. Aarhus: Aros Publishers, 1982, 38-47.

White, E. 'Bungan - A New Kayan Belief'. *Sarawak Museum Journal* 7:8 (December 1956), 472-475.

Whitier, H.L. 'The Kenyah'. In *World Within: The Ethnic Groups of Borneo.* Ed. Victor T. King. Reprint. Kuala Lumpur: S.A. Majeed & Co, 1994, 160-184.

Williams, C. Peter. *The Ideal of the Self-Governing Church: A Study in Victorian Missionary Strategy.* Studies in Christian Mission, Vol. 1. Leiden: E.J. Brill, 1990.

Williams, Peter. 'The Recruitment of Women Missionaries'. In *Women and Missions: Past and Present.* Eds. Fiona Bowie, D. Kirkwood, and S. Ardener. Oxford: Berg, 1993, 43-69.

Wolffe, John, Ed. *Evangelical Faith and Public Zeal.* London: Society for Promoting Christian Knowledge, 1995.

Worrall, B.G. *The Making of the Modern Church: Christianity in England since 1800.* London: Society for Promoting Christian Knowledge, 1988.

Wright, E. Mary. 'Eleven More years to go: Challenge facing the Borneo Evangelical Mission', *The Life of Faith* (26 August 1954), 575-576.

Yates, Timothy. *Christian Mission in the Twentieth Century.* Cambridge: Cambridge University Press, 1994.

Index

REGNUM EDINBURGH 2010 SERIES
Series Listing

David A. Kerr, Kenneth R. Ross (eds.)
Edinburgh 2010
Mission Then and Now
2009 / 978-1-870345-73-6 / xiv + 343pp (paperback)
2009 / 978-1-870345-76-7 / xiv + 343pp (hardback)

No one can hope to fully understand the modern Christian missionary movement without engaging substantially with the World Missionary Conference, held at Edinburgh in 1910. As the centenary of the Conference approaches, the time is ripe to examine its meaning in light of the past century and the questions facing Christian witness today. This book is the first to systematically examine the eight Commissions which reported to Edinburgh 1910 and gave the conference much of its substance and enduring value. It will deepen and extend the reflection being stimulated by the upcoming centenary and will kindle the missionary imagination for 2010 and beyond.

Daryl M. Balia, Kirsteen Kim (eds.)
Edinburgh 2010
Witnessing to Christ Today
2010 / 978-1-870345-77-4 / xiv +301pp

This volume, the second in the Edinburgh 2010 series, includes reports of the nine main study groups working on different themes for the celebration of the centenary of the World Missionary Conference, Edinburgh 1910. Their collaborative work brings together perspectives that are as inclusive as possible of contemporary world Christianity and helps readers to grasp what it means in different contexts to be 'witnessing to Christ today'.

Claudia Währisch-Oblau, Fidon Mwombeki (eds.)
Mission Continues
Global Impulses for the 21st Century
2010 / 978-1-870345-82-8 / 271pp

In May 2009, 35 theologians from Asia, Africa and Europe met in Wuppertal, Germany, for a consultation on mission theology organized by the United Evangelical Mission: Communion of 35 Churches in Three Continents. The aim was to participate in the 100th anniversary of the Edinburgh conference through a study process and reflect on the challenges for mission in the 21st century. This book brings together these papers written by experienced practitioners from around the world.

Brian Woolnough and Wonsuk Ma (Eds)

Holistic Mission

God's plan for God's people 2010 / 978-1-870345-85-9

Holistic mission, or integral mission, implies God is concerned with the whole person, the whole community, body, mind and spirit. This book discusses the meaning of the holistic gospel, how it has developed, and implications for the the church. . It takes a global, eclectic approach, with 19 writers, all of whom have much experience in, and commitment to, holistic mission. It addresses critically and honestly one of the most exciting, and challenging, issues facing the church today. To be part of God's plan for God's people, the church must take holistic mission to the world.

Kirsteen Kim and Andrew Anderson (Eds)

Mission Today and Tomorrow

2011/978-1-870345-91-0

The centenary of the historic and influential World Missionary Conference held in Edinburgh 1910 presented a unique opportunity for the whole church worldwide to come together in celebration, reflection and recommitment to witnessing to Christ today. Edinburgh 2010 also engaged in serious study and reflection on the current state of world mission and the challenges facing all those who seek to witness Christ today. The results of this research was presented and debated within the context of Christian fellowship and worship at the conference in June 2010. This record of that conference is intended to give the background to that Call, to share the spirit of the conference, and to stimulate informed and focused participation in God's mission in Christ for the world's salvation.

Tormod Engelsviken, Erling Lundeby and Dagfinn Solheim (Eds)

The Church Going Glocal

Mission and Globalisation 2011/978-1-870345-93-4

This book provides thought-provoking and inspiring reading for all concerned with mission in the 21st century. I have been challenged by its contributors to re-think our Gospel ministries in our new local contexts marked by globalisation and migration. With its biblical foundation, its missiological reflection and interaction with contemporary society I warmly recommend this volume for study and pray that it will renew our passion for the Gospel and compassion for people.

REGNUM Studies in Global Christianity

(Previously GLOBAL THEOLOGICAL VOICES series)

Series Listing

David Emmanuuel Singh (ed.)
Jesus and the Cross
Reflections of Christians from Islamic Contexts
2008 / 978-1-870345-65-1 / x + 226pp

The Cross reminds us that the sins of the world are not borne through the exercise of power but through Jesus Christ's submission to the will of the Father. The papers in this volume are organised in three parts: scriptural, contextual and theological. The central question being addressed is: how do Christians living in contexts, where Islam is a majority or minority religion, experience, express or think of the Cross? This is, therefore, an exercise in listening. As the contexts from where these engagements arise are varied, the papers in drawing scriptural, contextual and theological reflections offer a cross-section of Christian thinking about Jesus and the Cross.

David Emmanuuel Singh (ed.)
Jesus and the Incarnation
Reflections of Christians from Islamic Contexts
2011/978-1-870345-90-3

In the dialogue of Christians with Muslims nothing is more fundamental than the Cross, the Incarnation and the Resurrection of Jesus. This book contains voices of Christians living in various 'Islamic contexts' and reflecting on the Incarnation of Jesus. The aim of these reflections is constructive and the hope is that the papers weaved around the notion of 'the Word' will not only promote dialogue among Christians on the roles of the Person and the Book, but, also, create a positive environment for their conversations with Muslim neighbours.

Sung-wook Hong
Naming God in Korea
The Case of Protestant Christianity
2008 / 978-1-870345-66-8 / xiv + 170pp

Since Christianity was introduced to Korea more than a century ago, one of the most controversial issue has been the Korean term for the Christian 'God'. This issue is not merely about naming the Christian God in Korean language, but it relates to the question of theological contextualization—the relationship between the gospel and culture—and the question of Korean Christian identity. This book examines the theological contextualization of the concept of 'God' in the contemporary Korean context and applies the translatability of Christianity to that context. It also demonstrates the nature of the gospel in relation to cultures, i.e., the universality of the gospel expressed in all human cultures.

Hubert van Beek (ed.)
Revisioning Christian Unity
The Global Christian Forum
2009 / 978-1-870345-74-3 / xx + 288pp

This book contains the records of the Global Christian Forum gathering held in Limuru near Nairobi, Kenya, on 6 – 9 November 2007 as well as the papers presented at that historic event. Also included are a summary of the Global Christian Forum process from its inception until the 2007 gathering and the reports of the evaluation of the process that was carried out in 2008.

Paul Hang-Sik Cho
Eschatology and Ecology
Experiences of the Korean Church
2010 / 978-1-870345-75-0/ 260pp (approx)

This book raises the question of why Korean people, and Korean Protestant Christians in particular, pay so little attention (in theory or practice) to ecological issues. The author argues that there is an important connection (or elective affinity) between this lack of attention and the other-worldly eschatology that is so dominant within Korean Protestant Christianity. Dispensational premillennialism, originally imported by American missionaries, resonated with traditional religious beliefs in Korea and soon came to dominate much of Korean Protestantism. This book argues that this, of all forms of millennialism, is the most damaging to ecological concerns.

Dietrich Werner, David Esterline, Namsoon Kang, Joshva Raja (eds.)
The Handbook of Theological Education in World Christianity
Theological Perspectives, Ecumenical Trends, Regional Surveys
2010 / 978-1-870345-80-4/ 759pp

This major reference work is the first ever comprehensive study of Theological Education in Christianity of its kind. With contributions from over 90 international scholars and church leaders, it aims to be easily accessible across denominational, cultural, educational, and geographic boundaries. The Handbook will aid international dialogue and networking among theological educators, institutions, and agencies. The major objectives of the text are (1) to provide introductory surveys on selected issues and themes in global theological education; (2) to provide regional surveys on key developments, achievements, and challenges in theological education; (3) to provide an overview of theological education for each of the major denominational / confessional traditions; and (4) to provide a reference section with an up-to-date list of the regional associations of theological institutions and other resources.

David Emmanuel Singh & Bernard C Farr (eds.)

Christianity and Education

Shaping of Christian Context in Thinking

2010 / 978-1-870345-81-1/ 244pp (approx)

Christianity and Education is a collection of papers published in *Transformation: An International Journal of Holistic Mission Studies* over a period of 15 years. It brings to life some of the papers that lay buried in shelves and in disparate volumes of *Transformation,* under a single volume for theological libraries, students and teachers. The articles here represent a spectrum of Christian thinking addressing issues of institutional development for theological education, theological studies in the context of global mission, contextually aware/informed education, and academies which deliver such education, methodologies and personal reflections.

J.Andrew Kirk

Civilisations in Conflict?

Islam, the West and Christian Faith 2011- 978-1-870345-71-2

Samuel Huntington's thesis, which argues that there appear to be aspects of Islam that could be on a collision course with the politics and values of Western societies, has provoked much controversy. The purpose of this study is to offer a particular response to Huntington's thesis by making a comparison between the origins of Islam and Christianity; the two religions that can be said to have shaped, in contrasting ways, the history of the Western world. The early history of each faith continues to have a profound impact on the way in which their respective followers have interpreted the relationship between faith and political life. The book draws significant, critical and creative conclusions from the analysis for contemporary intercultural understanding, and in particular for the debate about the justification of violence for political and religious ends.

REGNUM STUDIES IN MISSION
Series Listing

Kwame Bediako

Theology and Identity

The Impact of Culture upon Christian Thought in the Second Century and in Modern Africa

1992 / 1-870345-10-X / xviii + 508pp

The author examines the question of Christian identity in the context of the Graeco–Roman culture of the early Roman Empire. He then addresses the modern African predicament of quests for identity and integration.

Christopher Sugden

Seeking the Asian Face of Jesus

The Practice and Theology of Christian Social Witness in Indonesia and India 1974–1996

1997 / 1-870345-26-6 / xx + 496pp

This study focuses on contemporary holistic mission with the poor in India and Indonesia combined with the call to transformation of all life in Christ with micro-credit enterprise schemes. 'The literature on contextual theology now has a new standard to rise to' – Lamin Sanneh (Yale University, USA).

Hwa Yung

Mangoes or Bananas?

The Quest for an Authentic Asian Christian Theology

1997 / 1-870345-25-8 / xii + 274pp

Asian Christian thought remains largely captive to Greek dualism and Enlightenment rationalism because of the overwhelming dominance of Western culture. Authentic contextual Christian theologies will emerge within Asian Christianity with a dual recovery of confidence in culture and the gospel.

Keith E. Eitel

Paradigm Wars

The Southern Baptist International Mission Board Faces the Third Millennium

1999 / 1-870345-12-6 / x + 140pp

The International Mission Board of the Southern Baptist Convention is the largest denominational mission agency in North America. This volume chronicles the historic and contemporary forces that led to the IMB's recent extensive reorganization, providing the most comprehensive case study to date of a historic mission agency restructuring to continue its mission purpose into the twenty-first century more effectively.

Samuel Jayakumar

Dalit Consciousness and Christian Conversion

Historical Resources for a Contemporary Debate

1999 / 81-7214-497-0 / xxiv + 434pp

(Published jointly with ISPCK)

The main focus of this historical study is social change and transformation among the Dalit Christian communities in India. Historiography tests the evidence in the light of the conclusions of the modern Dalit liberation theologians.

Vinay Samuel and Christopher Sugden (eds.)

Mission as Transformation

A Theology of the Whole Gospel

1999 / 0870345133/ 522pp

This book brings together in one volume twenty five years of biblical reflection on mission practice with the poor from around the world. The approach of holistic mission, which integrates proclamation, evangelism, church planting and social transformation seamlessly as a whole, has been adopted since 1983 by most evangelical development agencies, most indigenous mission agencies and many Pentecostal churches. This volume helps anyone understand how evangelicals, struggling to unite evangelism and social action, found their way in the last twenty five years to the biblical view of mission in which God calls all human beings to love God and their neighbour; never creating a separation between the two.

Christopher Sugden

Gospel, Culture and Transformation

2000 / 1-870345-32-0 / viii + 152pp

A Reprint, with a New Introduction, of Part Two of Seeking the Asian Face of Jesus

Gospel, Culture and Transformation explores the practice of mission especially in relation to transforming cultures and communities. - 'Transformation is to enable God's vision of society to be actualised in all relationships: social, economic and spiritual, so that God's will may be reflected in human society and his love experienced by all communities, especially the poor.'

Bernhard Ott

Beyond Fragmentation: Integrating Mission and Theological Education

A Critical Assessment of some Recent Developments in Evangelical Theological Education

2001 / 1-870345-14-2 / xxviii + 382pp

Beyond Fragmentation is an enquiry into the development of Mission Studies in evangelical theological education in Germany and German-speaking Switzerland between 1960 and 1995. The author undertakes a detailed examination of the paradigm shifts which have taken place in recent years in both the theology of mission and the understanding of theological education.

Gideon Githiga

The Church as the Bulwark against Authoritarianism

Development of Church and State Relations in Kenya, with Particular Reference to the Years after Political Independence 1963-1992

2002 / 1-870345-38-x / xviii + 218pp

'All who care for love, peace and unity in Kenyan society will want to read this careful history by Bishop Githiga of how Kenyan Christians, drawing on the Bible, have sought to share the love of God, bring his peace and build up the unity of the nation, often in the face of great difficulties and opposition.' Canon Dr Chris Sugden, Oxford Centre for Mission Studies.

Myung Sung-Hoon, Hong Young-Gi (eds.)

Charis and Charisma

David Yonggi Cho and the Growth of Yoido Full Gospel Church

2003 / 1-870345-45-2 / xxii + 218pp

This book discusses the factors responsible for the growth of the world's largest church. It expounds the role of the Holy Spirit, the leadership, prayer, preaching, cell groups and creativity in promoting church growth. It focuses on God's grace (charis) and inspiring leadership (charisma) as the two essential factors and the book's purpose is to present a model for church growth worldwide.

Samuel Jayakumar

Mission Reader

Historical Models for Wholistic Mission in the Indian Context

2003 / 1-870345-42-8 / x + 250pp

(Published jointly with ISPCK)

This book is written from an evangelical point of view revalidating and reaffirming the Christian commitment to wholistic mission. The roots of the 'wholistic mission' combining 'evangelism and social concerns' are to be located in the history and tradition of Christian evangelism in the past; and the civilizing purpose of evangelism is compatible with modernity as an instrument in nation building.

Bob Robinson

Christians Meeting Hindus

An Analysis and Theological Critique of the Hindu-Christian Encounter in India

2004 / 1-870345-39-8 / xviii + 392pp

This book focuses on the Hindu-Christian encounter, especially the intentional meeting called dialogue, mainly during the last four decades of the twentieth century, and specifically in India itself.

Gene Early

Leadership Expectations

How Executive Expectations are Created and Used in a Non-Profit Setting

2005 / 1-870345-30-4 / xxiv + 276pp

The author creates an Expectation Enactment Analysis to study the role of the Chancellor of the University of the Nations-Kona, Hawaii. This study is grounded in the field of managerial work, jobs, and behaviour and draws on symbolic interactionism, role theory, rolc identity theory and enactment theory. The result is a conceptual framework for developing an understanding of managerial roles.

Tharcisse Gatwa

The Churches and Ethnic Ideology in the Rwandan Crises 1900-1994

2005 / 1-870345-24-X / approx 300pp

Since the early years of the twentieth century Christianity has become a new factor in Rwandan society. This book investigates the role Christian churches played in the formulation and development of the racial ideology that culminated in the 1994 genocide.

Julie Ma

Mission Possible

Biblical Strategies for Reaching the Lost

2005 / 1-870345-37-1 / xvi + 142pp

This is a missiology book for the church which liberates missiology from the specialists for the benefit of every believer. It also serves as a textbook that is simple and friendly, and yet solid in biblical interpretation. This book links the biblical teaching to the actual and contemporary missiological settings with examples, making the Bible come alive to the reader.

Allan Anderson, Edmond Tang (eds.)

Asian and Pentecostal

The Charismatic Face of Christianity in Asia

2005 / 1-870345-43-6 / xiv + 596pp

(Published jointly with APTS Press)

This book provides a thematic discussion and pioneering case studies on the history and development of Pentecostal and Charismatic churches in the countries of South Asia, South East Asia and East Asia.

I. Mark Beaumont

Christology in Dialogue with Muslims

A Critical Analysis of Christian Presentations of Christ for Muslims from the Ninth and Twentieth Centuries

2005 / 1-870345-46-0 / xxvi + 228pp

This book analyses Christian presentations of Christ for Muslims in the most creative periods of Christian-Muslim dialogue, the first half of the ninth century and the second half of the twentieth century. In these two periods, Christians made serious attempts to present their faith in Christ in terms that take into account Muslim perceptions of him, with a view to bridging the gap between Muslim and Christian convictions.

Thomas Czövek,

Three Seasons of Charismatic Leadership

A Literary-Critical and Theological Interpretation of the Narrative of Saul, David and Solomon

2006 / 978-1-870345484 / 272pp

This book investigates the charismatic leadership of Saul, David and Solomon. It suggests that charismatic leaders emerge in crisis situations in order to resolve the crisis by the charisma granted by God. Czovek argues that Saul proved himself as a charismatic leader as long as he acted resolutely and independently from his mentor Samuel. In the author's eyes, Saul's failure to establish himself as a charismatic leader is caused by his inability to step out from Samuel's shadow.

Jemima Atieno Oluoch

The Christian Political Theology of Dr. John Henry Okullu

2006 / 1-870345-51-7 / xx + 137pp

This book reconstructs the Christian political theology of Bishop John Henry Okullu, DD, through establishing what motivated him and the biblical basis for his socio-political activities. It also attempts to reconstruct the socio-political environment that nurtured Dr Okullu's prophetic ministry.

Richard Burgess

Nigeria's Christian Revolution

The Civil War Revival and Its Pentecostal Progeny (1967-2006)

2008 / 978-1-870345-63-7 / xxii + 347pp

This book describes the revival that occurred among the Igbo people of Eastern Nigeria and the new Pentecostal churches it generated, and documents the changes that have occurred as the movement has responded to global flows and local demands. As such, it explores the nature of revivalist and Pentecostal experience, but does so against the backdrop of local socio-political and economic developments, such as decolonisation and civil war, as well as broader processes, such as modernisation and globalisation.

David Emmanuel Singh & Bernard C Farr (eds.)

Christianity and Cultures

Shaping Christian Thinking in Context

2008 / 978-1-870345-69-9 / x + 260pp

This volume marks an important milestone, the 25th anniversary of the Oxford Centre for Mission Studies (OCMS). The papers here have been exclusively sourced from Transformation, a quarterly journal of OCMS, and seek to provide a tripartite view of Christianity's engagement with cultures by focusing on the question: how is Christian thinking being formed or reformed through its interaction with the varied contexts it encounters? The subject matters include different strands of theological-missiological thinking, socio-political engagements and forms of family relationships in interaction with the host cultures.

Tormod Engelsviken, Ernst Harbakk, Rolv Olsen, Thor Strandenæs (eds.)

Mission to the World

Communicating the Gospel in the 21st Century: Essays in Honour of Knud Jørgensen

2008 / 978-1-870345-64-4 / 472pp

Knud Jørgensen is Director of Areopagos and Associate Professor of Missiology at MF Norwegian School of Theology. This book reflects on the main areas of Jørgensen's commitment to mission. At the same time it focuses on the main frontier of mission, the world, the content of mission, the Gospel, the fact that the Gospel has to be communicated, and the context of contemporary mission in the 21st century.

Al Tizon

Transformation after Lausanne

Radical Evangelical Mission in Global-Local Perspective

2008 / 978-1-870345-68-2 / xx + 281pp

After Lausanne '74, a worldwide network of radical evangelical mission theologians and practitioners use the notion of "Mission as Transformation" to integrate evangelism and social concern together, thus lifting theological voices from the Two Thirds World to places of prominence. This book documents the definitive gatherings, theological tensions, and social forces within and without evangelicalism that led up to Mission as Transformation. And it does so through a global-local grid that points the way toward greater holistic mission in the 21st century.

Bambang Budijanto

Values and Participation

Development in Rural Indonesia

2009 / 978-1-870345-70-5 / x + 237pp

Socio-religious values and socio-economic development are inter-dependant, inter-related and are constantly changing in the context of macro political structures, economic policy, religious organizations and globalization; and micro influences such as local affinities, identity, politics, leadership and beliefs. The three Lopait communities in Central Java, Indonesia provide an excellent model of the rich and complex negotiations and interactions among all the above factors. The book argues that the comprehensive approach in understanding the socio-religious values of each local community is essential to accurately describing their respective identity which will help institutions and agencies, both governmental and non-governmental, to relate to these communities with dignity and respect.

Young-hoon Lee

The Holy Spirit Movement in Korea

Its Historical and Theological Development

2009 / 978-1-870345-67-5 / x + 174pp

This book traces the historical and theological development of the Holy Spirit Movement in Korea through six successive periods (from 1900 to the present time). These periods are characterized by repentance and revival (1900-20), persecution and suffering under Japanese occupation (1920-40), confusion and division (1940-60), explosive revival in which the Pentecostal movement played a major role in the rapid growth of Korean churches (1960-80), the movement reaching out to all denominations (1980-2000), and the new context demanding the Holy Spirit movement to open new horizons in its mission engagement (2000-). The volume also discusses the relationship between this movement and other religions such as shamanism, and looks forward to further engagement with issues of concern in wider society.

Alan R. Johnson

Leadership in a Slum

A Bangkok Case Study

2009 / 978-1-870345-71-2 xx + 238pp

This book looks at leadership in the social context of a slum in Bangkok from an angle different from traditional studies which measure well educated Thais on leadership scales derived in the West. Using both systematic data collection and participant observation, it develops a culturally preferred model as well as a set of models based in Thai concepts that reflect on-the-ground realities. This work challenges the dominance of the patron-client rubric for understanding all forms of Thai leadership and offers a view for understanding leadership rooted in local social systems, contrary to approaches that assume the universal applicability of leadership research findings across all cultural settings. It concludes by looking at the implications of the anthropological approach for those who are involved in leadership training in Thai settings and beyond.

Titre Ande

Leadership and Authority

Bula Matari and Life - Community Ecclesiology in Congo

2010 / 978-1-870345-72-9 xvii + 189pp

This book proposes that Christian theology in Africa can make significant developments if a critical understanding of the socio-political context in contemporary Africa is taken seriously. The Christian leadership in post-colonial Africa has cloned its understanding and use of authority on the Bula Matari model, which was issued from the brutality of colonialism and political absolutism in post-colonial Africa. This model has caused many problems in churches, including dysfunction, conflicts, divisions and a lack of prophetic ministry. Titre proposes a Life-Community ecclesiology for liberating authority, where leadership is a function, not a status, and 'apostolic succession' belongs to all the people of God.

Frank Kwesi Adams

Odwira and the Gospel

A Study of the Asante Odwira Festival and its Significance for Christianity in Ghana

2010 /978-1-870345-59-0

The study of the Odwira festival is the key to the understanding of Asante religious and political life in Ghana. The book explores the nature of the Odwira festival longitudinally - in pre-colonial, colonial and post-independence Ghana - and examines the Odwira ideology and its implications for understanding the Asante self-identity. The book also discusses how some elements of faith portrayed in the Odwira festival could provide a framework for Christianity to engage with Asante culture at a greater depth. Theological themes in Asante belief that have emerged from this study include the theology of sacrament, ecclesiology, eschatology, Christology and a complex concept of time. The author argues that Asante cultural identity lies at the heart of the process by which the Asante Christian faith is carried forward.

Bruce Carlton

Strategy Coordinator

Changing the Course of Southern Baptist Missions

2010 / 978-1-870345-78-1 xvii + 268pp

In 1976, the Southern Baptist Convention adopted its Bold New Thrusts in Foreign Missions with the overarching goal of sharing the gospel with every person in the world by the year 2000. The formation of Cooperative Services International (CSI) in 1985 and the assigning of the first non-residential missionary (NRM) in 1987 demonstrated the Foreign Mission Board's (now International Mission Board) commitment to take the gospel message to countries that restricted traditional missionary presence and to people groups identified as having little or no access to the gospel. Carlton traces the historical development along with an analysis of the key components of the paradigm and its significant impact on Southern Baptists' missiology.

Julie Ma & Wonsuk Ma
Mission in the Spirit:
Towards a Pentecostal/Charismatic Missiology
2010 / 978-1-870345-84-2 xx + 312pp

The book explores the unique contribution of Pentecostal/Charismatic mission from the beginning of the twentieth century. The first part considers the theological basis of Pentecostal/Charismatic mission thinking and practice. Special attention is paid to the Old Testament, which has been regularly overlooked by the modern Pentecostal/Charismatic movements. The second part discusses major mission topics with contributions and challenges unique to Pentecostal/Charismatic mission. The book concludes with a reflection on the future of this powerful missionary movement. As the authors served as Korean missionaries in Asia, often their missionary experiences in Asia are reflected in their discussions.

S. Hun Kim & Wonsuk Ma (eds.)
Korean Diaspora and Christian Mission
2011-978-1-870345-89-7

As a 'divine conspiracy' for Missio Dei, the global phenomenon of people on the move has shown itself to be invaluable. In 2004 two significant documents concerning Diaspora were introduced, one by the Filipino International Network and the other by the Lausanne Committee for World Evangelization. These have created awareness of the importance of people on the move for Christian mission. Since then, Korean Diaspora has conducted similar research among Korean missions, resulting in this book. It is unique as the first volume researching Korean missions in Diasporic contexts, appraising and evaluating these missions with practical illustrations, and drawing on a wide diversity of researchers.

GENERAL REGNUM TITLES

Vinay Samuel, Chris Sugden (eds.)
The Church in Response to Human Need
1987 / 1870345045 / xii+268pp

Philip Sampson, Vinay Samuel, Chris Sugden (eds.)
Faith and Modernity
Essays in modernity and post-modernity
1994 / 1870345177 / 352pp

Klaus Fiedler
The Story of Faith Missions
1994 / 0745926878 / 428pp

Douglas Peterson
Not by Might nor by Power
A Pentecostal Theology of Social Concern in Latin America
1996 / 1870345207 / xvi+260pp

David Gitari
In Season and Out of Season
Sermons to a Nation
1996 / 1870345118 / 155pp

David. W. Virtue
A Vision of Hope
The Story of Samuel Habib
1996 / 1870345169 / xiv+137pp

Everett A Wilson
Strategy of the Spirit
J.Philip Hogan and the Growth of the Assemblies of God Worldwide, 1960 - 1990
1997 /1870345231/214

Murray Dempster, Byron Klaus, Douglas Petersen (eds.)
The Globalization of Pentecostalism
A Religion Made to Travel
1999 / 1870345290 / xvii+406pp

Peter Johnson, Chris Sugden (eds.)
Markets, Fair Trade and the Kingdom of God
Essays to Celebrate Traidcraft's 21st Birthday
2001 / 1870345193 / xii+155pp

Robert Hillman, Coral Chamberlain, Linda Harding
Healing & Wholeness
Reflections on the Healing Ministry
2002 / 978-1- 870345-35- 4 / xvii+283pp

David Bussau, Russell Mask
Christian Microenterprise Development
An Introduction
2003 / 1870345282 / xiii+142pp

David Singh
Sainthood and Revelatory Discourse
An Examination of the Basis for the Authority of Bayan in Mahdawi Islam
2003 / 8172147285 / xxiv+485pp

For the up-to-date listing of the Regnum books see www.ocms.ac.uk/regnum

regnum

Regnum Books International

Regnum is an Imprint of The Oxford Centre for Mission Studies
St. Philip and St. James Church
Woodstock Road
Oxford, OX2 6HR
Web: www.ocms.ac.uk/regnum